MW00560671

THE JOHN PHILLIPS COMMENTARY SERIES

Exploring THE PASTORAL EPISTLES

An Expository Commentary

JOHN PHILLIPS

Grand Rapids, MI 49501

Exploring the Pastoral Epistles: An Expository Commentary

Published in 2004 by Kregel Publications, a division of Kregel Inc., 2450 Oak Industrial Dr. NE, Grand Rapids, MI 49505.

Scripture quotations are from the King James Version of the Holy Bible.

Library of Congress Cataloging-in-Publication Data
Phillips, John.
Exploring the Pastoral Epistles: an expository commentary / by John Phillips.
p. cm.
Includes biographical references.
1. Bible. N.T. Pastoral Epistles—Commentaries. I. Title.
BS2735.53.P48 2003 227'.8307—dc22 2003021330

ISBN 978-0-8254-3394-8

Printed in the United States of America

8 9 10 / 26 25 24 23 22 21

Contents

Exploring
1 TIMOTHY

Introduction to 1 Timothy

Paul was Timothy's hero. The circumstances under which they met doubtless contributed to Timothy's high regard for the apostle. To appreciate fully the impact of that first encounter, we must understand something of Timothy's background.

His father was a Gentile. His Jewish mother and grandmother, however, reared him on Bible stories and instructed him in the messianic hope of the Jewish people. His father's influence was strong enough to prevent Timothy's being circumcised as a baby, but his mother, yielding on that issue, insisted on teaching her boy the great truths of the Jewish faith. So while his father doubtless told him tales about the Greek gods and Alexander the Great and acquainted him with the epics of the Roman Empire, Timothy's mother filled his impressionable heart with accounts of her heroes: Moses, Elijah, David, Daniel, and Joseph. She taught him Hebrew hymns and told him about the prophecies that spoke of a coming Redeemer.

Then Paul had come, invading Galatia with the gospel of Christ. He took by storm city after city—Pisidia, Antioch, Iconium, Lystra, Derbe. Paul's arrival in Lystra, which seems to have been Timothy's hometown, was both exciting and tempestuous. The whole city was turned upside down by Paul's dramatic healing of a local cripple, a man whom everyone knew to have been lame from birth (Acts 14:8–11). The amazed townsfolk at once proclaimed Paul and Barnabas to be incarnations of the pagan gods Mercury and Jupiter. The local priest prepared enthusiastically to sacrifice oxen in their honor. It had taken all of Paul's persuasive powers to prevent the people from offering the sacrifice.

We can well imagine how the events of that remarkable day were discussed around the supper table in Timothy's home. Soon Paul's thrilling news that the

Christ had come as prophesied in the Old Testament caught fire in Timothy's soul, and he capitulated to the claims of Christ.

Then there was another upheaval. Angry Jews from Antioch and Iconium descended on Lystra. They branded Paul as a heretic and troublemaker and succeeded in stirring up a riot. Paul was seized, stoned, dragged out of the city, and left for dead. Only when the Jews were convinced that he was dead did the riot cease.

Once the hubbub died down and the fickle mob dispersed, the disciples discovered that Paul was alive. Although battered, bruised, and bleeding, the apostle stood up! Perhaps he spent the night at Timothy's house before leaving the next day to continue his evangelistic activities in Derbe. When Paul left Lystra, he carried Timothy's heart with him. The apostle ruled in Timothy's affections to the end.

Paul may have written numerous letters to his young friend. Two of them have been immortalized as books of the Bible. Little did Timothy suspect when he became a Christian that his name would become a household word wherever the gospel was preached—to the ends of the earth and to the end of time. Yet, here we are on a continent of which no Caesar ever dreamed, nearly two thousand years after Timothy's death, preparing to weigh each word Paul wrote to Timothy in the first of the two letters that have survived.

Complete Outline of 1 Timothy

PART 1: INTRODUCTION (1:1–2)

- A. Paul and his signature (1:1a–b)
  - 1. His apostleship (1:1a)
  - 2. His authority (1:1b)
- B. Paul and his Savior (1:1c–e)
  - 1. The Savior is the One in whom we live (1:1c–d)
    - a. What He is (1:1c)
    - b. Who He is (1:1d)
  - 2. The Savior is the One for whom we look (1:1e)
- C. Paul and his son (1:2)
  - 1. Timothy's blessed relationship (1:2a)
  - 2. Timothy's boundless resources (1:2b)

PART 2: HOW TO BUILD AN EFFECTIVE CHURCH (1:3–3:15)

- A. The church and its doctrine (1:3–20)
  - 1. The loss of truth considered (1:3–4)
    - a. Timothy's residence (1:3a)
    - b. Timothy's responsibility (1:3b–4)
      - (1) To require sound doctrine (1:3b)
      - (2) To resist silly digressions (1:4)
        - (a) Gnostic tendencies exposed as foolish (1:4a–b)
          - i. Their fables (1:4a)
          - ii. Their fantasies (1:4b)
        - (b) Gnostic tendencies expelled as fruitless (1:4c–d)
          - i. What they invite (1:4c)
          - ii. What they inhibit (1:4d)

2. The law of God considered (1:5–11)
    a. Its fullest transformation (1:5)
    b. Its false teachers (1:6–7)
    c. Its foolish transgressors (1:8–11)
        (1) The goodness of God's law (1:8–9a)
        (2) The greatness of God's law (1:9b–11)
            (a) It exposes general sins (1:9b–g)
                i. Sins against government (1:9b–c)
                    a. The defiant (1:9b)
                    b. The disobedient (1:9c)
                ii. Sins against godliness (1:9d–e)
                    a. The impious (1:9d)
                    b. The iniquitous (1:9e)
                iii. Sins against goodness (1:9f–g)
                    a. Those without any sort of scruples (1:9f)
                    b. Those without any sense of sanctity (1:9g)
            (b) It exposes glaring sins (1:9h–11)
                i. The murderers (1:9h–i)
                    a. Those who kill their parents (1:9h)
                    b. Those who kill other people (1:9i)
                ii. The "mature" (1:10a–b)
                    a. Those who practice prostitution (1:10a)
                    b. Those who practice perversion (1:10b)
                iii. The menstealers (1:10c)
                iv. The manipulators (1:10d–11)
                    a. Those who sin against the spoken word (1:10d)
                    b. Those who sin against the sworn word (1:10e)
                    c. Those who sin against the sacred Word (1:10f–11)
3. The love of Christ considered (1:12–17)
    a. Paul's gratitude (1:12–14)
        (1) His present ministry (1:12)
        (2) His past malignancy (1:13–14)
            (a) The malice he expressed (1:13a)
            (b) The mercy he experienced (1:13b–14)
                i. His ignorance was forgiven (1:13b)
                ii. His ignorance was forgotten (1:14)

- *a.* In the grace that inundated him (1:14a)
- *b.* In the grace that inspired him (1:14b)

b. Paul's gospel (1:15–16)
- (1) Paul's affirmation (1:15a)
- (2) Paul's acceptation (1:15b)
- (3) Paul's attestation (1:15c–d)
  - (a) Of a historical fact (1:15c)
  - (b) Of a humbling fact (1:15d)
- (4) Paul's application (1:15e)
- (5) Paul's apprehension (1:16)
  - (a) The patience of God (1:16a)
  - (b) The pattern of grace (1:16b)

c. Paul's God (1:17)
- (1) His infinite greatness (1:17a–c)
  - (a) The King immutable (1:17a)
  - (b) The King immortal (1:17b)
  - (c) The King invisible (1:17c)
  - (d) The King infallible (1:17d)
- (2) His infinite glory (1:17e–f)
  - (a) It is evident glory (1:17e)
  - (b) It is everlasting glory (1:17f)

4. The life of faith considered (1:18–20)

a. The charge (1:18–19b)
- (1) The paternal appeal (1:18a)
- (2) The prophetic appeal (1:18b)
- (3) The practical appeal (1:18c–19b)
  - (a) Regarding the fight (1:18c)
  - (b) Regarding the faith (1:19a–b)
    - i. Truth viewed objectively (1:19a)
    - ii. Truth viewed subjectively (1:19b)

b. The challenge (1:19c–20)
- (1) The danger is exposed (1:19c)
- (2) The danger is exemplified (1:20)

B. The church and its devotions (2:1–15)

1. The practice of worship in the church (2:1–8)

a. Telling God about men (2:1–3)
- (1) Types of prayer (2:1a–d)

(a) Petitioning (2:1a)
(b) Personalizing (2:1b)
(c) Pleading (2:1c)
(d) Praising (2:1d)
(2) Topics for prayer (2:1e–2b)
(a) People in general (2:1e)
(b) People in government (2:2a–b)
i. Those who wield supreme authority (2:2a)
ii. Those who wield subordinate authority (2:2b)
(3) Targets in prayer (2:2c–3)
(a) The human dimension (2:2c–e)
i. A stable environment (2:2c)
ii. A steady encouragement (2:2d–e)
a. To godliness (2:2d)
b. To goodness (2:2e)
(b) The higher dimension (2:3)
b. Telling men about God (2:4–8)
(1) God and His mercy (2:4)
(a) His will (2:4a)
(b) His Word (2:4b)
(2) God and His mediator (2:5–6)
(a) His absolute exclusiveness (2:5)
(b) His abundant expiation (2:6)
(3) God and His messenger (2:7–8)
(a) Paul's appointment (2:7)
i. The scope of his appointment (2:7a)
ii. The surety of his appointment (2:7b)
iii. The sphere of his appointment (2:7c)
(b) Paul's appeal (2:8)
i. For an atmosphere of prayer (2:8a)
ii. For an attitude of prayer (2:8b–c)
a. Simple expectation (2:8b)
b. Self-examination (2:8c)
2. The place of women in the church (2:9–15)
a. They are to live in sobriety (2:9–10)
(1) What they should avoid (2:9)
(a) Regarding their dress (2:9a)

- (b) Regarding their deportment (2:9b)
- (c) Regarding their display (2:9c)
- (2) What they should avow (2:10)
  - (a) Personal godliness (2:10a)
  - (b) Practical goodness (2:10b)
- b. They are to learn in silence (2:11–15)
  - (1) The rule (2:11–12)
    - (a) What is foremost (2:11)
      - i. Silence (2:11a)
      - ii. Subjection (2:11b)
    - (b) What is forbidden (2:12)
      - i. Teaching (2:12a)
      - ii. Trespassing (2:12b)
  - (2) The reason (2:13–14)
    - (a) God's order in creation revealed (2:13)
    - (b) God's order in creation reversed (2:14)
      - i. Adam was disobedient (2:14a)
      - ii. Eve was deceived (2:14b)
  - (3) The response (2:15)
    - (a) The means of emancipation (2:15a)
    - (b) The measure of emancipation (2:15b)

C. The church and its duties (3:1–15)
- 1. The church's duties discussed (3:1–13)
  - a. The spiritual leadership of the local church—elders (3:1–7)
    - (1) The quest (3:1)
      - (a) The desire for the office (3:1a)
      - (b) The distinctive of the office (3:1b)
      - (c) The demands of the office (3:1c)
    - (2) The qualifications (3:2–7)
      - (a) The basic requirements for an elder (3:2)
        - i. The main requirement (3:2a)
        - ii. The marital requirement (3:2b)
        - iii. The moral requirements (3:2c–e)
          - *a.* His caution (3:2c)
          - *b.* His conclusions (3:2d)
          - *c.* His conduct (3:2e)
        - iv. The ministerial requirements (3:2f–g)

- *a.* Known for his social grace (3:2f)
- *b.* Known for his spiritual gift (3:2g)

(b) The broader requirements for an elder (3:3–7)

- i. His attachments (3:3a–c)
  - *a.* An elder must not be addicted to wine (3:3a)
  - *b.* An elder must not be addicted to wrath (3:3b)
  - *c.* An elder must not be addicted to wealth (3:3c)
- ii. His attitudes (3:3d–f)
  - *a.* An elder must not be choleric (3:3d)
  - *b.* An elder must not be contentious (3:3e)
  - *c.* An elder must not be covetous (3:3f)
- iii. His attainments (3:4–7)
  - *a.* In the parental sphere (3:4–5)
    - *1.* The rule (3:4)
      - (i) Where he rules (3:4a)
      - (ii) Whom he rules (3:4b)
    - *2.* The reason (3:5)
      - (i) The disquieting factor (3:5a)
      - (ii) The disqualifying factor (3:5b)
  - *b.* In the personal sphere (3:6)
    - *1.* The emphatic command (3:6a)
    - *2.* The enlightened comment (3:6b–c)
      - (i) The danger to be avoided (3:6b)
      - (ii) The downfall to be avoided (3:6c)
  - *c.* In the public sphere (3:7)
    - *1.* A good report (3:7a)
    - *2.* A good reason (3:7b)

b. The secular leadership of the local church—deacons (3:8–13)

(1) The deacon as a faultless man (3:8)

- (a) His temperament (3:8a)
- (b) His tongue (3:8b)
- (c) His temptations (3:8c–d)
  - i. Wine (3:8c)
  - ii. Wealth (3:8d)

(2) The deacon as a faithful man (3:9–10)

- (a) Possessing the truth (3:9)
  - i. His convictions (3:9a)

- ii. His conscience (3:9b)
- (b) Passing the test (3:10)
  - i. Proved (3:10a)
  - ii. Promoted (3:10b)
- (3) The deacon as a family man (3:11–12)
  - (a) His wife (3:11)
    - i. Her character (3:11a)
    - ii. Her conversation (3:11b)
    - iii. Her concern (3:11c)
    - iv. Her consistency (3:11d)
  - (b) His walk (3:12)
    - i. As a partner (3:12a)
    - ii. As a parent (3:12b)
- (4) The deacon as a farsighted man (3:13)
  - (a) His administration is assessed (3:13a)
  - (b) His advancement is assured (3:13b–c)
    - i. What he earns: a good degree in the faith (3:13b)
    - ii. What he learns: a growing daring in the faith (3:13c)
- 2. The church's duties displayed (3:14–15)
  - a. Paul's personal desire (3:14)
    - (1) His letter (3:14a)
    - (2) His longing (3:14b)
  - b. Paul's pastoral desire (3:15)
    - (1) A possible delay was envisioned (3:15a)
    - (2) A positive duty was enjoined (3:15b)
    - (3) A perfect description was enshrined (3:15c–d)
      - (a) The church's character (3:15c)
      - (b) The church's custodianship (3:15d)

PART 3: HOW TO BECOME AN EFFECTIVE CHRISTIAN (3:16–6:19)

- A. Walk with God (3:16–4:16)
  - 1. The mystery of godliness (3:16–4:7a)
    - a. The truth asserted (3:16)
      - (1) The mystery of Christ's person (3:16a–b)
        - (a) The virgin's womb: He came to live a human life (3:16a)
        - (b) The vacant tomb: He came to live a holy life (3:16b)

(2) The mystery of Christ's people (3:16c–d)
  (a) The heavenly host (3:16c)
  (b) The heathen heart (3:16d)
(3) The mystery of Christ's power (3:16e–f)
  (a) His triumph on this globe (3:16e)
  (b) His triumph in the glory (3:16f)

b. The truth assailed (4:1–7a)
  (1) The apostasy announced (4:1)
    (a) The day envisioned (4:1a)
    (b) The departure envisioned (4:1b–c)
      i. Its demonic inspiration (4:1b)
      ii. Its doctrinal deviation (4:1c)
  (2) The apostasy analyzed (4:2–5)
    (a) Its deceptive nature (4:2)
      i. Propagated by people devoid of character (4:2a)
      ii. Propagated by people devoid of conscience (4:2b)
    (b) Its destructive nature (4:3–5)
      i. Its attack upon marriage (4:3a)
      ii. Its attack upon meat (4:3b–5)
        a. A lying command (4:3b)
        b. A loving creator (4:3c)
        c. A loyal Christian (4:3d)
        d. A logical concept (4:4–5)
          1. A meat diet is scriptural (4:4a)
          2. A meat diet is sanctified (4:4b–5)
  (3) The apostasy anticipated (4:6–7a)
    (a) What to remember (4:6)
      i. The charge (4:6a)
      ii. The challenge (4:6b–c)
        a. The minister's diet (4:6b)
        b. The minister's development (4:6c)
    (b) What to repudiate (4:7a)

2. The manifestation of godliness (4:7b–16)
  a. By personal exercise (4:7b–11)
    (1) The question of proper exercise reviewed (4:7b–9)
      (a) A contrast (4:7b–8a)
        i. Exercising the spiritual man (4:7b)

- ii. Exercising the physical members (4:8a)
- (b) A conclusion (4:8b–9)
  - i. Godliness is profitable (4:8b–c)
    - *a.* For life on the earthly plane (4:8b)
    - *b.* For life on the eternal plane (4:8c)
  - ii. Godliness is preferable (4:9)
- (2) The question of painful experience reviewed (4:10–11)
  - (a) An exclamation (4:10)
    - i. Concerning our service (4:10a–b)
      - *a.* Our opportunities (4:10a)
      - *b.* Our opposition (4:10b)
    - ii. Concerning our salvation (4:10c–d)
      - *a.* God's salvation actively extended (4:10c)
      - *b.* God's salvation actually experienced (4:10d)
  - (b) An exhortation (4:11)
- b. By public example (4:12–16)
  - (1) A word of wisdom (4:12–13)
    - (a) Facing the problem (4:12a)
    - (b) Fighting the problem (4:12b–13)
      - i. Some first steps (4:12b–h)
        - *a.* The proposal expressed (4:12b)
        - *b.* The proposal expanded (4:12c–h)
          - *1.* Timothy's conversation to be exemplary (4:12c)
          - *2.* Timothy's conduct to be exemplary (4:12d)
          - *3.* Timothy's compassion to be exemplary (4:12e)
          - *4.* Timothy's character to be exemplary (4:12f)
          - *5.* Timothy's convictions to be exemplary (4:12g)
          - *6.* Timothy's cleanness to be exemplary (4:12h)
      - ii. Some further steps (4:13)
        - *a.* Keep growing mentally (4:13a)
        - *b.* Keep going ministerially (4:13b–c)
          - *1.* By exhorting the saints (4:13b)
          - *2.* By expounding the Scriptures (4:13c)
  - (2) A word of warning (4:14–16)

(a) Timothy and his gift (4:14)
- i. A reprimand (4:14a)
- ii. A reminder (4:14b)

(b) Timothy and his growth (4:15)
- i. A call to contemplate (4:15a)
- ii. A call to consecrate (4:15b)

(c) Timothy and his guard (4:16)
- i. Paul admonished him (4:16a)
- ii. Paul advised him (4:16b)

B. Witness for God (5:1–6:19)
1. The people of God (5:1–6:2)
   a. Fellowship of saints (5:1–2)
      (1) A message about the men (5:1)
         (a) The older men: emphasis on respect (5:1a)
         (b) The other men: emphasis on relationship (5:1b)
      (2) A word about the women (5:2)
         (a) The older women: emphasis on parenthood (5:2a)
         (b) The other women: emphasis on purity (5:2b)
   b. Fairness for widows (5:3–16)
      (1) The reliable widow (5:3–10)
         (a) The widow and her respect (5:3)
         (b) The widow and her resources (5:4)
            i. The rule (5:4a)
            ii. The reason (5:4b)
         (c) The widow and her reactions (5:5–7)
            i. The widow who reacts in a wise way (5:5)
               a. Her desolation (5:5a)
               b. Her dedication (5:5b–c)
                  1. Her dependence on God (5:5b)
                  2. Her devotion to God (5:5c)
            ii. The widow who reacts in a worldly way (5:6–7)
               a. What is noted (5:6)
               b. What is needed (5:7)
         (d) The widow and her relations (5:8)
            i. What is required (5:8a)
            ii. What is revealed (5:8b)
         (e) The widow and her reception (5:9)

i. The question of her maturity (5:9a)
ii. The question of her monogamy (5:9b)
(f) The widow and her reputation (5:10)
i. Is she a good person? (5:10a)
ii. Is she a giving person? (5:10b–f)
a. Look at her home (5:10b)
b. Look at her hospitality (5:10c)
c. Look at her humility (5:10d)
d. Look at her heart (5:10e)
e. Look at her helpfulness (5:10f)
(2) The reluctant widow (5:11–15)
(a) The refusal (5:11a)
(b) The reason (5:11b–12)
i. She will cast off her first love (5:11b)
ii. She will cast off her first faith (5:12)
(c) The recrimination (5:13)
i. Guilty of lazy living (5:13a)
ii. Guilty of haunting houses (5:13b)
iii. Guilty of telling tales (5:13c)
iv. Guilty of being busybodies (5:13d)
v. Guilty of doing damage (5:13e)
(d) The recommendation (5:14–15)
i. What Paul desired (5:14a–c)
The young widow should:
a. Betroth a new partner (5:14a)
b. Become a new parent (5:14b)
c. Beautify a new position (5:14c)
ii. What Paul deplored (5:14d)
iii. What Paul discerned (5:15)
(3) The related widow (5:16)
(a) A precaution (5:16a)
(b) A provision (5:16b)
(c) A proposal (5:16c–d)
i. The church and its resources (5:16c)
ii. The church and its responsibilities (5:16d)
c. Faithfulness to elders (5:17–25)
(1) A word to the people (5:17–22)

- (a) Acclaiming elders (5:17–18)
    - i. Their rule (5:17a)
    - ii. Their role (5:17b)
    - iii. Their reward (5:18)
        - *a.* An Old Testament reference (5:18a)
        - *b.* A New Testament reference (5:18b)
- (b) Accusing elders (5:19–20)
    - i. A precautionary requirement (5:19)
    - ii. A public rebuke (5:20)
- (c) Accepting elders (5:21–22)
    - i. A demand dramatized (5:21a)
    - ii. A difficulty disclosed (5:21b–c)
        - *a.* The issue of obedience (5:21b)
        - *b.* The issue of objectivity (5:21c)
    - iii. A danger displayed (5:22)
        - *a.* The possibility of making a hasty move (5:22a)
        - *b.* The possibility of making a horrible mistake (5:22b)

(2) A word to the pastor (5:23–25)
- (a) Timothy's sickness (5:23)
- (b) Timothy's situation (5:24–25)
    - i. Men who sin (5:24)
    - ii. Men who serve (5:25)

d. Firmness for servants (6:1–2)
- (1) Those with characteristic masters (6:1)
    - (a) The requirement expressed (6:1a)
    - (b) The requirement explained (6:1b)
- (2) Those with Christian masters (6:2)
    - (a) A danger (6:2a–b)
        - i. A blessing to be enjoyed (6:2a)
        - ii. A blame to be evaded (6:2b)
    - (b) A duty (6:2c–d)
        - i. A responsibility (6:2c)
        - ii. A reason (6:2d)
    - (c) A demand (6:2e)

2. The priority of godliness (6:3–6)
    - a. Godliness expounded (6:3–5)

- (1) The gold standard disclosed (6:3)
  - (a) How to mark the forger (6:3a–b)
    - i. By what he declares (6:3a)
    - ii. By what he denies (6:3b)
  - (b) How to measure the forgery (6:3c–d)
    - i. By the personal words of the Savior (6:3c)
    - ii. By the pure words of the Scripture (6:3d)
- (2) The guilt stains exposed (6:4–6)
  - (a) The examination of false teachers (6:4–5d)
    - i. Their personal exposure (6:4a)
    - ii. Their public exposure (6:4b–5d)
      - *a.* Their questions exposed (6:4b–c)
        - *1.* Such mundane observations (6:4b)
        - *2.* Such mischievous questions (6:4c)
      - *b.* Their quarrels exposed (6:4d–5d)
        - *1.* Their "ministry" (6:4d–f)
          - (i) Promotes covetousness (6:4d)
          - (ii) Promotes contentiousness (6:4e)
          - (iii) Promotes contemptuousness (6:4f)
        - *2.* Their mentality (6:4g–5c)
          - (i) The fruit of their thinking (6:4g–5a)
            - *(a)* Their mental squalor (6:4g)
            - *(b)* Their many squabbles (6:5a)
          - (ii) The root of their thinking (6:5b–c)
            - *(a)* The inherent badness of their minds (6:5b)
            - *(b)* The inherent bankruptcy of their minds (6:5c)
        - *3.* Their motives (6:5d)
  - (b) The excommunication of false teachers (6:5e)

b. Godliness extolled (6:6)

3. The peril of gold (6:7–10)
   - a. A basic fact (6:7)
   - b. A basic formula (6:8)
   - c. A basic folly (6:9)
     - (1) The temptation explained (6:9a–b)
       - (a) The hidden lure (6:9a)

- (b) The harmful lusts (6:9b)
- (2) The trap exposed (6:9c)
- d. A basic fallacy (6:10)
  - (1) What people dream (6:10a)
  - (2) What people discover (6:10b–d)
    - (a) The wrong love (6:10b)
    - (b) The wrecked life (6:10c–d)
      - i. The great seduction (6:10c)
      - ii. The great sorrow (6:10d)

4. The pursuit of goodness (6:11–19)
   - a. The challenge to Timothy (6:11–12)
     - (1) To flee (6:11a)
     - (2) To follow (6:11b–g)
       - (a) The divine character described (6:11b–c)
         - i. Integrity toward man (6:11b)
         - ii. Integrity toward God (6:11c)
       - (b) The divine character distilled (6:11d–e)
         - i. By the Word of God (6:11d)
         - ii. By the Spirit of God (6:11e)
       - (c) The divine character displayed (6:11f–g)
     - (3) To fight (6:12)
       - (a) A word of command (6:12a–b)
         - i. Don't give up! (6:12a)
         - ii. Don't let go! (6:12b)
       - (b) A word of commendation (6:12c–d)
         - i. Timothy had been perfectly true to his calling (6:12c)
         - ii. Timothy had been publicly true to his calling (6:12d)
   - b. The charge to Timothy (6:13–19)
     - (1) The exhortation (6:13a–b)
       - (a) The presence of God (6:13a)
       - (b) The power of God (6:13b)
     - (2) The example (6:13c–14)
       - (a) The Lord's confession (6:13c)
       - (b) The Lord's coming (6:14)

- (3) The exclamation (6:15–16)
  - (a) The moment of revelation (6:15a)
  - (b) The marvel of revelation (6:15b–16)
    - i. One who is absolute in power (6:15b–d)
      - *a.* As the ruling One (6:15b)
      - *b.* As the royal One (6:15c)
      - *c.* As the reigning One (6:15d)
    - ii. One who is ageless in person (6:16a)
    - iii. One who is awesome in presence (6:16b–c)
      - *a.* Inaccessible—bathed in fearful light (6:16b)
      - *b.* Invisible—beyond all finite sight (6:16c)
    - iv. One who is arrayed in praise (6:16d–e)
      - *a.* Everlasting acclaim is His (6:16d)
      - *b.* Everlasting authority is His (6:16e)
- (4) The expectation (6:17–19)
  - (a) The rich man and his gold (6:17)
    - i. What he must renounce (6:17a–b)
      - *a.* Triumphing in his money (6:17a)
      - *b.* Trusting in his money (6:17b)
    - ii. What he must recognize (6:17c)
  - (b) The rich man and his goal (6:18–19)
    He must keep an eye on:
    - i. His present responsibility (6:18)
    - ii. His prospective reward (6:19)

PART 4: CONCLUSION (6:20–21)

- A. A pleading word (6:20–21a)
  - 1. A duty recorded (6:20a)
  - 2. A detour recommended (6:20b–21a)
    - a. The danger is revealed (6:20b–c)
      - (1) Patently silly opinions (6:20b)
      - (2) Popular "scientific" oppositions (6:20c)
    - b. The danger is real (6:21a)
- B. A parting word (6:21b)

PART 1

Introduction

1 Timothy 1:1–2

A. Paul and his signature (1:1a–b)
   1. His apostleship (1:1a)

Paul, an apostle of Jesus Christ . . ." Thus, the first epistle to Timothy begins, and we are arrested at once. Why did Paul, in writing to his dear friend, think it necessary to add his title to his signature? (It was a common practice in those days to begin a letter with a signature.) However, when we write to our close friends, we do not put after our names the degrees to which we are entitled! That might be appropriate when we write official letters, but not when we write personal letters. So we are immediately alerted by Paul's use of his title. Evidently, 1 Timothy is not just a personal letter, although it might contain personal touches. It is a pastoral letter, intended to be read by not only Timothy but also those to whom he was ministering.

Timothy likely was in Ephesus at the time Paul wrote this letter, pastoring one of the greatest of Paul's churches. The "grievous wolves" about whom Paul had warned the Ephesian elders (Acts 20:29) had at last succeeded in invading the church. Paul had sent Timothy to deal with the situation. His letter was intended to strengthen Timothy's hand and guide him in the steps he should take. We can see God's overruling hand in preventing Paul's going to Ephesus himself, for had he gone, we would not have this letter in our Bible.

   2. His authority (1:1b)

Paul was an apostle "by the commandment of God." The word translated "commandment" emphasizes the authority behind the command. A Roman governor derived his authority from either the Roman senate or caesar; Paul's authority came from God.

The inclusion of the phrase "by the commandment of God" indicates something about the decline of the Ephesian church. Only half a dozen years had passed since Paul had sent the Christians in Ephesus the most magnificent letter ever written, one that enshrined the greatest truths ever revealed, yet Paul already found it necessary to exert his apostolic authority.

B. Paul and his Savior (1:1c–e)
   1. The Savior is the One in whom we live (1:1c–d)

Paul became an apostle by the commandment of "God our Saviour, and Lord Jesus Christ." God is called our Savior here and elsewhere in Scripture (Luke

1:47; 1 Tim. 2:3; Titus 1:3; 2:10; 3:4; Jude 25). Usually the title *Savior* is reserved for the Lord Jesus, whose name Paul immediately appended here, making an oblique reference to the deity of Christ. God, who is our Savior, and the Lord Jesus, who is equally our Savior, stood solidly behind Paul's apostleship.

We can picture Paul's striding into the cities of Galatia and Europe and into Asian Ephesus. He went as God's ambassador to lay siege to the court of the consciences of one and all in cities sodden with sin and corrupted by vile religions. How could one man and a few of his followers hope to make any serious impact on such places? Those cities lay in the lap of the evil one. Entrenched wickedness reigned in their governments and courts, in their colleges and universities, and in the homes and hearts of almost all of the residents. But Paul was backed by the power of God.

When Paul entered a city, he spied out the land for a good place to start his evangelistic efforts. If a synagogue was there, that is where he went first. If he could not find a synagogue, he looked for a handful of Jews by the river, perhaps, as in Philippi, or he obtained a job with a tent maker, as in Corinth. He made contacts, counting on God to bring hearts He had touched his way. However deeply entrenched Satan's power was, Paul carried with him a greater power and authority. He was an apostle commanded by God, who is our Savior, and by the Lord Jesus Christ, who is the "author and finisher of our faith" (Heb. 12:2).

Satan was no match for a man backed by such authority. His bastions crumbled. Souls were saved. A church sprang up. Lives were transformed. Entire families were redeemed. The weapons of Paul's warfare were "mighty through God to the pulling down of strong holds" (2 Cor. 10:4). Usually, all that the enemy could think to do was stir up persecution, but that only drove God's ambassador on to a new city, and the Christians who were left behind were strengthened, purified, and emboldened by Paul's example. Timothy recognized Paul's authority, as did the Ephesians.

2. The Savior is the One for whom we look (1:1e)

Having declared his apostolic authority, Paul softened the declaration by adding the words *which is our hope*. Thus, he turned his readers' eyes away from himself and young Timothy and focused them on the Lord Jesus and the sure hope that every believer has in Him.

During the time since Paul had written his epistle to the Ephesians, the world had become a much more dangerous place for Christians. Nero had set fire to Rome and, to cover his crime, blamed the fire on the Christians. They were a much more convenient scapegoat than the Jews. The Christians had no international organization, no people of great wealth and influence to speak for them, and no homeland ready to go to war with Rome for them. In fact, most Christians were slaves.

The fire of persecution was raging with fearful ferocity in Rome, and the flames were reaching out to the provinces. Doubtless, Paul knew that his days were numbered. The Jewish war with Rome had already broken out, a war that the Christians knew the Lord Himself had predicted (Luke 21:6–24).

No doubt, as the church read the word "hope" in 1 Timothy 1:1, most of the congregation thought of what Paul elsewhere called "that blessed hope, and the glorious appearing of the great God and our Saviour Jesus Christ" (Titus 2:13). As the days grew ever darker and the shadows lengthened, the hope of the Lord's return burned brighter. Thoughts of His coming again helped fortify believers against persecution and served as a healthy antidote to disorder and error in the church.

C. Paul and his son (1:2)
   1. Timothy's blessed relationship (1:2a)

Timothy had been about fifteen years old when Paul burst so dynamically and dramatically into his life in Lystra. Timothy was about thirty to thirty-five years old when he received this first epistle, but to "Paul the aged" (some thirty years Timothy's senior, Philem. 9), Timothy was still a youngster.

There can be no doubt about Paul's affection for his young friend. The apostle addressed his letter "unto Timothy, my own son in the faith." As far as we know, Paul was not married (1 Cor. 7:6–8) and had no son of his own. He found the son he longed for in Timothy. Paul reminded the Philippians how he and Timothy had worked together in Philippi: "As a son with the father, he hath served with me in the gospel" (Phil. 2:22). The word translated "son" in that verse is *teknon.* Paul's choice of that word indicates that he regarded Timothy as his own true child, as much as if he had been his natural-born son. When he wrote to the Corinthians, Paul called Timothy "my beloved son, and faithful to the Lord" (1 Cor. 4:17). Clearly, Paul derived joy and warmth from his relationship with Timothy, and Timothy was blessed to have a man like Paul as his mentor.

Paul was one of God's originals. He was as brave as a lion and had a mind made for the universe. Moreover, his giant intellect was captured and expanded by Christ. Paul was warmhearted, enterprising, energetic, and persuasive. He had a rare gift for making friends—and foes. He was born a Hebrew, raised a Pharisee, and trained to be a rabbi. He had lived in a Greek city and appreciated the Greek philosophers. He was also a Roman citizen—a rare thing in those days. He had traveled widely, knew all kinds of people, and had a keen zest for life. His convictions were crystal clear as a result of years of study of the Scriptures. Above all, he had met the risen Christ. What a fountain of wisdom he must have been! How stimulating his conversation must have been! What a man to have as a father in the faith and a personal friend!

2. Timothy's boundless resources (1:2b)

Paul reserved the salutation "Grace, *mercy,* and peace" for his personal and pastoral epistles to Timothy and Titus. It is a matter of conjecture as to why the apostle added "mercy" to his usual greeting of "grace and peace." Perhaps the reason lies in the difference between blessings and mercies. Blessings such as grace and peace are of a spiritual nature, whereas mercies are of a temporal nature. Not many people make this distinction. We often hear people say, "God has blessed me with a good wife, a comfortable home, and a steady job," but these provisions are not blessings; they are mercies. Our blessings are described in the Sermon on the Mount (Matt. 5:1–12) and in the Epistles (e.g., Eph. 1:3).

One clue as to why Paul included "mercy" in his greetings to his two young friends perhaps can be found in the political situation in the empire. Nero was on the rampage. It had become even more dangerous than before to be a Christian and doubly dangerous to be a church leader. Paul might well have invoked God's protective hand—His mercy—in view of the times.

In any case, it is sensible to remember that God's mercies are related to our temporal needs and can ebb and flow like the tide in accordance with His wisdom and will. We have no guarantee that we will never be sick, never be allowed to suffer, always be protected from our enemies, or always be in comfortable circumstances. Millions of God's people have been exposed to hardship and have grown in grace as a result. Our blessings, on the other hand, are all spiritual, eternal, and forever secure in Christ.

What Paul wrote after his salutation revolves around two major topics, one pastoral and the other personal. He told Timothy how to build an effective church (1:3–3:15) and how to become an effective Christian (3:16–6:19).

PART 2

How to Build an Effective Church

1 Timothy 1:3–3:15

A. The church and its doctrine (1:3–20)
   1. The loss of truth considered (1:3–4)
      a. Timothy's residence (1:3a)

Before getting down to business and dealing with doctrinal issues, Paul mentions the fact that Timothy was residing in Ephesus. The apostle had many happy memories of Ephesus—and some hair-raising ones as well.

He visited the city briefly at the end of his second missionary journey and left his colleagues Aquila and Priscilla there to prepare the way for his return (Acts 18:18–26). Paul made Ephesus the major site of his evangelistic activity during his third missionary journey. For three months, he preached in the synagogue and apparently made a number of Jewish converts. Then, when he was thrown out of the synagogue, he concentrated on reaching Gentiles during the next two years. A tremendous revival broke out, accompanied by apostolic signs and wonders. "So mightily grew the word of God and prevailed," commented Luke (Acts 19:20).

In the end, Demetrius and the silversmiths' guild instigated a citywide riot against Paul and the believers in Ephesus. The silversmiths made images of the goddess Diana (Artemis), whose foul pagan temple attracted a large number of tourists. So many people were turning to Christ that the sales of the images were falling, and the craftsmen became hostile.

Paul left Ephesus for Macedonia. A short time later, on his way to Jerusalem, the apostle met with the Ephesian elders at Miletus and urged them to continue his work and defend the faith. Later still, during his first Roman imprisonment, Paul wrote his epistle to the church at Ephesus. Evidently, the church there had continued Paul's evangelistic efforts because new churches had sprung up in surrounding communities such as Smyrna, Pergamos, Thyatira, Sardis, Philadelphia, Laodicea, Colosse, and Hierapolis.

After being released from his first imprisonment, Paul had Ephesus on his mind. Evidently, he wanted to go there himself, but other concerns took priority. So he sent Timothy, a young man he loved, to Ephesus, a city he loved.

We know by name quite a number of believers who had contact with the Ephesian church. They included Aquila and Priscilla of Pontus (Acts 18:18–19), Paul's loyal coworkers; Gaius of Macedonia (Acts 19:29); Aristarchus of Thessalonica (Acts 19:29; 20:4); the eloquent Apollus of Alexandria (Acts 18:24); Trophimus, a native of Ephesus (Acts 21:29); Onesiphorus (2 Tim. 1:16–18);

Erastus of Corinth (Acts 19:22); Fortunatus of Corinth, Stephanas, Achaicus, and Chloe (1 Cor. 1:11; 16:15–17, assuming that Paul wrote his first Corinthian letter from Ephesus); Timothy; and, later, the apostle John. Evidently, the church at Ephesus was as cosmopolitan as the city itself.

b. Timothy's responsibility (1:3b–4)
(1) To require sound doctrine (1:3b)

Paul instructed Timothy to "charge some that they teach no other doctrine." We do not know what rumors Paul had heard, but he was greatly concerned. By the time he wrote his second epistle to Timothy, Paul was able to list by name at least five people who had abandoned the faith: Hymenaeus and Alexander (1 Tim. 1:20), Phygellus and Hermogenes (2 Tim. 1:15), and Philetus (2 Tim. 2:17). Speaking more generally, Paul added, "All they which are in Asia (and presumably all in Ephesus) be turned away from me" (2 Tim. 1:15).

It always comes back to doctrine. The early church cut its teeth on doctrine (Acts 2:42). What we believe is vital. We must not be misinformed regarding the truth.

The story is told of a woman and her child who were traveling by train across the prairies in subzero weather. The woman kept on anxiously looking about her, worried about missing her stop. The conductor assured her that he would see her off the train at the right stop. A fellow traveler, a salesman, also tried to reassure her. "I travel this line frequently, lady," he said. "I know every station and whistle-stop. If the conductor forgets, I'll make sure you get off at the right place."

Soon the salesman said, "Yours will be the next stop." After a while the train came to a halt. There was no sign of the conductor. "This is where you get off, lady. I'll help you out with your bags."

It was dark and snowing hard, and there was no one in sight. The fellow passenger assured the frightened woman, "They'll have heard the train. They'll be along in a minute. This has to be your stop." He climbed back on board as the train pulled away.

Several minutes later, the conductor came through the car. "Where's the lady with the child?" he asked.

"I helped her off at the last stop," said the salesman. "That was her stop and you weren't here."

"That was not a station!" cried the conductor. "We were held up by a signal. There are no houses for miles around." The engineer stopped the train and backed it up. They found the woman and her child frozen to death. They were victims of false information.

People who teach false doctrine are as dangerous as that salesman. And people who listen to such teachers are in dire peril. So it was important for Timothy to put a stop to the propagation of false doctrine.

(2) To resist silly digressions (1:4)
  (a) Gnostic tendencies exposed as foolish (1:4a–b)

"Neither give heed," Paul wrote, "to fables and endless genealogies." The word translated "fables" here is *muthos,* which can be rendered "hoary old myths." People on the Judaistic side of gnosticism liked to dig up old Jewish legends (such as those we find in the Apocrypha) and to palm them off on gullible Gentiles as authentic gospel truth.

The word *genealogies* here does not refer to the legitimate, God-inspired chronologies and family trees that are scattered throughout the Bible. These scriptural genealogies serve useful purposes in the process of divine revelation. For instance, the nine chapters of names at the beginning of 1 Chronicles summarize the unfolding drama of redemption from Adam to Zedekiah.[1] That genealogy also served Ezra's purpose of assuring the discouraged Jews, repatriated from the captivity, that, although the throne of David was gone, the royal line remained intact. Moreover, the books of Chronicles were placed at the end of the Jewish canon by the Jews. Matthew began his gospel with a genealogy that traced the preservation of the royal Davidic line through the four silent centuries between Malachi and the Messiah. The genealogies found in 1 Chronicles link on to the genealogy in the gospel of Matthew. Together, the two form a natural bridge between the two major testaments.

Paul did not object to those genealogies because they are rich in instruction and are part of a God-breathed Book. What he had in mind was the foolish and imaginary emanations of the so-called aeons that the gnostics interposed between God and Christ. Those graded ranks of celestial beings were necessary to gnostic speculations because the gnostics considered matter to be evil and defiling. They invented a host of angelic beings, gradually descending in rank and slowly approaching a point at which one of their number would be so far from God that he could not defile His holiness, yet so powerful that he could bring

1. E. W. Bullinger, *The Companion Bible* (reprint, Grand Rapids: Kregel, 1990), 531 mar.

matter into being. Paul wrote off the whole scheme as utter foolishness and ordered Timothy to pay no heed to such high-sounding nonsense.

(b) Gnostic tendencies expelled as fruitless (1:4c–d)

Paul rejected all such speculations as fruitless because they *invite* "questions" and *inhibit* "godly edifying." Legitimate questions, of course, do exist. New converts who might be reading the Bible for the first time are naturally full of them. Indeed, some passages in the Bible challenge the understanding of even mature, well-taught believers. Paul did not object to legitimate questions. In fact, a segment of 1 Corinthians deals with practical and theological questions that the Corinthians had asked him. We would be the poorer if the apostle had not addressed them. The Lord Himself gave His great Olivet discourse (Matt. 24–25) in response to questions that the disciples asked.

What Paul denounced was the supercilious questions raised by those who trifle with the Word of God. When the Sadducees tried to trap the Lord with such a question, He bluntly told them that they were ignorant of both the Scriptures and the power of God (Matt. 22:23–29). Pilate was no better. He did not wait for an answer when he asked, "What is truth?" (John 18:38). The Athenians were trifling with the truth when they summoned Paul to Mars Hill (Acts 17:18–32). They sneered among themselves, "What will this babbler say?" Then they asked him, "May we know what this new doctrine, whereof thou speakest, is?" Luke commented that those philosophers "spent their time in nothing else, but either to tell, or to hear some new thing." Their insincerity was exposed when a little later they mocked at Paul.

Anyone who has been in the Lord's work for any length of time will have met people who come forward after a service to quarrel over a nonessential issue. Such quibbling is not edifying and does not promote godliness; it does not produce the orderly living that stems from true faith in the Lord. Christian doctrine has no place for silly arguments put forth by carnal, worldly-minded people. So Paul told Timothy to put a stop to pointless speculations.

2. The law of God considered (1:5–11)
   a. Its fullest transformation (1:5)

"Now the end of the commandment," wrote Paul, "is charity [love] out of a pure heart, and of a good conscience, and of faith unfeigned." The "commandment" to which Paul referred was the charge given to Timothy (1:3). The Greek word conveys the idea of a proclamation, command, or charge that is received from a superior and transmitted to others. The high priest used this word when he said to the apostles, "Did not we straitly command you that ye should not teach in this name?" He employed a particularly strong expression that could be rendered, "Did not we command with a command . . . ?" The disciples, unawed by Caiaphas and his crowd, replied, "We ought to obey God rather than men" (Acts 5:28–29).

Paul's rigorous command was that Timothy quell the gnostics and legalists in Ephesus and promote unquenchable love, unqualified goodness, and unquestionable faith. The "wolves" (Acts 20:29) wanted to promote questions and quarrels, but the old *dos* and *don'ts* of the legalizers had been replaced by the law of love. The law of love, which Timothy was charged to uphold, transcends the old law with its rules and rituals.

Some time ago when I was in Panama City, I stayed in a motel with a view of the waterfront. When I first looked out the window, the tide was low; and the seagulls and other tidewater birds were busying themselves around stranded pools of water. Then the sea came in, inundating all of the little puddles, and the birds were able to rejoice in a limitless supply of water. That is a picture of what happened to the old law when the tide of God's love came in at Calvary. Rules and regulations were inundated by the sea of God's limitless love. The Law was fulfilled in Christ, and now it is fulfilled in us by His Holy Spirit. It is no longer a duty to do this and that; it is our delight. Paul charged Timothy to make the law of love clear for the legalists were still exerting a strong influence, as Paul went on to show.

b. Its false teachers (1:6–7)

Paul continued, "From which (gospel truth) some having swerved have turned aside unto vain jangling; desiring to be teachers of the law; understanding neither what they say, nor whereof they affirm" The word translated here means "to miss the mark," which is exactly what legalists do. They miss the whole point of our new life in Christ, which is love, a pure conscience, and sincere faith. It is not a matter of whether a person parts his hair this way or that or dresses thus and so.

The word translated here as "turned aside" is *ektrepomai,* which is also used in Hebrews 12:13. There, the author, just before his final warning passage, urged believers to "make straight paths for your feet, lest that which is lame *be tuned out of the way*" (italics added).

The word translated "vain jangling" in 1 Timothy 1:6 is *mataiologia,* which refers to foolish talking. The legalists and other false teachers, having forgotten what true Christianity is all about, were losing themselves in a sea of words. The expression *vain jangling* reminds us of the Lord's complaint in Malachi 2:17. Just before He closed the Old Testament and withdrew into a four-century-long silence, He inspired His prophet to write His complaint: "Ye have wearied the Lord with your words."

c. Its foolish transgressors (1:8–11)
   (1) The goodness of God's law (1:8–9a)

Legalists, who major on the minors and insist on their petty little shibboleths, not only miss the point of genuine Christianity but also demean the law itself. The law served a great purpose in its day and is still of great value when its limitations are understood. Paul wrote, "We know that the law is good, if a man use it lawfully" (1 Tim. 1:8). Here, as in Romans 7:12, the apostle emphasized the essential goodness of God's law.

In Old Testament times, the law served a double function. First, it provided a *system,* a manner of life for Old Testament believers. The law probed every nook and cranny of their lives. It demanded obedience at all levels and threatened dire penalties for failure to keep it. It maintained a large body of ritualistic rules and regulations; upheld a system of sacrifice; sustained an elaborate ceremonial priesthood connected to an earthly sanctuary; and designated feast days, fast days, new moons, and Sabbaths. The law as a system was abolished at Calvary; God rent the temple and rendered Judaism obsolete.

Second, the law provided a *standard* for Old Testament believers. The Ten Commandments, which were amplified in many other detailed demands spelled out heaven's minimum for human behavior. The moral laws enshrined changeless principles for all divine and human relationships. Mandates such as those requiring worship of God alone; total freedom from idolatry and profanity; obedience to parents; and abhorrence of murder, adultery, theft, lying, and covetousness are changeless and nonnegotiable.

The law as a standard is as much in effect in our age of grace as it was in Old Testament times. What has changed is God's attitude toward the sinner. At Calvary He provided a perfect redemption for sinners. And on the Day of Pentecost He provided a perfect means of living a new life in Christ; the Christian can now live above the law in a realm ruled by love.

So Paul could say that "the law is good." However, he added, ". . . if a man use it lawfully." The apostle knew people who used the law unlawfully. The rabbis, for example, added the requirements and regulations of the budding Talmud to the simple but adequate edicts of the Torah. By the time of Christ, they had already hedged in the Sabbath with scores of burdensome rules of their own invention. Eventually, they would hem in every mandate of the law with encyclopedic rabbinical rules.

Paul fought tooth and nail against any attempt to fasten this unbearable yoke on the necks of Christians, particularly the Gentile believers. Even Peter and James conceded that Gentiles should be exempt (Acts 15). Yet, legalists in the church have in all ages sought to add lists of requirements and prohibitions to simple faith in Christ and obedience to His Word.

The law was intended to show us what holiness is; it was not intended to make us holy. The command in Leviticus 11:45 to "be holy, for I am holy" was appended to a long list of dietary rules. It is the Lord, not the law, who makes us holy (1 Peter 1:13–16).

First Timothy 1:9 adds the thought that "the law is not made for a righteous man." In its narrower sense, this statement means that the believer who is robed in the impeccable righteousness of Christ lives above the law positionally and should live above the law practically. By obeying the law of love (Rom. 13:8–10), the believer automatically obeys the law of God. The indwelling Holy Spirit makes his new life in Christ possible (Rom. 8:1–4).

In its broader sense, Paul's statement that the "the law is not made for a righteous man" means that the person who does not break specific demands of the law has nothing to fear from the law. Its penalties are directed against murderers, thieves, perjurers, and the like. Thus, Paul could insist on the goodness of God's law. Jesus said, "I am not come to call the righteous, but sinners to repentance" (Matt. 9:13).

(2) The greatness of God's law (1:9b–11)

(a) It exposes general sins (1:9b–g)

Just as those who break the law of the land can expect to face its penalties, the law of God with all of its penalties still threatens those who live in sin. Paul gave a series of illustrations of this truth, beginning with general sins.

i. Sins against government (1:9b–c)

The law is made to expose *the defiant* (lawless) and *the disobedient.* The word translated "lawless" in 1:9 is *anomos,* which can be translated "men without law" and refers to those who have contempt for the law. Peter used this word on the Day of Pentecost when he charged Israel with the murder of their Messiah. "Him . . . ye have taken," he said, "and by wicked *[anomos]* hands have crucified and slain" (Acts 2:23). Paul used the same word in 2 Thessalonians 2:8 to describe the coming antichrist as "the lawless one" or "that wicked" (one) in the King James Version. Such men may defy all human laws, but they cannot escape God's law.

The word translated "disobedient" in 1 Timothy 1:9 is *anupotakos,* which refers to people who are not under subjection. They are undisciplined. Whereas the lawless person refuses to recognize any law, the undisciplined person refuses to obey any law. Just the same, the law was made for such people.

ii. Sins against godliness (1:9d–e)

The law was also made for *the impious* and *the iniquitous,* or as Paul put it, "for the ungodly and for sinners." The word translated "ungodly" here means "impious" and refers to those who are devoid of reverence for God. Such people are not simply irreligious; they act in ways that are contrary to God's demands. They might think of themselves as clever and completely emancipated, but God's law will catch up with them sooner or later, as it did with Charles Darwin.

Darwin began his career by training for the ministry. For a long time, he debated whether he should publish his book on evolution and did so only when he discovered that a rival was about to beat him to it. He hesitated because he was afraid he might fall down between two stools and end up castigated by theologians and scientists alike. He need not have worried. Men such as T. H. Huxley saw at once the potential of Darwin's book; it was a valuable weapon in the war against God because it provided men like him with a working hypothesis for atheism. Darwin's theory enabled atheists to explain the universe without God.

Darwin was popularized and publicized, voted a scholar, canonized as a saint by the anti-God community, and hailed as a jolly good fellow. But he couldn't live with his conscience. He became chronically ill, made excuses for himself, and half apologized to God. Darwin made his intellect his god, but God's law—"Thou shalt have no other gods before me" (Exod. 20:3)—found him out. Darwin sought balm for his guilty conscience in the accolades that a godless world eagerly bestowed on him, the man who had liberated them from the Bible.

The word translated "sinners" in 1 Timothy 1:9 conveys the idea of missing the mark, of wandering from the right path, of doing wrong. God views going astray as iniquity. His law was made for such people; it points to the proper path. Isaiah wrote, "All we like sheep have gone astray; we have turned every one to his own way." Thankfully, he showed us the way back—"The Lord hath laid on him the iniquity of us all" (Isa. 53:6).

iii. Sins against goodness (1:9f–g)

Referring to *those without any sort of scruples* and *those without any sense of sanctity,* Paul called them the "unholy and profane." The law was made for them as well. The word translated "unholy" here is *anosios,* which suggests the opposite of holiness. The concept of holiness includes the idea of being separated to God; the believer is "called . . . unto holiness" (1 Thess. 4:7). The unbeliever is a stranger to holiness.

The word translated "profane" in 1 Timothy 1:9 stems from a Greek term meaning "threshold." A threshold is something on which people tread, so a profane person is one whose life can be trampled on by every evil impulse and influence. Essentially irreligious, he is common and unhallowed. The classic biblical example is Esau (Heb. 12:16).

(b) It exposes glaring sins (1:9h–11)

i. The murderers (1:9h–i)

Next, Paul showed how God's law is specifically targeted against people who become involved in crimes such as murder. The law is designed to expose *those who kill their parents* and *those who kill other people.* The apostles called them "murderers of fathers," "murderers of mothers," and "manslayers." People who attack their parents and commit patricide and matricide come under the curse of the Mosaic Law.

The word translated "manslayers" here simply means "murderers." In our society, many murderers are never caught, and many others escape the full penalty of our laws by invoking pleas of insanity, by receiving lenient sentences and early parole, by turning state's evidence, by taking advantage of legal loopholes, by bribing corrupt judges, or by intimidating witnesses or jurors. But murderers cannot escape the penalties of God's laws or avoid the coming Great White Throne judgment (Rev. 20). Unless, of course, they turn to Christ and have their sins forgiven (1 Cor. 6:9–11).

ii. The "mature" (1:10a–b)

God's law is also designed for people in our pornographic society who classify themselves as "mature" or "adult." This category includes *those who practice prostitution* and *those who practice perversion.* Paul called them "whoremongers" and "them that defile themselves with mankind." The word translated "whoremongers" here refers to a person who indulges in fornication. This is akin to the Greek word for "harlot."

To change the label on a bottle of poison and call it "essence of peppermint" might be aesthetically pleasing to some people, but it does not change the nature of the bottle's contents. Likewise, calling those who watch pornographic movies "mature" does not make them so. The false label only makes the bottle and its lethal contents more dangerous. People who engage in immoral activities expose themselves to the penalties of God's law. Nowadays, those penalties often include disgusting, debilitating, and deadly diseases.

The word translated "them that defile themselves with mankind" refers to people who practice sodomy. Our laws regarding sodomy are becoming increasingly lax. Nowadays, lesbians and homosexuals parade with pride and use the political system to win approval from society and gain the protection of its laws. God's laws against sodomy, however, remain unchanged.

iii. The menstealers (1:10c)

Paul said that the law was made for "menstealers" as well. The word translated "menstealers" refers to slave dealers and kidnappers. It stems from a word that describes a slave captured in a war. The word *andrapodon* was offensive to the Greeks because of its likeness to *tetrapoda,* which referred to a quadruped; the implication was that slaves differed from animals only in the number of their feet. The Holy Spirit bluntly used the derivative of a disliked word to emphasize His disapproval of the sin of menstealing.

iv. The manipulators (1:10d–11)

God's law was also made for the manipulators, those who play fast and loose with the given word. *Those who sin against the spoken word* were called "liars" by Paul.

Those who sin against the sworn word were called "perjured persons." The apostle was also referring to *those who sin against the sacred Word* when he spoke of "any other thing that is contrary to sound doctrine; According to the glorious gospel of the blessed God, which was committed to my trust."

When a case is brought to trial, one of the important functions of the court of law is to determine who is speaking the truth. Truth is essential in all forms of communication. Lies, however, spring readily to many people's lips. Because all human transactions are based on trust, lies destroy the foundation of society. The lie is the idiom of Satan's language, for he is "the father" of lies (John 8:44).

Heavy penalties await witnesses who lie under oath in court. The sorriest case of perjury in all history is found in the record of the trial of the Lord Jesus before the Jewish Sanhedrin. We read in Matthew 26:59–61:

> Now the chief priests, and elders, and all the council, sought false witness against Jesus, to put him to death; But found none: yea, though many false witnesses came, yet found they none. At the last came two false witnesses, And said, This fellow said, I am able to destroy the temple of God, and to build it in three days.

A more corrupt court would be hard to find. At the same trial, Jesus was put under oath by the high priest, who said, "I adjure thee by the living God, that thou tell us whether thou be the Christ, the Son of God" (26:63). Jesus responded truthfully, knowing full well that He would die as a result.

The worst lies are those that are told in relation to the Word of God. No greater communication exists: God has spoken to man! What He has revealed by means of plenary, verbal, and inerrant inspiration of the Holy Spirit is preserved in the Bible. To tamper with that body of absolute truth, to handle the Word of God deceitfully, is the sin of sins (Rev. 22:18–19). So Paul wrote about manipulators who teach things "contrary to sound doctrine." Sound doctrine is basic to any exposition of God's Word.

The word translated "sound" in 1 Timothy 1:10 means literally "to be in good health." Our doctrine must be healthy, and it can be healthy only if it is based on an unwavering commitment to the authority and inerrancy of Scripture and on an unimpeachable method of interpretation. We must take the position that God says what He means and means what He says and that what He says is to be interpreted literally, grammatically, culturally, and contextually.

The unifying factor in such a system of interpretation is the recognition that God does all things for His own glory. Thus, the truth committed to Paul by the Holy Spirit is described in 1 Timothy 1:11 as "the glorious gospel of the blessed God," or, as the phrase could also be rendered, "the gospel of the glory of the blessed God."

3. The love of Christ considered (1:12–17)
   a. Paul's gratitude (1:12–14)
      (1) His present ministry (1:12)

Note Paul's gratitude: "I thank Christ Jesus our Lord, who hath enabled me, for that he counted me faithful, putting me into the ministry." The apostle was grateful that God counted him worthy, especially in view of his past.

The Holy Spirit was able to entrust Paul with so much marvelous truth—He enabled him to write fourteen New Testament epistles, counting Hebrews—because of his personal integrity. The apostle was absolutely trustworthy, and the Lord "counted" him faithful. The word translated "counted" here carries the idea of pondering or considering carefully a course of action and taking into account the various issues at stake.

In the zealous young persecutor of the church, the Lord Jesus saw an equally zealous preacher of the gospel. God saw Saul's potential, just as He had seen the potential of Jonah. God knew the fiber of Jonah's soul; He knew that the same fiery disposition that prompted him to flee to Tarshish, regardless of the consequences, would make him a powerful missionary to Nineveh. The burning passions of Jonah's heart that were set on fire by hell needed to be extinguished and set on fire again by God.

The prophet who later stalked the streets of Nineveh in the name of God was the same man who recklessly urged the sailors to heave him overboard. In the midst of the storm, he reasoned that if he were dead he could not go to Nineveh; if he did not go to Nineveh and preach imminent judgment, then God's judgment would assuredly fall. Nineveh would be overthrown, and Israel would no longer have to fear that enemy. God knew that after Jonah had been through a death, burial, and resurrection (possibly in fact, certainly in type) his voice would shake Nineveh to its foundations.

God saw as much in Saul of Tarsus as He had seen in Jonah. He "counted" Paul faithful. And God did not count on Paul in vain.

(2) His past malignancy (1:13–14)
   (a) The malice he expressed (1:13a)

Paul had once been an avowed enemy of New Testament truth. "[He] was before a blasphemer, and a persecutor, and injurious." As Saul of Tarsus, he was a Pharisee, a rabbinically trained Jew, a brilliant controversialist, a militant activist, and a passionate nationalist. He was absolutely convinced that Jesus of Nazareth was an imposter, that Christianity was a dangerous cult, and that pacifism would never wipe it out. Christianity, Saul believed, needed to be rooted up, by violence if necessary.

He became the accredited agent of the Sanhedrin to destroy Christianity, and he persecuted Christians to the death at home and abroad. He described his crusade thus:

> I persecuted this way unto the death, binding and delivering into prisons both men and women. . . . I verily thought with myself, that I ought to do many things contrary to the name of Jesus of Nazareth. Which thing I also did in Jerusalem: and many of the saints did I shut up in prison, having received authority from the chief priests; and when they were put to death, I gave my voice against them. And I punished them oft in every synagogue, and compelled them to blaspheme; and being exceedingly mad against them, I persecuted them even unto strange [foreign] cities. (Acts 22:4; 26:9–11)

The Holy Spirit described Saul's activities as "breathing out threatenings and slaughter against the disciples of the Lord" (Acts 9:1). Furthermore, the initiative was his, although Caiaphas doubtless was only too willing to have such a zealous tool.

(b) The mercy he experienced (1:13b–14)

i. His ignorance was forgiven (1:13b)

"But," wrote Paul, "I obtained mercy, because I did it ignorantly in unbelief." Even in his unregenerate days, Paul was not guilty of intellectual dishonesty. He was wrong in his estimate of Christ and the church, but he was honestly wrong. He was ignorant, the victim of wrong information. Moreover he was not without the courage of his convictions.

His revered old rabbi, Gamaliel, suggested caution in dealing with Christians (Acts 5:34–40), but Saul saw clearly that Judaism and Christianity were not compatible. It had to be one or the other. He allowed his intellectual honesty to work out its logical conclusion; because Christianity and Judaism were mutually exclusive, the innovation (Christianity) would have to be nipped in the bud—no matter what the cost. Carrying his logic one step further, he reasoned that because no one else seemed prepared to take the radical measures required he would.

When he looked back, Paul wondered why God had not smitten him and concluded that it was because of his ignorance. Of course, ignorance is not a valid plea in a court of law, but under grace it is weighed and accepted as a reasonable excuse when it is offered along with a repentant, broken heart. Probably the face of Stephen, the first Christian martyr, caused doubt to take root in Saul's soul (Acts 6:15). That seed of doubt grew and grew until the light dawned in a blaze of glory on the Damascus road. Thereafter, Paul knew the truth, and he became the boldest believer of them all.

ii. His ignorance was forgotten (1:14)

Paul's ignorance was swallowed up in the overwhelming grace of God. "The grace of our Lord was exceeding abundant with faith and love which is in Christ Jesus" (1:14). *Grace, faith,* and *love* became the best-loved words in Paul's new vocabulary. He could never get over the fact that his blasphemies had been removed by God's grace, his desire to persecute Christians had been replaced by faith, and his injurious behavior had been revolutionized by God's love.

In his unregenerate days, Paul had had a savage tongue; he had been a "blasphemer." The verb form of the word translated "blasphemer" in 1:13 means "to revile, to rail," especially against Christ. Paul doubtless had said terrible things about the Lord.

He had also been a "persecutor." The word translated "persecutor" occurs only in 1:13 in the New Testament. Its verb form means "to put to flight, to pursue." Paul was like a savage hound snarling at the heels of fleeing Christians, who scattered everywhere to escape his fury (Acts 8:1–4).

Before he was converted, Paul had been "injurious" as well. The word translated "injurious" means "an insulter." Saul's venomous tongue had often been busy making insolent and contemptuous remarks about the Lord Jesus Christ.

The sins of his past had been forgiven and forgotten. Paul could not forget them, but the Lord could and did. The wonderful thing about God's forgiveness is that when He forgives He forgets. God said, "I, even I, am he that blotteth out thy transgressions for mine own sake, and will not remember thy sins" (Isa. 43:25). Because He controls all of the factors of space and time, He can sovereignly dismiss our sins from His mind and banish them from the universe. So far as God is concerned, they are as nonexistent as they would be if they had never been committed (Heb. 8:12). Our troubled hearts and accusing consciences can rest on that truth.

b. Paul's gospel (1:15–16)

"This is a faithful saying, and worthy of all acceptation, that Christ Jesus came into the world to save sinners; of whom I am chief." First Timothy 1:15 is one of the great gospel texts of Scripture. It ranks with Isaiah 53:6; 11, John 3:16 and Romans 10:9.

(1) Paul's affirmation (1:15a)

"This is a faithful saying." First and foremost, Paul would have us know that the gospel of Christ is based on fact. The gospel is completely reliable and should be given universal acceptance. Paul's affirmation was based on his own investigation of its truth and his personal meeting with the risen Christ.

What is recorded in the four Gospels is true. Matthew, Mark, Luke, and John were credible, reliable witnesses whose testimony would stand up in any law court in the civilized world, as Simon Greenleaf demonstrated.

Greenleaf, once the dean of Harvard Law School, was one of America's greatest authorities on the laws of evidence; his treatise on the subject was a standard textbook for a hundred years. When he was a mature lawyer of sixty-three years of age, he decided to examine the four gospel writers to see if their statements were completely reliable. He brought Matthew, Mark, Luke, and John into court, as it were, and cross-examined them. He used the accepted rules of evidence in a court of law as the basis of his inquiry. He compared meticulously their various accounts of the events with which they claimed to have been personally acquainted. He subsequently recorded his findings in a lengthy book titled *The Testimony of the Evangelists, Examined by the Rules of Evidence Administered in Courts of Justice.* In his opening remarks, which were addressed to members of the legal profession, he wrote,

> Our profession leads us to explore the mazes of falsehood, to detect its artifices, to pierce its thickest veils, to follow and expose its sophistries, to compare the statements of different witnesses with severity, to discover truth and separate it from error.[2]

After putting the testimony of the four Evangelists to the test, he concluded that they had recorded the simple, unvarnished truth about the extraordinary life of Jesus. Their claims would stand up in court. As Paul affirmed, the gospel message is completely reliable.

(2) Paul's acceptation (1:15b)

That "faithful saying," Paul wrote, is "worthy of all acceptation." The startling events recorded in the Gospels really happened. A babe was born in Bethlehem, and angel choirs heralded His birth. He was who He claimed to be, the Son of God. He did go about doing good, and He did perform all kinds of marvelous miracles. He did teach truth in a particularly pungent, undiluted form and with divine authority. He was crucified and buried. He did rise from the dead and ascend bodily into heaven. The Gospels are not "cunningly devised fables" (2 Peter 1:16); they contain documented historical facts.

The events in the life of Christ might be overwhelming, but how could we have expected anything less astounding to happen when the Creator of the universe became a man? To dismiss the facts of the gospel is to reject the truth, truth that is verifiable in a court of law and vital to our eternal well-being.

(3) Paul's attestation (1:15c–d)

(a) Of a historical fact (1:15c)

The fact is that Christ Jesus came into the world. Other people are *born* into the world, but He *came.* He is the only person in history who chose the time, place, and circumstances of His own advent. In coming, He fulfilled a series of specific prophecies concerning His birth, life, and death. Only an ignorant person would deny that such a person as Jesus of Nazareth existed. He came into the world and lived on our planet. We do not know whether He ever visited other worlds as He did ours, even before His incarnation, but we do know that He visited Earth. And we know what happened to Him when He came.

2. Simon Greenleaf, *The Testimony of the Evangelists* (Grand Rapids: Baker, 1965).

(b) Of a humbling fact (1:15d)

He came "to save sinners." Christ Jesus came from the mansions of glory, "out of the ivory palaces, into a world of woe."[3] He came because we were lost, enslaved in sin, and unable to save ourselves. We faced the wrath of God; hell awaited us. More than anything else, we needed a savior. So He "came into he world to save sinners."

We must acknowledge that we are numbered among those whom Christ came to save, that we are sinners. The word translated "sinners" in 1:15 (as in 1:9) points to "those who miss the mark." It reminds us that we have all "come short of the glory of God" (Rom. 3:23). We fail to come up to God's standard; we cannot reach the goal He has set in His law.

With infinite compassion the Son of the living God vacated His throne in the highest heaven, bade farewell to the angel throng, descended to this planet, was "contracted to the span of a virgin's womb," and came into this world to do what had to be done to save sinners.

We were slaves of sin, in bondage to wickedness, so we needed to be *redeemed.* We were unregenerate, following the dictates of fallen human nature, so we needed to be *regenerated.* We were ignorant of God's Word, averse to His presence, in love with the world, conquered by lust, and deceived by Satan; in other words, we were enemies of God, so we needed to be *reconciled.* We needed to be justified, sanctified, adopted, and glorified. So Paul's attestation was good news: "Christ Jesus came into the world to save sinners."

(4) Paul's application (1:15e)

The dark shadow of Paul's past fell once again upon his heart. Having mentioned sinners, he added, "of whom I am chief." God allowed him to append this personal application because of the hope and encouragement it would give to countless other sinners. They would reason that if God had already saved the chief of sinners there is no one whom Jesus cannot save, if he acknowledges that he is a sinner.

There is, of course, another requirement: he must accept God's offer of salvation. It is indeed "worthy of all acceptation." The word translated "acceptation" means "to receive heartily." The pardon that God offers should be received gladly

3. From the hymn "My Lord Has Garments" by Henry Barraclough.

and welcomed warmly. The tragedy is that many sinners do not respond positively as Paul did to the offer of salvation.

Even in the secular realm, pardon must be accepted. Consider the case of George Wilson. In 1830, a court in the eastern district of Pennsylvania condemned this man to death for armed robbery of the U. S. mail, and a date was set for his execution. However, he was pardoned by President Andrew Jackson. For some unknown reason, Wilson refused to accept the pardon. His lawyers demanded a stay of execution and declared, "You cannot execute a man who has been pardoned." Eventually, they carried the case to the Supreme Court.[4] Here, in part, is the Court's decision:

> A pardon is a deed, to the validity of which delivery is essential, and delivery is not complete without acceptance. It may then be rejected by the person to whom it is tendered; and if it be rejected, we have discovered no power in a court to force it on him.
>
> It may be supposed that no being condemned to death would reject a pardon; but the rule must be the same in capital cases and in misdemeanors.[5]

Likewise, God's offer of salvation has to be accepted. We could paraphrase the Court's decision as follows: "It may be supposed that no being condemned to a lost eternity would reject God's pardon, but if it is rejected, the rule must be the same." Our pardon was purchased at Calvary at infinite cost, and the only sensible response is to receive heartily God's gracious offer.

(5) Paul's apprehension (1:16)

Verse 16 reveals Paul's grasp of the meaning of verse 15. He understood that *the patience of God* and *the pattern of grace* were displayed in his case: "For this cause I obtained mercy, that in me first Jesus Christ might shew forth all longsuffering, for a pattern to them which should hereafter believe on him to life everlasting." Paul was saying, "If He could save *me,* He could save anyone." What

---

4. Written up in court records by Richard Peters. See *Reports of Cases Argued and Adjudged in the Supreme Court of the United States Term, 1883,* vol. 7, case 150, *The United States vs. George Wilson.*
5. Stephen K. Williams, *Cases Argued and Decided in the Supreme Court of the United States,* bk. 8, ed. Lawyers (Rochester, N.Y.: Lawyers Co-operative, 1883), 644.

impressed the apostle most was the patience God had shown toward him—the restraint He had used, the long-suffering He had shown.

No doubt, as Saul of Tarsus, he had argued about doctrine with the early Christians and probably with Stephen, a man full of wisdom and the Holy Spirit. Then Saul, infuriated by his inability to prove the Christians wrong, had grown increasingly vindictive and violent. He ended up making "havoc" of the church (Acts 8:3). The word translated "made havoc of" is *lumainomai,* which means "to maltreat and outrage." It was used to describe a boar ravaging a vineyard by tearing up tender saplings by the roots.

For more than half a dozen years, Saul had acted like a madman. During his rampage, homes had been wrecked, wives had been widowed, children had been orphaned, and believers had been made to blaspheme. The church had been broken up and scattered, the name of Christ had been profaned, and the Jews had been confirmed in their unbelief. Many believers had been stripped of their wealth and had become a financial burden to the church at Jerusalem. The persecution had gone on and on, yet God was long-suffering with Paul. God's marvelous patience overwhelmed the apostle and offers hope to all of us. Paul's experience is a wonderful illustration of God's grace as revealed in the gospel.

c. Paul's God (1:17)
   (1) His infinite greatness (1:17a–c)

With thoughts of God's grace overwhelming him, Paul could not restrain himself. In one of the Bible's great doxologies, he cried out, "Now unto the King eternal, immortal, invisible. . . ."

Saul had finally recognized that the Lord Jesus was King. The Jews had denied Him and the throne of David, although He was its rightful claimant. He descended from David through both His mother and His foster father, as the chronologies of Matthew and Luke proved. Those genealogies were easily verifiable from the temple records in those days. The wise men from the East proclaimed the Lord Jesus to be King; and Pilate, scoffing skeptic though he was, also named Him King (Matt. 2:1–11; 27:37).

Now the King reigned supreme in Paul's heart, and he anticipated the day when every knee would bow to Him (Phil. 2:5–11). Already, thousands upon thousands had owned Him as King, and, in time, millions more around the globe would worship Him. The hymn writer captured the contrast between His rejection and His acclamation:

Sinners in derision crowned Him,
Mocking thus the Savior's claim;
Saints and angels crowd around Him,
Own His title, praise His name.[6]

One of these days, the Lord Jesus is coming back to reign, to be owned as "King of kings, and Lord of lords" (Rev. 19:16). Now He is seated on His Father's throne in heaven (Heb. 1:3), but He is coming back to sit on "the throne of his father David" (Luke 1:32) and to reign "from the river unto the ends of the earth" (Ps. 72:8). Meanwhile, believers around the world pray daily for His return (Matt. 6:10, 13).

(a) The King immutable (1:17a)

Christ is "the King eternal." The phrase could be rendered "King of the ages" because the word translated "eternal" signifies a period of indefinite duration. The Lord Jesus is the absolute Ruler of all of the ages of time.

He was there in the dateless, timeless past before the rustle of an angel's wing ever disturbed the silence of eternity. He was there when countless stars and their satellites were hurled out into intangible space, to travel on prodigious orbits at inconceivable velocities and with mathematical precision. He was there when our planet was fitted to be man's future home. He was there in the Garden of Eden to stoop down and fashion Adam's clay. He was there when Adam fell. He was there when the Flood inundated the planet, when the builders of Babel were scattered, and when Abraham was given a vision of a celestial city and called to be a pilgrim and stranger on earth. Christ was there in Egypt when the Exodus took place. He was there at Sinai when the Law was given. He was there when David was crowned king of Israel and when the messianic dynasty began. He was there when Assyria overran Israel, when Babylon ended the Judean monarchy, and when Persia condoned the rebirth of the Jewish state. He was there when Alexander conquered the world and when Rome rose to power. He was there when Jerusalem fell. He will be there when the church is raptured. He will be there when the millennial age ends and time will be no more. The Lord Jesus is "the King eternal."

6. From the hymn "Look, Ye Saints, the Sight Is Glorious!" by Thomas Kelly.

(b) The King immortal (1:17b)

Christ is also the King "immortal." We usually connect the idea of exemption from death with the word *immortal,* and, of course, Jesus has conquered death and all of its powers (Rev. 1:18). But the Greek word translated "immortal" in 1 Timothy 1:17 is *aphthartos,* which means "uncorrupted or not liable to corruption or decay." The Lord demonstrated His immortality in that sense in His tomb. The horrors of the grave could not visit Jesus' sepulcher because it had been decreed: "Thou wilt not leave my soul in hell [sheol]; neither wilt thou suffer thine Holy One to see corruption" (Ps. 16:10).

When the Lord stood at the door of Lazarus's tomb and commanded that the stone be removed, Martha was horrified. "Lord, by this time he stinketh," she said, "for he hath been dead four days" (John 11:39). Death and decay are inevitable consequences of sin. These companions of death found no footing in the Lord's tomb. He was immortal.

(c) The King invisible (1:17c)

Christ is the King "invisible." The word translated "invisible" here is *aoratos,* which means "unseen." The Lord had the power to appear or vanish at will, as He did in the house of two of His disciples in the village of Emmaus (Luke 24:31). Another instance is His sudden appearance in the Upper Room (John 20:19). Paul had personally experienced the Lord's ability to become visible and invisible, for he had been converted when the Lord had visibly appeared to him from heaven (Acts 9:3–4).

(d) The King infallible (1:17d)

To be eternal, incorruptible, and invisible are attributes of God. Jesus shares these attributes because He is God. Indeed, Paul describes Him as "the only wise God." All other gods worshiped by men are foolish. They are products of human imagination and demonic deception. They are foolish gods because they are false gods.

The Jesus of the New Testament, who is the Jehovah of the Old Testament, is "the only wise God." Paul reminded the Colossians that in Him "are hid all the treasures of wisdom and knowledge" (Col. 2:3). The Old Testament prophet Isaiah described Him as "Wonderful, Counselor, The mighty God, The Everlasting Father, The Prince of Peace" (Isa. 9:6).

How wonderfully wise He is! He is wise enough and knowledgeable enough to plan the creation of the universe and to plan the size and composition of everything from galaxies to subatomic particles. He has wisdom enough to decide the size, speed, and orbits of a hundred billion galaxies. He has wisdom and knowledge enough to hold positively charged protons together in an atom's heart; enough wisdom and knowledge to invent DNA, the very code of life itself; and wisdom and knowledge enough to control all the factors of time, matter, and space and to hold them in proper balance so that all things work out according to the counsels of His will.

The Lord has wisdom and knowledge enough to comprehend and countermand the entire "mystery of iniquity" (2 Thess. 2:7). He has wisdom and knowledge enough to fathom the mind, malice, and motives of the Prince of Darkness and to overrule unerringly all of his deep and diabolical schemes. He has wisdom and knowledge enough to be aware of the mind, heart, will, hopes, fears, aspirations, potential, limitations, thoughts, words, and actions of every creature in all ages of time. He has wisdom and knowledge enough to foresee the future and make all things work together ultimately for our good and His glory.

He is the only wise God. No god lolling or lusting on fabled Mount Olympus had wisdom. No pagan god about whom we read in the sacred Scriptures had knowledge. No Baal, Ashtoreth, Moloch, or Dagon had understanding. No god in the tangled Hindu pantheon is wise. We worship the only God who is wise, and His name is Jesus.

(2) His infinite glory (1:17e–f)

God's glory is *evident* and *everlasting.* To Him we should ascribe "honour and glory forever and ever." These words *honor and glory* are linked together in Hebrews 2:7–9; 2 Peter 1:17; Revelation 4:9, 11; 5:12–13; 19:1 in describing the divine glory. Our beloved Lord receives little enough honor from most people here on earth. His blessed name is often used as a curse word and linked with the foulest language that unregenerate people can dredge up from the dark sewers of their minds. But He does have some people who honor Him.

The word translated "honour" here relates to the value we place on things. Only believers can really appreciate, and even they only to a limited degree, the inestimable worth of the Lord Jesus. As Peter wrote, "Unto you therefore which believe he is precious: but unto them which be disobedient, the stone which the builders disallowed." The word translated "precious" is *entimos,* which means "of great price, costly in the superlative degree." It is used in the same context in connection with precious stones. Having picked up the word, Peter seemed reluctant to put it down, for he used it three times in four verses (1 Peter 2:4–7).

The word translated "glory" in 1 Timothy 1:17 is *doxa.* It is often used in the New Testament in relation to the nature and acts of God as He reveals Himself, especially in the person of Christ, through whom this glory shines (John 17:5). *Doxa* is used to describe the brightness and splendor that pours out from God (Luke 2:9), to portray the awesome transfiguration of Christ (2 Peter 1:17), and to ascribe praise to God (Luke 17:18).

Overwhelmed by the grace and glory of God, Paul poured out his doxology. Then as though there were no more words to be said, he wrote "Amen."

4. The life of faith considered (1:18–20)
   a. The charge (1:18–19b)

Like the Lord and His disciples (see Matt. 17:1–16), Paul came down from the mount. Mountaintop experiences and outpoured doxologies have their place, but soon the practicalities of life demand their due. We remember that a demon-possessed boy, a group of powerless believers, and a collection of sneering enemies were waiting for the Lord in the valley when He came down from the Mount of Transfiguration. So Paul, after his outburst of praise, still had to face the difficult situation in the Ephesian church. So he followed his doxology with a new, threefold charge to his young colleague in Ephesus.

(1) The paternal appeal (1:18a)

"This charge I commit unto thee, son Timothy," Paul began. There is something tender and touching about this appeal because the word translated "son" here is *teknon,* which means "child." Wolves prowled in Ephesus (Acts 20:29–30) and there was a growing lukewarmness (Rev. 2:4), and, in some respects, Timothy was only a child. But sometimes it pays to be childlike (Matt. 18:1–6). A great prophet was inspired to write, "A little child shall lead them" (Isa. 11:6). When the newly crowned Solomon, weighing his awesome responsibilities and his desperate need for wisdom, confessed to God, "I am but a little child" (1 Kings 3:7), he received the gift of great understanding.

Timothy might have been a child, but he had Paul for a spiritual father. All of the apostle's authority, wisdom, and experience were at Timothy's disposal. Indeed, much of this wisdom can be found in the pages of this epistle. Paul had a personal, paternal concern for Timothy and did not hesitate to let it be known.

(2) The prophetic appeal (1:18b)

Paul's charge was committed to Timothy "according to the prophecies which went before on thee." The apostle was reminding him of the prophecies made at the time he was ordained to the ministry (4:14). Although Paul might paternally regard Timothy as a child, and the sophisticated intellectuals and legalists in the church might patronizingly regard him as a child, he was armed with impressive gifts and credentials. Let the Ephesians who underestimated Timothy beware. Everyone was to heed the Lord's warning in Matthew 18:6.

Paul's words in 1 Corinthians 14:20 doubtless applied to Timothy: "Brethren, be not children in understanding: howbeit in malice be ye children, but in understanding be men." That was the approach Timothy needed to take. Although he was young, he had been around Paul for more than fifteen years and had learned much. Doubtless Timothy knew Paul's epistles by heart (his name is included in half a dozen of them). So, child though he was, Timothy was well equipped to undertake whatever charge Paul laid on him.

(3) The practical appeal (1:18c–19b)

(a) Regarding the fight (1:18c)

"This charge I commit unto thee," Paul wrote, "that thou by them mightest war a good warfare." The word *them,* of course, refers to the prophecies and gifts that Timothy received when the believers back home first commended him to full-time Christian work. The apostle had already written to the Ephesians about the war that was raging and had urged them to "put on the whole armour of God" so that they would be victorious in the fight (Eph. 6:11–17).

Timothy needed no reminder that perilous times had come. He had heard the terrible stories being told about the persecution of Christians in Rome. It was becoming increasingly dangerous to be a believer. Moreover, as if attacks from without were not bad enough, heretics within the church were becoming bolder. But Paul charged Timothy not to surrender but to "war a good warfare." He was to stand up for the truth, come what may.

When Solomon said, "To every thing there is a season, and a time to every purpose under heaven," he ended his diverse list with "a time of war, and a time of peace" (Eccl. 3:1, 8). The time for trying to reach an understanding with those who taught false doctrines had ended. The time for trying to pacify hostile government officials was over. It was time to wage war. The battle lines had been drawn both inside the church and in the world. Paul made clear that Timothy had to be prepared to fight to the death because that is what warfare is all about.

(b) Regarding the faith (1:19a–b)

i. Truth viewed objectively (1:19a)

When Paul wrote, "Holding faith *[pistis]*," he had in mind not only the great body of truth that we call "the faith" but also faith as the living, divinely implanted principle that sees us through. John wrote, "This is the victory that overcometh the world, even our faith *[pistis]*" (1 John 5:4).

ii. Truth viewed subjectively (1:19b)

"A good conscience" must accompany that dynamic faith when we wage war on the spiritual plane. Shakespeare wrote, "Conscience doth make cowards of us all."[7] The person who has a guilty, accusing conscience is terribly handicapped in doing the Lord's work. He might be able to put on a good front and brazen things out for a while, but he has no real power because he does not deceive the Holy Spirit.

b. The challenge (1:19c–20)

(1) The danger is exposed (1:19c)

Paul became more specific regarding the challenge that Timothy faced in Ephesus: "Some having put away concerning faith have made shipwreck." The word translated "put away" is a strong expression in the original and means "to thrust away." It implies that some people had willfully violated their consciences. Stephen used the word when he was describing the initial rejection of Moses by the enslaved Israelites in Egypt: "He that did his neighbour wrong thrust him away, saying, 'Who made thee a ruler and a judge over us?'" (Acts 7:27). Paul used the same word when the Jews in the synagogue at Pisidian Antioch, who were envious of his success, began to contradict him and blaspheme: "Then Paul

7. Shakespeare, *Hamlet,* 3.1.

and Barnabas waxed bold, and said, It was necessary that the word of God should first have been spoken to you: but seeing ye put it from you (thrust it away from you) . . . lo, we turn to the Gentiles" (Acts 13:46).

The situation at Ephesus was not simply that some people had begun to entertain doubts. Rather they had deliberately rejected the truth they once professed to believe. In other words, they had become apostates. They had rejected not only their personal faith but also *the* faith, the divinely revealed body of truth that constitutes Christian doctrine.

As a result of contemptuously thrusting away truth and throwing over their good consciences, those individuals had "made shipwreck." The idea is that of a ship being run into the rocks.

(2) The danger is exemplified (1:20)

Paul named two of the apostates: Hymenaeus and Alexander. The apostle mentioned both of these men again in his second epistle to Timothy. Paul said that Hymenaeus's teaching was cancerous in nature and that his heretical teaching on the Resurrection had overthrown the faith of some (2 Tim. 2:17–18). And Paul identified Alexander as a coppersmith who did him much evil, probably during his trial. The apostle prayed that he might be rewarded "according to his works" (2 Tim. 4:14). Both men were blasphemers.

In 1 Timothy 1:20, Paul said, "I have delivered [Hymenaeus and Alexander] unto Satan." Nothing in this life could be more solemn than to be apostolically handed over to Satan. Such excommunication from the church thrust the offender back into the world, where Satan is lord and god (John 12:31; 14:30; 16:11; 2 Cor. 4:4) and where the offender would be exposed to Satan's malignity and hate. Such apostolic discipline was exercised sparingly and in the hope that the offender would recover. Paul had dealt thus with the incestuous brother at Corinth (1 Cor. 5:5). Hymenaeus and Alexander were excommunicated so that they could "learn not to blaspheme." Evidently, they did not learn their lesson.

B. The church and its devotions (2:1–15)
   1. The practice of worship in the church (2:1–8)
      a. Telling God about men (2:1–3)

Prayer is "first of all" an act of worship. We must never underestimate the importance of public prayer. Paul wrote, "I exhort therefore, that, first of all, supplications, prayers, intercessions, and giving of thanks, be made for all men" (2:1). Telling God about men is a great privilege.

(1) Types of prayer (2:1a–d)
(a) Petitioning (2:1a)

The word translated "supplications" in 2:1 has to do with asking God for something specific. Supplications are petitions that have our personal needs in view rather than God's ability to meet our needs. Paul had in mind here those needs that are a result of the policies of the governments under which we live. We can readily understand his emphasis when we remember that in Paul's day Nero governed the empire, and he was on a rampage against the church.

Most people in the Western world live under relatively benign governments that respond reasonably well to the will of the people. Christians are not widely persecuted, oppressed, abused, or discriminated against. But many of God's people live in lands where intolerant governments put all kinds of pressure on their people, especially Christians. Communism still controls the lives of vast numbers, and others are held in the grip of Islamic fundamentalism. Persecuted Christians must have numerous supplications to present to God.

God hears and heeds such petitions, although He works according to a timetable and on a scale that are beyond our comprehension. For instance, God said to Moses, "I have surely seen the affliction of my people which are in Egypt . . . for I know their sorrows" (Exod. 3:7). God's time for intervention came after years of oppression and suffering, during which countless petitions must have ascended on high. Doubtless *individual* prayers were answered while God waited before acting on behalf of the *nation* of Israel. Take, for an example, the impassioned supplications of Amram and Jochebed for the tiny infant whom they hid in an ark of bulrushes and concealed among the reeds; God marvelously took care of their needs even before the foreknown moment came when He directly intervened in the Egyptian-Hebrew crisis.

(b) Personalizing (2:1b)

The word translated "prayers" in 2:1 refers to prayers offered to God. Such prayers involve an awareness of God's power and an emphasis on *personal* devotion.

Prayer is a spiritual force that is as real as any physical force such as gravity, magnetism, and electricity. God controls all of the forces of nature. Wind, wave, and weather are His to command (as we learn from the book of Jonah). He regulates the energy output of every star. He holds the earth as it rotates on its axis and takes its annual journey around the sun. Tides and tempests, tornadoes and earthquakes, droughts and downpours are all under His ultimate rule. Although Satan wields power over the forces of nature, his power is subservient to God's power. God also controls the rise and fall of nations: "The king's heart is in the hand of the LORD, as the rivers of water: he turneth it whithersoever He will" (Prov. 21:1). And He controls the unseen angelic and demonic powers who seek to influence human affairs.

We do not know how prayer works, but we know that it does. We pray; God hears. He gives our prayers their due weight as He balances all of the forces and factors involved in the situation about which we are praying. Sometimes He says yes; sometimes He says no; sometimes He says to wait. We can rest assured that He is too wise to make mistakes, too loving to be unkind, and too powerful to be thwarted.

(c) Pleading (2:1c)

The word translated "intercessions" in 2:1 is *enteuxis,* which *The Companion Bible* says has to do with "confiding access to God, giving prominence to child-like confidence in prayer."[8] *Enteuxis* occurs only here and in 4:5 in the New Testament. It conveys the idea of drawing near to a person to converse familiarly with him, just as the Lord drew near to His two discouraged disciples on the road to Emmaus to talk with them (Luke 24:13–15). The word initially meant "meeting"; it came to mean "conversation" and then "petition." *Enteuxis* later became the technical word for approaching a king and at last the word for coming to God to intercede.

To intercede is to come into the presence of God on behalf of others. The classic example of intercession is the prayer of Moses after the children of Israel sinned so terribly by making and worshiping the golden calf. "Oh, this people have sinned a great sin, and have made them gods of gold," he cried. "Yet now, if thou wilt forgive their sin—; and if not, blot me, I pray thee, out of thy book which thou hast written" (Exod. 32:31–32).

It is the privilege of God's children to draw near to their heavenly Father to converse familiarly with Him about others. In the New Testament, we see the

8. See *The Companion Bible,* app. 124:2.

great Intercessor acting as His people's Great High Priest and pouring out His heart in petitions for His disciples (John 17).

(d) Praising (2:1d)

The word translated "giving of thanks" in 2:1 is *eucharistia,* which communicates the idea of expressing gratitude. The sad truth is that we are far more prone to come to God to ask for something that we need or that someone we love needs than we are to return thanks for the boundless benefits that His goodness and grace bestow so lavishly on us.

(2) Topics for prayer (2:1e–2b)

(a) People in general (2:1e)

Paul gathered up all of these types of prayer and said that we should exercise them on behalf of "all men." No person exists on this crowded planet in whom God does not have a personal interest. He would have us enlarge our narrow horizons, expand the breadth of our vision, increase the area of our concern, and be ready to pray for anyone anywhere at any time.

My first wife, Jean, was an indefatigable prayer warrior. Christian schools and organizations, missionaries and mission boards, churches, interest groups espousing various worthy causes, family, friends, and even strangers would send her prayer requests. She must have been on scores of mailing lists. Every day the postman brought her more and more letters. She had a big three-ring notebook in which she filed all of these reminders, and she patiently prayed her way through them. She took the time to pause at each name, consider each request, and formulate an intelligent prayer.

The tough part of responding to such requests is praying for "Alfonso, who is facing persecution for daring to get baptized" or "Umbopa, who is about to marry a pagan." To us, the Alfonsos and the Umbopas are only names with a splash of local color. How can we become genuinely interested in people who are almost entirely unknown, who live far away, whose faces remain unseen, and whose personalities are blank? It takes imagination and time. Maps and pictures can clothe unfamiliar names with flesh and features, surroundings and color. And it helps to remember that God knows every detail of every life and every situation. One word from us speaks volumes to Him. So Jean prayed until, under the ravages of inoperable cancer, it became too much. I remember the day, when faced with a new batch of prayer requests, she finally gave up. She put down her heavy, oversized three-ring notebook with the words, "There You are, Lord. I can't do it anymore. You'll have to pray for them Yourself."

(b) People in government (2:2a–b)

i. Those who wield supreme authority (2:2a)

Paul also exhorted Timothy to pray "for kings"—in other words, for Nero.

The mighty had already fallen. Julius Caesar had been assassinated in 44 B.C. After defeating Antony at Actium in 31 B.C., Octavian became the first Roman emperor in 27 B.C., and the heralded *Pax Romana* (two hundred years of peace) began. Political rot soon set in as Tiberius, Caligula, Claudius, and Nero succeeded Octavian. These men illustrated repeatedly the fact that absolute power tends to corrupt absolutely. The name *Nero* became a synonym for terror and tyranny. By the time Paul wrote this letter to Timothy, thousands of Christians had died horrible deaths under his rule. Yet, Paul said in effect, "Pray for him. He is the king."

The apostle, during his first Roman imprisonment, had sent his Ephesian friends a request for prayer: "Praying always . . . for me, that utterance may be given unto me, that I may open my mouth boldly, to make known the mystery of the gospel, For which I am an ambassador in bonds: that therein I may speak boldly, as I ought to speak" (Eph. 6:18–20). Now, free again for a little while, Paul wrote to Timothy, who was ministering to those same people. This time, instead of saying, "Pray for me," Paul said in effect, "Pray for Nero." Although the emperor had all of the might of imperial Rome at his command, Paul was the more powerful of the two. As the apostle had already reminded the Ephesian believers, the child of God—all outward appearances to the contrary notwithstanding—is "strengthened with might by his Spirit in the inner man" (Eph. 3:16).

During Paul's first Roman imprisonment, his case might have been heard by a court judge, but it is possible, even likely, that the apostle appeared before Nero himself and gave his testimony directly to the emperor. If so, what a scene it must have been! There sat the emperor, dressed in royal robes and surrounded by luxury, pomp, and power. There stood the sentries and the senators. There stood the sycophants who toadied to the man who murdered countless people with the utmost barbarity. And there stood Paul, alone and dressed in homespun. We can see Nero as he stared scornfully at the battered-looking Jew whose bodily appearance some people described as "weak" and whose speech they said was "contemptible" (2 Cor. 10:10). Nero, haunted by a guilty conscience for crimes already committed, was capable of any act of wickedness. Nevertheless, Paul boldly told him about Christ, His cross, the power of His resurrection, and the new life that is available to all.

However, at the time Paul wrote to Timothy, he was no longer in custody. He knew, however, that one of these days Nero, whose decadence was deteriorating into unrestrained depravity, would summon him to answer for his crime of propagating Christianity. Paul's name must have been high on Nero's hit list. After all, he was the boldest and most eloquent and vocal of all of the detested Christians. Paul's interval of freedom would soon end. The next time he was arrested, he would be treated not as a Roman but as a criminal. He knew what that would mean—he would face rigorous incarceration and certain death. He was living on borrowed time. "Pray for Nero," Paul said.

So we are to pray for those who wield supreme authority. We might not like the decisions made by those in power, but we are to pray for those who make them. Our complaints and criticisms of those who rule over us should be aired in heaven at God's throne.

ii. Those who wield subordinate authority (2:2b)

We are to pray for "all that are in authority." When Paul gave this exhortation, he had everyone in mind who wielded power, everyone from senators who held power in Rome, to soldiers who were visible on provincial streets; everyone from the senators in Rome to the local magistrates in the provinces.

The church was already familiar with persecution. The Jerusalem church had been persecuted by Herod Agrippa I. He murdered James and then tried to murder Peter. Peter became an urgent target for prayer as he lay bound and guarded in his prison. "Prayer was made without ceasing of the church unto God for him," wrote Luke (Acts 12:5). But who had prayed for lost Herod?

Paul had been in the hands of political and religious authorities many times. He had stood before a criminal high priest, a corrupt Felix, a compromising Festus, and a careless Herod Agrippa II. Paul understood their need for prayer. He himself had once been one of them, a persecutor of the church. As Saul of Tarsus, he had used his authority to persecute the church (Acts 22:5). Who had prayed for him? Perhaps Andronicus and Junia had done so (Rom. 16:7).

(3) Targets in prayer (2:2c–3)

(a) The human dimension (2:2c–e)

i. A stable environment (2:2c)

Paul said that we should pray "that we may lead a quiet and peaceable life." The word translated "quiet" here means "tranquil" and refers to tranquility arising from without, from the absence of outward disturbance and persecution. We can well believe that Christians everywhere were fervently imploring the throne of God for that kind of rest, especially when Nero was on the rampage. Many times in the long history of the church, Christians have prayed for such tranquility. We tend to take it for granted when we have it.

The word translated "peaceable" refers to tranquility arising from peace within. When storm tides rise, and when the world is torn apart by war and woe, when tyrants come to power and people are tormented, peace is still a fruit of the Spirit for the child of God.

The Lord Jesus could sleep amid the storm (Matt. 8:24) and walk in triumph over heaving waves (Matt. 14:25). Unlike Peter, He was never ruled by circumstances. Peter tried to walk on water himself. At the Lord's bidding, he stepped out of the boat onto the nearest wave. He made momentary progress in a revolutionary new life of faith. But then he took his eyes off the Lord and, overwhelmed by the howling wind and heaving sea, cried out in terror. Peter still had to learn that all of those things that were over his head and that threatened to overwhelm him were already under the Master's feet.

ii. A steady encouragement (2:2d–e)

a. To godliness (2:2d)

We pray for tranquility without and within "that we may lead a quiet and peaceable life in all godliness and honesty." The word translated "godliness" here is *eusebeia,* which comes from a word meaning, "to be devout, to adopt an attitude that is pleasing to God." *Eusebeia* occurs often in Paul's Pastoral Epistles but does not occur in his earlier letters.

Why does godliness surface as a theme in these epistles that were written during the time of Neronic persecution? Perhaps the reason is that one mark of godliness is love for one's enemies (Matt. 5:43–48). Who but a godly Christian could love a Nero? We can be sure that Paul loved his enemies and prayed for them. The Lord Jesus loved Pilate as much as He loved Peter. He loved Judas as much as He loved John.

b. To goodness (2:2e)

The word translated "honesty" in 2:2 denotes gravity or dignity and conveys the idea of decency and decorum. Why shouldn't believers be clothed with dignity? Why shouldn't we have the deportment of those who are sons and daughters of the living God, the aristocracy of the universe? We do not need to put on airs, but we do need to be like Jesus. He always moved among men as One who was royal. We cannot imagine His being vulgar, uncouth, or cheap. We cannot think of His trying to win an argument or stooping to squabble. He was always—at all times, in all places, in all company—a perfect gentleman in the best sense of the word.

(b) The higher dimension (2:3)

God views with the utmost favor our prayers toward the ends we have been discussing: "this is good and acceptable in the sight of God our Saviour."

Again we read the expression "God our Saviour" (2:3; 1:1), which can also be translated "our Saviour, God." The word translated "Saviour" was claimed by Nero, who claimed to be the world's savior and god. It was a pitiful claim. Our Savior *is* God so we can have every confidence that our prayers are heard and heeded and that they will, directly or indirectly, affect the course of events. A verse of song admirably embodies the power and dignity of prayer:

Thou art coming to a King;
Large petitions with thee bring;
For His grace and power are such,
None can ever ask too much.[9]

b. Telling men about God (2:4–8)
(1) God and His mercy (2:4)

God "will have all men to be saved, and to come unto the knowledge of the truth," wrote Paul. "All men" included even the Nebuchadnezzars, Neros, and

9. From the hymn "Come, My Soul, Thy Suit Prepare" by John Newton.

Napoleons of this world. According to *The Companion Bible,* the word translated "will" here means "to wish or desire." It is the emotional element that leads to consequent action. It is therefore stronger than *boulomai* [deliberate determination], because the natural impulse is stronger than the reasoned resolve.[10] So it is God's gracious desire, *His will,* for all men to be saved.

Some people however, are not willing to accept His "so great salvation" (Heb. 2:3); thus, they remove themselves from the blessing. Sometimes their preconceived ideas, the bent views of their perverted minds, keep them from salvation. Sometimes it is their ingrained love of sin or their stubborn, rebellious wills.

God would have all men "to come unto the knowledge of the truth." To that end, He has given us *His Word* and has sent His Holy Spirit into the world.

Because God has endowed the human race with the power of choice, making us free moral agents, He will not violate the will of any man. Nor will He allow Satan to do so. Satan can persuade, but he cannot push, as we see in the temptation of Eve (Gen. 3). Similarly, God woos, but He will not ravish. The Holy Spirit enlightens, quickens, and pleads, but He does not force. Nevertheless, God's great heart yearns over lost people as the Spirit of God once brooded over the darkness of the deep in the morn of creation (Gen. 1:2).

(2) God and His mediator (2:5–6)
(a) His absolute exclusiveness (2:5)

"There is one God, and one mediator between God and men, the man Christ Jesus." The word translated "mediator" refers to "a go-between." The old patriarch Job, in the midst of his suffering, longed for such a mediator. He cried out, "[God] is not a man, as I am, that I should answer him and we should come together in judgment. Neither is there any daysman betwixt us, that might lay his hand upon us both" (Job 9:32–33).

The longed-for Mediator has now come. He is God over all, blessed forevermore, self-existing, and coeternal and coequal with the Father and the Spirit. The second person of the Godhead became a man and lived among men on this planet in space. He was truly man and truly God and free from sin. He was conceived of the Holy Spirit and born of the Virgin Mary. As a true human being, He grew up, went to school, lived in a human home, had brothers and

10. *The Companion Bible,* app. 102.

sisters, worked as a village carpenter, and went about doing good. He knew what it was like to be hungry, thirsty, and tired. He experienced joy and sorrow, grief and pain. He prayed. He suffered, bled, and died. He was man while never ceasing to be God. As God, His mind, heart, and will were coextensive with those of the Father. He knew that He was God (Luke 2:48–50) and emphatically declared Himself to be God (John 8:57–59).

The Lord Jesus told Nathanael that He was the ladder between earth and heaven, the link between man and God (John 1:47–51). He was alluding to the ladder in Genesis 28:12. Jacob dreamed of a ladder with its foot resting on earth and its top reaching into heaven, and he saw the angels of God ascending and descending the shining stairway.

The Lord Jesus knows all there is to know about God because He *is* God; He knows all there is to know about man because He *is* man. He can lay His hands on both God in heaven and man on earth. The great gulf has been spanned. Christ is our Great High Priest (Heb. 4:14) and our Advocate with the Father (1 John 2:1).

Jesus is the only Mediator between God and man. Rome would make Mary an immaculate virgin, the queen of heaven, coredemptrix with Christ, and our mediator. Devout Catholics put her image in their churches, pray to her, and light candles to her. They consider her to be their go-between, the one who mediates between the sinner and an angry Christ. They make her a partner with Christ in the salvation that He bought with His own most precious blood.

But for Mary to be a mediator, she would have to be a sinless woman rather than a woman who confessed her need of a Savior (Luke 1:46–47). She would also have to be God, able to hear and heed an endless stream of prayers offered simultaneously in hundreds of languages. She must be able to understand a babel of tongues, receive thousands of petitions pouring in from all over the world. She must weigh the merits of each one. She must have perfect knowledge of each individual's circumstances and unerringly grant or deny each request. Those who pray to Mary assume that she has all of these attributes of deity. They make her a goddess. As good and as blessed as she is, however, she has none of the attributes of deity.

Mariolatry is an invention of fertile religious minds. One solid text, 1 Timothy 2:5, demolishes any amount of human tradition: "There is . . . *one* mediator," God said (italics added)—not the angels, not canonized Roman saints, not the Virgin Mary. There is one and only one Mediator, "the man Christ Jesus."

(b) His abundant expiation (2:6)

Christ Jesus "gave himself a ransom for all." The word translated "ransom" here is *antilutron. Lutron* is the usual word for the redemption price of a slave. It occurs in the New Testament only in Matthew 20:28 and Mark 10:45, which, incidentally, is the key verse in Mark's gospel. In 1 Timothy 2:6, Paul added the prefix *anti-*, which signifies substitution and means "instead of."

At Calvary, exposed to God's judgment, the Lord Jesus gave Himself in expiatory sacrifice. He thus provided a ransom whereby those who receive Him as their Redeemer obtain deliverance from the penalty of sin. The provision was universal, "for all." However, the sacrifice becomes operational only in the lives of those who accept Christ.

This wondrous ransom was "to be testified in due time." The expression *in due time* in 2:6 is a translation of *kairos idios.* The word *kairos* refers to a fixed, definite period of time. Throughout history, God has pursued His purposes during fixed periods of time. When great turning points are reached, His purposes, which have been maturing slowly, come to full flower and fruit. Decisive events take place. One dispensation ends; another begins. At one epochal turning point, the Son of God became the Son of Man. After that, life on this planet could never be the same. An event of cosmic and eternal significance had taken place.

The word *idios* means "private, unique, the only one of its kind." So *kairos idios* points to a special, unique period when the good news of a ransom paid would be proclaimed. That period was anticipated in the Old Testament by the types and shadows in the law and by the preaching of the prophets; it was heralded by John the Baptist and Jesus, it actually began with the descent of the Holy Spirit at Pentecost, and it will run its course until the end of time.

(3) God and His messenger (2:7–8)

(a) Paul's appointment (2:7)

i. The scope of his appointment (2:7a)

"Whereunto," Paul wrote, "I am ordained a preacher, and an apostle." The word translated "ordained" means "to appoint," and the word translated "preacher" means "to herald." A herald was given authority to deliver official messages from his sovereign to kings or government officials and to make formal public proclamations. Each of the messages with which he was entrusted was to be delivered exactly as it was given to him. The herald was not to add to any of it or subtract from it. Paul was appointed to be a herald.

He was also appointed to be an apostle—that is to say, Paul was God's "sent one." Along with this commission came the power of an apostle to perform miracles when required, to execute judgment when necessary, and to speak with firsthand knowledge of Christ, whom he had met personally.

ii. The surety of his appointment (2:7b)

"I speak the truth in Christ, and lie not," wrote Paul. He evidently felt the need to reaffirm his integrity as God's chosen herald and ambassador. Probably some of those who had so viciously attacked his credentials and credibility in Corinth had carried their criticisms to Ephesus. Paul doubtless deplored the need to put himself under oath, but he did so when necessary. He understood that an attack on the messenger was an attack on the message.

iii. The sphere of his appointment (2:7c)

Paul was appointed to be "a teacher of the Gentiles." The Jews despised him for that. Unconverted Jews hounded him out of their synagogues and whipped up opposition to him in city after city. Believing Jews held him at arm's length; they were content to let him do a work they scorned to do, and they viewed with great suspicion the emancipating truths that he preached. But God's time had come. A new epoch had dawned. God needed someone to tell the whole world that Satan's slaves had been ransomed, and He chose Paul to be His herald.

Paul taught the Gentiles "in faith and verity." He preached with unwavering faith in the gospel. He gave people a truthful account of the gospel, the gospel he believed because he had seen the print of the nails in the palms of the great Redeemer's hands.

(b) Paul's appeal (2:8)

Coming back to his starting point in 2:1, Paul appealed for *an atmosphere of prayer* and *an attitude of prayer:* "I will therefore that men pray every where, lifting up holy hands, without wrath and doubting" (2:8). With persecution mounting to a crescendo, many people must have been full of secret rage at the evil emperor and his supine senators. Many people, even Christians, must have been giving in to doubt. We can hear them asking, "How can God be all-powerful and all-loving and allow monsters like Nero to torture innocent people to death? How can He stand by while Nero propagates odious and atrocious lies about

Christians and the church? If God is all-loving, He cannot be all-powerful; if He were both, He would stop the persecution of Christians. If He is all-powerful, He cannot be all-loving because He sits impassively on His throne and watches the indescribable sufferings of His people and countless others." The same agnostic arguments are common today.

Paul's answer to the angry and the doubtful was, "Pray every where." Everyone could pray. Some of his own best praying had been done in prison (Eph. 1:15–23; 3:14–21).

The word translated "men" in 1 Timothy 2:8 refers to an adult male or husband. In the Greek, it has a definite article and therefore should be translated "the man." In other words, the male is to take the lead in public prayer. Paul seems to have been preparing the way here for what would follow, namely, a discussion of the place of women in the public worship of the church.

Paul's words about "lifting up holy hands" suggest that it was customary in the early church for people to lift up their hands when they prayed, just as it was customary for them to kneel (Acts 20:36). Such outward demonstrations of humility may well have been cultural.

However, "holy hands" may be a symbolic reference. Psalm 24:3–4 says that it is "he that hath clean hands, and a pure heart" who will "ascend into the hill of the LORD" and "stand in his holy place." Clean hands symbolize an impeccable outward life; a pure heart symbolizes a clean inward life. So lifting up holy hands may be an open, symbolic declaration of a clean life.

In any case, Paul's emphasis is on holiness rather than on hands. Holiness is one of the conditions of successful prayer. Successful prayer comes from a person whose life meets with God's approval (Ps. 66:18).

2. The place of women in the church (2:9–15)

People often accuse Paul of being antagonistic toward women. Such critics cite his instructions regarding widows and virgins (1 Cor. 7) and his silencing of women in the Corinthian church (1 Cor. 14:34–35). Feminists also object to his further instructions about the place of women in the local church (1 Tim. 2:9–15). These verses have nothing to do with male chauvinism. The feminists' fight is not with Paul but with God. The instructions, which are inspired by the Holy Spirit, are part of God's Word. Paul was simply the teacher. The truth came from God. Paul simply wrote, under direct and inerrant inspiration by the Spirit of God, what God wanted him to say about women.

In fact, Paul had a warm regard for women in the church. For instance, he spoke highly of Phoebe (Rom. 16:1–2) and an unknown woman named Mary (Rom. 16:6). He wrote glowingly about the mother of Rufus (Rom. 16:13) and Timothy's mother and grandmother (2 Tim. 1:5). One of his dear friends was Lydia of Philippi (Acts 16:14–15). Only those who are ignorant can accuse Paul of being a woman hater. Yet, he did make some firm statements about the role of women in the church.

a. They are to live in sobriety (2:9–10)
   (1) What they should avoid (2:9)
      (a) Regarding their dress (2:9a)

Paul taught that women should avoid immodesty and "adorn themselves with modest apparel." The word translated "adorn" primarily means "to arrange, to put in order." Our English word *cosmetic* is derived from it. The corresponding noun refers to "a harmonious arrangement of things" and came to signify the world and the universe as divinely set in order. The word for *modest* means "orderly," or well arranged. The word for *apparel* points to the flowing outer garment worn by kings and members of the nobility. In summary, Paul conveys the idea that a woman should dress in ways becoming to a Christian. No room exists for immodesty on the one hand or flashy display on the other. Paul was too wise to go into details; he simply stated the principle.

(b) Regarding their deportment (2:9b)

Paul also taught that women should avoid behavior that is not in keeping with "shamefacedness and sobriety." The word translated "shamefacedness" is best defined as "modesty." The English word *shamefacedness* has come to mean "sheepishness," which is certainly not what Paul had in mind. The word points to the kind of attitude that would keep a person from unbecoming behavior.

The word *sobriety* means "self-control, complete command of one's passions." It refers to the inner discipline that erects barriers to prevent one's natural lust from stampeding. Paul used the word in his reply to Governor Festus's rude outburst: "Festus said with a loud voice, 'Paul, thou art beside thyself; much learning doth make thee mad.' But [Paul] said, 'I am not mad, most noble Festus; but speak forth the words of truth and *soberness*'" (Acts 26:24–25).

As he gave these instructions, Paul envisioned quietly dressed women whose demeanor was modest and well controlled. We can imagine that Mary, the Lord's mother, was just such a woman.

(c) Regarding their display (2:9c)

Paul taught that women should also avoid "braided hair, or gold, or pearls, or costly array." The word for "braided hair" refers to plaits or braids and can also be translated "elaborate coiffure." The believer's body is the temple of the Holy Spirit and is not to be the vehicle for elaborate display of worldliness and wealth. Christian women have other, nobler ways of accenting their personal beauty. Paul went on to describe those ways in verse 10.

(2) What they should avow (2:10)

Christian women should display *personal godliness* and *practical goodness.* They should adorn themselves "(which becometh women professing godliness) with good works." Dorcas was so adorned (see Acts 9:36–40). "There was at Joppa," Luke wrote, "a certain disciple named Tabitha, which by interpretation is called Dorcas [the name means 'gazelle']: this woman was full of good works and almsdeeds which she did. And it came to pass in those days, that she was sick, and died." Peter was summoned from Lydda to Joppa to comfort the believers in their loss of one so noble. "When he was come," Luke continued, "they brought him into the upper chamber: and all the widows stood by him weeping, and shewing the coats and garments which Dorcas made, while she was with them."

Dorcas was adorned as God wants all Christian women to be adorned. Her beauty was so great in the sight of God that the Holy Spirit empowered Peter to raise her from the dead; she was allotted more time so that she might go on professing godliness with good works.

Anyone can wear a wig or, if naturally endowed, create an elaborate hairdo. Anyone with money can buy rings, diamonds, golden ornaments, and pearls. Such outward beauty can be *bought.* The beauty God wants to see, however, has to be *wrought*—that is, it has to be worked out in a believing woman's life by the Holy Spirit.

b. They are to learn in silence (2:11–15)

(1) The rule (2:11–12)

(a) What is foremost (2:11)

"Let the woman learn in silence with all subjection," wrote Paul. The words *silence* and *subjection* stir the wrath of women's rights advocates. "Why should women have to be silent in the church?" they demand. "Why should they have to be in subjection?" The reason lies within the mind, heart, and will of God, who is the Author of their being and One who surely knows best what is right and proper for women in the home, in society, and (supremely) in His church. His rules are not arbitrary. Because the Bible is the divinely inspired and absolutely inerrant Word of God, the instructions it contains must be accepted as being inherently right, proper, and best for all concerned.

Suppose that a woman purchases a complicated, costly appliance. When it is installed in her home, she is given a warranty and a book of instructions. The first page has a diagram that illustrates how various parts are related. The second page shows how the equipment is to be operated. Bold red letters warn, "Press button A *before* you press button B." That is the fundamental rule, the rule of order based on the nature and structure of the appliance. It takes into account the way it was made and how it works. Obviously, the manufacturer knows more about these things than the purchaser does. The basic rule is followed by a disclaimer: "The manufacturer is not responsible for damage done to this appliance if this warning is disregarded. The manufacturer's warranty applies only when this instruction is observed."

Now suppose that the woman becomes angry and rebellious when she reads the rule. She chooses to regard the mandatory instruction as an infringement of her civil rights, as an arbitrary and unwarranted rule of chauvinistic engineers who are determined to interfere with a purchaser's right to do what she pleases with her appliance. She asserts her sovereign rights and deliberately presses button B before she presses button A. There is a brief pause during which nothing happens. Then there is a whir, a bang, and a puff of smoke. The appliance is ruined. She now possesses a nonfunctioning piece of equipment for which she has no warranty. She might tinker with it. She might use it for storing odds and ends. She might say foolish things about the manufacturer, but she has no one but herself to blame.

The church is a far more complex entity than a mere appliance. The church is an organism. It is rooted in eternity; it is made up of people from all walks of life and every part of the world. The church comes with a set of instructions found, especially, in the New Testament Epistles. It also comes with its Maker's warning. His order must be observed if the church is to function properly. In the church, both men and women have their place. Both are equally important, but the order spelled out in 1 Corinthians 11 must be observed. We must concede that all of our "rights" notwithstanding, God knows what is best for His own church.

First Timothy 2:11 simply reminds us that God has an inviolable rule for the proper functioning of His church. The woman's role, which involves silence and subjection, is not based on an arbitrary whim. It is based on the nature of the church and God's inerrant knowledge of the nature of men and women. Those who choose to ignore God's instructions damage the church. They keep the church from being as God intended it to be.

When the patriarch Abraham realized that Sarah was too old to give him the heir that God had promised, he married Hagar. She was Sarah's maid. The idea came from Sarah herself, but it was a disastrous expedient. Once it became obvious that Hagar was pregnant, Sarah became bitter and persecuted Hagar. Goaded to desperation, Hagar ran away into the wilderness. There she met "the angel of the LORD," the second person of the Godhead in angelic guise. He said to her, "Return to thy mistress, and submit thyself under her hands" (Gen. 16:9). There were numerous good reasons why God gave Hagar this command,[11] but she did not understand them. Undoubtedly nothing God could have demanded of her could have been harder than to "return" and "submit."

The God who, in His infinite wisdom and boundless love, confronted Hagar with those two inflexible words now confronts all women in the church with two similar uncompromising words: *silence* and *subjection.* How a woman responds to the rule of the Holy Spirit of God on this issue is an indication of her growth in Christ.

The word for "silence" in1 Timothy 2:11 denotes tranquility from within. The adjective form is translated "peaceable" in 2:2. Luke used the word in his description of the reaction of the mob in the temple precincts in Jerusalem when Paul addressed them in their native language: "When they heard that he spake in the Hebrew tongue to them, they kept the more silence" (Acts 22:2). In other words, *silence* means "silence," like it or not.

The word for "subjection" in 1 Timothy 2:11 is a military term referring to those of lesser rank in an army. Luke used this word to describe Paul's absolute refusal, in the face of all of the hierarchy in the Jerusalem church, to be put in subjection to false teachers who wished to subordinate Gentile believers to Jewish legalism (Gal. 2:5).

---

11. See John Phillips, *Exploring Genesis* (Grand Rapids: Kregel, 2001).

(b) What is forbidden (2:12)

Teaching and *trespassing* are forbidden to women. Paul wrote, "I suffer not a woman to teach, nor to usurp authority over the man, but to be in silence."

Paul's words could be put, "I don't allow a woman to teach." His *I,* of course, refers to him as the inspired apostle writing under the direct revelation and inspiration of the Holy Spirit. According to *The Companion Bible,* in 2:12, as in 2:7, the word *not* expresses "full and direct negation, independently and absolutely; not depending on any condition expressed or implied."[12] Wuest pointed out, "The correct understanding of Paul's words, 'I suffer not a woman to teach,' are dependent upon the tense of the Greek infinitive and the grammatical rule pertaining to it." He concluded that Paul meant, "I do not permit a woman to be a teacher."[13] W. E. Vine has pointed out that the infinitive to teach can be used absolutely or transitively; he also indicated that in 2:12 it is used absolutely and means "to give instruction."[14]

Paul was speaking in the context of teaching in the local church. He did not prohibit women from teaching other women (Titus 2:3–4) or from teaching children (1 Tim. 2:15; 5:10). Neither is censure directed against Priscilla who, along with her husband, privately taught Apollos "the way of God more perfectly" (Acts 18:24–28). But the apostle absolutely reserved the teaching role in the church for men. He went on to explain why.

(2) The reason (2:13–14)

(a) God's order in creation revealed (2:13)

"For Adam was first formed, then Eve," Paul explained. Liberal theology denies the truth taught in the opening chapters of Genesis. The Holy Spirit ignores their skeptical views and takes us back to Adam and Eve to explain Romans 5 and 1 Corinthians 15:45–49 and the prospect of resurrection. Adam and Eve were real people and are referred to by the Spirit of God as the parents of the human race.

The word translated "formed" (v. 13) means "to form or mold something as

12. *The Companion Bible,* app. 105:1.
13. Kenneth S. Wuest, *The Pastoral Epistles in the Greek New Testament* (Grand Rapids: Eerdmans, 1952), 48.
14. W. E. Vine, *An Expository Dictionary of New Testament Words,* 4 vols. (London: Oliphants, 1963), 4:111.

from clay or wax. It is used in Romans 9:20, where Paul (quoting from Isa. 45:9) asks, "Shall the thing formed say to him that formed it, 'Why hast thou made me thus?'" The emphasis is on the unquestionable right of God to order things as He sees fit.

God created Adam first, then Eve. Adam was a direct creation of God; Eve was formed from that which was taken from Adam (Gen. 2:21–25). In so doing, God established an order, a primacy, a headship in human affairs (1 Cor. 11). And God's order prevails throughout creation, from the greatest galaxy to the smallest atom.

According to God's order for the human race, "Adam was first formed, then Eve." This is a biblical fact. It is foolish to quarrel with facts. The only way a person can get away from this fact is to deny the divine inspiration of Scripture. A person who thus denies the Bible might be on some church roll, but he cannot really call himself a Christian. Therefore, he is not in the true church. His views about Paul's teaching here are therefore irrelevant.

(b) God's order in creation reversed (2:14)

Adam's sin and Eve's sin are presented as being radically different from each other: "Adam was not deceived, but the woman being deceived was in the transgression." *Adam was disobedient,* whereas *Eve was deceived.*

To understand the difference, we must go back to the beginning. Adam was created first, then Eve was formed from Adam. Moreover, Adam was given the headship and was crowned by God (1 Cor. 11:3). The man was created to be ruled by his head, and the woman was created to be ruled by her heart. Anyone who has had an argument with his or her spouse has experienced this essential difference between the man's approach to issues and the woman's approach.

Of course, the fact that a woman is ruled by her heart does not mean that a woman cannot think; we have all met some women who can outthink some men. And the fact that a man is ruled by his head does not mean that a man cannot feel. We have all met some men who can feel more deeply than some women. Generally speaking, however, a man's center of action is his mind, and a woman's is her heart.

In the temptation of Adam and Eve, Satan twisted God's order. The Devil first aimed the temptation at Eve's head and engaged her in intellectual discussion as to whether it was right for her to do something that God had said was wrong. Eve's sole defense was the Word of God. Accordingly, Satan's first words were an outright attack on it. He raised the first question in human history: "Yea, hath God said. . . ?" (Gen. 3:1).

Satan's attack was along three lines. First, he assailed the *authority* of the Word of God: "Yea, hath *God* said?" In other words, "How do you know that it really is the Word of God? After all, you weren't there when this supposed Word of God was given."

Then Satan assaulted the *accuracy* of God's Word: "Yea, hath God said, Ye shall not eat of *every* tree of the garden?" In other words, "How do you know that the Word is an accurate and inerrant account of what God said? After all, you have only what has been handed down to you. You do not have the original. How do you know that something has not been lost in the transmission?"

The third attack was on the *acceptability* of the Word of God. Satan directed Eve's gaze toward the forbidden fruit and filled her mind with longing. She "saw that the tree was good for food, and that it was pleasant to the eyes, and a tree to be desired to make one wise" (Gen. 3:6). The Devil persuaded her that it was simply unacceptable for her to heed a supposed demand of God that interfered with her independence and prevented her from doing as she pleased. After all, she was a mature, rational woman with a mind and will of her own. So Eve was deceived—cleverly deceived, but deceived nonetheless.

Eve was vulnerable to Satan's attack because she handled the Word of God carelessly. Her Bible was small (only two verses), but it was quite adequate. It said, "And the LORD God commanded the man, saying, 'Of every tree of the garden thou mayest freely eat: But of the tree of the knowledge of good and evil, thou shalt not eat of it: for in the day that thou eatest thereof thou shalt surely die" (Gen. 2:16–17). To each of Satan's suggestions, Eve simply had to say, "Thus saith the Lord," and Satan would have been unable to subvert her. Instead, she was careless. She made three mistakes when she quoted God's Word. Twice she subtracted from the Word, and once she added to it. Satan knew from the way she handled Scripture that she could be deceived and defeated easily.

When Satan said, "Yea, hath God said, Ye shall not eat of every tree of the garden?" Eve replied, "We may eat of the fruit of the trees of the garden." That is not what God had said. He had said, "of *every* tree of the garden thou mayest *freely* eat." She left something out.

Eve continued, "But of the fruit of the tree which is in the midst of the garden, God hath said, Ye shall not eat of it . . . lest ye die." That is not what God had said. He had said, "Thou shalt *surely* die" (italics added, compare Gen. 2:17 and

3:3). Again, she left something out. In comparing those verses, we also note that Eve added "neither shall ye touch it." God had said no such thing.

So, in effect, Eve abandoned the original text of Scripture and used a paraphrase, a free rendering, a version that she made up for herself. Many modern "translations" of the Bible do the same thing. They leave things out, put things in, and generally distort the Word of God.

When Eve left out the word *freely* ("Thou mayest freely eat"), she minimized God's goodness and lavish generosity. When she left out *surely* ("Thou shalt surely die"), she minimized the severity of God and the certainty of punishment. When she added *neither shall ye touch it,* she exaggerated the one restriction that God had placed on her.

The more we study Eve's careless handling of God's Word, the more we see the serpent's subtlety in addressing her intellect and thus appealing to her vanity. When she ate the forbidden fruit, she showed that she considered her own opinion to be more valid than God's Word. As Paul wrote to Timothy, she was "deceived." Satan directed his temptation to Eve's head and triumphed. That is God's reason for His prohibition against women teachers in the church.

On the other hand, Adam was not deceived. He knew perfectly well what he was doing. He was disobedient, and thus Paul wrote, "By one man's disobedience many were made sinners" (Rom. 5:12, 19).

Whereas Satan had aimed temptation at Eve's head, he directed temptation toward Adam's heart. In actuality, the Devil did not tempt Adam directly; he let Eve do it. "When the woman saw that the tree was good for food, and that it was pleasant to the eyes, and a tree to be desired to make one wise, she took of the fruit thereof, and did eat, and gave also unto her husband with her; and he did eat" (Gen. 3:6). She assumed the leadership role.

Evidently, when Adam saw Eve in her fallen condition, his heart went out to her. Perhaps in some twisted way, she had become even more desirable than she had been in her innocence. In any case he looked on her in her lostness and loneliness and loved her just the same. He knew that his next act would be one of flagrant disobedience. He was not deceived concerning the step he was about to take. He followed his heart into sin; and because he was to be the head of the entire human race, he drew the race with him into the Fall.

God put the responsibility for the Fall on Adam, not Eve. Just the same, Eve did not escape the consequences of her sin. Nor did womanhood escape. As Paul wrote in 1 Timothy 2:14, "The woman being deceived was in the transgression." The words translated "was in" are *gegonen* (in the perfect tense) and *en;* they indicate that Eve had fallen into transgression. The word translated "transgression" carries the idea of "stepping aside" or "overstepping." That is what Eve did. She stepped over a forbidden boundary line.

The word translated "deceived" in 2:14a means "cheated, beguiled." The word for "being deceived" in 2:14b means "being completely or thoroughly deceived." Eve was completely taken in. The serpent actually beguiled her into believing that by partaking of the forbidden fruit she would benefit herself and the human race. Hence, the divine ban on women becoming pastor-teachers in the church.

(3) The response (2:15)

Because Eve was deceived, Paul barred women from becoming teachers in the church, but he added, "Notwithstanding she shall be saved in childbearing, if they continue in faith and charity and holiness with sobriety."

The word translated "saved" here is by no means confined in the New Testament to salvation from sin. It is used in connection with deliverance from danger in Matthew 8:25, from death in Luke 23:35, and from sickness in Matthew 9:22. Therefore, we should not be surprised that the word is used in 1 Timothy 2:15 in reference to salvation from something other than sin.

Note the transition in 2:15 from the personal (Eve) to the generic (woman), as indicated by the change from a singular to a plural pronoun ("she" then "they"). In Eve's case, the immediate penalty for her transgression was expressed thus: "I will greatly multiply thy sorrow and thy conception; in sorrow thou shalt bring forth children" (Gen. 3:16). As far as womankind is concerned, a subsidiary penalty is that women are barred from teaching roles in the church.[15]

Possibly, 1 Timothy 2:15 means that in childbirth women are "saved" from this subsidiary penalty, for as mothers they can certainly teach their children the truths of the gospel. Timothy was a prime example of a son being instructed in the Scriptures from childhood by his mother and grandmother (2 Tim. 3:15). This emancipation is all the more effective when mothers' lives are marked by faith, love, holiness, and sobriety. Their doctrine is thus adorned by godly lives. To welcome the opportunity to teach children is one way to react to the prohibition against women being teachers in the church. This is much better than a carnal response of resentment or outright rebellion.

---

15. See 1 Corinthians 11:5 and the commentary on this verse in John Phillips, *Exploring 1 Corinthians* (Grand Rapids: Kregel, 2002).

C. The church and its duties (3:1–15)

1. The church's duties discussed (3:1–13)

Paul turns now to a different topic, the organization of the church. The local church needs both spiritual and secular leaders to conduct its ministry effectively, so the apostle discussed two kinds of offices: elders and deacons. He outlined for Timothy the qualifications that elders and deacons must have.

Paul ignored the qualifications that most modern churches think are important. Today, many churches are eager to fill the positions with bankers, businessmen, professionals, people in high society, and those who wield influence in government, commerce, and entertainment. However, some "poor wise man" (Eccl. 9:15) full of the Holy Spirit (Acts 6:3) would be more qualified to be an elder or a deacon than a carnal, worldly-wise businessman would be.

a. The spiritual leadership of the local church—elders (3:1–7)

(1) The quest (3:1)

(a) The desire for the office (3:1a)

Paul started, "If a man desire the office. . . ." Everything begins with the desire. The word translated "desire" here is *oregomai,* which means "to stretch out." To desire is to long after something, to set one's heart on it, to reach out for it. *Oregomai* is translated "coveted" in 6:10, where Paul warned against coveting money.

In 3:1, the apostle did not have the desire for position or power in mind. He was referring to the desire to shepherd a flock. One does not become an elder in a church because his name appears on a list of nominees and he manages to collect enough votes; he begins his quest for this position because he has an inward longing, put in his heart by the Holy Spirit, to be a shepherd.

(b) The distinctive of the office (3:1b)

What is desired is "the office of a bishop." When people think of a bishop, they think of a high-ranking powerful church dignitary. They picture a man arrayed in distinctive garments, residing in a palace, in charge of a diocese, ruling like a prince over a number of churches, and in some countries entitled to a seat in parliament. That concept of a bishop comes from Rome, not from the New Testament. The use of such a loaded word in the King James Version reflects the mind-set of the translators, many of whom were members of the clergy.

The word translated "office" in 3:1 carries the idea of visitation, as in 1 Peter 2:12. The word translated "bishop" in 3:2 carries the idea of watching over a flock. The word for "elders" in Acts 20:17 refers to the same function of shepherding but indicates the degree of spiritual maturity needed for that work; Peter and John called themselves "elders" (1 Peter 5:1; 2 John 1; 3 John 1). According to the New Testament, each individual church is to have its own elders (bishops) (Acts 14:23; 20:17; Phil. 1:1; Titus 1:5).

(c) The demands of the office (3:1c)

The work to which an elder is called is "a good work." And it is work! Paul described the duties of elders in Acts 20, which records his charge to the leaders of the Ephesian church. In addition to hard work, shepherding calls for time, patience, and wisdom. It involves teaching the Word of God, helping people, visiting the flock, and looking out for the spiritual and physical well-being of those entrusted to the elder's care.

(2) The qualifications (3:2–7)
(a) The basic requirements for an elder (3:2)
i. The main requirement (3:2a)

"A bishop then must be blameless." The word used means "irreproachable." There must be nothing open to censure in an elder's life. His character and reputation must be stainless. Character is as important as competence.

What happens when a person who holds a public office in the local church does not have an impeccable standing in the community? He will be unable to discharge his duties because he dwells with a grieved Holy Spirit, and he will bring dishonor and scorn upon the church. When David lost his reputation for being a man after God's own heart because of his sin with Bathsheba, the prophet rebuked him with these words: "Thou hast given great occasion to the enemies of the LORD to blaspheme" (compare 1 Sam. 13:14 and 2 Sam. 12:14). So Paul put "blameless" at the top of the list of requirements for an elder.

ii. The marital requirement (3:2b)

Next on Paul's list is "the husband of one wife." What a blow to the Roman Catholic policy of enforced celibacy for its clergy!

A great deal of discussion has centered on this verse. Some scholars think that it prohibits polygamy; and that would be the most logical view, especially in view of the fact that polygamy was widely tolerated in the Old Testament. Other scholars think that the verse means that an elder must be married to only one woman at a time and therefore that a widowed believer who remarries can still be an elder. An unmarried man cannot be. Still others think that Paul was forbidding a second marriage or ruling out a divorced man, or a man married to a previously divorced woman.

Wuest suggested the following translation of 3:2b: "a one-wife sort of husband" or "a one-woman sort of a man."[16] In other words, anyone who holds public office in the church should be above reproach in his conduct—scrupulously scriptural in his, or her, marital relationship.

Wuest's translation reminds me of Mark Twain, who saw a man tying a rope around the neck of a dog. He asked the man what he was doing. The man replied, "That there dog runs after any man or boy who whistles to him, so I'm going to drown him. I've no use for a dog like that." The man wanted a one-man dog, like an Airedale who becomes attached to only its master. Similarly, God wants a man to hold a church office only if he is attached solely and wholly to his wife. Nothing will ruin a man's ministry more quickly than infidelity or philandering. Sad to say, some men in the ministry learn this lesson too late or not at all.

Legalists in the church often legislate against all divorced people, including those who are the innocent parties and who have biblical grounds for divorce. They ignore the "except-it-be-for-fornication" rule, found in both the Lord's definitive statement on divorce (Matt. 19:9) and the Sermon on the Mount (where, throughout, the highest imaginable standards are upheld, Matt. 5:32). This exception clause defends the innocent party from blame and from discrimination. It is grossly unscriptural and unfair to treat the innocent party as though he, or she, were the guilty party.

What destroys marriage is the infidelity of the one who commits adultery, breaking vows and remaining unrepentant. When such a case comes to court, the judge acts on behalf of the state to make the divorce legal in the eyes of the law.

The question of the innocent party's freedom to remarry, without blame or shame, is taken up by the Lord in Matthew 19:11–12.

16. Wuest, *Pastoral Epistles in the Greek New Testament,* 53.

Particularly objectionable is the legalist's claim that a remarriage following a scriptural divorce involves "two living husbands" (or wives, as the case may be). This claim is tantamount to accusing the remarried person of being either a bigamist or a polygamist. Such an accusation is both untrue and libelous.

People who make this accusation often appeal to Romans 7:1–2 as their ground for accusing remarried divorcées (or divorcés) of living in sin. This passage has to do with (1) our bondage, as believers, to our old Adamic nature; (2) the role that the Mosaic Law plays in aggravating that bondage; and (3) how God used death—not our death, but the death of Christ—as His instrument to set us free. To introduce divorce into all of this is confusing and contrary to sound exegesis.

In the Old Testament, God permitted divorce. The Lord commented that all divorce arises from hardness of heart (Matt. 19:8). Divorce itself was a gracious concession, under the Mosaic Law, to dissolve a marriage that had degenerated into chaos. The Jewish rabbis had tinkered with the divorce issue so that, by the time of Christ, one school held cast-iron legalistic views, which barely tolerated divorce at all, whereas the other school held such lax, liberal views that a man could divorce his wife for burning his toast. The Lord refused to take either side and instead expounded His own balanced view.

The pity today is that many churches go to one extreme or the other. Hardness of heart rules in some churches. Their synods—or their local elders, deacons, and pastors—develop such hardness toward those victims of hellish marriages, who have sought refuge in divorce, as to impose all kinds of sanctions upon them—regardless of whether they are the innocent ones.[17]

iii. The moral requirements (3:2c–e)

The office of elder has three moral requirements. Elders must be "vigilant, sober, of good behaviour." The word translated "vigilant" here suggests the idea of wise *caution.* Paul was saying that an elder must possess self-control.

Gamaliel demonstrated this quality in his advice to the Sanhedrin (Acts 5:34–39). When the members, enraged by the apostles' teaching, were talking about killing them, Gamaliel, the esteemed grandson of the revered scholar Hillel, interrupted the discussion. Gamaliel is described in Acts as "a doctor of the law, had in reputation among all the people." He reminded the Sanhedrin of some would-be messiahs who had come and gone, leaving scarcely a ripple behind

17. See John Phillips, *Exploring the Gospels* (Neptune, N.J.: Loizeaux, 1999), 381–82.

them. Then he brought the council back to the subject of the apostles, whose ministry was causing a stir in Jerusalem: "Now I say unto you, Refrain from these men, and let them alone: for if this counsel or this work be of men, it will come to nought: But if it be of God, ye cannot overthrow it; lest haply ye be found even to fight against God." Gamaliel's advice illustrates the wise caution that God expects of elders.

The word for "sober" in 1 Timothy 3:2 describes a person who is sober-minded and serious, one who has a sound mind and draws wise *conclusions.* He likes to have all of the facts before making a decision. So an elder should be known for his discretion, he should not be given to frivolity, and he should not jump to conclusions.

We make all kinds of mistakes when we speak before we know all of the facts—as did a man some years ago when traveling cross-country by train. He was in a sleeping car; and in the compartment across from him, another man was trying to hush a crying baby. The noise of the little one got on the first man's nerves. Angrily, he said to the distraught father, "Can't you keep that child quiet? How is anyone supposed to get any rest with this noise going on? That child needs his mother. Where is his mother, anyway?"

The father replied, "This child's mother is in the baggage car, in her coffin."

Elders must avoid hasty words. They also need to be wise in their *conduct;* they must be "of good behavior *[kosmios].*" The Greek word, which can also be translated "orderly," suggests a man who has a disciplined life. Who could respect an elder who has slovenly habits and whose behavior is undisciplined and disorderly? A man who is always late for meetings, forgets appointments, breaks promises, is careless about his physical appearance, and constantly misplaces important papers does not qualify for a leadership position in the church.

iv. The ministerial requirements (3:2f–g)

There are two ministerial requirements for an elder. First, he must be *known for his social grace,* or, as Paul puts it, he must be "given to hospitality." The expression is a translation of the adjective *philoxenos,* which in its noun form means "love of strangers." Paul was saying that to be hospitable is to open one's home to visitors without thought of reward.

Xenos is the usual word for "stranger." The Lord Jesus used it of Himself in Matthew 25:31–40. In describing the coming judgment of the nations in the valley of Jehoshaphat, He said, "Then shall the King say . . . I was a stranger *[xenos],* and ye took me in." These words will be addressed to those who are kind to a Jew during the dark days of the Great Tribulation. Astonished, they will reply, "When saw we thee a stranger *[xenos]?*" The King will answer, "Inasmuch as ye have done it unto one of the least of these my brethren, ye have done it unto me." Conversely, the Lord will judge those who are not hospitable to a Jew as being inhospitable to Him. Those who treat His people coldly as strangers will "go away into everlasting punishment."

"Be not forgetful to entertain strangers: for thereby some have entertained angels unawares," wrote the apostle in Hebrews 13:2. Abraham, Lot, Manoah, and Gideon all entertained angels. Regardless of whether we ever entertain angels, we can be sure that when we show hospitality to the Lord's people, we are actually showing hospitality to Him.

Elders should regard hospitality not as a duty but as a delight. They should love to entertain. When Paul wrote to Timothy (and probably when Hebrews was written as well), Nero's persecutions were raging across the empire. Many Christians were homeless refuges. To receive them into one's home might well have been dangerous, but godly elders, addicted to hospitality, scorned any danger and offered bed and board to these "strangers" who were far from home.

The second ministerial requirement is that an elder must be *known for his spiritual gift.* He must be "apt to teach" those gathered in the local church or around his table. The word translated "apt to teach" is *didaktikos,* which means "skilled in teaching."

The ability to teach the Word, like all other skills, is not acquired overnight. The Bible is a library of books, and it takes years of diligent study to acquire a thorough, working knowledge of its contents and to become familiar with sound hermeneutical principles. A teacher must understand the Bible's broad movements; meet its many people; master its major doctrines; apply its vital principles; weigh its geography, history, cultures, and themes; think about the languages in which it was written; study its structure; attend to the context of any given verse; and compare various passages. An elder must aim to be skilled in all of these aspects of teaching.

We must not forget that a difference exists between acquired teaching skills and a Holy Spirit-endowed spiritual gift. Just because a person has acquired the necessary knowledge and techniques does not necessarily mean that he will be a good teacher, even in the secular realm. We have all listened to boring doctors and been moved by eloquent chimney sweeps. The mere acquisition of knowledge certainly does not necessarily mean that a person has the anointing of the

Spirit. It takes a spiritual gift and Holy Spirit anointing to perceive spiritual truth and impart it such that people are enlightened and energized to experience behavioral change. Apart from the anointing and gifting of the Spirit, the impartation of mere knowledge can be sterile.

(b) The broader requirements for an elder (3:3–7)

i. His attachments (3:3a–c)

Adding some negatives to his list of qualifications, Paul mentioned three addictions that must be conspicuously absent from the life of an elder. First, *an elder must not be addicted to wine.* The word translated "given to wine" is *paroinos,* which can be translated "brawler" (drunkenness causes some people to be brawlers) or "quarrelsome over wine." The book of Proverbs contains numerous warnings against strong drink (23:29–35; 31:4–7). A person who is given to alcohol is not fit to be an elder in a church.

Second, *an elder must not be addicted to wrath.* The word translated "striker" conjures the picture of a quarrelsome person who is always ready with his fists. Such a man is unfit to shepherd God's flock.

Third, *an elder must not be addicted to wealth.* In Paul's words, he must not be "greedy of filthy lucre." "Filthy lucre" is a synonym for money. A money-grabbing individual is disqualified from being a church elder. After all, "the love of money is the root of all evil" (1 Tim. 6:10).

ii. His attitudes (3:3d–f)

Paul next spoke of a "patient" attitude. Put in negative terms, the requirement is that *an elder must not be choleric.* The word translated "patient" here suggests gentleness and fairness, reasonableness. What a desirable quality for an elder!

The word describes someone who is not unduly rigorous and who does not clamor for his due. A person who has to deal with people and their problems must not be irascible. He must not always insist on the full application of the letter of the law. Situations can be aggravated by a choleric person and easily become inflamed. What is needed is a soft touch and, when firmness is required, a gentle hand. "A soft answer turneth away wrath," wrote the wise man (Prov. 15:1).

Paul also indicated that *an elder must not be contentious.* He must not be a "brawler." The word translated "not a brawler" in 1 Timothy 3:3 is *amachos,* which means literally "not fighting." An elder must not be a combative person, ready to fight at the slightest provocation. He should lead his flock as an Eastern shepherd leads his sheep. He does not drive his flock or herd it with dogs. On the contrary, he establishes a friendly relationship with the animals that are committed to his care. He knows them by name, helps them over difficult places, guides them into green pastures and beside still waters, tends to their hurts, cares for their little ones, and defends them from their enemies. If the shepherd fights, he fights with wolves, not sheep.

Moreover, *an elder must not be covetous.* The word translated "not covetous" here is *aphilarguros,* which means "not money-loving," so an elder must be free from the love of money. Covetousness focuses a person's attention on things rather than on people, on this world rather than on the world to come. It has been well said that there are two kinds of people: those who love things and use people and those who love people and use things. There is, of course, nothing wrong with having money, but there is everything wrong with loving money and coveting it.

iii. His attainments (3:4–7)

a. In the parental sphere (3:4–5)

In 3:4, Paul stated *the rule* for attainments in the parental sphere: An elder must be "one that ruleth well his own house, having his children in subjection with all gravity." The word for "subjection" here is the same word used in 2:11 to describe the subjection of women in the church to the authority of men. As noted before, it is primarily a military term. It is a simple scriptural principle that children are to learn obedience in the home, where parents are to exercise authority and rule over their offspring. When children are defiant, argumentative, and self-willed and are allowed to get away with disobedience and temper tantrums, it is evident that their parents have lost control.

The word *gravity* in 3:4 suggests venerableness and dignity. It is the quality that inspires respect and awe in children as they contemplate their fathers. Such a response, of course, has to be earned. A father does not earn respect by bullying or beating his children. Firmness and fairness are more effective.

The reason for the rule is stated in 3:5: "If a man know not how to rule his own house, how shall he take care of the church of God?" The answer to that question is obvious.

When God looks for elders to whom He can entrust the oversight of His church, He looks for men like Abraham. Abraham was one of the greatest men in the Old Testament. Great in terms of his *faith,* he became "the father of all them that believe" (Rom. 4:11). He was also great in terms of his *future,* both temporal (Gen. 12:1–3; 15:18) and eternal (Heb. 11:8–10). And he was great in terms of his *family.* God could reveal future events to Abraham for this very reason. He said, "Shall I hide from Abraham that thing which I do . . . ? For I know him, that he will command his children and his household after him, and they shall keep the way of the LORD" (Gen. 18:17–19).

b. In the personal sphere (3:6)

Paul gave an *emphatic command* about attainments in the personal sphere: an elder must not be "a novice, lest being lifted up with pride he fall into the condemnation of the devil." The word for "novice" here is derived from two terms, one meaning "new" and the other meaning "to spring up." So an elder is not to be one newly sprung up, that is, not a new convert. An inexperienced person is simply not qualified to be a church leader. He might be well established in business; he might be a learned man by the world's standards and competent in many ways; but if he has only recently been saved, he is disqualified from being an overseer in the church.

This prohibition is as much for the man's own good as for the good of the church. If he is promoted too quickly, the new convert might become "lifted up with pride." The word for "lifted up" means literally "to raise a smoke." Smoke draws attention to itself but is wholly without substance.

If the new convert becomes puffed up, he is in danger of falling "into the condemnation of the devil." It was because of pride that Lucifer was transformed into the Devil and cast out of heaven (Isa. 14:12–15).

c. In the public sphere (3:7)

In the public sphere, an elder "must have a good report of them which are without; lest he fall into reproach and the snare of the devil." Similarly, one of the three basic requirements for the first deacons was that they be "men of honest report" (Acts 6:3). Nothing could be worse for the testimony of a local church than to choose an elder with a bad reputation. The world quickly spots a phony. A man who has a foul mouth on the job, or does not pay his bills, or has an extramarital affair, or is embroiled with the law, or abuses his family simply has no right to be an elder. Public opinion must be taken into account.

b. The secular leadership of the local church—deacons (3:8–13)

Paul turned his attention to those who are appointed to take care of the more mundane duties connected with leading a local congregation. The Jerusalem apostles described the work of the deacons as waiting on tables (Acts 6:2), but there are a thousand other routine tasks that have to be handled as well. Paul envisioned a special group of men being consecrated for this kind of service. Although their duties might be secular, their qualifications are spiritual and on a par with those outlined for elders.

The word for "deacon" in 1 Timothy 3:8 points to a servant who is engaged in his work. Paul used the word twenty-two times in his epistles. It is not found even once in the book of Acts, although in that book Luke did record the first tentative step toward establishing a diaconate. In Acts 6:1–6, he wrote about the setting apart of certain able, spiritually qualified men to function as servants of the local church. The seven men chosen for this office were solemnly ordained by the apostles.

The word *diakonos* needs to be distinguished from the other common New Testament word translated "servant," *doulos* ("bond slave"). A writer who uses *doulos* has in mind the relationship between the servant and his master; a writer who uses *diakonos* has in mind the relationship between the servant and his work. Paul used *diakonos* when he was writing to Timothy about the ministry of a deacon, for a deacon must be a servant of the church, and he must be willing to work.

The work of waiting on tables to which Luke referred related to the grand experiment of sharing in which the church was then engaged. Believers in those early days had all things in common, anticipating by nearly two thousand years the communist slogan "From each according to his ability; to each according to his need." However, human nature being what it is, the share-and-share-alike idea did not work.

Before the experiment failed, however, many of the new converts (out of gratitude for their salvation) sold their possessions and put the proceeds into a common fund. The money was then used to meet the material needs of the Lord's people. Soon, however, some people began to complain that this practice was working to the advantage of some and the detriment of others. To put an end to the perceived inequalities (whether they were actual or imagined was beside the point), the apostles advocated the consecration of seven men of proven integrity, ability, and spirituality to handle "this business." They would thus relieve the apostles of an impossible administrative burden. By delegating the tasks of managing money and serving tables, the apostles could devote themselves to the more spiritual side of their ministry. By the time Paul wrote to Timothy and Titus, the function of deacons needed to be formalized.

Nowadays, the work of a deacon includes not only the administration of his church's funds but also the management of its buildings, business transactions, and charities. Assuming that deacons are chosen properly, the elders need to be only marginally involved in such matters. The spiritual leaders can be more profitably employed in prayer, Bible study, evangelism, pastoring, and teaching. That is not to say that a deacon is to be less spiritual than those who are called to teach and preach the Word. Indeed, Paul's list of qualifications for a deacon is nearly as long as his list for elders, and some of the qualifications are the same.

(1) The deacon as a faultless man (3:8)

(a) His temperament (3:8a)

"Likewise," Paul wrote, "must the deacons be grave *[semnos]*." Paul used the same word in Philippians 4:8 (his masterly summary of the true "power of positive thinking"), where he told the brethren to think on "whatsoever things are true, whatsoever things are honest *[semnos]* . . ." The word refers to that which is honorable, venerable, and grave. Being a deacon is a serious matter. The office is not for a prankster.

The position of deacon in the New Testament sense calls for hard work and often, long hours. A deacon must be as diligent in his sacred work as he is in his secular employment. It is astonishing how some deacons put their hearts and souls into their careers and then turn around and render indifferent service to the church.

(b) His tongue (3:8b)

The next qualification Paul listed is that a deacon should not be "doubletongued." The word for "doubletongued" occurs only here in the New Testament and means "saying the same thing twice," or "given to repetition." A double-tongued person says something to one person and then, when talking to another person, puts an altogether different slant on the subject. Today, instead of saying that someone is double-tongued, we might say that he is fork-tongued (like a serpent) or that he talks out of both sides of his mouth.

Nothing could be more destructive in a local church than a double-tongued deacon. A deacon has to be a man of the highest integrity because he often has to deal with sensitive matters. He must be able to control his tongue, even when being pumped by another, including his wife. It is better for him to say nothing at all than to say one thing to one person and something else to another. A man who earns the reputation of being conversationally unreliable is rendered useless in his office, for no one really wants to confide in a loose-tongued deacon.

David's wife, Michal, is one biblical example of a double-tongued person (see 1 Sam. 19:10–17). Once when her father, King Saul, tried to kill David, David ran home in a panic. Michal, full of sympathy, said, "If thou save not thy life to night, to morrow thou shalt be slain." David fled, and when Saul's officers arrived at his house with a warrant for his arrest, Michal said, "He is sick." Not long afterward, when she was face-to-face with her angry father, she told an altogether different story. Instead of standing up for David, she lied about him. In effect, she said, "He threatened to kill me if I hindered his escape." She later sided with her father by supinely agreeing to marry a man named Phalti while she was still legally married to David (1 Sam. 25:44). God wants no such vacillating, reprehensible double-talk in one called to serve the people of God.

Outside the pages of the Bible, we find illustrations of double-tongued people everywhere. In *Treasure Island,* Robert Louis Stevenson introduces us to the eloquent pirate Long John Silver; again and again the old scoundrel uses his forked tongue to subvert and deceive or to talk himself out of a tight corner. In *Perelandra,* C. S. Lewis introduces us to Weston, the Devil's eloquent surrogate on the planet Venus; he uses his forked tongue to persuade the woman of the place to abandon her loyalty to the Lord Maleldil. In *Colonel Quaritch* by Sir Henry Rider Haggard, we see the duplicity of Quest, the village lawyer. In *Oliver Twist,* Charles Dickens introduces us to crafty old Fagin, who uses his tongue in an effort to subvert poor, orphaned Oliver from the path of moral integrity.

On the highway of life we all have personally met people who have spoken to us eloquently out of the wrong side of their mouths. But what can we expect of pirates, mad scientists, unscrupulous lawyers, and crooked businessmen? The world might afford them grudging admiration when success seems to crown their lies, but the Holy Spirit says that double-tongued people are not even fit to wait on tables in the church of God.

(c) His temptations (3:8c–d)

i. Wine (3:8c)

A deacon, Paul said, must not be "given to much wine." The word translated "wine" here is *oinos.* It is the usual New Testament word for wine. The same word is used in Ephesians 5:18 (where intoxication is evidently in view); in John 2:10; and in 1 Timothy 5:23 (where Paul advises his young colleague to use wine moderately for medicinal purposes).

A deacon must never overindulge. What could be worse than a drunken deacon? Although the Bible does not specifically demand total abstinence, it most certainly militates against drunkenness in the strongest terms (1 Cor. 6:9–10; Gal. 5:19–21). The New Testament's warning against indulging in anything that might cause a brother to stumble practically rules out the use of wine altogether (Rom. 14:21).

The requirements for deacons are illustrated in the Old Testament law of the Nazarite. Like the New Testament deacon, the Old Testament Nazarite was a man set apart for God, although there were differences in their consecration. The Nazarite was consecrated to God by vows; the deacon was consecrated by vocation. The Nazarite's vow set him apart for a specific period; the deacon's consecration set him apart for a specific purpose. There were only three lifelong Nazarites: Samuel, Samson, and John the Baptist.

The Nazarite had to let his hair grow long; he was forbidden to touch any dead body (even that of a loved one); and he was prohibited from any use of wine. His long hair declared that his *appearance* was on the altar. He could be picked out in a crowd; he was conspicuously set apart for God. The Nazarite's detachment from all dead bodies declared that his *affections* were on the altar. Not even his closest relatives or friends were allowed to come between him and God. The Nazarite was set apart from all contact with a dead world.

His total abstinence from wine declared that his *appetites* were on the altar. Even the legitimate use of wine was forbidden to him. Indeed, all products of the vine were placed out of bounds. He was to hunger and thirst after righteousness. Disregard for this prohibition was one reason that God handed Israel over to the Assyrians for punishment. In Amos 2:12, the prophet solemnly stated God's accusation: "Ye gave the Nazarites wine." God would not put up with drunken Nazarites or with a nation that had so lost its sense of divine purpose that it deliberately tried to subvert those who were consecrated to that purpose. God took the Old Testament vows seriously, and surely He takes the vocation of a deacon just as seriously. There must be no drunken deacons.

ii. Wealth (3:8d)

The deacon must also be faultless in the matter of wealth. He must not be "greedy of filthy lucre," said Paul. The word translated "greedy" conveys the picture of someone who is eager to make money. We recognize in the old-fashioned word *lucre* the root of our modern word *lucrative*. No deacon should be in the ministry merely to make money. God does not want greedy deacons any more than He wants drunken deacons. If someone wants to be well paid for his service, he is probably disqualified.

One of the Lord's disciples was "greedy of filthy lucre." His name was Judas. He held the bag, kept accounts for the apostolic fellowship, was in charge of its charities, bought the groceries, and paid the bills. The trouble was that he had a habit of dipping into the bag to feather his own nest. He figured that he had a right to do so; being a disciple was not proving to be as lucrative as he had expected. So far, all he had been able to get his hands on was small change.

When Judas first joined the messianic movement, he was full of high hopes. Doubtless, he envisioned himself receiving a well-paying position in the millennial kingdom. Possibly he saw himself becoming the secretary of the treasury. But when those hopes began to dim, he decided to cash in by selling Jesus to His enemies. Judas didn't get much, just the price of a female slave. He was a deacon "greedy of filthy lucre," and he ended up a suicide.

Because a deacon often helps manage the finances of his local church, he is sometimes exposed to the temptation to steal. In our day, considerable sums of money are sometimes involved, and the temptation might well overpower a greedy man. Thus, it would be best to keep him away from the diaconate.

Some time ago, when I was swapping trivia with another preacher, he remarked, "A hog cannot look up." That is true. A hog is focused on what this world has to offer. The same is true of some men who are deeply involved in finance, sports, or entertainment. The love of money increasingly fastens their attention on this world so that more and more they cease to look up. It happened to Solomon; it can happen to anyone. Jesus said, "Ye cannot serve God and mammon" (Matt. 6:24). A fixation on wealth disqualifies a man from being a deacon.

(2) The deacon as a faithful man (3:9–10)

(a) Possessing the truth (3:9)

i. His convictions (3:9a)

A deacon must be a man of the Word. Paul wrote that he must be able to hold "the mystery of the faith." The word translated "mystery" here refers to a sacred secret. In the New Testament it refers to the great plans and purposes of God that were not revealed in the Old Testament but are the subject of the New Testament revelation (Rom. 16:25; Eph. 3:5, 9; Col. 1:26). Various mysteries surface in the New Testament: the hidden mysteries of the kingdom (Matt. 13:10–11), the mystery of Israel's blindness during this present age of grace (Rom. 11:25), the mystery of the rapture of the church (1 Cor. 15:51), the mystery of the church itself (Eph. 3:9–11), the mystery of iniquity (2 Thess. 2:7), the mystery of godliness (1 Tim. 3:16), and the mystery of Babylon (Rev. 17:5).

ii. His conscience (3:9b)

It is incumbent on deacons to have at least a basic working knowledge of these truths and hold them with absolute integrity—"in a pure conscience." The word translated "pure" here means "cleansed, free from any mixture with impurity, unblemished." Paul called for purity of conscience in deacons because a conscience can be warped, deadened, and seared.

The only thing that Adam and Eve brought out of the Garden of Eden was a conscience; they left the garden with an awareness of guilt before God and with the burdensome knowledge of right and wrong. Conscience in and of itself might be a good goad, but it is not always a good guide; therefore, it has to be monitored by the Word of God and motivated by the Spirit of God.

(b) Passing the test (3:10)

"And let these," said Paul of the deacons, "also first be proved; then let them use the office of a deacon, being found blameless." They are to be *proved* before they are *promoted.* In other words, deacons are to be put to the test before being put in trust. The word for "proved" here means "to test with the expectation that the test results will prove to be favorable." Such a probation requirement makes sense in any walk of life.

When I finished high school in Britain and applied for a job with a large banking institution, I was given a written exam and then a personal interview with one of the bank officials. A few days later, the bank sent me a letter stating that my application had been approved and that I was being put on three months' probation. The bank was cautious about hiring people and wanted to ensure that prospective employees would be worthy of the training and trust to be invested in them. The bank was equally cautious about promoting its employees. If secular institutions are circumspect regarding personnel, how much more should the church be!

God put Moses through a long probationary period before promoting him. Having been adopted into the Egyptian royal family, he spent the first forty years of his life acquiring the finest education Egypt could offer. He "was learned in all the wisdom of the Egyptians, and was mighty in words and in deeds" (Acts 7:22). Then came the test, and Moses failed miserably. He intended to become a missionary; instead, he became a murderer and was forced to flee into the wilderness (Exod. 2:11–15). For the next forty years, he had to learn how to shepherd a flock. Only after he passed that test could God use him.

Likewise, David had a long probation. He was about sixteen years old when Samuel first anointed him to be Israel's next king, but he was thirty years old when he was anointed king by the tribe of Judah and thirty-eight years old when he was anointed king over all Israel. Many of the intervening years were marked by hardship, suffering, and persecution. During his apprenticeship, he had to spend time *in the country* minding sheep, *in the camp* confronting Goliath, *at the court* serving Saul, and *in the cave* dodging danger. If God required such rigorous preparation for a man who was to run an earthly kingdom, why would he require less "proving" for those called to lead a heaven-born, heaven-bound church?

In ancient Israel, Levites were taken into apprenticeship when they were twenty-five years old (Num. 8:24), but they did not begin their actual service until they reached thirty years of age (Num. 4:2–4). Joseph was thirty years old when he began his ministry in Egypt (Gen. 41:46). So was the Lord Jesus when he began His public ministry (Luke 3:23). God wants mature, tried men to serve Him as officers of His church.

He also wants them to be "blameless." The word used describes a person whose way of life is so blameless that he cannot be called to account. There should be nothing in a deacon's life that could be dug up by a public investigation and held against him. No basis for a charge should exist. Paul lived a blameless life, as the Ephesians and Timothy knew (Acts 20:17–38).

(3) The deacon as a family man (3:11–12)
 (a) His wife (3:11)
  i. Her character (3:11a)

"Even so must their wives be grave," wrote Paul. Note that one of the first qualifications for a deacon is also the first quality listed for his wife. A deacon and his wife are in the ministry together, so the wife must be as honorable as the husband. A deacon's ministry can easily be compromised by an irresponsible wife.

ii. Her conversation (3:11b)

Deacons' wives must not be "slanderers." The word translated "slanderer" is *diabolos,* which means "accuser, slanderer", and is one of the names for the Devil. This title is used for the Evil One some thirty-four times in the New Testament. In the Garden of Eden, the Devil slandered God when he was talking to man. In the book of Job, the Devil slandered man when he was talking to God. So when God insists that a deacon's wife not be a slanderer, He implies that a slanderous woman does the Devil's work and thus disqualifies her husband for the office of deacon.

The classic biblical example of a slanderer is Ziba, who tried to undermine Mephibosheth's integrity before David. Ziba was largely successful, in spite of the protest of Mephibosheth, who said, "He hath slandered thy servant unto my lord the king" (2 Sam. 19:27). Slanderers are dangerous people. Pity the man who is qualified in every other way to be a deacon, but is disqualified by his wife's malicious tongue.

iii. Her concern (3:11c)

A deacon's wife must also be "sober." The word translated "sober" here is translated "vigilant" in 3:2. It can also be rendered "temperate." So Paul was saying that a deacon's wife must be a steady, self-controlled person. A hysterical or immoderate wife would handicap a deacon.

iv. Her consistency (3:11d)

Furthermore, a deacon's wife must be "faithful in all things." She must be dependable. Possibly Paul had in mind the model wife described by Solomon in Proverbs 31. Maybe the woman whom Solomon described there was the Shulamite who had enough sense to turn him down.[18] In spite of all of Solomon's wit and wealth, he was most unfortunate in his choice of wives, who proved to be his undoing in his later years.

18. See John Phillips, *Exploring the Love Song of Solomon* (Grand Rapids: Kregel, 2002).

(b) His walk (3:12)

Paul next considered the deacon *as a partner* and *as a parent.* "Let the deacons," wrote the apostle, "be the husbands of one wife, ruling their children and their own houses well." This requirement is similar to that incumbent on elders.

The home is the basic, God-ordained unit of society. As the home goes, so goes the nation. In his roles as husband and father, a man develops the attitudes, discipline, compassion, and skills that enable him to be a leader in the church. In the home, he learns how to show love, loyalty, sympathy, and understanding. In the home, he learns how to handle authority, power, and money. The home is the proving ground for elders and deacons.

The model deacon in the New Testament is Philip the Evangelist (Acts 6:5). Luke had nothing but good to say about him. In Acts 21:8–9, Luke wrote, "And the next day [toward the end of Paul's third missionary journey] we that were of Paul's company departed, and came unto Caesarea [the Roman capital of Palestine]: and we entered into the house of Philip the evangelist, which was one of the seven; and abode with him. And the same man had four daughters, virgins, which did prophesy." Philip was not only hospitable but also had a houseful of daughters who were able to articulate the Word of God. Paul must have been delighted to see his idea of the model deacon personified.

(4) The deacon as a farsighted man (3:13)

When the model deacon's *administration is assessed,* his *advancement is assured:* "They that have used the office of a deacon well purchase to themselves a good degree, and great boldness in the faith which is in Christ Jesus." In other words, the office of the deacon is not to be regarded as an end in itself. It can be a stepping-stone to greater things in the work of God. Those who diligently discharge their duties as deacons make a great investment in their own future.

The word for "purchase" here means "to gain possession, acquire." Paul used the same word when personally addressing the Ephesian elders at Miletus. He was impressing upon them the solemn responsibility that they had assumed by becoming elders. They were never to forget that they were shepherds and overseers of "the church of God, which he hath purchased [same word] with his own blood" (Acts 20:28).

The word translated "degree" in 1 Timothy 3:13 is *bathmos,* which refers to a step, stair, or threshold. *Bathmos* occurs only here in the New Testament and suggests perhaps a picture of a deacon going up a rung on the ladder of success.

We see such advancement illustrated in the lives of two of the seven deacons appointed by the Jerusalem church: Stephen and Philip.

Stephen went on to become the church's first martyr. We know nothing about how he discharged his duty of waiting on tables, though doubtless he did his work well. Luke picked up his story a little later when "Stephen, full of faith and power, did great wonders and miracles among the people" (Acts 6:8). At that point, Stephen was already behaving more like an apostle than a deacon. The Bible says that a man's gift will make room for him (Prov. 18:16), and Stephen's certainly did. He was mighty in word and deed.

"Then," we read, "there arose certain of the synagogue, which is called the synagogue of the Libertines, and Cyrenians, and Alexandrians, and of them of Cilicia and of Asia, disputing with Stephen" (Acts 6:9). The reference to Cilicia leads us to think that Saul of Tarsus was one of those who tried to confound Stephen in debate. If so, even before his conversion Paul had firsthand knowledge of the formidable power and persuasiveness of a Spirit-filled, God-promoted deacon.

Unable to silence Stephen in debate, the enemies of the gospel decided that they had best silence him in death. Their decision was a tacit confession of defeat. Saul of Tarsus seems to have been one of the leaders of those enemies during this dark chapter of Jewish national life. Stephen's eloquent defense of the gospel during his trial and his subsequent triumphant death became significant but subliminal factors in the equation of Saul's subsequent conversion.

Our other example of advancement is Philip the Evangelist and deacon. He went on to become the church's first missionary. The Great Commission, given by the risen Lord to the apostles, had been clear enough: "Ye shall be witnesses unto me both in Jerusalem, and in all Judea, and in Samaria, and unto the uttermost part of the earth" (Acts 1:8). The apostles, however, seem to have been content to remain in Jerusalem (Acts 8:1). After all, the believers in the Jerusalem church now numbered in the thousands, so there was ample opportunity for a dozen men to minister. Why should they go elsewhere? It remained for a deacon to demonstrate obedience to the Lord's command.

"Philip went down to the city of Samaria, and preached Christ unto them" (Acts 8:5). He was the first to take seriously the Samaritan part of the missionary agenda. Not one of the apostles seemed eager to cross the frontier of Samaria. After all, the Samaritans were regarded by all self-respecting Jews with ineffable contempt. As a result of Philip's daring, however, a tremendous revival broke out in Samaria. So noteworthy was the response that the apostles were obliged to acknowledge it and bestir themselves (8:14).

Later, the Holy Spirit used Philip to lead an important Ethiopian to Christ (8:26–39) and to evangelize the coastal cities of Palestine from Azotus (the ancient Philistine city of Ashdod) to Caesarea. In that important, cosmopolitan, Gentile city, he became a resident evangelist.

Such were the farsighted early deacons!

2. The church's duties displayed (3:14–15)
   a. Paul's personal desire (3:14)

Paul's desire was to fulfill his apostolic duty to visit Ephesus. His *letter* to Timothy said, "These things write I unto thee, hoping to come unto thee shortly." Timothy was already there to deal with whatever the problem was, and Paul's letter would guide him and strengthen his hand. But evidently the Ephesian situation was serious enough to warrant an apostolic visit.

Paul's decision making was often governed by circumstances and common sense, along with the leading of the Holy Spirit. Circumstances led him to take Silas rather than Barnabas on his second missionary journey (Acts 15:37–41), and circumstances led him to choose Timothy to replace Mark as his personal attendant. Circumstances often governed Paul's missionary activities (13:50–52; 14:19–20). At the time he wrote the first epistle to Timothy, the apostle was "hoping to come," but circumstances in the shape of growing Neronic persecution were about to take over with a vengeance. Through it all, Paul never lost sight of the fact that all circumstances were under the control of the Holy Spirit, the true "Lord of the Harvest" (Luke 10:2).

Paul's *longing* was to hurry off to Ephesus to see his dear young friend. He also longed to fellowship with the Ephesians, many of whom he had personally led to Christ. He longed to fortify the believers there because the coming storm would soon break in fury on the church near and far.

   b. Paul's pastoral desire (3:15)
      (1) A possible delay was envisioned (3:15a)

Paul's desire was to visit Ephesus, but he hinted to Timothy that circumstances might detain him. Envisioning a possible delay, he wrote, "But if I tarry long . . ." The word for "tarry long" means "to delay or be slow." In other words, Paul was telling Timothy not to count on his coming.

Because Paul might not be able to visit, he wanted Timothy to heed the instructions written in his letter. How thankful we should be that Paul took the precaution of writing this epistle! What important practical instruction and magnificent doctrinal teaching we would have missed if, instead of writing to Timothy, Paul had simply dropped everything and hurried off to Ephesus!

(2) A positive duty was enjoined (3:15b)

Paul told Timothy, "[I write} that thou mayest know how thou oughtest to behave thyself in the house of God." The word translated "behave" here is rendered "conversation" in 2 Corinthians 1:12 and could be translated "lifestyle." In the Corinthian passage, Paul used the word in describing his own unimpeachable behavior.

(3) A perfect description was enshrined (3:15c–d)

(a) The church's character (3:15c)

Paul added a twofold description of "the house of God." First, he called it "the church of the living God." The word translated "church" points to a special company of called-out ones. The word is used by the Holy Spirit to describe both the entire company of those who trust in Christ and any local gathering of His people.

Most people have a poor opinion of the church. If they think of it at all, they think of the vast organized system of religion that began to develop about the third century and is now represented by the Roman Catholic, Greek Orthodox, and Russian Orthodox churches; apostate liberal churches; the various Protestant state churches; numerous nonconformist and independent churches; and a miscellaneous assortment of odd cults. That conglomeration is not the church but Christendom—what men see and identify as the church. They listen to its babble of voices, witness its dissensions and wars, notice its meddling in politics and interfering with science, and observe its futile struggles to unite under an ecumenical banner. They see Christendom and despise the church.

The true church, however, is quite different from that conglomerate. The church is the mystical body of Christ (1 Cor. 12:13), which is comprised of all blood-bought believers from all of the centuries since Pentecost. The church has its home in heaven, and its members come from all nations on the earth. They come from all walks of life. To the hosts of hell, the church is, indeed, as "terrible as an army with banners" (Song 6:4, 10).

The church, the bride of Christ, is already seated with Him in the heavenlies. It is the body of Christ through which He carries on His work in the world. "The church of the living God" is the creation of the Holy Spirit of God and shares the life of God. The church has no equal in all of the annals of time and eternity. It ranks higher than angels, cherubim and seraphim, principalities and powers, thrones and dominions, and every name that is named. It is infinitely precious to God because He purchased it with His blood. We must never underestimate the church.

Ever since Pentecost, the church has been the apple of God's eye. Woe betides those who tamper with it. Satan works away at his nefarious schemes. He sows false philosophies and cultic religions into the world and corrupts the minds of men. Then God sends revival through the church, and Satan's house of cards comes tumbling down. Satan begins again. He brings along a tyrant to sow misery and mayhem on earth. War, famine, pestilence, and persecution convulse the world, then suddenly God sends revival through the church again and makes the wrath of man to praise Him (Ps. 76:10). Again and again Satan has set the stage for the coming of his "man of sin" (2 Thess. 2:1–4), but times without number God has sent revival through His church and foiled Satan's plans for another generation. Satan knows about the church. He hates and fears it. It is "the church of the living God!"

(b) The church's custodianship (3:15d)

The second part of the twofold description of "the house of God" states that the church is "the pillar and ground of the truth." The word translated "pillar" is *stulos,* which refers to a column designed to support a building. The word translated "ground" actually refers to a support or bulwark. In some medieval churches, the vast expanse of the roof is supported by flying buttresses that shore up the considerable weight. That is a picture of what "the church of the living God" is intended to do for truth.

Truth is constantly under attack in this world. Satan has a fertile mind for inventing doctrinal error, and he never stops spreading deceptions and falsehoods. Amid all of these attacks, the church stands as a bulwark and buttress of truth. The church is the guardian of the truth contained in the thirty-nine books of the Old Testament and the twenty-seven books of the New Testament.

PART 3

How to Become an Effective Christian

1 Timothy 3:16–6:19

A. Walk with God (3:16–4:16)
1. The mystery of godliness (3:16–4:7a)
a. The truth asserted (3:16)

In 3:16, Paul summarized the essential elements of the truth of which the church is the custodian: "Without controversy great is the mystery of godliness: God was manifest in the flesh, justified in the Spirit, seen of angels, preached unto the Gentiles, believed on in the world, received up into glory." These are the truths that Satan hates and assails (see 4:1–7).

A whole book could be written on 1 Timothy 3:16 alone. It is an amazing verse. It begins with Jesus as God and ends with Jesus in glory. It begins with His incarnation and ends with His ascension.

(1) The mystery of Christ's person (3:16a–b)
(a) The virgin's womb: He came to live a human life (3:16a)

The first part of the verse refers to the mystery of Christ's person: "Without controversy great is the mystery of godliness: God was manifest in the flesh." The word translated "without controversy" means "confessedly" or "by common consent." The truths enshrined in 3:16 were the basics of a common confession of faith in the early church, so the verse is a kind of general and agreed-upon creedal statement. The great "mystery of godliness" is the revelation of godliness as incarnated in the person of the Lord Jesus Christ.

Major Ian Thomas says that Jesus had to come as He came to be what He was (both God and man). He had to be what He was to live as He lived (wholly dependent as man on His Father as God). He had to live as He lived (He lived an absolutely holy and perfect life) to do what He did (He gave that life first in service and then in sacrifice).

God is manifest in flaming suns and burning stars, in changing seasons, in the rainbow's hues, and in the sunset's scarlet rays. He is manifest in the glory of the galaxies and in the pale, silver face of the moon. Now He has been manifest in flesh. Deity is robed in humanity. The Son of God has become the Son of Man. Our planet has been invaded from outer space by the glorious Son of the living God; the Creator of the universe; the One whom angels worship; the eternal, uncreated, self-existing second person of the Godhead! The manger in Bethlehem cradled the One who was God, now appearing as a child of Adam's race.

Jesus was man as God always intended man to be: man inhabited by God. Christ's human spirit was so filled with the indwelling Spirit of God and His work was so anointed by the Spirit of God that He was described by the Holy Spirit as "the image of the invisible God" and "the express image of [God's] person" (Col. 1:15; Heb. 1:3). It could be truly said of Him that "in him dwelleth all the fullness of the Godhead bodily" (Col. 2:9).

(b) The vacant tomb: He came to live a holy life (3:16b)

Christ came to live not only a human life but also a holy life. That life received accolades from heaven from time to time (Matt. 3:17; 17:5) but did not receive its full endorsement until He rose from the dead. Paul wrote in Romans 1:4 that the Lord Jesus was "declared to be the Son of God with power, according to the spirit of holiness, by the resurrection from the dead." In Romans 8:10–11, the apostle says that Christ was raised from the dead by the power of the Holy Spirit. It was thus and then that Christ was "justified in the Spirit" (1 Tim. 3:16).

The word translated "justified" here is the general word used for declaring a sinner to be righteous. It means "to be vindicated, or to be proved or pronounced righteous." The Lord Jesus, "who knew no sin," was made "sin for us" (2 Cor. 5:21). The wicked men who contrived His death thought that they had triumphed. They gathered together at Calvary to mock Him as He died. But God had the last word. Three days later, Jesus was "justified in the Spirit" by being raised from the dead. Vindicated in life and death, He declared, "I am he that liveth, and was dead; and, behold, I am alive for evermore, Amen; and have the keys of hell and of death" (Rev. 1:18).

(2) The mystery of Christ's people (3:16c–d)

(a) The heavenly host (3:16c)

Christ was "seen of angels," wrote Paul. Angels have a great interest in the events that surrounded the incarnation, crucifixion, resurrection, ascension, intercession, and coronation of the Lord. As 1 Peter 1:12 puts it, these are "things the angels desire to look into."

Angels announced Christ's birth and heralded His coming (Luke 1:26–38; 2:8–15). They ministered to Him after His temptation (Matt. 4:11) and during His agony in the Garden of Gethsemane (Luke 22:43). Jesus told Peter that He had more than twelve legions of angels who would defend Him against His foes, were He to summon them (Matt. 26:52–54). Angels are mentioned in connection with His resurrection (Matt. 28:1–10; John 20:11–14) and His going home to heaven (Acts 1:9–11). Angels will accompany Him at His return (1 Thess. 4:16) and will administer judgment during the days after the church's rapture (Rev. 7:1–3; 8:1–13; 12:7–9; 14:1–18:21; 19:11–20:3).

The heavenly hosts have watched with keenest interest the unfolding drama of redemption. After all, the "mystery of iniquity" (2 Thess. 2:7) began not on earth but in heaven. It did not begin with Adam and Eve; it was born in the breast of Lucifer, the highest archangel in glory (Isa. 14:9–14; Ezek. 28:12–15).

Moreover, the number of Scripture references to things that happened "from [or before] the foundation of the world" (e.g., Matt. 13:35; 25:34; Eph. 1:4; Rev. 13:8) suggests that God sovereignly chose our planet to be the place in the universe where the whole question of iniquity would be settled once and for all, to His entire and eternal satisfaction. So the heavenly hosts watch our planet with more than common interest. They kept their eyes riveted on the Lord Jesus from the moment He stepped off His Father's throne on high to come to earth until the moment when He arrived back in heaven as described in Psalm 24.

(b) The heathen heart (3:16d)

First Timothy 3:16 is a hymn of contrasts: between the womb and the tomb, between the angelic hosts of heaven and the lost Gentiles of earth, and between this globe and the glory. But surely no greater contrast can be drawn than that between the sinless sons of light, whose hallelujahs awaken the echoes of the everlasting hills as they sing Christ's praise, and the pagan Gentiles, besotted with sin, bound by superstition and sophistry, and blinded by an enslaving worship of graven images.

Christ was "preached unto the Gentiles," wrote the great Apostle to the Gentiles. The Jews in Jerusalem and throughout the far-flung Diaspora could never forgive Paul for breaking all of their religious taboos and throwing in his lot with the Gentiles. Even the believing Jews resented Paul's Gentile ministry, especially as increasing numbers of Gentiles poured into the church, making the Jews an ever-shrinking minority. Peter had to be convinced by a vision that God was determined to reach out to the Gentiles with the same love and compassion that He had shown to the Jews (Acts 10:9–11:18). The Jewish believers in Jerusalem were barely restrained from trying to force Gentiles to become Jews before they could become Christians (Acts 15). Even after that issue was settled, Jewish missionaries dogged Paul's steps, invaded his churches and sought to convince Gentile converts to embrace Judaism and legalism.

To preach to the Gentiles was a bold move, one of the distinguishing marks of a new dispensation in God's dealing with man. Descendants of Ham, Shem, and Japheth—the three racial families—were made one in Christ by this movement of the Spirit of God. In Acts 8, we read of the conversion of an Ethiopian, a descendant of Ham; in Acts 9, we read of the conversion of Saul of Tarsus (a "Hebrew of the Hebrews," Phil. 3:4–7), a descendant of Shem; and in Acts 10, we read of the conversion of the Roman soldier Cornelius, a descendant of Japheth.

From Acts 11 to the end of the book (the great missions handbook of the church), the focus is on Paul and his monumental ministry of preaching the unsearchable riches of Christ to the Gentiles. His three great missionary journeys embraced about fifteen years of travel in ever-expanding circles. From Antioch to Corinth, he planted church after church in city after city. A long line of churches sprang up in one major city after another, each surrounded by densely populated areas. By the time he wrote to the Romans, he could tell believers in the capital that "from Jerusalem, and round about into Illyricum" he had "fully preached the gospel of Christ" and that in so doing he had scrupulously avoided building "upon another man's foundation" (Rom. 15:19–20). Paul claimed to have fully evangelized an area stretching fifteen hundred miles up through Syria, across Asia Minor, into Macedonia, down into Greece, and up into Illyricum (the old-world name for Yugoslavia, the northern Balkan Peninsula). Moreover, he was making plans to go on to Spain (Rom. 15:24).

Half a dozen decades after Pentecost, Jews were outnumbered by Gentiles in the church, but the task of reaching the Gentiles was far from complete. Nearly two thousand years later, the God who has been "manifest in the flesh" is still being "preached unto the Gentiles." The world is still a mission field.

The least evangelized countries, including communist China, are located in what is often called "the resistant belt." It reaches all of the way from West Africa to East Asia and lies between the latitudes of ten degrees north to forty degrees north. The world's largest and most gospel-resistant religions—Islam, Buddhism, and Hinduism—are dominant in this zone. Roughly two-thirds of the world's population live in the belt, although it contains only one-third of the world's land area. Some sixty countries and about fifty of the world's least evangelized megacities are in this zone. The megacities (including Calcutta, Tokyo, Tel Aviv, and Istanbul) are home to many millions of people. Moreover, the poorest of the poor live in this belt, too. Many of the resistant countries are closed to missionaries, but the gospel gets in through radio, literature, and other means.

(3) The mystery of Christ's power (3:16e–f)

(a) His triumph on this globe (3:16e)

Christ's triumph here is that He is "believed on in the world." In spite of setbacks, people are believing. The mystery is why some people *don't* believe. After all, the gospel is the best news ever proclaimed on this planet. The Son of God became the Son of Man so that the sons of men might become the sons of God! We are offered full and free salvation, a place in the family of God, a home in heaven, and a standing in Christ above all thrones, dominions, principalities, and powers. The only explanation for unbelief is that the gospel is intended in this age simply to "call out a people" (Acts 15:13–14). The church is a company of called-out ones, the true aristocracy of the universe.

The results of evangelism might look small to us, but God is satisfied. The Holy Spirit is the Lord of the harvest. He makes no mistakes; He knows what He is doing. The history of the church since Pentecost is proof that the Lord Jesus is being "believed on in the world."

We call to witness John Wesley, who went to America as a *missionary* to convert the Indians and discovered that he himself was not converted. After he went back home to England, he became a believer and a great herald of the gospel.

We call to witness the *martyr* Hugh Latimer, who was called "the honestest man in England." He was led to Christ by Thomas Bilney, a nobody who was brought to Christ by reading the works of Erasmus. When Latimer was burned at the stake, he proclaimed that his martyrdom would light a candle in England that would never be put out. He was right.

We call to witness King George VI, *monarch* of England, and the British Empire, a man who knew and loved the Lord. Before he became king and thereby the titular head of the Church of England, he had more liberty than his older brother Edward, who was the crown prince. A humble believer, George took advantage of his freedom to meet with a small group of like-minded believers for the sole purpose of participating in conversational Bible reading.

We call my *mother* to witness. She was an ordinary woman who loved the Lord from her childhood days. She was a devout believer. My earliest recollection is of her rocking me to sleep to the tune of old-fashioned hymns. When she died years ago in a Florida retirement home, the Bible on her bed table was open to

Psalm 23. On a piece of paper marking that passage, she had written, "The secret of a happy life! The secret of a happy death! The secret of a happy eternity!" With those thoughts in her mind, she went from grace to glory.

We call to witness Evan Roberts. He was an unknown *miner* who became a well-known revivalist. As a believer, he was bowed down by the crying need of the age for spiritual renewal and devoted himself to intercession. Revival came to Wales. It influenced Britain and spread to the Welsh coal miners in Pennsylvania. It transformed lives and cleaned up society.

We call to witness the *murderer* Saul of Tarsus. He hated Christ and detested Christianity. He considered Christ to be a blasphemer and Christianity to be a cult. Saul dedicated his life to blotting out the church and became the Sanhedrin's chosen agent to get rid of as many believers as possible. Acts 9:1 says that he breathed out "threatenings and slaughter." The word translated "slaughter" there is *phonos,* which means "murder." *Phonos* occurs ten times in the New Testament and, except in Acts 9:1 and Hebrews 11:37, is always translated "murder." Paul himself said that he voted for the death of many believers (Acts 26:9–11). But one glimpse of the risen Lord was enough to make him believe.

We call to witness former *mobster* Jim Vaus, who was an electronics wizard in the early day of that technology. He was born in a Christian home and had a believing wife, but he accepted the pay of gangsters and racketeers who found his skills useful. Then he went forward to accept Christ at a Billy Graham crusade. He quit the mob at the risk of his life, went to prison to pay his debt to society, and became a missionary.

We call to witness the *merchant* D. L. Moody, a shoe salesman, who came from New England to Chicago to make his fortune. He was led to Christ in the back of the shoe store where he was working. The bold, brash salesman who was on his way up in the world became a bold, brash believer who threw himself as enthusiastically into soul winning as he had into shoe selling. He heard someone say that the world had yet to see what God could do through a man who was wholly yielded to Himself, and he responded, "By the grace of God, I'll be that man." Moody became one of the world's great revivalists, and through him the Lord Jesus was "believed on in the world" by many. To this day, through the Moody Bible Institute, the work he began goes on to the ends of the earth.

We call to witness the *mariner* John Newton. A born rebel, he ran away to sea and sank to the uttermost depths of degradation and despair; indeed he became the slave of a slave. Then during a storm at sea it seemed to him that the Lord stood by him on the heaving deck of the ship and looked into his soul, and he was saved. He quit the sea and became a preacher and hymn writer. His song "Amazing Grace" is sung the world over to this day.

Finally, we call to witness a *menial,* Sophie the scrubwoman. She was an uneducated nobody who wanted to become a missionary. Her pastor, Dr. A. B. Simpson, knew of no missionary society that would accept an application from her. When she came to ask his advice, he told her to go home and pray about it. She came back the next week. Dr. Simpson saw her coming and wondered what he could say to her. He discovered that the Lord had said all that was needed. God had directed her attention to the Chinese laundryman on the corner, to the Italian tailor across the way, and to the Greek vegetable vendor who pushed his cart up her street. They had all come to New York, the Lord told her, so that she could be a missionary to them. So Sophie reached out to people of many ethnic groups and nationalities who lived in her great city. At her funeral, people kept jumping to their feet to testify that Sophie had led them to Christ. By Sophie's converts and an innumerable multitude of others, Christ is "believed on in the world."

(b) His triumph in the glory (3:16f)

Paul concluded 3:16 by affirming that Christ was "received up into glory." Think of the *majesty* of that triumph. For forty days and forty nights, Jesus waited for the great day. During that time, He appeared here and there, showing "himself alive after his passion by many infallible proofs" (Acts 1:3). Finally, He gathered together about 120 people, those who believed in Him, and led them through the gate of the city, across the Kidron, past the Garden of Gethsemane, and up to the brow of Olivet. What a picture! The apostles and the other believers were following a resurrected man as He took His last walk on earth.

They arrived at the brow of Olivet. He raised His hands in a parting benediction and began to rise toward the sky. We can see them as they stood and stared, craning their necks. Nothing like this has ever happened before. Enoch, as far as we know, was alone when he was raptured. Elijah had ascended with an angel escort, but only one person had seen him go. Jesus, however, ascended in full view of about six score people. The nail prints in His feet were the last thing they saw as the glory cloud wrapped around Him.

Up He went until the gates of the celestial loomed ahead. He gave the triumphant command recorded by David in Psalm 24 and entered the city of God. On He went amid the hosannas of the angels to the Great White Throne of God.[1]

---

1. See John Phillips, *Exploring the Psalms,* 2 vols. (Grand Rapids: Kregel, 2002), 1:180–85.

Think, too, of the *mystery* of Christ's triumph. Now there is a man in a glorified but battle-scarred body seated on the throne of God in heaven! He has every right to be there because He is God over all, blessed forevermore. Stephen saw that ascended Christ and became the church's first martyr. Saul saw Him and became the church's foremost missionary.

If an ordinary British citizen or a foreign visitor were to try to sit on Queen Elizabeth's throne, he would be hauled away at once. But Jesus, the One born in Bethlehem, verily the Son of Man, sits in splendor on God's throne, ruling the universe and receiving the homage of the angels! The human race now has a kinsman on the throne of God. Well might Satan and all of his host tremble.

Think also of the *ministry* of Christ's triumph. We now have a Great High Priest in Glory, One touched with the feelings of our infirmities, to intercede for us. "We have an advocate with the Father" (1 John 2:1) who is able to silence all of the accusations of the enemy. Through our Great High Priest we have access to God (Rom. 5:1–2); we can come into the Holy of Holies in heaven because of Him (Heb. 10:19–22).

Suppose that Christ had stayed here instead of being "received up into glory." Suppose that He had said to His disciples, "I'm going to build a palace here in Jerusalem. I will grant audience to those who wish to come to see Me. You can take care of the arrangements. Schedule people in the order of their applications. Each one can have fifteen minutes." What chance would we ever have to get an appointment with the King? And what could be said and done in a scant quarter hour?

But we have something far better than that. Jesus has returned to heaven, and we can come into His presence whenever we like, stay as long as we like, and tell Him whatever we like. Such is "the mystery of godliness."

It would seem, from what follows in 1 Timothy 4:1–7, that Paul had heresy in mind when he made the doctrinal statement recorded in 3:16. The Gnostic heresy that later came to full flower and fruit had already raised its head.

The gnostics denied that God had manifested Himself in the flesh. Some of them denied Christ's manhood outright. They said that His body was a phantom, a delusion, or a mirage, or that, quite unlike our bodies, it was composed of celestial substances. All gnostics attacked the Godhead of Jesus; they believed that He was some kind of inferior deity or angelic being (aeon).

Some gnostics declared that Jesus was just an ordinary human being on whom "the Christ" (a mighty aeon or spirit) descended at the time of His baptism and that by union with "the Christ," Jesus became "Jesus Christ." According to this heresy, "the Christ" left Jesus before the Crucifixion; on the basis of that teaching, the Gnostics denied the reality of Christ's death. Likewise, they denied that Jesus was "justified in the Spirit" (as suggested earlier, this reference to the Spirit likely points to the resurrection of Christ, which was effected by the Holy Spirit).

As we have already seen in 2:5, Paul wrote emphatically about "the *man* Christ Jesus" and, opposing the Gnostic theory of many emanations or intermediary angels, declared Him to be the "*one* mediator" (italics added). Moreover, Paul had already urged the Ephesian elders, "Feed the church of *God,* which he hath purchased with *his own blood*" (Acts 20:28, italics added). He had reminded them of the reality of both the deity and humanity of Jesus and of His atoning death. The dangerous Gnostic heresy is refuted not only here but also in Colossians and the first epistle of John.

b. The truth assailed (4:1–7a)
   (1) The apostasy announced (4:1)
      (a) The day envisioned (4:1a)

The apostasy that was already taking root during apostolic times will reach full and final development in the end times. Paul prophesied, "The Spirit speaketh expressly, that in the latter times some shall depart from the faith." The word translated "expressly" occurs only here in the New Testament and means "in specific terms." The Holy Spirit bears witness to this end-times prophecy, not in vague terms or symbolic language but in plain, unambiguous words.

The word translated "letter" occurs as an adjective only here in the New Testament. It refers to "that which comes after." Although "latter times" doubtless includes postapostolic times, it also anticipates end-times conditions. The word translated "times" here is *kairos.* It refers not to time (as does *chronos*) but to the critical turning points in history, all of which are under God's control.

The word translated "depart" means literally "to apostatize." The definite article preceding the word *faith* makes clear that there will be an abandonment of *the* faith, the body of Christian doctrine that Paul capsulized in 3:16.

In 4:1, the focus is on the end-times abandonment of the faith that will precede the rapture of the church and create a global climate conducive to the coming of the Antichrist (2 Thess. 2:3). Those who lead the way into the end-times apostasy, which will pave the way for the coming "strong delusion" (2 Thess. 2:11), will be people who have known the truth and even professed the faith but who have deliberately abandoned it. Such departure from the faith is exemplified in Hymenaeus and Alexander, who "made shipwreck" concerning the faith (1 Tim. 1:19). Elsewhere, Paul described such apostasy as an "overthrow" (2 Tim. 2:18).

To leave Christianity for paganism, as the Roman emperor Julian did, is apostasy. An apostate holds to a false religion, one that is inconsistent with the revealed truths of Christianity. Such abandonment of truth was a characteristic of the days of Noah (Gen. 4–6), and it is becoming an increasingly evident feature of our modern era (Matt. 24:37–39). The false Christ will spring out of such apostasy.

(b) The departure envisioned (4:1b–c)

Paul envisioned that those who abandon the faith in the end times will be "giving heed to seducing spirits, and doctrines of devils." The word translated "seducing" is *planos,* which means "causing to wander, leading astray."

In one of His parables, the Lord taught that after a time, during which Satan will seem to have been vanquished and driven out of his stronghold, he will come back stronger and more wicked than before. A wicked "generation" will welcome him, a generation seven times more possessed by Satan than at the first (Matt. 12:45; Luke 11:26). Many indications exist that our own generation may well be that generation. It is preparing the way for that final departure from God that is the prophetic hallmark of Christendom in the end times.

The progression of apostasy can be illustrated by developments in Germany. The country that gave us Martin Luther later gave us the so-called "higher critics" and then Adolph Hitler. The regime of this demon-controlled man was one of Satan's dress rehearsals for end-times events. Hitler regularly consulted horoscopes and established Germany's Federal Commission of Occultism. This was the first time a modern state officially recognized occultism and created a governmental department to oversee it. Britain took Hitler's occultism seriously enough to retain the services of Walter Stein, a German occultist and medium who informed the authorities about what the astrologers were telling Hitler. Hitler was initiated into satanism by Dietrich Eckart, a founder of the Nazi party. This evil man opened Hitler's soul to possession by powerful evil spirits who lured him and Germany to destruction. So apostasy gave rise to Nazi Germany.

We have already mentioned the disastrous effect Darwin's theory on Darwin himself. The disastrous effect that it has had on the world will never be calculated this side of eternity. It was at the heart of both Nazism and Communism.

Professor Sedgewick, a Cambridge geologist, saw through Darwin's book at once. He described it as "a dish of materialism, cleverly cooked and served up merely to make us independent of the Creator." He declared that if and when Darwin's theory was generally accepted, it would lead to the brutalization of the race.[2]

The theory of evolution has also given rise to modern humanism. Secular humanists occupy key positions in our schools, courts, legislatures, and media; and they seek to establish what is basically a new religion based on science. In the new world order that they envision, man is to be his own god; the state is to be supreme; the leading ideas of all religions are to be synthesized to give the world a common creed; the true church and biblical Christianity (obscurantist institutions, in their view) are to be uprooted; genetic engineering is to produce a superior brand of human beings; children are to be indoctrinated from the time they are two years old until they have finished college; and the mass media, courts, educational systems, churches, and all governmental agencies are to be enlisted in the cause. It is a formula for the Antichrist.

Man is not a machine. He has a soul, a conscience, and an inbred hunger for God, so the materialism of the humanists is unappetizing fare. Modern man has largely abandoned the Christian faith, so people have to look for something else to fill the inner void. What has arisen is another factor in the end-times apostasy that will prepare the world for the Antichrist: the New Age movement. This occult movement is attracting a growing and potentially threatening conglomerate of people devoted to astrology, witchcraft, demonism, psychic phenomena, supernaturalism, hauntings, extrasensory perception, spiritism, and the worship of Satan. The movement is made somewhat palatable by its enthusiasm for ecological and environmental reform, its zeal for natural foods uncontaminated by pesticides, and its strong leanings toward a supposedly healthy vegetarian diet. (Vegetarianism is a must for all in-depth occult experience.)

Interest in the New Age movement received considerable impetus from such media productions as the book and movie versions of *Rosemary's Baby*, a story of a young woman who gave birth to a child of the Devil. When the film premiered on the West Coast, newspaper ads blasphemously pleaded, "Pray for Rosemary's baby." The movie *The Exorcist*, another occult production, captured the imagination of millions. Daily radio and television programs that feature psychics and fortune-tellers are attracting increasing numbers of people.

The occult world has never been far away. The Bible warns against occultism.

---

2. R. E. D. Clarke, *Darwin, Before and After* (Grand Rapids: Grand Rapids International Publications, 1958).

Such practices as witchcraft and necromancy were capital offenses under the Mosaic Law (Exod. 22:18; Deut. 18:10). King Saul consulted a witch to his own undoing (1 Sam. 28:6–19).

Three great eruptions of demonic activity are noted in the historical sections of the Bible. The first was an unprecedented outbreak of satanism in the days of Noah. The second was in the land of Canaan just before the Hebrew conquest. Both of these eruptions produced a giant, demon progeny on the earth. The third outbreak greeted the public ministry of Christ. In fact, the first recorded miracle of the Gospels of Mark and Luke involved an encounter with an evil spirit. The advent of Christ threw the satanic world into a tumult and provoked an epidemic of demon activity.

A fourth eruption will occur as the coming of the Antichrist approaches. We are living today in the shadow of end-times events, and the increasing interest in the occult in our day, the most sophisticated scientific age in history, shows how close we are.

Modern spiritism was launched in 1848 by Margaret and Kate Fox (ages twelve and nine, respectively), who lived in Hydesville, New York. These sisters heard rappings on the wall of their home and established a system of responsive raps whereby they could communicate with the haunting spirit. The spiritist movement attracted outstanding advocates, including Sir Oliver Lodge, the eminent British scientist, and Sir Arthur Conan Doyle, creator of the famous fictional detective Sherlock Holmes.

Although a considerable amount of fraud has plagued the movement, there can be little doubt that spiritists do make contact with intelligences in the world beyond. They assume that they are contacting the spirits of dead people, but the fact is that they are communicating with demons who impersonate dead people. The demons involved in the deception are called "familiar spirits" because they are familiar with some of the details of the lives of the dead people whom they pretend to be. These evil spirits crave embodiment, and they possess the bodies of their victims whenever the opportunity arises. Motivated by an implacable hatred of the human race, the demons are eager to lure their victims to destruction.

A classic modern example of such a victim is the rationalistic bishop James A. Pike, a learned but controversial leader of the American Episcopal Church. He was a lawyer, who became a clergyman, who became an apostate, who became a dupe of evil spirits. His total disbelief in the bodily resurrection of Christ caused his denomination to charge him with heresy.

Pike had a son who became addicted to psychedelic drugs and committed suicide at age twenty. The bishop had his son's body cremated and his ashes scattered on the ocean just beyond San Francisco's Golden Gate Bridge. Then he went to Cambridge, England, and stayed in the same apartment where he and his son had enjoyed time together on a previous occasion. The stage was thus set for demons to entrap the apostate bishop. Strange things began to happen that convinced the bereaved father that his dead son was trying to get in touch with him. The idea became an obsession, so he sought out the services of a certain Mrs. Twigg in East Acton, London. She had the reputation of being one of England's foremost mediums.

Pike became convinced that the Cambridge apartment, which held nostalgic memories for him, was haunted by the ghost of his son. The deceiving spirit he had contacted urged him to be bold in his battle against those who were charging him with heresy. The bishop was then visited by what he took to be the ghost of Paul Tillich, a German-American theologian who had been one of his friends. The spirit impersonating Tillich thanked Pike for dedicating a book to him and urged him to continue his campaign against Christian doctrine.

Having become a believer in spiritism, Pike returned to the United States, resigned from the church, and championed the occult. In the end, the evil spirits that controlled him lured him to his death in the burning desert that surrounds the Dead Sea.[3] As Paul wrote in his warning to Timothy, "Some shall depart from the faith, giving heed to seducing spirits, and doctrines of devils."

Spiritism is well established in today's religious world. It is supported and augmented by the invasion, into the West, of oriental religions that have always been heavily influenced by the occult. Spiritism has a face-saving mask in the New Age movement, which has some plausible, popular advocates. People are being deceived.

Right from its start, modern spiritism has been freighted with fraud and trivia. Even its strongest proponents have confessed being appalled at the incompetence and brazen wickedness of the spirits they have contacted: Homers who cannot write passable Greek, Shakespeares who cannot speak Elizabethan English, and Sir Isaac Newtons who cannot solve simple arithmetic problems. Spiritists admit that most of the phenomena they have encountered—noises, raps, taps, movements of tables, inane answers to questions—are childish, trivial, vulgar, and often downright ridiculous.[4]

---

3. See Merrill Unger, *The Haunting of Bishop Pike* (Wheaton: Tyndale, 1971).
4. See *Dawn,* 15 January 1943, 462.

The existence of intelligent beings in the spirit world who seek to influence mankind is no longer in question. The question is, who are they? Sir Oliver Lodge confessed, "Occasionally there are direct impersonations."[5] He also admitted, "The only alternative [to the return of the dead in a séance] is to imagine a sort of supernormal mischievousness, so elaborately misleading that it would have to be stigmatized as vicious or even diabolical."[6] That, of course, is exactly what it is.

Stainton Moses was an Oxford clergyman who was made an apostate by his familiar spirits. The leading spiritist of the nineteenth century, he confessed that the spirits with whom he was in contact were "without moral consciousness." He said, "There is an organized plan on the part of the spirits who govern these manifestations to act on us, and on the religious thought of the age. The central dogmas of the Christian faith seem especially attacked, and it was this that startled me."[7]

Sir Arthur Conan Doyle confessed much the same: "We have, unhappily, to deal with cold-blooded lying on the part of wicked intelligences."[8] Had he believed the apostle Paul and heeded his warning, Doyle would not have had to become their victim.

Today's renewed interest in the occult heralds the approach of the "latter times" of which Paul wrote. The testimony of Charles D. Lamme is particularly significant, and its value is not diminished by the fact that he gave it a number of years ago.

Before his conversion, he was an initiate of the inner circle of theosophy. He soon became aware that great power was at work but was disturbed by its lack of dependability. Being a non-Christian, he did not believe in a personal devil as the source of all evil. But he did know that he was in touch with great spirit intelligences that were preparing the world, even in his day, for the coming False Prophet and for the Antichrist.

There is a great expectancy, he says, that a great teacher is coming shortly. Satan's supernatural aids are preparing for the Man of Sin.

He had heard such men as C. Jindarapodasa, a Buddhist, deliver messages containing secret information outlining the knowledge that had come to them

5. Oliver Lodge, cited in *Strand*, June 1917.
6. Oliver Lodge, *Raymond* (New York: George H. Doran, 1916), 347.
7. Stainton Moses, *Spirit Identity*, cited in *Dawn*, 15 October 1928, 295–96.
8. Arthur Conan Doyle, *The New Revelation*, 123, cited in *Spiritualism: Its Origin and Character* (London: Thynn and Jarvis, 1923), 22.

from the unseen realms regarding the coming of a great leader. He had heard Hindu seers say that a great world teacher must come as the reincarnation of some "master" of the remote past. He knew that Buddhist monks tell of the rise of a world Buddha who will be a holy and supremely enlightened one. He knew also that the masterminds of Buddhism claim to have come in contact with unseen beings who have sent out the information that one is coming.

The coming Antichrist will meet the demands of the occultists of all shades of thought who are predicting that a god-emperor will manifest himself. The method of his appearing is to take possession of a body chosen by himself and prepared for his use. In other words, the occultists are looking for a man whose spirit will incarnate itself in a human body.[9]

The occultists of the Thule Group, to which Hitler and many other leading Nazis belonged, were sure that the long-awaited Messiah was Hitler himself. Since then, the Western world has been invaded by numerous Hindu and Buddhist gurus, and their teachings and expectations have made significant inroads into a society that has largely abandoned Christianity. But accurate information regarding the coming world Messiah is found only in the Bible.

We can be sure of one thing: Satan will not be allowed to produce that superman—the one called for by Nietzsche, heralded by the Nazis, anticipated in the New Age movement, expected by initiates of oriental religions, and foretold in the Bible—until God's time comes. The Holy Spirit, in the church, acts as the great restrainer. Satan's plans are constantly hindered, in spite of repeated optimistic announcements to his duped human followers that the time is at hand. The hinderer (the Holy Spirit) is still here (2 Thess. 2:7–8).

So are the "seducing spirits." And the "doctrines of devils" abound. False cults are multiplying their memberships. Weird messiahs are able to persuade their followers to commit mass suicide by drinking poison or by immolating themselves and their children in the flames of a fiery holocaust. Eastern gurus entrap people in mind-controlling cults. Even the professing church has largely abandoned traditional Christianity in favor of either a Bible-denying liberal theology or a cultic theology that elevates experience and depreciates doctrine; such overemphasis on experience is a flirtation with the occult.

9. Charles D. Lamme, "Spirit Expectancy," *Dawn,* 15 September 1933, 261–63.

(2) The apostasy analyzed (4:2–5)

(a) Its deceptive nature (4:2)

Analyzing the end-times apostasy, Paul pointed out that it will be *propagated by people devoid of character,* by people guilty of "speaking lies in hypocrisy." In other words, they will be liars. The word translated "speaking lies" here is *pseudologos,* which means "speaking false words." The word translated "hypocrisy" is *hupokrisis,* which conveys the idea of playacting. The description "speaking lies in hypocrisy" might apply to the evil spirits who will inspire apostasy or perhaps to the people who will spread it—or possibly to both.

Demons seem to be totally depraved beings who love sin and delight in leading people into sin. The demons' human agents are wolves in sheep's clothing but against whom the church has been adequately warned (Matt. 7:15; Acts 20:29). These deceivers are not victims of delusion; they act deliberately against known truth and conscience.

In fact, Paul declared that the end-times apostasy will be *propagated by people devoid of conscience.* He described them as "having their conscience seared with a hot iron." This will be a mark of those evil spirits and human beings who deliberately and knowingly promote apostasy. Although they know that the end result of their teaching will be blasphemy against God, unbridled licentiousness, and unrestrained violence, they will persuade people that only their teaching promotes true holiness. (See 2 Peter and Jude for further descriptions of the life and evil influence of full-fledged apostates.)

The word translated "seared" here is a term that gives us our English word *cauterize.* In the old days, wounds were seared (cauterized) with a hot iron. The word can also be translated "branded." Just as we brand cattle with a red-hot iron, so Satan will brand his agents in their consciences. They will be beyond the reach of the convicting work of the Holy Spirit.

How far the latter-days apostasy has already shaped our modern society can be seen in the types of movies being produced and promoted. Numerous examples could be given of the unbridled lust and violence that has become the daily fare of many people who frequent theaters and watch movies on cable television. *The Last Temptation of Christ,* which attracted millions of viewers and which is offered in home-video catalogs from time to time, portrays the Son of God as an adulterer and Judas Iscariot as a hero. A few decades ago, no one, no matter how bitter toward Christ, would have dared to make such a movie. Now such blasphemous productions are box office hits that are widely advertised and acclaimed in the press.

(b) Its destructive nature (4:3–5)

Paul mentioned two more marks of demon-inspired apostasy: "Forbidding to marry, and commanding to abstain from meats" (4:3). Apostasy is marked by its attack on *marriage* and its attack on the eating of *meat.* The twofold prohibition arises from demonic teaching that was seen in the gnosticism that plagued the early church. It will be seen more and more as the end times approach. Asceticism will come into its own.

Some people believe that these marks of apostasy are seen in Romanism because the prohibitions may be either partial or total. The Roman Catholic Church does enforce celibacy on its priests and those who enter monasteries; monks and nuns are sometimes required to abstain from meat; and at one time the Roman Catholic Church required all of its members to abstain from eating meat on Fridays. However, the Roman Catholic Church certainly has not undermined marriage as such. Although Catholic dogma is cluttered with many additions to New Testament doctrine and gives many of its traditions the same weight as Scripture, Rome does hold to the articles of faith mentioned in 1 Timothy 3:16. It believes that Jesus is God manifest in the flesh and that He died, rose again, and ascended into heaven.

"Forbidding to marry" is the first attack mentioned in 4:3. The word *forbidding* underlines the authority to be assumed by the apostate teachers, an authority derived from the demons they will serve. In spiritism, demons teach people to be united only with a "spiritual affinity"; that teaching has wrecked many homes.[10] Gnostic doctrine held that marriage itself was evil.

The second attack is "commanding to abstain from *meats.*" The word *meat* in our society primarily refers to animal flesh. The Greek word used here, however, refers to food in general, but it is likely that the demonic prohibition applies particularly to eating meat. Spiritists believe that eating meat inhibits the development of the power that mediums need to convey messages from the dead to the living.

Until the Flood, God restricted people to a vegetarian diet. Although Adam was given dominion over fish and fowl and every other living thing, his diet was restricted to fruits and vegetables. God said, "I have given you every herb bearing seed, which is upon the face of all the earth, and every tree, in the which is the fruit of a tree yielding seed; to you it shall be for meat." After the Fall, certain animals were used in sacrifice; but no provision was made for them to be used as food (Gen. 1:28–29; 4:1–5).

After the Flood, however, man's diet was suddenly and drastically changed.

---

10. See E. W. Bullinger, *The Companion Bible* (reprint, Grand Rapids: Kregel, 1990), app. 118:2.

God said, "Every moving thing that liveth shall be meat for you; even as the green herb have I given you all things." The one restriction was that blood should not be eaten (Gen. 9:3–4).

This change in diet seems to be related to the fact that, before the Flood, there was a massive occultic invasion of this planet. Fallen celestial beings found ways to produce on earth a monstrous hybrid race of giants (Gen. 6:1–5). The word translated "giants" is *nephilim,* which means "fallen ones." Their appearance was accompanied by a sudden increase of wickedness along with an explosion of knowledge. The allowance for a meat diet may have been connected to this antediluvian occultism if eating meat was seen as inhibiting spiritism, demonism, witchcraft, and satanism.

So prohibitions against eating certain kinds of food, especially meat, are just what we would expect from teaching that comes from evil spirits who are eager to break down all barriers that hinder the spread of the end-times apostasy. We can see the impact of all of this in oriental religions that are often heavily involved in occultism and that demand that abstinence from eating meat be a rule of life. The current surge in popularity of vegetarian food fads is just another indication that the end-times apostasy is approaching.

In 1 Timothy 4:3–5, Paul elaborated on God's goodness and wisdom in making an omnivorous diet available to us. He emphasized the fact that we should eat whatever we like as long as our eating is accompanied by proper thankful acknowledgement of God's goodness in providing for our needs.

The Lord Jesus ate meat. He partook of the Passover lamb, for instance; and He fed a hungry multitude with a little lad's loaves and fish. When He appeared in the Upper Room after His resurrection, He deliberately ate broiled fish to prove that He was not a spirit but a real human being. When, after His resurrection, He met Peter and his companions by the shore of the Sea of Galilee, He provided them a breakfast that included fish.

(3) The apostasy anticipated (4:6–7a)

(a) What to remember (4:6)

Paul *charged* Timothy to remind the Christians in Ephesus of the anticipated apostasy. Already the wolves were among the sheep. He had warned the Ephesian elders what to expect. "Of your own selves shall men arise, speaking perverse things, to draw away disciples after them" (Acts 20:30). Paul had already warned them, so he urged Timothy to "put the brethren in remembrance of these things."

In Paul's mind, the dangers that were beginning to threaten the church from within were far more serious than those that were threatening it from without. He barely mentions the Neronic persecutions because they were of small and transient significance in contrast to the rising Gnostic heresies. The church could outlive its Neros; it could only barely survive its apostasies.

Among Paul's greatest apostolic triumphs was the planting of the church in Ephesus because that city was one of Satan's capitals. Magic arts flourished there, and its citizens served with fervor the repulsive image of their goddess (Acts 19:13–20, 23–41). In this moral and religious quagmire, the church stood out like a lovely lily, fair and unsullied, as bright as the sun. It stood in great contrast to the vile temple of Diana and its foul worship. Paul knew that the church could survive the persecution of the paganism that surrounded it on the outside, but if the paganism and occultism seeped in, its straits would be dire indeed.

So the apostle charged Timothy not to teach some new error but to remind the Ephesians of what they already knew. If he warned them against these things, he would prove himself to be "a good minister of Jesus Christ" (1 Tim. 4:6).

The falling away from the faith evidently had begun, so the believers needed to be "nourished up." The word translated "nourished" in 4:6 is *entrephomai,* which means "trained or nurtured." We cannot do without physical food for long; neither can we do without spiritual food for long. The Ephesians needed to be fed spiritually, and so did their minister, Timothy. To feed Timothy, Paul sent this God-breathed epistle to him. In so doing, the apostle provided spiritual food that would nourish God's people from that day to this.

In 4:3–5, Paul had discussed the table that God habitually spreads to meet the physical needs of His people. Now, in 4:6, he mentioned the table that is spread to meet their spiritual needs. He *challenged* Timothy to nourish the believers with "the words of faith and of good doctrine." These "royal dainties" (Gen. 49:20) would fortify God's people against error and eventual apostasy.

It is dangerous to neglect doctrine, so Paul kept on emphasizing it (1 Tim. 4:6, 13, 16). We cannot build our souls on songs, choruses, and testimonies. The clamor and sensationalism of some movements is a poor substitute for solid doctrine. That is why, in the early church, the sign gifts were withdrawn as soon as they had accomplished their purpose (1 Cor. 13:8–12). The great question that overshadows the story of Job was this: "Will his experience triumph over his theology, or will his theology triumph over his experience?" This question hangs over all who leave doctrinally sound churches to embrace emotion-driven groups.

We can nourish our souls by means of intensive personal Bible study and extensive Scripture reading. We can sit at the feet of those who have been taught of God. We can read the books of the great pulpit masters of the ages.

Timothy had won Paul's approval as both a student and a teacher of God's Word. Paul wrote, "Whereunto thou hast attained" (1 Tim. 4:6). The word translated "attained" here is in the past tense. It means "attended closely." Timothy had paid close attention to the apostolic teaching he had received from Paul and followed closely in Paul's footsteps. Mark used the same word to depict the way signs and wonders would follow the early preaching of the gospel: "These signs shall 'follow' them that believe" (Mark 16:17). Luke used the word to indicate how closely and carefully he had followed up his sources of information when he was preparing to write his gospel: "Having had perfect understanding [same word] of all things" (Luke 1:3). Paul used the word to affirm that Timothy had followed fully his example and instruction.

(b) What to repudiate (4:7a)

Timothy was not to let anything turn him aside from pursuing "good doctrine." Paul warned him to "refuse profane and old wives' fables." Evidently, they were in vogue at Ephesus. The word translated "fables," *mythos,* has various shades of meaning, but here it carries the idea of fiction and refers to Gnostic error. Paul had already used this word in reference to Jewish fables (1:4). Clearly, Timothy was not to waste his time on the silly, godless fictions of the Gnostics.

How foolish it would be for us to waste our time on such fables. We have the Bible. It is God-breathed and deathless. Made of the same stuff as eternity, it will outlast all of the stars of space. It will take all of eternity for us to explore its depths, scale its heights, and traverse its boundless domains. We have authoritative, ageless, and absolute truth in our hands.

"Profane and old wives' fables" have no affinity with the Word of God. The word translated "profane" here is also used in 1:9. The word for "old wives'" occurs only here. It can be rendered "old womanish." Of course, old women do not have any monopoly on talking nonsense (Acts 17:18–21). In any case, we should not waste our time discussing the foolish notions of people who have grown old in error.

Timothy was to "refuse" to argue with people who were wedded to their follies. The word translated "refuse" can also be rendered "beg off" or "ask to be excused." We do not have to be rude to such foolish people, but we certainly have to be firm with them. We don't have time to argue with people who say that the world is flat, that the United States did not really land men on the moon, or that the Nazi holocaust never happened. We do not want to become involved in way-out arguments of a religious nature when people ask, "How many angels can stand on the head of a pin?" or "If God made everything, who made God?" or "Where did Cain get his wife?" Still less do we want to become involved in philosophical discussions or in wild speculations of weird cults.

Because we have far better things to do, we should excuse ourselves from all such involvements. We should confront people who raise foolish issues with the truths of God's Word and leave it at that. Usually, intellectual arguments do not convince people to become Christians. They become Christians because the Holy Spirit convicts them of their utter lostness without Christ (John 16:7–11).

2. The manifestation of godliness (4:7b–16)
   a. By personal exercise (4:7b–11)
      (1) The question of proper exercise reviewed (4:7b–9)
         (a) A contrast (4:7b–8a)
            i. Exercising the spiritual man (4:7b)

The time and effort spent arguing with the unsaved people over mystical and metaphysical vagaries can be better invested by the believer in physical and spiritual exercise. "Exercise thyself rather unto godliness," Paul told Timothy. The word for "exercise" here gives us our English word *gymnasium*. The Greek term suggests the idea of going into training.

Paul would have Christians be just as determined and energetic in training their inner man as some people are in training their bodies. Gyms are full of people exercising to develop their muscles and improve their coordination. They set goals and work toward achieving their objectives. Some of them spend considerable sums of money on expensive equipment so they can work toward their objectives at home too. Believers should be just as intent on developing their spiritual well-being. They should set realistic goals that become progressively more difficult to achieve. There are no shortcuts. Exercises "unto godliness" need to be done every day.

A famous violinist was asked how many hours a day he practiced. The answer was a considerable number of hours. He was then asked what would happen if he stopped practicing. "If I do not practice for one day," he said, "I know it. If I do not practice for two days, the conductor knows it. If I do not practice for three days, everybody knows it."

Likewise, if we stop exercising the spiritual man, the world will notice. We will fail to reach our ultimate objective, which is to manifest godliness. We cannot waste the time we should be spending in developing our spiritual lives. We certainly do not have time to play mental tiddledywinks with people who want to discuss weird philosophies that they have embraced.

ii. Exercising the physical members (4:8a)

By way of contrast, Paul wrote, "Bodily exercise profiteth little." The reference seems to be to gymnastic exercises. Paul was saying that developing physical fitness has value, but it is relatively unimportant compared with spiritual exercise.

Paul had spent many years among the Greeks. In fact, his hometown was part of the Greek world, so he knew of their devotion to gymnastics and their enthusiasm for the Olympic games and other sporting events held in various city stadiums. He knew that, for some Greeks, bodily exercise was an all-absorbing preoccupation. Doubtless, many of Paul's Greek converts brought their passion for physical exercise into their church life. He did not deny them their participation in gymnastics, but he did put it in its place. He warned them never to allow it to encroach on their pursuit of godliness.

(b) A conclusion (4:8b–9)

i. Godliness is profitable (4:8b–c)

Paul explained, "Godliness is profitable unto all things, having promise of the life that now is, and of that which is to come." In other words, godliness is profitable both *for life on the earthly plane* and *for life on the eternal plane.* Some of Paul's readers might have thought that he was belittling bodily exercise, but he was not. He simply wanted them to keep things in proper balance.

The word for "profitable" means "useful." Modern medical science would say that bodily exercise is useful in helping to keep arteries open and cholesterol down and in warding off strokes and heart attacks. Paul would agree that physical fitness has value for this life, but athletics did not greatly interest him. His interest was in spiritual fitness, which has value for both this life and the life to come.

Godliness affects all areas of life, including athletics, as the popular movie *Chariots of Fire* illustrates. The movie tells the story of a young Scot, Eric Liddell, who was chosen to run for Britain in the Olympic games. He and his teammates left Britain amid the cheers of supporters, but then a crisis came when Liddell was told that his event was scheduled for a Sunday. Breaking the Sabbath would violate his convictions, so he adamantly refused to run. The coach, his teammates, and the authorities were astounded. Liddell found himself isolated, misunderstood, and abused. Every pressure was brought to bear to persuade him to change his mind. He was even brought before Edward, Prince of Wales, who turned his considerable charm on Liddell, but the athlete quietly stood his ground. Even those who were most upset by this stand admired his courage and respected his convictions. In the end, the impasse was resolved. He ran in a different event and won the race without bringing any reproach on his Christian testimony. His godliness triumphed over all.

Godliness is an adornment, regardless of one's age, social standing, or walk in life. A physically handicapped saint is undoubtedly a better man than one who is a magnificent physical specimen but a moral leper. Godliness can grace a plowman's cottage as fittingly as a bishop's palace, a barrack room as well as the halls of Congress. Godliness brings beauty to pulpit and pew. It silences the scoffer, shames the profane, confounds the critic, exposes the hypocrite, and refutes the unbeliever. Bodily exercise, at best, profits a person for the seventy or eighty years of his life span; but godliness, which has its roots in eternity, outlasts the galactic empires of space. It comes from God and lasts forever.

Godly Enoch was translated to heaven so "that he should not see death" (Heb. 11:5; see also Gen. 5:21–24; Jude 14–15). Was it because he was rich or powerful or clever (if he was)? No! He was raptured because "he had this testimony, that he pleased God." In that, he was just like Jesus (Matt. 3:17). Enoch has been in heaven for thousands of years, the living type of all those who have "promise of the life that now is, and of that which is to come."

ii. Godliness is preferable (4:9)

Having stated that godliness is preferable, Paul wrote, "This is a faithful saying and worthy of all acceptation." We noted another of his "faithful sayings" in 1:15: "This is a faithful saying, and worthy of all acceptation, that Christ Jesus came into the world to save sinners." In 1:15, Paul affirmed the ground of godliness; in 4:9, he affirmed the greatness of godliness. In the first "faithful saying," he told us how to get godliness; in the second saying, he told us where it will get us. The first one reminds us of our old nature as sinners; the second one reminds us of our new nature as saints. The first one reminds us that the Lord Jesus came into the world to redeem us; the second one reminds us that the Lord Jesus will come back to receive us.

In 4:8, Paul wrote of "the life that . . . is to come" and then added in 4:9, "This is a faithful saying." In other words, there is no doubt about it at all!

(2) The question of painful experience reviewed (4:10–11)

(a) An exclamation (4:10)

At this point, Paul made a brief comment that probably refers to the persecution that was gaining momentum throughout the Roman Empire: "Therefore we both labour and suffer reproach, because we trust in the living God, who is the Saviour of all men, specially of those that believe." The word translated "Saviour" here was used of the emperor by those who followed the state religion. Nero claimed to be both savior and god. Christians, who refused to acknowledge him as either, were regarded as traitors and apostates and were persecuted savagely. Nero found them to be convenient scapegoats on whom he could heap the blame for his own crimes.

The believers suffered reproach because they trusted in the living God. However, they refused to deny Him no matter how savagely they were persecuted. The word translated "suffer reproach" can also be rendered "are reviled." The expression conveys the idea of defamation of character. Paul chose to use that word because he knew that Christians were being falsely charged with the most atrocious crimes by their enemies. Even at a time when they were called upon to endure the scorn and slander of the world, the believers sought to live godly lives. They carried on with the Lord's work and put their confidence in the living God.

Paul described God as "the Saviour of all men." He is the Savior of all men in the sense that He stays His hand. He does not punish each transgression immediately, as He did in the case of Ananias and Sapphira (Acts 5:1–10). That judgment was exemplary, a terrible warning concerning the holiness of the Spirit of God and the heinousness of human sin. Were God to punish our sins the moment they are committed with the full penalty they deserve, the human race would come to a quick end. Note that before God sentenced Adam and Eve, He sentenced the serpent—and that sentence contained a clause concerning the coming Redeemer for the human race. That made possible a stay of execution and a provision for Adam and Eve's salvation and covering (Gen. 3:14–21).

All people live under a suspended sentence while God's grace holds back His wrath. The Holy Spirit is abroad in the world, dealing with all men everywhere.

Thus, John wrote of "the true Light, which lighteth every man that cometh into the world" (John 1:9). Only when people deliberately reject the Light do they become fully culpable (John 3:19–20).

First John 2:1–2 puts it thus: "If any man sin, we have an advocate with the Father, Jesus Christ the righteous: And he is the propitiation for our sins: and not for ours only, but also for the sins of the whole world." In other words, the sacrifice of Calvary is *sufficient* for all men; and all are brought provisionally under its umbrella until they reach the point of decision and accountability.

First John 1:8–9 describes the activating principle: "If we say that we have no sin, we deceive ourselves, and the truth is not in us. If we confess our sins, he is faithful and just to forgive us our sins, and to cleanse us from all unrighteousness." When people believe, God's salvation becomes fully operative in the soul. The sacrifice of Calvary becomes *efficient* to save fully and forever when people respond properly to it. The Lord Jesus is the Savior "specially [most of all] of those that believe."

(b) An exhortation (4:11)

"These things command and teach," wrote Paul. Young Timothy was to exercise authority and preserve accuracy in his teaching. He was to impress on his people the truths that Paul had brought to his attention. He was to counter with Pauline doctrine the cultic tendencies creeping into the church.

Timothy had been around Paul long enough to know his views on most matters. He had been with Paul in Corinth when the apostle wrote his doctrinal masterpiece to the Romans (Rom. 16:21), a treatise that we might well label "the gospel according to Paul." Timothy is mentioned in 1 Corinthians 16:10 and is united with Paul in the opening greetings of 2 Corinthians, Philippians, Colossians, 1 Thessalonians, and 2 Thessalonians. We can take it for granted that Timothy had the monumental teachings of those great Epistles at his fingertips.

Timothy had accompanied Paul on the mission field, so he knew firsthand the apostle's methods and was well acquainted with the soul-saving, life-transforming, world-evangelizing, church-building, mind-expanding, heartwarming truths that Paul taught. These truths were the Holy Spirit's safeguard against Gnostic, Judaistic, and cabalistic heresies. Certainly, Timothy would have his hands full teaching these truths and would have no time to debate foolish trivia.

b. By public example (4:12–16)
   (1) A word of wisdom (4:12–13)
      (a) Facing the problem (4:12a)

Timothy's personal exercise in the things of God had to be demonstrated by public example, regardless of people's attitude toward his youthfulness. "Let no man despise thy youth," wrote Paul. The word translated "youth" here is used in the Gospels to describe the rich young ruler, who approached Christ eagerly but went away sorrowful once the terms of discipleship were explained to him (Matt. 19:20; Mark 10:20; Luke 18:21). The only other place this word is used in the New Testament is Acts 26:4, where Paul made a passing reference to his own youth. (We could profitably compare these three youths: the eager and youthful ruler with all of his riches, young Saul of Tarsus with all of his religion, and young Timothy with all of his responsibility.)

Timothy, though described as a youth by Paul, was no teenager. He was probably in his late thirties. However, he would be dealing with elders in the Ephesian church who were much older than he was, so Paul told him not to let the difference in age get in his way. Timothy might not be bowed by years, but he was mature in experience. And age is relative. Forty is considered old for most professional athletes, yet it is considered young for the chief executive of a corporate conglomerate and very youthful indeed for a president or prime minister.

The word translated "despise" means "to think slightingly of someone." Evidently, Paul expected some people in Ephesus to try to intimidate Timothy. Any pastor who has ministered to people who are richer, more clever, more successful, more talented, and more influential than he is understands how it feels to be intimidated.

The classic biblical example of despising a man's youth is found in the story of David. He was recommended to Saul in glowing terms by a servant who was more discerning than the king. "I have seen a son of Jesse the Bethlehemite," the servant said, "that is cunning in playing [David's competence], and a mighty valiant man [David's courage], and a man of war [David's conquests], and prudent in matters [David's caution], and a comely person [David's charisma], and the LORD is with him [David's character]" (1 Sam. 16:18). These were high words of praise indeed! Saul sent for David and looked him over, but he saw only a boy.

In time, David went back home to the family farm. Fortunately for King Saul, however, he came back when Goliath showed up. Saul took the measure of Goliath and decided that he was too big to fight; David took the measure of Goliath and thought that he was too big to miss! So he volunteered to take on the giant. Saul was skeptical. After all, David was only about seventeen years old, and he had three older brothers in the army. The Holy Spirit emphasized his youth, saying, "David was the youngest" (1 Sam. 17:14).

All Saul could see was a bit of a boy offering to do a man's job. "Thou art not able to go against this Philistine to fight with him," he said, "for thou art but a youth, and he a man of war from his youth" (17:33). The giant made the same mistake: "When the Philistine looked about, and saw David, he disdained him: for he was but a youth" (17:42). It was the biggest mistake Goliath ever made.

Timothy was also a comparatively young man, but he stood tall in Paul's estimation. In spiritual development, as in many other areas of development, age is no proof of maturity. It is foolish to reject a man simply because he is young.

(b) Fighting the problem (4:12b–13)

i. Some first steps (4:12b–h)

a. The proposal expressed (4:12b)

Having told Timothy to face his problem, Paul went on to tell him how to fight it. The apostle described the first step: "Be thou an example of the believers." An exemplary life ought to silence the most vociferous of critics.

The word translated "example" here is *tupos,* which is derived from a word meaning "to strike." *Tupos* sometimes refers to the mark made by a blow. Thomas used the word when he announced that he would not believe in Christ's resurrection unless he could see and feel "the print *[tupos]* of the nails" in His hands (John 20:25).

Elsewhere, Paul used the word to point out an Old Testament "type." A type is a highly specialized Old Testament illustration of a New Testament truth. After describing some of the wilderness experiences of the nation of Israel, Paul made his point: "These things were our examples *[tupos],* to the intent we should not lust after evil things, as they also lusted" (1 Cor. 10:6). Timothy was to be a type of Christ to his congregation. Those to whom he ministered ought to be able to look at him and be reminded of Christ.

b. The proposal expanded (4:12c–h)

Paul listed half a dozen ways in which Timothy should be an example. If he followed Paul's advice, he could overcome the handicap of his youthfulness.

First, Paul said, "Be thou an example of the believers, in word." Timothy's *conversation* was to be exemplary. "Word" is a translation of *logos,* which suggests the spoken word. In his speech, Timothy was to impress people with his likeness to the One who was the Word made flesh. Timothy's everyday speech was to be of such character, consistency, and content that it would make people think of Jesus.

Second, Paul said, "Be thou an example . . . in conversation." The meaning of the English word *conversation* has changed since the King James Version of the Bible was published. The word is a translation of a Greek word that means, in today's English, "lifestyle." When Paul reminded the Galatians that they were fully conversant with his "conversation," he was referring to his way of life (Gal. 1:13). Peter used the word in the same way when he said that Lot was vexed every day by "the filthy conversation [lifestyle] of the wicked" (2 Peter 2:7). So Paul's advice to Timothy was that his *conduct* should be exemplary. His lifestyle was to be an advertisement of the gospel of Christ. Timothy's manner of life was to be beyond rebuke.

Third, Paul said, "Be thou an example . . . in charity." Timothy's *compassion* was to be exemplary. The Greek word that is translated "charity" here really signifies love of the highest kind. Timothy no doubt knew by heart Paul's great poem on love (1 Cor. 13), so he knew what Paul expected of him. Timothy was to be like Jesus in showing love to one and all. Jesus was the only person whose life was a moment-by-moment, audiovisual, three-dimensional demonstration of this highest kind of love. Timothy was to be like Him.

Fourth, Paul said, "Be thou an example . . . in spirit." He meant that Timothy's *character* was to be exemplary. His human spirit was to be so inhabited and filled by the Holy Spirit that his whole being would radiate the life of God. Timothy was to take up his dwelling place in Romans 8. If we, like Timothy, are to be examples, our spirits must cooperate with God's Spirit. Only through the Spirit of God can we understand the Word of God, do the will of God, accomplish the work of God, properly engage in the worship of God, and display the wisdom of God.

Fifth, Paul said, "Be thou an example . . . in faith." Timothy's *convictions* were to be exemplary. Through the centuries, generation after generation, God has raised up people who have set examples of faith before an unbelieving world and a half-believing church. One such giant was George Müller of Bristol, who deliberately set out to demonstrate who God is and that He is "a rewarder of them that diligently seek him" (Heb. 11:6). It was said of Müller that in his day agnosticism did not dare raise its head in his town. Numerous stories are told about this man who had the courage of his convictions. One such story is about an occasion when a baby started to cry while Müller was preaching. The mother stood up and started to take the child out of the meeting, but Müller asked her to sit down. "We'll just ask the Lord to put the baby to sleep," he said. Timothy was a man like that.

Sixth, Paul said, "Be thou an example . . . in purity." Timothy's *cleanness* was to be exemplary. The word translated "purity" in 1 Timothy 4:12 is *hagneia,* which comes from the same root as the word translated "holiness." Timothy was to keep himself from defilement in an impure environment. Ephesus, like Corinth and Antioch, was a morally polluted place. Its temple of Diana (Artemis) was known far and wide for the pornographic character of the worship it sustained. Many Gentile converts to Christianity came from grossly immoral backgrounds. The purity of the Christians was what first astonished the pagan world, then enraged it, and finally conquered it. Paul called on Timothy to set the standard in purity.

If Timothy exemplified what it meant to be a Christian in these six ways, he would not need to worry about his youthfulness.

ii. Some further steps (4:13)

a. Keep growing mentally (4:13a)

"Till I come, give attendance to reading," Paul added. We do not know whether Paul ever came, but we do know that this advice is timeless. Timothy would begin, of course, by reading his Bible, and so should we.

The Bible is a big book, and no one can hope to know it from just one reading, especially if he reads at a fast pace. It must be read over and over. The Bible rewards slow, thoughtful, contemplative reading. To familiarize ourselves with the Bible as a whole, we must survey its books, mark its movements, and master its major themes. We must also approach each book analytically, learning how chapters, paragraphs, and verses are structured and put together. Using sound hermeneutical principles, we must rightly divide the Word of truth (2 Tim. 2:15) and make a difference where God makes a difference. We must recognize the figures of speech that God uses in communicating His Word in our tongue. We must have at least a nodding acquaintance with the languages in which the Bible was written and become familiar with its cultural, geographical, and historical settings. As we thus develop a working knowledge of the Bible, we begin to see where its thousands of details fit together to present a consistent, comprehensive whole.

To "give attendance to reading," we will turn to books and commentaries written by gifted godly men. We must be discriminating in our choice of commentaries, however, for not all authors with famous names are reliable guides.

As we read, we will find ourselves accumulating a library of useful books. Our interests will widen to include many subjects related to topics mentioned in the Bible. We will begin inquiring into the histories of Israel, the church, and the nations and empires that surrounded them. We will probe into natural history, astronomy, and other subjects that have a peripheral bearing on the Bible. The list of books that we want will keep growing. By reading, we, like Timothy, can overcome the handicap of chronological or spiritual youth.

b. Keep going ministerially (4:13b–c)

Paul also urged Timothy to "give attendance to . . . exhortation, to doctrine." In other words, his work as a minister was to involve *exhorting the saints* and *expounding the Scriptures.* It was not enough for Timothy to be widely read; he had to pass on to others the fruit of his studies by means of exhortation.

The word for "exhortation" here means both "exhortation" and "consolation." Luke used the word in Acts 4:36 to describe Paul's friend, Barnabas, as "the son of consolation." The Lord used a related word when He described the Holy Spirit as the Comforter, "one called alongside to help" (John 14:16). Exhortation, therefore, is not simply a matter of urging people to be and do what they ought; it also involves entreating, encouraging, and consoling.

A pastor is to be a shepherd, leading his flock beside still waters into green pastures. He must lead them in the paths of righteousness. He is to be with them in the dark valley to comfort and console. He is to defend them from the foe (Ps. 23).

A pastor could easily let his reading become an end in itself, but there has to be a practical outlet if his studies are to do any good. Exhortation is the great work of the pastor. Attending to doctrine is the great work of the teacher. Today, many people are more concerned with experience than with doctrine. They say that doctrine is divisive; they are willing to compromise on doctrinal differences and unite around shared emotional experiences. On nonessentials Paul was the most conciliatory of men (Acts 21:18–27), but on matters of vital doctrine he was adamant (Acts 15:1–18; Gal. 1:1–14).

(2) A word of warning (4:14–16)
(a) Timothy and his gift (4:14)
i. A reprimand (4:14a)

Paul warned Timothy, "Neglect not the gift that is in thee." The word translated "gift" here is *charisma,* which means "a free gift." It occurs seventeen times in the New Testament, where it is reserved for reference to God's gifts. Although we are not told expressly what Timothy's spiritual gifts were, they certainly included the pastoral and teaching gifts. It seems likely that he also had the gifts of exhortation and ruling (Rom. 12; 1 Cor. 12).

The word translated "neglect" here can mean "contemptuous neglect" or "careless neglect," or "not caring for something." A gift has to be cared for and exercised or it shrivels up, just as does an unused muscle. "Use it, or lose it" is one way to put it. Paul's use here of the present imperative form of the verb in the Greek implies that the neglect he was forbidding had already been going on. The word is used in Hebrews 2:3 in connection with those who "neglect so great salvation." It is also used by the Lord Jesus in Matthew 22:5 to describe those who "made light of" the king's invitation to his son's wedding.

Evidently, Paul saw a flaw in Timothy's character. Apparently, the young man needed to be prodded from time to time because he had a tendency to settle down. Paul warned Timothy to resist the temptation to allow his gift to lie smoldering. Everyone who has had a fireplace knows why tongs, a shovel, and a poker are necessary equipment. The poker, especially, is necessary because logs and coals need to be stirred up occasionally to allow air to circulate and keep the flames leaping. Paul's reprimand was intended to prod Timothy to action.

Spiritual gifts are given "for the perfecting of the saints, for the work of the ministry, for the edifying of the body of Christ" (Eph. 4:12). When a man who has the gift of evangelism, for example, speaks to people personally or preaches from the pulpit, people get saved. Suppose, however, that he neglects his gift. It withers, and the church is a poorer place as a result. He secularizes his gift, so to speak, and uses it to become a successful salesman. The same traits that the Holy Spirit energized to make him a successful spokesman for the gospel are employed in selling cars or in promoting the interests of a political party or some other group. The church has lost an evangelist, and the world has gained another salesman or politician.

It is a serious error to neglect one's spiritual gift. The consequences of the error will be revealed at the judgment seat of Christ where all ministry will be evaluated by One who knows all of the factors involved (1 Cor. 3:11–15).

ii. A reminder (4:14b)

Timothy's gift was given to him "by prophecy, with the laying on of the hands of the presbytery." Apparently, the phrase *by prophecy* is a reference to the divine enlightenment given to Paul at the time he called Timothy to be a partner in the ministry of the Word. Possibly, the elders in the Galatian cities of Lystra and Iconium were given a similar prophetic intimation of the suitability of young Timothy for this responsible work (Acts 16:1–3).

The word translated "presbytery" here is *presbuterion.* In the New Testament, the related word *presbuteros* means simply "elder" and describes those who are older than others. Among the Jews, this word was used to signify the tribal heads. The Sanhedrin was composed of chief priests, scribes, and "elders." In the church, the word signifies those who are raised up and qualified by the Holy Spirit to oversee the spiritual aspects of a local church. Whereas *episkopos* indicates the nature of the elder's work, *presbuteros* draws attention to the elder's spiritual maturity.

In 1 Timothy 4:14, Paul reminded Timothy of the ordination ceremony that had confirmed him as being commended to the work of the ministry by the united laying on of the hands of the elders. The ceremony had been marked by the bestowal of the spiritual gift that Timothy was now in danger of neglecting. Paul and Barnabas had been similarly commended to the work of foreign missions some time earlier (Acts 13:1–4); John Mark's joining them is mentioned only as a sort of footnote in 13:5; Silas had been ordained by the Antioch church (Acts 15:40).

The ordination of Timothy had been particularly important to Paul because of John Mark's defection. No ordination exercise had accompanied the decision of John Mark to attach himself to the mission enterprise, nor had Paul and Barnabas required it. The apostle ensured that no such neglect accompanied Timothy's selection as Mark's replacement.

Timothy himself was not likely to forget his ordination because, about that time, Paul had circumcised him to make him more acceptable to Jews who needed to be evangelized. Timothy's willingness to submit to that painful procedure had proved to Paul that Timothy had courage and fortitude and was not likely to quit when the going became rough.

(b) Timothy and his growth (4:15)

i. A call to contemplate (4:15a)

Paul challenged Timothy to "meditate upon these things." The word translated "meditate" means "to ponder, to be diligent." The same word is used in Acts 4:25, which records part of the prayer of the early church on an occasion when the Sanhedrin raised its menacing voice in threats. In their prayer, those believers quoted from Psalm 2:1: "Why did the heathen rage, and the people *imagine* vain things?" Paul's call to Timothy was to keep turning over in his mind the great truths of the gospel.

Meditation, or contemplation, leads to mature, reasoned conclusions. It considers the various factors in an equation and gives them their due weight. Contemplation is a worthwhile occupation, and it cannot be hurried. Galloping through the Bible in a year does give one a broad view of Scripture; but it is rather like driving from Portland, Maine, to Portland, Oregon, in a week. It can be done. Much ground can be covered, and many interesting sights can be passed at top speed. A traveler will see the country that way, but he will not get to know it.

When I first came to North America from London as a new employee of the Bank of Montreal, I reported to the bank's headquarters in Montreal, but the officers decided to send me to Vancouver on the opposite side of Canada. A branch manager of the bank from Vancouver, who was in Montreal at the time, had just bought a new car. He called into the main office. "Did they have some young fellow they were transferring to British Columbia who could help him with the driving?" The bank sent me with him. My letters home sounded like this:

> We left French-speaking Canada today and crossed into Ontario. Caught my first glimpse of the Great Lakes. They resemble an inland sea.
>
> This morning we crossed over into the United States at a place called Sault Ste. Marie. The bank manager says that American roads are better than Canadian roads.
>
> Prairie! There seems to be no end to it. We drive westward hour after hour. Everything is so flat and bare at this time of year.
>
> Drove through the Badlands, rolling hills of dead rock and earth. Saw my first cowboy riding a horse, all complete with traditional hat and rope.

> The Rocky Mountains can now be seen straight ahead. How they must have appalled the early pioneers heading west! The mountains are magnificent, the lower slopes all fir-coated, the upper reaches bedrock granite peaks, with snow.
>
> Back into Canada! Will reach Vancouver tomorrow. Caught a glimpse of the ocean, so have come from the Atlantic to the Pacific.

I saw the continent, but I didn't learn much about it! To get to know a country, one has to take time, go slowly, stop frequently, ask questions, talk to people, buy books, visit places, compare notes, form impressions, and check conclusions.

Likewise, to get to know the Bible, one must read it as Paul must have reread his Old Testament with new eyes after he met Jesus on the Damascus road. Off he went to the silences of Sinai; he carried his parchments in his bag, and a vision of a resurrected man with nail-scarred hands dominated his thoughts. Day after day, week after week, month after month, he sat where Moses had sat and stood where Elijah had stood. Mount Sinai towered close by him. Moses! The Law! David! The prophets! Paul thought everything through in the fresh light of Calvary. The brief vision of the risen Christ made Paul a believer; the months of contemplation in the wilderness made him an apostle.

Time for meditation is what Paul coveted for Timothy. The apostle advised him never to get too busy to meditate. Only by heeding Paul's call in 1 Timothy 4:15a would the young man's beliefs be transformed into convictions based on the living Word of God.

ii. A call to consecrate (4:15b)

Consecration is the natural outcome of conviction. "Give thyself wholly to [these things]," Paul said to Timothy. Spare time is not adequate for the study of the Scriptures and the ministry of the Word, although any time devoted to these activities will be time well spent.

When I first joined the staff of Moody Bible Institute, the radio pastor of the MBI network was an older believer named Robert J. Little. This godly man was a walking encyclopedia of Bible knowledge and was much in demand as a conference speaker. After speaking at one local church, he was approached by a man about his own age who said, "Mr. Little, I wish I had your knowledge of the Bible."

R. J. looked at the man for a moment, then said, "My friend, you are too late.

You look like you are about my age, so I'd say you are about fifty years too late. To acquire my knowledge of the Bible, you should have started fifty years ago and studied diligently every day. That's how long it took me to acquire my knowledge of the Bible. You are too late—but you can still make a start."

Timothy was a comparatively young man, so it was not too late for him to acquire a thorough knowledge of the Bible if he gave himself wholly to the things of God.

Paul advised him, "Give thyself . . . that thy profiting may appear to all." The word translated "profiting" here was also used by Paul when he told his friends in Philippi how God had sovereignly used his Roman imprisonment in the salvation of souls: "The things which happened unto me have fallen out rather unto the furtherance [same word] of the gospel" (Phil. 1:12). Instead of his imprisonment being the hindrance that Satan had intended, it became a means of reaching people whom Paul never would have met otherwise, including members of the Praetorian guard.

The idea behind the word *profiting* is that of making progress. W. E. Vine noted, "Originally the word was used of a pioneer cutting his way through brushwood."[11] Paul wanted Timothy to make progress in the things of God. It was not enough for him, as a minister, to be zealous for the spiritual progress of others; he had to make progress himself. Moreover, his progress was to be evident to all. So Paul used the phrase *eimi phaneros* (translated "may appear" in the KJV). It means "to be visible, open to sight," or "be made manifest."

When the children of Israel left Egypt for Canaan, their early progress could have been marked on a map. They went from Rameses to Succoth with the fiery, cloudy pillar marching on ahead. They camped at Pi-hahiroth between Migdol and the Red Sea. At the sea, God performed another mighty miracle, and soon they had crossed over, having been "baptized unto Moses in the cloud and in the sea." They had left Egypt and its bondage forever. Three days later, they came to Marah, where they learned that God can make bitter experiences sweet. On they went to Elim and discovered that not all of the experiences of the life of faith are testings and trials. Then came the formidable Wilderness of Sin. On they went, and soon they came to Rephidim, where God gave them water from the rock. On they went through the desert until they came to Mount Sinai itself. They halted there for a considerable time because they had much to learn about the walk, warfare, and worship of the life of faith. Then, at last, they traveled on to

---

11. W. E. Vine, *An Expository Dictionary of New Testament Words,* 4 vols. (London: Oliphants, 1963), 2:138.

Kadesh-barnea and the border of the Promised Land. They were now to be confronted with the great crisis and turning point of their pilgrimage. Each place marked a step in their spiritual development, and at each place they learned lessons (1 Cor. 10:1–11).

Similarly, Paul desired to plot Timothy's spiritual progress. He said that it should be open for all to see. The same holds true for us. No matter how far we have come, "there remaineth yet very much land to be possessed" (Josh. 13:1).

(c) Timothy and his guard (4:16)

i. Paul admonished him (4:16a)

Again Paul admonished Timothy, "Take heed unto thyself, and unto the doctrine." The apostle had some fears for Timothy, for the new cults that were arising were very subtle. The old-fashioned legalism that Paul had combated in his letter to the Galatians was a fairly minor threat compared with the mix of intellectualism, ritualism, legalism, mysticism, and asceticism with which he had dealt in his letter to the Colossians. But even that form of Gnosticism was mild compared with what was now infiltrating the church at Ephesus.

Timothy needed to "take heed" because the Devil himself was masterminding the mental and moral attack on the church. The old serpent was after everyone who professed to be a believer, especially missionaries, ministers, and other church leaders. He was abroad as a roaring lion. Timothy could not afford to neglect his daily quiet time or his continuing study of the Word.

"Take heed . . . unto the doctrine," Paul said. There it is again: that word *doctrine.* Doctrine is of supreme importance. We cannot afford to be like the man who, when asked what he believed, replied, "I believe what the church believes."

"Well," someone challenged, "what does the church believe?"

"Why," he said, "the church believes what I believe."

His questioner persisted, "Then what do you both believe?"

"To be sure," replied the undaunted believer, "we both believe the same!"

That attitude will not see us through the perils and pitfalls that await us.

ii. Paul advised him (4:16b)

"Continue in them," Paul advised, "for in doing this thou shalt both save thyself, and them that hear thee." Here the apostle was not referring to salvation in the evangelistic sense of salvation of sinners or in the sense of preservation of the faith of believers. Every time the word *save* is used, its sense has to be defined by the context in which it is found. The salvation in 4:16 evidently has to do with being delivered from the false but diabolically clever teachings of demon-inspired cultists.

Timothy, by taking heed to himself and his doctrine, would save himself and his people from becoming enmeshed in cultic sophistries. Uncertainty in the pulpit will certainly be reflected in the pew and will usually be compounded. No greater stumbling block exists than a fallen minister, one who has succumbed to immorality or infidelity.

Consider, for example, the results when a minister takes an extreme Calvinistic doctrinal position. He claims that because man is dead in trespasses and sins, he is incapable of any response to the gospel. The sovereignty of God is what leads Him to decide who will be saved and how and when. If God does not choose to save a person, that person is damned. A minister who proclaims such dogma in the pulpit might find it worked out with dreadful thoroughness by those in the pew.

In one such case that I observed, a father reasoned, *If my children have been chosen to be saved, they will be saved. There is nothing I can do about it. If they have not been chosen, they will not be saved. The matter is out of my hands.* As a result of this pew-level interpretation of what was taught in the pulpit, this man's children were allowed to grow up totally unevangelized. Now only one or two of them show interest in the things of God. They are a living condemnation of ultra-Calvinism. Whoever taught this father will surely be held accountable at the judgment seat of Christ.

Paul warned Timothy to guard himself against false doctrine, "for in doing this thou shalt both save thyself, and them that hear thee." We have seen the converse is also true: failure to hold and teach sound doctrine leads to the spiritual downfall of both those who teach false doctrine and those who are taught it and apply it.

B. Witness for God (5:1–6:19)
 1. The people of God (5:1–6:2)
  a. Fellowship of saints (5:1–2)
   (1) A message about the men (5:1)
    (a) The older men: emphasis on respect (5:1a)

Paul continues his instruction on how to become an effective Christian. He told Timothy, "Rebuke not an elder, but intreat him as a father." *Epiplēssō,* the forceful word translated "rebuke," occurs only here in the New Testament and means literally "to strike at." *Presbuteros,* the word translated "elder," refers here not to an office but to old age.

Young people, who forget that one day they will be old, tend to be impatient with and intolerant of the slowness, conservatism, and impediments that come with old age. In fact, the way some young people speak to and treat older people is sometimes the equivalent of a blow to the face. Older men who have earned the respect and trust of the church must be treated with honor. Paul made clear that we are not to chide, treat harshly, or rebuke older people. The church is for the weak, the aged, and the infirm just as much as it is for the young, active, and strong.

David knew the value of old men. That is why he urged eighty-year-old Barzillai to come to Jerusalem with him and take an honored seat at his table (2 Sam. 19:31–38). Barzillai had proved his worth, and there was an empty seat at the table, now that wicked old Ahithophel had committed suicide. No doubt, David was disappointed at Barzillai's unwillingness to join his inner circle of counselors. He agreed to take young Chimham with him instead—and David treated him well—but he would have preferred old Barzillai.

Old age is treated with honor and dignity throughout the Bible. Abraham was seventy-five when God first called him (Gen. 12:4). Moses was eighty when he received his call to emancipate the Hebrew people from bondage in Egypt (Exod. 7:7). Tough old Caleb was eighty-five when he asked to be given a mountain to conquer (Josh. 14:10). Daniel was about eighty-eight when he began to pray to the Lord about ending the Babylonian captivity.

It is wise to cultivate the counsel of men who have grown old in the things of God. They provide continuity with the past and often, as a result of rich experience, are fountains of wisdom. But even when, because of infirmity, they are no longer able to function in a useful capacity, they are still to be honored, loved, and cared for. The world all too often treats old people—especially in our busy, materialistic, pragmatic Western culture—with scant respect. Sometimes men are retired from business at the peak of their usefulness; they are pensioned off or simply fired, allowed to drift from retirement home to nursing home, and visited as seldom as conscience will permit.

(b) The other men: emphasis on relationship (5:1b)

Paul moved on, saying, "Intreat . . . the younger men as brethren." Timothy, in his pastoral capacity, was to show respect to the older man and treat the other men as equals in the family of God.

The word translated "brethren" here is one of the universal titles by which those who trusted Christ were known in the early church. The New Testament church had no denominational titles. Those who belonged to Christ were disciples, saints, believers, Christians, or brethren. They were fellow members of a new heaven-born and heaven-bound community. They knew a common salvation, shared a common allegiance to the risen Lord, and were united by a common family bond.

The Bible first refers to brethren in connection with Cain and Abel. Genesis 4:1–2 tells us that "Eve . . . bare Cain . . . and again bare his brother Abel." These were the first two brethren to live on earth. All they had was each other during those early days. But sin is a great destroyer. The first sin divided man from God; the second sin divided man from man. The first sin put man out of the family circle of God; the second sin put Cain out of the family circle of men.

We have a further reference to Cain and Abel as brethren in Genesis 4:8–10: "Cain [with murder in his heart] talked with Abel his brother." Then he slew him. Later, God demanded of Cain, "Where is Abel thy brother?"

Cain insolently responded, "Am I my brother's keeper?"

God replied, "The voice of thy brother's blood crieth unto me from the ground."

In contrast to Cain, who was driven away from his family to become a "fugitive and a vagabond," Abraham and Lot became "strangers and pilgrims" (Gen. 4:12; Heb. 11:13). They were uncle and nephew by natural ties, but when they became pilgrims, a new tie was formed. Abraham and Lot became brothers in the Lord. They are one of the most important pairs of brethren in the Bible.

Abraham appealed to this fraternal relationship when their followers quarreled. "We be brethren," he said to Lot. As the older and more mature believer, Abraham assumed the humble place. Eager for harmony, willing to surrender his rights, willing to make any sacrifice to maintain a good testimony, he entreated his brother. Subsequently, Lot took advantage of Abraham, but when Lot found himself in dire circumstances, Abraham still loved him as a brother and came to his rescue (Gen. 14:14).[12]

People talk about the brotherhood of man. However, there can be no brotherhood of man apart from the Fatherhood of God, and God, contrary to popular

12. For further discussion of Lot's disastrous backslidings, see John Phillips, *Exploring Genesis* (Grand Rapids: Kregel, 2001).

belief, is not the Father of all men. God is the Creator of all men, but He is the Father of only those who are born into His family by the regenerating work of the Holy Spirit (John 1:11–13). Having thus become sons of God, the young men in the Ephesian church were Timothy's brothers, and he was to treat them as such.

(2) A word about the women (5:2)

(a) The older women: emphasis on parenthood (5:2a)

Paul told Timothy to "intreat . . . the elder women as mothers." What a delightful concept of the relationship between a young pastor and the older women who were entrusted to his care. Timothy was to look upon them as mothers.

One of Paul's mothers in Christ was the mother of Rufus. Rufus and his mother were mentioned by Paul in his final greetings to the church at Rome. If this Rufus was the Rufus mentioned by Mark, he was one of the sons of Simon the Cyrenian, who was forced by the Romans to carry Christ's cross to Calvary (Mark 15:21). Simon likely was a black man and possibly was the elder of the church at Antioch who is referred to as "Simeon that was called Niger" in Acts 13:1. If so, Paul knew Rufus and his family well and perhaps had been a guest in their home. Paul had probably been the recipient of many kindnesses and services there, so it is no wonder that he referred to Rufus as "chosen in the Lord" and sent greetings not only to him but also to "his mother and mine" (Rom. 16:13). Timothy was to treat the older women in his congregation with similar regard.

We are reminded of one occasion when Peter said to Jesus, "Behold, we have forsaken all, and followed thee; what shall we have therefore?" Jesus replied, "Every one that hath forsaken houses, or brethren, or sisters, or father, or mother, or wife, or children, or lands, for my name's sake, shall receive an hundredfold [10,000 percent!], and shall inherit everlasting life" (Matt. 19:27–29). Like Peter, Paul had forsaken all to follow Jesus, and he had found the Lord's promise to be wonderfully true. He had ten thousand mothers in Christ—and the mother of Rufus was one of them (Matt. 19:2–9).

Timothy, too, had given up earthly advantages to become a full-time servant of the Lord. He had left his mother and grandmother to become a missionary and eventually a pastor in a far-off land—and he had as many mothers in Christ as Paul had. Among them were the older women in his congregation in Ephesus, and Timothy was to treat them with regard. Doubtless, he had already discovered how they liked to mother him. Should he have any cause to exhort one of them, he was to "intreat" her with the same filial respect that he would show to his mother, Eunice (Acts 16:1; 2 Tim. 1:5). Paul's rule is a good one.

(b) The other women: emphasis on purity (5:2b)

Paul told Timothy to relate to the younger women "as sisters, with all purity." Brothers usually associate their sisters with companionship, confidences, and care. The feeling of a brother for a sister is usually that of protective love. It is tender but not without its toughness. The closeness of a brother-sister relationship has well-defined limits. A sister is not a wife. A healthy brother-sister relationship involves not so much as a thought of trespassing beyond the boundaries set by both nature and the Word of God.

In the church, born again women are sisters in Christ. Their relationship with their brothers in Christ, though close and companionable, has strict limits. Hence, Paul warned Timothy that, in all of his contacts with younger women in the church, he must be on his guard. Purity was the standard. There was to be no undue familiarity.

Paul had already reminded Timothy that he was to be an example "in purity" (4:12). The same word *hagneia* ("purity") is used in both 4:12 and 5:2 and occurs only in these two places in the New Testament.

Hagneia speaks of a chastity that forbids all physical and spiritual impurity, whether of manner or act. The word is derived from the same root as *hagios,* which means "holy," and *hagnos,* which means "pure from defilement." Men in the church can be friendly with young women, but they must keep their distance. This is especially true for those who have pastoral responsibility. They need to be doubly careful.

Pastoral counseling is especially fraught with peril. The strictest safeguards must be in place and kept in good repair. Expository preaching ought to take care of most of the congregation's needs. Because people with emotional needs often fasten on to a counselor, pastors must curtail counseling sessions with members of the opposite sex. Interviews should be granted only in an open area where passersby can be an added security.

Some time ago, a woman approached me at the close of a meeting. A story I had told about our son's early rebellion and how he found Christ struck a responsive chord. My sermon had touched a need in her life, and she wanted me to set some time aside to counsel her. I said, "I do not counsel women. My wife does. She was involved in all aspects of the story I told in my message. She has a woman's viewpoint. She can counsel you better than I can. Here is our phone number. Call her."

Far too many ministers and preachers have made shipwreck of their lives by not heeding Paul's advice to Timothy regarding his relationship to young women in the church. Any private exhortation should be handled in the same way a brother would counsel or correct a sister.

b. Fairness for widows (5:3–16)

Paul had great compassion for widows. As the arch-persecutor of the church in his unregenerate days, he had made many women widows. Doubtless they were always on his conscience. The rules he laid down for Timothy, however, were not based on sentiment; they were based on sanctified common sense.

In pagan cultures, widows are often treated harshly. Many stories have been told of the terrible plight of the Native American widow in the old West; usually regarded as an encumbrance, she was robbed of her possessions and left to fend for herself until death overtook her. Anyone who has read the history of India knows how unhappy has been the lot of Hindu women, especially widows. Even among the Hebrews in Old Testament times, widows were married off to the next of kin regardless of their feelings in the matter. It was the gospel of Christ that raised widowhood to an honorable status in society.

(1) The reliable widow (5:3–10)

(a) The widow and her respect (5:3)

Under the Law of Moses, a woman who was left widowed and childless was automatically married to the brother of the deceased, and the first child born of this marriage took the name of the widow's first husband to keep that name alive in Israel (Deut. 25:5–6). It was by means of just such a marriage—the marriage of Ruth and Boaz—that Jesus came into this world (Ruth 1–4). Just the same, the Jews regarded widowhood and barrenness with horror (Isa. 54:4). The Levitical marriage provided some protection for destitute widows, but the custom was really a device to keep property in the right family. Paul freed widows from unwelcome and forced second, third, or fourth marriages when he told Timothy to "honour widows that are widows indeed" (1 Tim. 5:3).

The word translated "honour" means "to estimate or fix the value, revere, venerate." As used here, the word conveys the idea of appreciating the widow's worth as a sister in Christ and paying proper respect to her. The word translated "indeed" can be rendered "truly," so Paul was referring here to widows who were totally bereft and left without any financial support. Later, Paul appended some duties that the church ought to expect widows to perform if they were supported by church funds.

We meet one such godly widow in the record of the events surrounding our Lord's birth (Luke 2:22–38). Her name was Anna, a member of the tribe of Asher. She had been a widow for eighty-four years. Her husband had died after only seven years of marriage, but instead of seeking remarriage, she devoted herself to spiritual ministry. She found a nook in the temple and made God's house her home, marrying herself, as it were, to Him. Called a "prophetess" (Luke 2:36), she "served God with fastings and prayers night and day."

Anna stands in stark contrast to "that woman Jezebel" in the church at Thyatira. She called herself a "prophetess," but she dedicated herself to the corruption of the people of God (Rev. 2:20). The contrast is more than a coincidence because Luke 2:36 and Revelation 2:20 are the only two places in the New Testament where the word *prophetess* occurs.

Anna was in the temple when Joseph and Mary brought the infant Christ to Jerusalem to present Him to the Lord when Mary's forty-day purification period was over. Anna was standing by when the aged Simeon recognized "the Lord's Christ." Instantly, Anna gave thanks and then launched a new ministry: she "spake of him to all them that looked for redemption in Jerusalem." Surely Anna was exactly the kind of widow that Paul had in mind when he spoke of "widows indeed."

(b) The widow and her resources (5:4)

i. The rule (5:4a)

Paul turned his attention to the case of widows who were not entirely destitute. "If any widow have children or nephews," he said, "let them learn first to shew piety at home, and to requite their parents." The word translated "children" here is *teknon,* which refers to a child (boy or girl) of natural descent. The word translated "nephews" is *ekgonos,* which occurs only here in the New Testament and refers to grandchildren or other descendants. The meaning of the English word "nephews" has changed with the passing of time. When the King James Version of the Bible was translated, it meant "grandchildren." We see the same obsolete use of *nephews* in Shakespeare's *Othello.*

The word translated "shew piety" means "to treat reverently." In the New Testament, it is used only here and in Paul's speech on Mars Hill in Athens, where he told the gullible Greek intellectuals that he had noted their superstitious *worship* of "the unknown God" (Acts 17:23). So the use of *eusebeō* in 1 Timothy 5:4 is a solemn reminder to children and grandchildren of their obligation to God to express their worship of Him in a practical way by taking care of their family members.

The phrase translated "requite" means "to recompense" or "to repay." In light of all of the love and care, all of the sacrifice and tireless devotion that mothers pour into their children, no wonder God expects His children to repay their widowed mothers in the same way.

Our society is impoverished by its departure from this Pauline principle. Social welfare is a poor substitute for spiritual welfare; a state or private institution is a cold replacement for a loving home. A widowed mother who lives in one's home can be a benediction. She can also be a trial, as well as a spur to her family to grow in grace.

My grandmother lived with my parents for as long as I can remember. An institution in our family, she had her own place at the table and her own corner by the fire. She was always there with her knitting, her smiles, her comfort, and her little treats. Sometimes we rebelled against Mom and Dad, but we always loved and obeyed Grandma. She was a center of peace, quietness, and godliness. That dear old lady with otherworldly ways loved us and helped pray us into the kingdom of God. Grandma went to her eternal rest many years ago, but I still remember her old-fashioned black dresses, her lace-up boots, her round wire spectacles, and her gray hair done up in a bun.

Grandma did all of the darning, and she was always in charge on Mondays when the boiler was lit and the week's accumulation of soiled clothes and bedding were washed. She made the most marvelous toast I have ever eaten; it was browned by the red coals of the kitchen fire and buttered on both sides! Every Sunday morning, we were awakened by Grandma's weekly treat: a cup of properly brewed English tea and wafer-thin slices of bread and butter sprinkled with sugar! She really shone at Christmas when she made the plum puddings and a big cake iced with marzipan and sugar. Moreover, Grandma was always available to play a game of dominoes or to lend a hand with a jigsaw puzzle. And she was always good for a small contribution out of her tiny pension to augment one's pocket money. That was Grandma. She belonged.

Paul was right. A widowed mother belongs in the home of one of her children.

My wife and I kept my mother in our home for some years until shortly before her death. Her presence certainly required changes, and we lost a small measure of freedom. But what was that compared with the love she gave us and the prayers she prayed for our children?

ii. The reason (5:4b)

We should care for our parents because "that is good and acceptable before God." In this statement of the reason for the rule, we can almost hear an echo from Paul's dictum to the Romans regarding the will of God. He told them it was "good, and acceptable, and perfect" (Rom. 12:2). Certainly, it is God's will that believers support their aged, widowed mothers. Our piety is phony if it does not include taking care of such an obvious and elementary duty.

The scribes and Pharisees displayed their hypocrisy and earned the Lord's scathing denunciation by the way they circumvented their duty to their parents. Rabbinical tradition allowed them to pretend that they could not afford to support their parents because they had dedicated so much of their income to God (Matt. 15:4–9). Jesus denounced both their hypocrisy and their tradition.

(c) The widow and her reactions (5:5–7)

i. The widow who reacts in a wise way (5:5)

Paul returns to the case of the totally bereaved widow. He mentions her *desolation,* her *dedication,* her *dependence* on God, and her *devotion* to God. The apostle noted, "She that is a widow indeed, and desolate, trusteth in God and continueth in supplications and prayers night and day." Where can she go, but to the Lord?

The word translated "desolate" is *monoomai,* which occurs only here in the New Testament and means "left alone." Jesus met a lone widow at the gate of Nain, and Luke recorded the incident. "Behold," he wrote, "there was a dead man carried out, the only son of his mother, and she was a widow." She was accompanied by a large crowd, but that was no guarantee of generous support. People scatter quickly after a funeral, and even those who return to the house do not stay long. But Jesus did something about her desolate situation. First, He dried her tears, and then He gave her back her son (Luke 7:11–17). And He has not ceased to care for widows. Today, He uses the church, His mystical body, to carry on His work of compassion and care.

The desolate widow who reacts wisely "trusteth in God." The word translated "trusteth" here is in the perfect tense. It means "to hope." The implication is that the widow has made it a habit to rest her hope in God, so it is not about to be upset by her bereavement. Her hope has become unshakable trust, which expresses itself in a life on continuing supplication and prayer. She has always trusted God, and now she trusts Him even more.

Jesus told a story about another widow in Luke 18:1–8. "There was in a city a judge," He said, "which feared not God, neither regarded man: And there was a widow in that city; and she came unto him saying, Avenge me of mine adversary. And he would not for a while: but afterward he said within himself, Though I fear not God, nor regard man; yet because this widow troubleth me, I will avenge her, lest by her continual coming she weary me."

The point of the parable was that "men ought always to pray, and not to faint." God is not like that unjust judge who, in spite of the many articles of the Mosaic Law and elsewhere that protected widows (Exod. 22:22; Deut. 10:18; Isa. 1:17, 23; Mal. 3:5), acted on her behalf only out of self-interest. God may indeed delay His response to our prayers, but such a delay has a divine and all-wise purpose. From heaven's viewpoint God responds "speedily."

The widow who responds wisely will simply go on trusting God and continue to look to Him to answer in His own good time.

ii. The widow who reacts in a worldly way (5:6–7)

a. What is noted (5:6)

Paul noted, "She that liveth in pleasure is dead while she liveth." The widow who seeks to drown her sorrow (or express her relief) at the death of her husband by plunging into all of the world's pleasures does irreparable damage to her soul.

The expression "liveth in pleasure" here is used by James in denouncing the ungodly rich: "Ye have lived in pleasure on the earth, and been *wanton*" (James 5:5). The word means "to live luxuriously." It could properly be applied to the Prodigal Son (Luke 15:13).

The widow who turns to sinful pleasure, said Paul, is "dead while she liveth." This expression can also be rendered "is killing her own soul." A recently widowed person is brought face-to-face with the dread reality of death, so for her to plunge headlong into a round of pleasure seeking is perhaps to court death. Her danger is illuminated in Mark 8:35, where the Lord said, "Whosoever will save his life shall lose it." If it is possible to lose one's life while trying to save it, how much more must it be possible to lose one's life while deliberately throwing it away!

b. What is needed (5:7)

In view of such danger, some rules are needed to guide the local church in its practical ministry to the bereaved. The guidelines are already established according to apostolic standards. "These things give in charge," Paul told Timothy, "that they be blameless." Ministers are constantly to command that the rules be observed.

The word translated "give in charge" also occurs in Acts 1:4, where the Lord "*commanded* [same word]" His disciples "that they should not depart from Jerusalem, but wait for the promise of the Father." The word translated "blameless" conveys the idea of not giving an adversary anything to seize as the basis of an accusation.

If the elders of a local church subsidize the lifestyle of a worldly widow, the church might be blamed for condoning that kind of lifestyle. Whereas the pious widow is to be supported by the church, the pleasure-seeking widow, by choosing a worldly lifestyle, cuts herself off from such support.

(d) The widow and her relations (5:8)

i. What is required (5:8a)

Paul comes back to the widow who does have relatives. He envisions a case in which a family member who professes to be a believer refuses to shoulder his responsibility to provide for the widow. Paul had little patience with such an empty profession of faith. He wrote, "If any provide not for his own, and specially for those of his own house, he hath denied the faith, and is worse than an infidel." This is pretty strong language, but Paul was as adamant as James in insisting that believers have a belief that behaves.

The word for "provide" here communicates the idea of anticipating, thinking of something beforehand, and of caring. In Paul's view, it was plain common sense for a person to anticipate having to care for a family member if the need should arise. Even unbelievers know how to show natural affection to family members. A Christian cannot adopt a lower standard of caring than an unsaved person does. The believer should show the kind of love described in 1 Corinthians 13; such love is at the heart of the Christian faith.

The professing Christian who does not show this kind of love can be compared to the servant in the Lord's story recorded in Matthew 18:23–35. The servant owed the king ten thousand talents; and although he pleaded for more time and made vague promises to put things right, he obviously had no way of meeting this enormous indebtedness. So the king canceled his debt. However, as soon as this unscrupulous man was set free, he sought out a fellow servant who owed him a hundred pence. He abused his fellow servant, demanded immediate payment, and flung the unfortunate debtor into prison. When other servants brought the matter to the king's attention, he summoned the man back to court. "O thou wicked servant," the king said, "I forgave thee all that debt, because thou desiredst me: Shouldest not thou also have had compassion on thy fellowservant, even as I had pity on thee?" Then the king thrust the wicked servant into prison until he could pay his enormous debt in full.

The same principle applies to the treatment of widows. The professing believer has drawn on the bank of heaven for forgiveness of all his debt of sin. God has shown him enormous love, kindness, and grace and now expects him to show similar kindness and compassion to other people. He owes a debt of love, especially to members of his family.

ii. What is revealed (5:8b)

The man who acts unfeelingly toward his needy relatives is branded by the Holy Spirit as an unbeliever. "He hath denied the faith," wrote Paul, "and is worse than an infidel." Refusing to extend the love of Christ to a widowed mother, aunt, sister, or niece demonstrates a hard heart and negates any profession of faith.

The word translated "infidel" here is *apistos.* The word translated "faith" here is *pistis.* The letter *alpha (a)* placed in front of a Greek word gives it a negative meaning. Sometimes the same is true in English. For example, the word *theist* refers to someone who acknowledges that there is a God, but if we put an *a* in front of it, we form the word *atheist,* which refers to someone who denies that there is a God. So the Greek letter *alpha* changes *pistis* ("faith") to *apistos* ("infidel").

(e) The widow and her reception (5:9)

Paul gave Timothy two divinely indicated guidelines for a church that is considering providing charity for a particular widow. The elders are to take into account the widow's *maturity* and her *monogamy:* "Let not a widow be taken into the number under threescore years old, having been the wife of one man." The word translated "taken into the number" is *katalegomai,* which occurs only here in the New Testament. In classical Greek, the word was used in reference to enrolling or enlisting soldiers. The English word *catalog* is derived from *katalegomai.*

Only a mature widow was to be enrolled as a recipient of church funds. After being placed on the church's charity roll, she was to be especially consecrated to the Lord's work; having put her hand to this plow, she was not to turn back. By accepting the church's financial support, the widow made a commitment to serve the church, particularly in the sphere of hospitality. Perhaps the younger widows were excluded because they would find it harder to resist the temptations that might arise in this sphere of service. The sixty-year rule would also prevent younger widows from becoming entangled by vows and commitments that they had not carefully considered and the weight of which they had not fully realized when recently bereaved and heartsore. The age of sixty was significant in the Mosaic Law regarding vows (Lev. 27:1–4, 7).

To be enrolled for church support, the widow was not only required to be mature. She was also required to have been married only once. Presumably, a widow who has been married twice or more would have a broader base of relatives from whom some financial support could reasonably be expected. In addition, her monogamy would be proof of her fidelity and constancy.

(f) The widow and her reputation (5:10)

i. Is she a good person? (5:10a)

Paul stated two basic questions that need to be asked before putting a widow on the roll. The first is very practical: Is she "well reported of for good works"? In other words, does she have a well-founded reputation for having lived a good life?

The phrase *good works* occurs often in the Pastoral Epistles (1 Tim. 2:10; 3:1; 5:10, 25; 6:18; 2 Tim. 2:21; 3:17; Titus 1:16; 2:7, 14; 3:1, 8, 14). In the Sermon on the Mount, the Lord declared that good works should be one of the hallmarks of His disciples—a hallmark that would be especially convincing to the unsaved (Matt. 5:16). His own life and ministry were marked by good works (John 10:32–33). Peter, who personally observed many of the Lord's works, told Cornelius that Jesus "went about doing good" (Acts 10:38).

Good works are more than good intentions (Matt. 21:28–31). Love is not a good work. Feeding the hungry, clothing the naked, and visiting the sick are good works (Matt. 25:35–36). Unsaved people can, of course, do good works—and often they hope that such activities will get them into heaven—but that is no reason to depreciate good works. The believer does good works, not *to be* saved but *because* he is saved. So Paul told elders to look for such evidence in the lives of widows who wanted to be the permanent beneficiaries of church bounty.

ii. Is she a giving person? (5:10b–f)

a. Look at her home (5:10b)

The second question listed five areas that elders should check before deciding to support a widow financially. For instance, they should look at her home and ask "if she have brought up children." The word translated "brought up children" occurs only here in the New Testament. The word is said to imply that the children must have been her own. The idea seems to be that the widow in question must have brought up her own children well and been a good mother to them; there would doubtless have to be good reasons why her children could not support her, as 5:3–4 requires. Or perhaps widows who had been good mothers were especially prized by the church, so much so that their full-time ministry was seen as an asset worth securing by offering financial support (1 Cor. 9:9; 1 Tim. 5:18). Certainly, a widow with a good track record as a mother is to be encouraged to serve in the local church.

b. Look at her hospitality (5:10c)

When checking the qualifications of a widow, the elders should also determine "if she have lodged strangers." This is the second of five *ifs* in this verse. In each case, the word *if* is followed by the indicative mood. *The Companion Bible* explains that "the hypothesis is assumed as an actual fact, the condition being unfulfilled, but no doubt being thrown upon the supposition."[13] The same usage is found in 1 Corinthians 15:16–17: "*If* the dead rise not, then is not Christ raised: And *if* Christ be not raised, your faith is vain" (italics added).

The word translated "lodging strangers" occurs only here in the New Testament, but the cognate word *xenos* ("strangers") occurs four times in a row in the Lord's parable of the sheep and the goats (Matt. 25:35, 38, 43, 44). In the story, the

13. Bullinger, *Companion Bible,* app. 118:2.

Lord described Himself as "a stranger" in the very world His hands had made, and the way people treated strangers was taken to be an indication of how they treat Him. The parable's interpretation refers to the period of the Great Tribulation and the subsequent judgment of the nations at the Lord's return in the valley of Jehoshaphat (Matt. 24:15–22; Joel 3:2). The parable's application can be relevant to the case of the worthy widow whose kindness to visitors is noted by the elders of her church.

c. Look at her humility (5:10d)

When considering the case of a widow, the elders should also note "if she have washed the saints' feet." Some churches make foot washing a ritual, but Paul did not have a ritual in mind. He was simply dealing with the realities of his day. People wore open sandals, and the roads and byways were hot and dirty, so feet soon became weary and soiled. It was a mark of good hospitality to set water at the door so that a slave might cleanse and refresh visitors' feet as they entered the house.

Water was placed in the Upper Room by the owner of the building so that a slave could thus minister to the Lord and His disciples upon their arrival at the Last Supper. But they had no slave, and none of the disciples was willing to humble himself to perform this menial task. So the Lord took the slave's place and washed all of their feet—much to their secret chagrin and Peter's outspoken dismay (John 13:3–17). The Lord used the incident as an opportunity to press home the lesson of humility and service.

On an earlier occasion, when Jesus had been invited to the home of a Pharisee, the disdainful man had not offered this common courtesy to his guest. However, the Pharisee's lack of cordiality was more than compensated for by the arrival of a sinful woman who bathed His feet with her tears and wiped them with her hair. The Lord indicted the Pharisee when He said to him, "Thou gavest me no water for my feet" (Luke 7:44).

Paul, then, was simply telling Timothy that a worthy widow would be one who did not shrink from performing even the most menial of tasks in the line of duty and devotion.

d. Look at her heart (5:10e)

In judging the worthiness of a widow, the elders should determine "if she have relieved the afflicted." The word translated "relieved" here is another word that is rarely used. It conveys the idea of giving succor to people hard-pressed by circumstances. Many of the widows in the ancient pagan world had experienced adverse circumstances themselves. A widow who had overcome such obstacles would have thus given evidence of her trust in the Lord, strength of character, and hard work, and could now busily engage herself in helping others overcome their difficulties.

We meet just such a widow in the story of Elijah. In spite of her obvious destitution, this courageous soul was willing to give what she had to the visiting prophet. How she was rewarded is one of the delightful stories of the Old Testament (1 Kings 17:8–24).

God is no man's debtor. The widow who overcomes her difficulties is like the faithful deacon who earns "a good degree, and great boldness in the faith which is in Christ Jesus" (1 Tim. 3:13), and thus she qualified to become a deaconess on the church payroll and to minister to others in need.

e. Look at her helpfulness (5:10f)

Finally, in evaluating a widow, the elder should determine, "if she have diligently followed every good work." The word translated "diligently followed" here is used in Mark 16:20 in reference to the apostolic signs that followed hard on the heels of the preaching of the early church. The same word is used in 1 Timothy 5:24 in reference to sins that follow after those who are guilty of them. In 5:10, the word suggests persevering in every good work. Anyone can do an occasional kind or generous act, but the worthy widow conscientiously does all of the good she can.

(2) The reluctant widow (5:11–15)

(a) The refusal (5:11a)

Paul turned his attention to younger widows who had not yet proved themselves to be qualified or who had already proved themselves to be unworthy of church support. He began bluntly enough: "But the younger widows refuse." The word translated "refuse" here is *paraiteomai,* which means "to avoid, beg off." Paul used the same word in 4:7 when warning Timothy to "refuse profane and old wives' fables."

Paul was well acquainted with life. Doubtless, he had known many widows, young and old. He had observed that, as soon as their grief subsided, the young widows often turned their attention toward finding another husband. There was, of course, nothing wrong with a widow remarrying. In the Old Testament, remarriage was the usual way of taking care of a childless widow. But the desire of young widows to remarry mitigated against their being put on the church payroll because commitment to the Lord's work was a requirement.

(b) The reason (5:11b–12)

A hasty commitment by a young widow to the cause of Christ could become an irksome burden to her, especially if vows were involved. As a result of her discontent, she might *cast off her first love* and *cast off her first faith.* Foreseeing such an outcome, Paul wrote, "When [the younger widows] have begun to wax wanton against Christ, they will marry, Having damnation, because they have cast off their first faith."

The word translated "begun to wax wanton" occurs only here in the New Testament. Behind the word is the idea of running riot. Cognate words are used in Revelation 18:3, 7, 9 ("delicacies," "lived deliciously") to describe the luxurious, wanton lifestyle of the Antichrist's Babylon. Trench rendered the word as "petulance"—petulance arising from fullness, like the wicked behavior of Jeshurun who "waxed fat, and kicked" (Deut. 32:15).[14] Paul was using strong language indeed.

The apostle could envision a young widow grieving over her loss and anxious about her future. Who would support her? She considers making a vow to live solely for Christ. Although she is sure that her faith and love will never wane, she might well be in danger of making promises to the Lord that she will not be able to keep.

She makes her vow. Then an attractive man comes along. She becomes interested in him and begins to rebel against the restraints imposed upon her by her vow. More and more she resents the life of sacrifice and supplication that she has assumed. One likelihood is that she will remarry. Another is that she might plunge into the round of the worldly pleasure she renounced when her heart was still sore. The young woman exposes herself to "damnation" by casting off her first faith.

Paul's advice was that the church keep such a widow off the payroll. During her recent bereavement, the Lord may well have become very real to her. She

14. Richard C. Trench, *Synonyms of the New Testament* (London: Macmillan, 1876), 193–95.

might indeed have felt sure that she would love and trust Him fervently. He had filled her heart with comfort. But Paul was too experienced an evangelist and pastor to place too much confidence in a love and trust based on emotion. The elders should wait and see. Getting her to make commitments to gain financial support would be self-defeating and could compound her problems later.

As Paul said, the young widows who make rash vows might have "damnation, because they have cast off their first faith." The word for "cast off" means "to render null and void, to reject, to break faith, to disappoint." The word for "damnation" occurs twenty-eight times in the New Testament and is usually rendered "judgment," "damnation," or "condemnation." This verse in no way implies that the young widow who breaks her vows will lose her salvation. What is implied is that if she renounces her promises to the Lord to remarry, she will carry over into her new marriage a haunting sense of guilt and self-reproach, and she will expose herself to the condemnatory comments of critics. This can all be avoided. Church elders should follow Paul's instructions and not make financial commitments to young widows and not solicit lifelong commitments from them.

(c) The recrimination (5:13)

Evidently, Paul felt strongly about making vows to God. After all, complete surrender to Christ and total commitment to His cause, which tolerates no rivals and no refusals, is a serious matter. Such a commitment involves not only the emotions but also the intellect and the will, along with a watchful conscience. Paul envisioned that all sorts of complications could arise if the church tried to capitalize on the emotional susceptibility and financial needs of young widows.

i. Guilty of lazy living (5:13a)

Paul also recognized the danger that a young widow who is supported by the church might "learn to be idle." The word translated "idle" is *argos,* the negative form of the word translated "work." Once the necessity for work is removed, all kinds of mischief can follow. God never intended people to be idle. Even when perfect conditions prevailed in Eden, God gave Adam work to do (Gen. 2:15). After the Fall, God increased that to hard work (3:17–19).

Paul was a firm believer in hard work. As he had already reminded the Ephesian elders, he was always ready to go back to tent making to support himself and his immediate colleagues in evangelism (Acts 20:34). He could see no point in relieving young, able-bodied widows of the necessity of working to support themselves. The saying "The devil always finds work for idle hands to do" contains much truth.

ii. Guilty of haunting houses (5:13b)

Another danger was that idle young widows would go "wandering about from house to house." With no financial worries, they might fall into bad habits, the mildest of which would be dropping in on their neighbors and friends to waste time. The expression *wandering about* is a translation of *perierchomai,* which can be rendered "strolling." It is used in Acts 19:13 to describe certain "vagabond" Jews who tried to imitate Paul's miracles by casting out demons—with disastrous results to themselves. In Acts 28:13, the word is translated "fetched a compass," but it can also be rendered "having tacked about." The context is Luke's description of a journey on a sailing ship. As we read the passage, we can picture the ship's turning this way and that to take advantage of the wind.

The older widows who were supported by the church were expected to do house-to-house visitation to minister to people materially and spiritually. The younger widows, however, might meet all kinds of temptation in their going in and out of the various houses.

iii. Guilty of telling tales (5:13c)

There was also the danger that the young widows would become "tattlers" *(phluaros),* that is, silly talkers. The verb form of the Greek word means "to babble." Tattlers are garrulous people; they are gossipy and have excessively busy tongues.

Silly talk soon degenerates into idle accusations, baseless charges, and malicious words. As James wrote, "Behold, how great a matter a little fire kindleth!" (see James 3:5–10). Paul was horrified at the thought of young widows spending their time in such unprofitable and disastrous conversations, especially while being supported by church funds.

iv. Guilty of being busybodies (5:13d)

Still another danger was that young widows might become "busybodies" *(periergos),* meddling in matters that were of no concern to them. The kindred verb *periergazomai* means "to be busy about useless matters" and suggests the idea of wasting labor. It occurs in 2 Thessalonians 3:11, where Paul denounced slackers: "We hear that there are some which walk among you disorderly, working not at all, but are busybodies." *Periergos,* rendered "curious arts" in Luke's account of the burning of the books of magic in Ephesus (Acts 19:19), suggests going beyond that which is legitimate.

Paul did not see any reason for the church to be encouraging meddling by subsidizing young widows. They would be better off seeking gainful employment.

v. Guilty of doing damage (5:13e)

The final danger was that the young widows would start "speaking things which they ought not." Paul was afraid of the damage they could do as they went in and out of houses. Gathering bits and pieces of gossip and retailing their news and views, they could undermine the fellowship and destroy the local church. "No," cried Paul in effect, "ten thousand times no! Never let a widow be so well supported by the church that she has nothing better to do with her time than that."

(d) The recommendation (5:14–15)

i. What Paul desired (5:14a–c)

Paul offered some practical, commonsense suggestions for the young widow. Because it would be better for all concerned for her to remarry, he suggested that she *betroth a new partner.* The apostle's rational, well-pondered desire was "that the younger women marry." A young widow has already tasted married life and might not be constituted for celibacy, so it would be best for her to find a new husband.

Paul went on to suggest that she *become a new parent,* that she "bear children." That is the natural, logical result of marriage. There is a great need for Christian mothers. And who can tell what kind of future church leaders might be born to remarried widows? For example, Obed was the son of a second marriage (Ruth's marriage to Boaz), and he turned out to be the grandfather of David!

The young widow should *beautify a new position.* Her role is to "guide the house," Paul said, for that is where a woman comes into her own. The word translated "guide the house" occurs only here and means "to manage and direct household affairs." At the heart of the word is the idea of ruling.

The home is the woman's domain. To rule a home well is a full-time job, especially when children are involved. The godly wife and mother, reigning as a queen over her own little world, holds the destiny of nations in her hands. How true is the claim that the hand that rocks the cradle rules the world! Blessed be Jochebed, who rocked the cradle of the infant Moses! Blessed be Jesse's wife, who rocked the cradle of David! Blessed be Mary, who rocked the cradle of Jesus!

ii. What Paul deplored (5:14d)

Paul deplored giving the enemy even the slightest ground for maligning the church, so he wanted the young widows to "give none occasion to the adversary to speak reproachfully." He knew the wiles of the Evil One. He knew how Satan could exploit the trauma and emotional upheaval of a recently widowed woman. Steps had to be taken to safeguard both the widow and the church from attack.

The word translated "adversary" here is *antikeimai.* The same word is used to describe the Antichrist as the one "who opposeth *[antikeimai]* and exalteth himself above all that is called God" (2 Thess. 2:4). It is also used to describe the opposition of the Holy Spirit to the flesh and the opposition of the flesh to the Holy Spirit: "These are contrary *[antikeimai]* the one to the other," wrote Paul (Gal. 5:17). In the Septuagint, the word is used in Zechariah 3:1 in reference to Satan.

The adversary that Paul mentioned in 1 Timothy 5:14 could be either Satan or human enemies of the gospel. With Nero on the rampage against Christians in the Roman Empire, it was doubly important to ensure that nothing was said or done to discredit the church. Enough malicious slander was already being circulated; the church should avoid giving the enemy any live ammunition.

The word translated "occasion" means "a starting point." According to Vine, the word denotes "a base of operations in war."[15] Paul was afraid that careless behavior on the part of young widows might give Satan a launching pad from which to mount an offensive against the faith.

The word *reproachfully* here can be rendered "reviling." The enemies of the gospel were already reviling Christians. Nero had accused them of starting the fire that burned Rome. They were also being accused of practicing the most terrible abominations. Paul feared that young widows, freed from the obligation to earn a living, might unwittingly by thoughtless behavior do what David had done: he gave "occasion to the enemies of the Lord to blaspheme" (2 Sam. 12:14).

15. Vine, *Expository Dictionary of New Testament Words,* 3:127.

iii. What Paul discerned (5:15)

Some widows, Paul discerned, had "already turned aside after Satan." This was not mere conjecture; the apostle knew of actual cases.

Satan, one of the names of the Devil, actually means "adversary." He is our great enemy and vigilantly opposes all that God is doing in the world. Satan was the unseen instigator of the heretical teachings that were making inroads into the church. He was the author of the terrifying Neronic persecution raging in Rome. He is the one who lays traps for the unwary. He has no respect for the grief and vulnerability of young widows; on the contrary, he tries to exploit them and, as Paul declared, had been only too successful with some.

The words *turned aside* here take us back to Paul's opening warning to Timothy: "Some having swerved have turned aside *[ektrepomai]* unto vain jangling" (1:6). Paul's heart went out to the widows, especially the young ones. He longed to protect them from the adversary who would beguile them into paths of folly. His words of warning and advice were prompted solely by a desire to help young, vulnerable widows become strong, saintly believers.

(3) The related widow (5:16)

(a) A precaution (5:16a)

Referring again to widows who do have relatives who are able to provide support, Paul wrote, "If any man or woman that believeth have widows. . . ." First and foremost, widows are a family responsibility; Paul place the onus on the widow's relatives.

A believer is duty bound to take care of his or her bereaved relatives. At the heart of this injunction is the concept of the extended family. The idea was strong among the Jews (Heb. 11:8–9), it is still strong in many Third World countries today, and it ought to be strong among God's people. The family unit is God ordained, and its breakdown always heralds the collapse of a society. The family ought to be the first line of support for the bereaved, the unemployed, the sick, and the poor.

(b) A provision (5:16b)

"Let them relieve them," wrote Paul. That might not be the way it *is,* but that is the way it *ought* to be. In our day, disaster has overtaken family life. As Vance

Havner said, the automobile took the family out of the home; and television brought the world into the home. As a result of the advent of automobile and television, old-fashioned family life has vanished, taking with it the ideal of being responsible for one's dependents.

Paul's decree, however, remains in force. A believer—man or woman—is responsible to care for his or her own family members. That obligation remains undimmed by time and technology. The family is God's first sphere of provision for the needs of its members.

(c) A proposal (5:16c–d)

Paul added, "Let not the church be charged; that it may relieve them that are widows indeed." Such is Paul's teaching regarding widows. Church funds must be reserved for helping those who have no other means of support.

The stories of a number of widows are told in Scripture, and collectively they make an interesting study.[16] At the judgment seat of Christ, the church and believers will be judged for their treatment of widows, so let us take heed to our roles and responsibilities.

---

16. Tamar (Gen. 38:6–7), *the designing widow,* was set on receiving her rights. In consequence, God honored her by allowing her to become an ancestress of the Lord Jesus. Through her, Judah was judged.

    The widow of Tekoah (2 Sam. 14:4–5), *the discerning widow,* was hired by Joab to persuade David to relax the law in favor of Absalom. By so doing, David opened Pandora's box and received payment in kind, under the judgment of God, for his seduction of Bathsheba and murder of Uriah.

    Hiram's mother (1 Kings 7:13–14) was *the distinguished widow* of whom we know very little. She was originally of the tribe of Dan, a tribe associated with judgment (Gen. 49:16). She married a man of Naphtali who was also known as "a man of Tyre," an utterly pagan Phoenician city. Perhaps he died young under God's judgment. The pair had a son, Hiram (evidently named after the king of Tyre), who was extraordinarily gifted. Solomon hired Hiram to help build the temple.

    Zeruah (1 Kings 11:26), *the destructive widow,* was the mother of Jeroboam, who led the revolt that divided the nation of Israel. The division of the kingdom was a divine judgment on Solomon for his idolatries. Jeroboam brought into existence the idolatrous northern kingdom, which faced nothing but judgment throughout its history.

    The widow of Zarephath (1 Kings 17:9), *the desperate widow,* ministered to Elijah. When her son died, she accused the prophet of bringing her sin to remembrance and of slaying her son. Desperately poor, she was rewarded by God with her daily bread as well as the miraculous resurrection of her son.

c. Faithfulness to elders (5:17–25)
  (1) A word to the people (5:17–22)
    (a) Acclaiming elders (5:17–18)

Returning to the subject of elders, Paul discussed the local church's responsibility to acclaim these God-appointed men for *their rule.* "Let the elders that rule well . . . ," he began (5:17). The word translated "rule" here is the same one used in 3:4 to describe an elder's rule over his house. The word is *proistēmi,* which means "to superintend."

The local church is not a democracy where action is decided by a majority vote. A democracy might be man's view of the ideal form of government, but God's ideal is an absolute monarchy in which all power rests in the hands of Jesus. In the church, Christ is the Head, and the Holy Spirit is the Executor. The Holy Spirit raises up elders who are to make decisions as He leads and who are to be given honor if they do their tasks well. Thus, the church is to be ruled by men who have been gifted, proven, and appointed by the Holy Spirit. The Ephesian elders were well aware of this fact (Acts 20:17, 20).

Elders are also to be acclaimed for *their role.* They are to "be counted worthy of double honour, especially they who labour in the word and doctrine" (1 Tim. 5:17). Although it is desirable that all elders be "apt to teach" (3:2), some of them are more gifted than others and therefore devote more time to teaching. All elders are to be honored, and those who excel in teaching the Word of God and sound doctrine are to be doubly honored. The reason for the double honor is that God's Word is of supreme importance in the corporate life of a local church. God has magnified His Word even above His own illustrious name (Ps. 138:2). The world might not think so, but no nobler task exists on earth than to make known the Word of God.

The poor woman mentioned in Mark 12:42 was *the delightful widow* whose magnificent generosity earned her the commendation of the Lord Jesus. Whatever judgment she had tasted was thus swallowed up in blessing.

Anna (Luke 2:36–37), *the devoted widow* of long-standing, was one of the first people to recognize the advent of God's Son.

The widow of Nain (Luke 7:12) was *the destitute widow* whose unutterable sorrow was turned into unspeakable joy. We do not know what judgment had deprived her of both her husband and her son. We do know that Jesus wiped away her tears.

The determined widow of Luke 18:3 overcame the unjust judge and his wicked judgment and triumphed gloriously.

Elders are to be acclaimed for *their reward.* In 1 Timothy 5:18 Paul explained, "For the scripture saith, Thou shalt not muzzle the ox that treadeth out the corn" (see Deut. 25:4). And, "The labourer is worthy of his reward" (see Matt. 10:10). Evidently, Paul envisioned elders being paid for their service to the local church because the word translated "reward" means literally "pay." The word for "labour" suggests growing weary, becoming exhausted from toil and effort. The word used here, *labourer,* is sometimes used in reference to a farmhand or a manual laborer. Evidently, elders are expected to earn their financial support by sheer hard work and are to be remunerated accordingly.

(b) Accusing elders (5:19–20)

i. A precautionary requirement (5:19)

It is extraordinary how ready people are to gossip about church leaders, how eagerly they entertain stories—true or false—and pass them on to others. Church members who gripe about decisions that elders make foment dissent and dissatisfaction. To stop such talk, Paul laid down one simple rule: "Against an elder receive not an accusation, but before two or three witnesses." Paul himself had been unmercifully and unfairly attacked at Corinth and elsewhere, and Timothy had doubtless received his share of abusive treatment at Ephesus.

Moses was subjected to criticism throughout his career as leader, shepherd, and teacher of God's people. The Israelites constantly murmured against him and Aaron. At times, God had to intervene to vindicate and protect His faithful servants (Exod. 14:11–12; 15:24; 16:2, 7, 9, 12; 17:3; 32:1; Num. 11:1, 9–15; 12:1; 14:1–5; 16:11–32, 41–46; 21:4–5). David, too, faced criticism, as did Jeremiah. The prophet's life was made a burden to him by the intransigence of the majority of the nation.

So it was not unusual for the leaders of a congregation to be abused. To deal with this tendency, Paul simply said that any charge against an elder must be made formally and must be substantiated by at least two—preferably three—witnesses (see Deut. 19:15). This Old Testament principle was reinforced by the Lord's dictum in Matthew 18:16.

Any accusations against an elder must be received only when they are submitted properly. That is the rule. To accept accusations without proper proof is to undermine the authority of God-appointed leaders and to act contrary to God's Word. The word translated "accusation" has to do with legal procedure. Note that Paul did not use the word for slander. He put the emphasis, rather, on speaking against a person in public, especially before a tribunal. Paul's idea seems to be that we are not to entertain any accusation against an elder unless the accuser comes with the required number of witnesses who are able and willing to back up the charge.

ii. A public rebuke (5:20)

Because of their public position, church leaders who do sin should be rebuked publicly. Paul said, "Them that sin rebuke before all, that others also may fear." The word translated "rebuke" means "to convict of or to reprove." The implication is that the conviction will lead to confession. When a church leader is arraigned, accused, convicted, and sentenced publicly, the effect on the other elders is bound to be salutary. Fear is almost as strong as love as a motivating force.

Sometimes the decree in 5:20 is invoked against ordinary members of the congregation. Sinning individuals are hauled before the church and rebuked publicly. But this does not seem to be what Paul had in mind here. The context has to do with elders, not rank-and-file members who do not hold a public position.

(c) Accepting elders (5:21–22)

i. A demand dramatized (5:21a)

Apparently Paul had some reservations about Timothy's moral courage, so the apostle addressed himself directly, plainly, and bluntly to his young friend: "I charge thee before God, and the Lord Jesus Christ, and the elect angels . . ." The solemnity of this charge is evident.

We can understand why Paul would adjure Timothy before God and the Lord Jesus Christ. But why did Paul also adjure him before "the elect angels"? This is the only place in the Bible where angels are called "elect." Doubtless, Paul was drawing a contrast between the fallen angels, who help administer Satan's vast empire, and the holy angels, who are used by God in His sovereign rule over the created universe. However, to understand why the apostle mentioned the angels in 5:21, we must review some of their functions.

Angels often act as God's messengers (Luke 1:5–22, 26–38; Matt. 28:1–7). They serve as mighty warriors and interfere directly with Satan's schemes (Dan. 10:10–21; Rev. 12:7–8). They control the elements (Rev. 7:1–3). They administer God's judgments on earth (Rev. 8–9;16). They watch over children (Matt. 18:10), minister to God's people (Heb. 1:14), and attend to the needs of individual believers (Acts 12:6–11; 27:21–25). Angels are keenly interested in the redemptive purposes of God (1 Peter 1:12) and watch over worship in the church (1 Cor. 11:10). If we take literally the repeated references to angels in the letters to the seven churches (and we take them literally everywhere else in the Apocalypse), each church has its own attending angel (Rev. 2–3). The church on earth is in enemy territory and under constant attack from Satan's hosts (Eph. 6:11–13), so we should not be surprised if the holy angels are somehow involved in hindering Satan and helping saints. This activity in the spirit world helps explain why Paul summoned "the elect angels," along with God and His Son, to be witnesses to his charge to Timothy.

ii. A difficulty disclosed (5:21b–c)

Setting before Timothy the issue of *obedience* and *objectivity,* Paul stated his charge: "Observe these things without preferring one before another, doing nothing by partiality." The word translated "observe" means "to guard, to watch, or to beware." Timothy was to watch out. He was especially to guard against "preferring" someone and showing "partiality." The word translated "preferring" is *prokrima,* which occurs only here in the New Testament and means "prejudging, showing prejudice." The word translated "partiality" here is *prosklisis,* which also occurs only here and means literally "inclination toward" someone or something.

Evidently, Timothy was in danger of being swayed by some of the more influential, persuasive, or personable believers in Ephesus. Paul, who probably knew some of the people who might try to influence his coworker, seems to have been afraid that Timothy would allow himself to be intimidated by them and not be governed by God's revealed will regarding widows and elders, for instance. The apostle feared that Timothy might prejudge some issues without weighing the evidence properly and that he might be swayed to deal with some people differently than he dealt with others. So before divine and angelic witnesses, Paul solemnly adjures Timothy to treat everyone alike and not to incline the scales of judgment to one side or the other.

iii. A danger displayed (5:22)

a. The possibility of making a hasty move (5:22a)

Paul warned his young pastor friend, "Lay hands suddenly on no man." The interpretation of this verse is determined by what Paul says to Timothy elsewhere in this regard (1 Tim. 4:14; 2 Tim. 1:6). In both of these places, the reference is to ordination. So it seems that in 1 Timothy 5:22 Paul was warning against being too hasty in promoting a person in the Lord's work.

A Christian must prove himself before he is identified with the public ministry of the local church. Many a man has been lionized because he has some spectacular-sounding testimony or because he displays extraordinary gifts or zeal. He rides the crest of public applause for a while—only to fall into disgrace. Paul, of course, was familiar with the long apprenticeship required of Old Testament priests before they were formally ordained (Num. 4:1–3; 8:24). Their probationary period began at age twenty-five, and their consecration was not celebrated until they were thirty years old. Similarly, the Lord Jesus was about thirty years of age when He began His ministry (Luke 3:2). Paul and Barnabas also proved themselves thoroughly before the Antioch church ordained them as official missionaries (Acts 11:19–26; 13:1–3).

Certainly the principle in 1 Timothy 5:22 is sound. Paul's injunction cautions against haste in three types of situations: (1) in consecrating an elder, a deacon, or some other officially recognized servant of the Lord; (2) in arresting a person for arraignment before the church's governing body; (3) in restoring a disciplined church member to full fellowship. Natural impulses are to be held in check. It is too easy to make a mistake when we are hasty.

b. The possibility of making a horrible mistake (5:22b)

Paul continued, "Neither be partakers of other men's sins: keep thyself pure." Those who are overeager to ordain someone to the ministry or commend someone to full-time Christian service must share the blame and responsibility if the results are disastrous. Likewise, those who are too quick in reconciliation share responsibility for any negative results that follow. In a case of hasty restoration, the offender might get the impression that his offense was not so serious after all. Other people might get the same message and follow the example of the offender.

The word translated "pure" in 5:22 is *hagnos,* which conveys the idea of not being contaminated. Paul's warning to Timothy to keep himself "pure" was, in other words, a warning to guard against inducting unfit men into the ministry. Today, the whole church suffers because Paul's commonsense spiritual counsel was not followed.

(2) A word to the pastor (5:23–25)
(a) Timothy's sickness (5:23)

Paul turned for a moment to a collateral issue and admitted that Timothy did not enjoy good health. It seems as if the apostle suddenly remembered that his dear young friend was often ill and was not blessed with a tough physique. Perhaps Paul was making a somewhat belated allowance for the fact that poor health might have contributed to Timothy's tendency to take the line of least resistance.

Paul advised Timothy to "drink no longer water, but use a little wine for thy stomach's sake and thine often infirmities." In Paul's day, nothing was done to prevent the local water supply from harboring bacteria and parasites, so water might have caused Timothy's "infirmities." (The word translated "infirmities" is *astheneia,* which is used here in the sense of weakness, sickness, or attacks of illness.) Water supplies in many countries are still often contaminated. Travelers from the United States to Latin America, for example, are well-advised to steer clear of tap water in even the most reputable hotels. In some places, fresh fruits and vegetables that have been washed in local water can cause dysentery.

Paul showed good common sense in advising Timothy to drink "a little wine" instead of water. Wine, with its antiseptic qualities, was much safer to drink. The word translated "wine" here means wine, not grape juice; there is no escaping that. The same word is used in such well-known passages as Matthew 9:17; John 2:10; and Ephesians 5:18. However, the word *little* in 1 Timothy 5:23 needs to be emphasized. Paul was not writing a prescription for drunkenness; that would have been contrary to his teaching elsewhere (Gal. 5:19–21). He was suggesting that Timothy, who apparently was a total abstainer, use "a little wine" for medicinal purposes.

(b) Timothy's situation (5:24–25)
i. Men who sin (5:24)

As Paul concluded this section of his letter, he tried to stiffen Timothy's resolve as a pastor by reminding him that sin is a serious matter. The apostle wrote, "Some men's sins are open beforehand, going before to judgment; and some men they follow after." Paul might still have had in mind those hastily ordained individuals who make swift public shipwreck of their lives. Or he might have been thinking about sins in general.

Some men's sins are flagrant, requiring no investigation to uncover them. Such sins march ahead of the guilty person to the place of judgment. Other sins are covered up and are not exposed without careful investigation. Some people manage to conceal their guilt all of their lives, but their sins, which follow them as a weasel follows a rabbit, will catch up with them at the judgment seat of Christ. The sin of Simeon and Levi, for example, was flagrant, heralding the need for judgment (Gen. 34:25–31; 49:5–7). The sin of Reuben, however, was concealed, so he mistakenly thought that he had gotten away with it—until it was exposed publicly by Jacob on his deathbed (49:3–4).

ii. Men who serve (5:25)

"Likewise," wrote Paul, "the good works of some are manifest beforehand; and they that are otherwise cannot be hid." We have all known people whose godliness, gifts, and greatness have earned them public recognition in this life. Men flocked to the standard raised by Martin Luther. Queen Mary of Scotland feared John Knox and his preaching more than she feared all of the armies of England. David Livingstone was honored in life and death by an admiring nation. George Müller's funeral closed down Bristol. Millions of people from all walks of life have acknowledged Billy Graham as an evangelist-statesman. Church history books are full of the stories of such people. Paul himself was confident of the reward that awaited him at the judgment seat of Christ (2 Tim. 4:6–8).

By the same token, those who have opposed, attacked, and slandered the giants of the faith will one day receive their due reward, as did Shimei in the Old Testament. He cursed David, secretly at first but then openly, and he lived to rue the day (2 Sam. 16:5–13; 19:16–23; 1 Kings 2:8–9, 36–46). Those whose opposition has been secret and treacherous will be exposed openly.

d. Firmness for servants (6:1–2)
(1) Those with characteristic masters (6:1)

In the early days of the church, a high percentage of believers were slaves, most of whom had unsaved masters. Some of the masters were kind, but others were cruel. Some were fair, but others were tyrants. Some were indulgent, but others were harsh. In any case, slaves had no rights. Sometimes they had privileges, but their legal status was clear: they were pieces of property, bought and paid for, body and soul.

How was a Christian slave to act toward an unsaved master? (In our culture the question would be, "How should a Christian employee act toward an unsaved employer?") Paul said, "Let as many servants [*doulos,* 'slaves'] as are under the yoke count their own masters worthy of all honour, that the name of God and His doctrine be not blasphemed." Whether a person is a slave or a freeman is not what is important. What matters is that the person does nothing to bring the gospel into disrepute and thereby hinder the salvation of even the most cruel master.

Paul believed strongly in constitutional authority at all levels of life. He told citizens to obey the law, honor those in authority, and pray for them (Rom. 13:1–7; 1 Tim. 2:1–4). He told wives to obey their husbands, husbands to love their wives, children to obey their parents, and parents not to provoke their children (Eph. 5:21–6:4). He told believers to be mindful of church elders and to acknowledge their rule (Heb. 13:7; 1 Tim. 5:17).

The constitution of the Roman Empire upheld slavery. Although Paul's heart went out to slaves—and he struck at the heart of the issue in his letter to Philemon—he never tried to change the law. Instead, he tried to change the hearts of both the slaves and their owners.

Paul's instructions in 1 Timothy 6 were in keeping with his conviction that social ills had a spiritual cause and that as an apostle and preacher his primary calling was to deal with the spiritual dimension. Paul knew that a slave who radiated Christ was far more likely to see his circumstances change than was a slave who was surly. The radiant slave was also more likely to see his unsaved master get saved. In any case, by manifesting the spirit of Christ, the slave could live above his circumstances.

Paul strung together a number of words here that reveal his understanding of the slave's lot in life. He had been a prisoner in bonds and knew of the irksomeness of bondage. The slaves whom he mentioned in 6:1 were "under the yoke." By adding these words to the word *servants,* Paul implied that their bondage was harsh and wretched.

The word *yoke* brings to mind an ox or a horse that is harnessed and obliged to toil in the traces at the will of its owner. The human spirit revolts against such servitude, so slave owners had ways of breaking a slave, just as men have methods of breaking a horse. Such means ought not to be necessary for breaking a Christian slave. The bondage was doubtless galling, but God had higher purposes than emancipating slaves; He was at work emancipating sinners. The emancipation of slaves would follow as a matter of course.

The word translated "masters" here is significant. It is the root of our English word *despot* and implies absolute ownership and uncontrolled power. The use of the word suggests that Paul particularly had in mind Christian slaves who were in bondage to tyrannical masters.

What were slaves who had harsh masters to do? Paul demanded what was virtually impossible, humanly speaking: even in their unhappy circumstances, they were to "count" their masters as worthy of all honor. The word translated "count" means "to lead the way, to lead before the mind." It conveys the idea that a slave was to respond to his master not on the basis of emotion, for that could lead him into all kinds of difficulty, but on the basis of a careful consideration of the issues. The facts were simple enough: he was a slave and would remain so unless his master freed him or sold him to someone who would, and all of the weight of the Roman law was on the master's side. The system—as cruel, inhuman, and unjust as it was—had the upper hand. The slave had to accept that reality.

Another fact was that his master was entitled to honor by virtue of his position, if for no other reason. The word translated "honour" here primarily has to do with evaluation of worth and refers to the esteem due a person who ranks higher than the person who renders that esteem. *Personally* a master might be despicable; *positionally* he ought to command respect and honor; *potentially* he was a soul for whom Christ had died and thus was a candidate for salvation.

Yet another fact was to be considered. Humanly speaking, the Christian slave might indeed find it impossible to render deference and honor to an unfit master. As a new man in Christ, however, the slave was indwelt by the Spirit of God and had all of the resources of the Godhead at his disposal to enable him to do what was humanly impossible. Thus, poor Uncle Tom in Harriet Beecher Stowe's famous story was enabled to live a Christlike life before the cruel and vindictive Simon Legree.

Paul lifted the whole issue of slavery from the natural level to the spiritual level and added still another fact to be weighed and evaluated objectively: a Christian must never do anything detrimental to the gospel. A cruel master might not become a Christian, but he was never to be given a weapon to wield in support of his unbelief—a weapon such as a bad attitude in his Christian slave.

One last fact must be remembered: God is still on the throne! Take, for example, the case of Joseph. When he was sold into slavery, he lived such a godly life that his master, Potiphar, put him in a position of trust, honor, and power (Gen. 39:3–6). When Joseph was accused falsely and thrown into prison, he lived such a godly life that he was given free access to all parts of the facility so that he could witness and minister to the inmates (Gen. 39:21–40: 23).

(2) Those with Christian masters (6:2)
(a) A danger (6:2a–b)

Some slaves were fortunate enough to have Christian masters, just as some believers today work for Christian employers. But Paul recognized a danger and gave a word of warning for such slaves: "They that have believing masters, let them not despise them, because they are brethren." The word for "despise" here means "to think down upon" someone or "to think slightingly" of someone.

Being "brethren," master and slave sat at the feet of the same Bible teachers. Indeed, the slave might well have been the teacher, for God is no respecter of persons in the dispensing of the gifts of the Spirit. Slave and master sat at the same Communion table and together worshiped the same Lord. They had a common interest in the things of God. The danger was that on Monday the slave might think that he had the same rights socially that he had enjoyed spiritually on Sunday. In a word, he might presume upon the fact that his master was a believer. Paul warned against such presumption.

I once worked for a friend who owned a large business and was a wealthy, influential member of his community. The fact that I was often a guest in his palatial home on Sunday gave me no right to barge into his office on Monday to tell him how to run his business or to demand preferential treatment. On the contrary, I had to be especially careful not to offend the other employees. They knew about the Sunday relationship that I had with both the owner of the company and its general manager and would have been quick to resent any attempted exploitation of my unique position, and it would have been unfair if I had tried to exploit it. Similarly, a slave did not have the right to take advantage of a Christian master in the workaday world.

(b) A duty (6:2c–d)
i. A responsibility (6:2c)

Paul also recognized the duty of slaves who had Christian masters. "Do them service," he said. Instead of demanding privileges and concessions, a Christian slave ought to be the best of all of his master's slaves—the best in diligence, loyalty, productivity, and attitude. Likewise, a Christian employee should strive to excel in serving his employer.

The word translated "do . . . service" here means "slave." In other words, Paul was saying that a slave should serve as a bondsman. As we would say today, he should *slave* for his master. No task was to be considered too arduous or tedious. The slave was to go the extra mile gladly (Matt. 5:38–48). The world thinks such service is foolish. The world hails Spartacus, who led a slave rebellion and ended up being crucified. The Christian, however, sees things from the perspective of a different world.

ii. A reason (6:2d)

Paul said that slaves should serve well "because they are faithful and beloved, partakers of the benefit." The word for "partakers" refers here to the kindly acts and generous benefits that Christian masters bestowed on their slaves. These benefits were another reason for the slaves not to take advantage of their masters.

(c) A demand (6:2e)

Paul demanded, "These things teach and exhort." His practical teaching was not simply high-flying philosophy at which Timothy and the local church elders could nod and wave and then forget. Paul's epistle was solid, Holy Spirit-inspired doctrine to be taught diligently and pressed home by exhortation.

What Paul wrote would not be popular with the rank-and-file slaves who often made up the bulk of a congregation in the early church. Some of them doubtless hoped that the apostle would use his pen, personality, and powers of persuasion to urge action against slavery or, at least, to demand that Christian masters manumit their slaves. But Paul did nothing of the kind. Redressing social ills would have been (and often is) counterproductive. The apostle was not in the business of turning men against their masters. In a later century, Marx, Engels, and Lenin would try that experiment at enormous cost in lives, misery, global unrest, and bankruptcy of nations.

Paul had a better plan: bring masters and slaves alike to Calvary, and let Christ change the thoughts, feelings, and decisions that made slavery possible in the first place. Let Christ be all in all, and social ills would be resolved swiftly and permanently in an atmosphere of love, not hatred. So Timothy must not hesitate to teach and exhort even unpopular truths.

2. The priority of godliness (6:3–6)
   a. Godliness expounded (6:3–5)
      (1) The gold standard disclosed (6:3)
         (a) How to mark the forger (6:3a–b)

Godliness was Paul's theme in 3:16–4:16, and now he came back to it. When all is said and done, godliness is what the Christian life is really all about. Expounding on the subject, the apostle reminded believers of the gold standard and exposed forgers whose teachings do not meet that standard. A forger, Paul implied, is betrayed *by what he declares* and *by what he denies.* He is exposed by his teaching when it runs counter to the inspired teaching of Paul. The way to detect a forged painting, document, or coin is to compare it with the genuine article. Paul's doctrine was the real thing, so any teaching that painted a different picture of Christ, a different creed, or a different set of values was a forgery.

Paul said that "if any man teach otherwise, and consent not to wholesome words," he is marked. Because the *if* here in 6:3 is followed by the indicative mood, the hypothesis is assumed to be an actual fact. Paul knew perfectly well that some people were teaching the opposite of what he taught and it is confirmed by Paul's use here of a word that means to "teach otherwise." It indicates that their declarations were different from his.

The phrase *wholesome words* means the same as "sound doctrine" in 1:10. The word translated "wholesome" means "healthy"—our English word *hygiene* is derived from it. The teaching of deceivers always contains something tainted or unwholesome.

Paul had no doubts that many lesser men would deny and scoff at his teaching to make immediate inroads at his expense. The apostle's high ethical standards and his ability to see both sides of an issue—beyond the immediate to the ultimate, beyond the temporal to the eternal, beyond the sensual and social to the spiritual—made him seem insensitive, impractical, or unacceptable to some people.

The Jerusalem church looked askance at the tremendous freedom that Paul had preached for both Jew and Gentile. Jewish Christians as a whole lacked Paul's breadth of vision. They favored legalism. They were wrong and Paul was right. The implementation of their views would have made Christianity nothing more than another Jewish sect, wholly unattractive to Gentiles. Not long after Paul fought for full Christian liberty from Judaism in all of its forms, Jerusalem was caught up in an unwinnable war with Rome and soon ceased to have influence over the Christian church—except as a place for tourists and pilgrims to visit.

(b) How to measure the forgery (6:3c–d)

The touchstone of all teaching is "the words of our Lord Jesus Christ." We are to compare all teaching to "the doctrine which is according to godliness" because the Lord's teaching promoted godliness—that is, a proper attitude toward God. Paul's ethical, moral, and practical teaching measured up to the gold standard of the Sermon on the Mount. His prophetic teaching was in harmony with the Lord's parables and prophecies.

(2) The guilt stains exposed (6:4–6)
(a) The examination of false teachers (6:4–5d)
i. Their personal exposure (6:4a)

When we reread Paul's marvelous epistle to the church at Ephesus, where Timothy was pastoring, we find it almost incredible that the believers there could have succumbed so quickly to false teachers. The Ephesian Christians had been well warned that such "wolves" were coming (Acts 20:17, 28–31), and come they did—swiftly and apparently successfully. Hence, Paul wrote to Timothy to strengthen his stand against false teachers.

Paul told Timothy that one mark of a false teacher is that "he is proud" (1 Tim. 6:4). The word for "proud" here means literally "to wrap in smoke or mist, to befog," which is what cult leaders do. They cloud their own minds with smoke and then befog the crystal-clear issues in the minds of those who listen to them. False teachers are also full of conceit, thinking themselves to be extremely clever and the sole possessors of truth.

Paul further described false teachers as "knowing nothing." The word translated "knowing," *epistamai,* has to do with the ability to understand something and thus points to the thought process that results in understanding. False teachers do not have the facts, and they are unable to arrive at the knowledge of the truth (1 Cor. 2:12–16). The word for "nothing" here means "nothing at all." False teachers think that they know it all, but they know nothing at all.

ii. Their public exposure (6:4b–5d)
a. Their questions exposed (6:4b–c)

Continuing his exposure of false teachers, Paul described them as "doting about questions and strifes of words." The word translated "doting" here is *noseō,* which means "sick" or "diseased." As far as the apostle was concerned, those who taught things that were contrary to sound doctrine and divinely revealed truth were sick in the head. One translator referred to such a teacher as a "conceited idiot!"[17]

17. J. B. Phillips, *The New Testament in Modern English* (New York: Macmillan, 1972) 442.

The church can judge false teachers just by listening to them. When they speak, all they have to offer is "questions and strifes of words." The word translated "questions" primarily means "seeking." The word has to do with the curiosity of the natural mind and its restless desire to probe into matters that lead nowhere. The term translated "strifes of words" is *logomachia,* which comes from *logos* ("a word") and from a word that means "to fight." Paul was saying that teachers of error not only have endless unprofitable questions but also like to fight over words.

False teachers are dangerous. A typical trick of theirs is to take good gospel words and give them different meanings. They say the things that believers say, but they do not mean what we mean. A New Age teacher, for example, would endorse our claim that people must be born again, but he would not mean what we mean by the phrase *born again.* We mean that people are born spiritually dead and need to accept Christ as their personal Savior and be regenerated by the Holy Spirit. New Age teachers, however, mean that people have to be reincarnated countless times to work out their destinies.

Another example would be a Mormon who speaks about the priesthood of Melchizedek, but he does not mean the royal priesthood of the Lord Jesus. Similarly, Christian Science has redefined almost all of the gospel terms and uses them to preach the mysticism and metaphysics of a deluded woman. Satan is the source of all such verbal jangling.

b. Their quarrels exposed (6:4d–5d)

1. Their "ministry" (6:4d–f)

Three words summarized the "ministry" of cultists: *envy, strife,* and *railings.* The word translated "envy," *phthonos,* has to do with a wicked feeling of ill will produced by witnessing or hearing about the promotion or prosperity of someone else. A false teacher looks with a jaundiced eye on the success of another preacher, for instance. So we can say that the "ministry" of cultists *promotes covetousness.*

The word translated "strife," *eris,* refers to contention that stems from sheer enmity. The activity of cultists *promotes contentiousness.* False teaching engenders the kind of quarreling that can turn a peaceable assembly of God's people into a battlefield.

The word translated "railings" here gives us our English word *blasphemy.* Blasphemy, an outpouring of contempt for God, is an abusive evil speaking. The activity of cultists produces "railings." It *promotes contemptuousness.*

Such is the dubious activity of false teachers. Lacking the power of the Holy Spirit, they manifest the power of Satan to stir up trouble, discontent, arguments, quarrels, and insults.

2. Their mentality (6:4g–5c)

(i) The fruit of their thinking (6:4g–5a)

By mentioning the fruit of "evil surmisings," Paul was referring to the *mental squalor* of false teachers. The word for "surmisings" here means "suppositions or conjectures." The phrase *evil surmisings* conveys the idea of thinking the worst about people. It has been rendered as "malicious innuendoes."[18]

By mentioning the fruit of "perverse disputings," Paul was referring to the *many squabbles* of false teachers. The word translated "perverse disputings" here occurs only here in the New Testament and refers to incessant wrangling. The Greek word suggests that Paul had in mind the wearing effect of constant friction. Squabbling is the fruit of a false teacher's efforts to win a following for himself. One can hardly imagine anything more unlike the godliness promoted by Paul. And how unlike "the mind of Christ" is the thinking of false teachers (1 Cor. 2:16; Phil. 2:5–11)!

(ii) The root of their thinking (6:5b–c)

In the phrase *men of corrupt minds,* Paul gave us a glimpse of *the inherent badness of their minds.* The word translated "corrupt" indicates that the false teachers are utterly corrupted, through and through. Their minds are warped.

In the phrase *destitute of the truth,* Paul gave us a glimpse of *the inherent bankruptcy of their minds.* The word translated "destitute" means "to be defrauded, robbed." W. E. Vine said that in 1 Timothy 6:5 the word suggests that false teachers who once knew the truth have been retributively robbed of the truth through the corrupt condition of their minds.[19] In other words, they are apostates.

The man who robs another person of his money, or even his life, is not nearly so criminal in the light of eternity as the man who robs another person of revealed truth and thus imperils that person's immortal soul. Throughout the Bible, the strongest language is reserved for those who lead other people astray.

18. Ibid.
19. Vine, *Expository Dictionary of New Testament Words,* 1:287.

3. Their motives (6:5d)

As might be expected, false teachers have financial motives. "Supposing that gain is godliness," they act as they do to obtain money from their followers. They hope to make a profit from the Christian faith. Teaching false doctrine is just another profession to them, one that they hope will be lucrative. To Paul, such a motive was the last straw. It was bad enough that the false teachers of his day were propagating dangerous errors and teaching what they knew to be lies. What capped it all was that they were doing so to make money.

(b) The excommunication of false teachers (6:5e)

"From such withdraw thyself," wrote Paul. We are to have nothing to do with false teachers. We are to leave them for God to deal with in His own time and way.

b. Godliness extolled (6:6)

Paul turned to a subject suggested by the greed and guilt of the false teachers: "Godliness with contentment is great gain." Gain is not godliness; the two often dwell far apart. True riches are to be found not in material things but in spiritual things.

Paul was a model of "godliness with contentment." Regarding money matters, the apostle was frank with his friends at Phillipi, as he was with everyone. He told them candidly that he had known times of plenty and times of poverty and that he had learned how to be content with either (Phil. 4:10–13). Paul also told them that he had "suffered the loss of all things" (3:8). Perhaps he was disinherited by his family for preaching the gospel.

Paul handled large sums of money in the course of his ministry. More often than not, he was simply a channel through which gifts could be sent to those in need (Acts 11:29–30). Godly Paul was just as willing to turn his hand to manual labor as he was to accept money for himself (20:33–35).

I have known many godly people. These Christlike individuals radiate goodness. Having learned patience, they abide in an atmosphere of peace, joy, purity, benevolence, love, and serenity. They live in 1 Corinthians 13 and seem to have a childlike trust in God that is undisturbed by passing events. Most of them are, if not actually poor, in modest financial circumstances. They are humble, holy, and happy. So free from guile are they that I cannot imagine their harboring evil in their hearts. They are approachable, unsophisticated (though not necessarily uneducated), and unworldly.

The Lord Jesus seems to be very real to these individuals. They know Him well and talk to Him often—and about Him as opportunities arise. Being people of the Book, they often have keen insights into its deeper truths. When they differ with someone, they express themselves charmingly, courteously, and unpretentiously. When I have been in the presence of one or another of these godly people, I left with the feeling that I had been in the presence of God.

"Godliness with contentment is great gain." The world cannot give it, nor can it take it away. Moreover, it is not for sale. The word translated "contentment" in 1 Timothy 6:6 is *autarkeia,* which means literally "satisfaction with what one has." Such satisfaction takes the hassles out of life. Godly contentment lifts a person out of the realm of the physical, material, and temporal and into the realm of the spiritual and eternal. People who have learned to be content resemble majestic mountain peaks; clouds and storms might swirl around their feet, but their eyes gaze on a realm where the sun always shines and storms cannot reach.

3. The peril of gold (6:7–10)
   a. A basic fact (6:7)

Gold and godliness do not often dwell together. Even when they do, it is only temporarily because the usefulness of gold is limited to this life. The value of godliness, however, lasts forever. To emphasize the fact that material things are useful for only a short time, Paul stated a basic and obvious fact: "We brought nothing into this world, and it is certain we can carry nothing out."

We have the example of Job. He was very rich. He had enormous flocks comprised of seven thousand sheep. He also had three thousand camels, vast caravans to carry on his commerce near and far. That would be like having three thousand rigs on the road today. In addition, he had five hundred "she asses" and five hundred yoke of oxen with which to plow and plant his farms. Moreover, he had many servants and was blessed with ten children, whom he loved dearly. If ever a man had it all, that man was Job.

Then disaster struck. He was stripped of all of his possessions, his children were killed by a tornado, his wife turned against him, and his friends accused him of being wicked. Job learned the emptiness of the things of this world. He prostrated himself before God and said, "Naked came I out of my mother's womb, and naked shall I return thither" (Job 1:21). He emerged from the womb with nothing, and he would enter the tomb with nothing. Paul expressed the same truth in 1 Timothy 6:7. We might say, "You can't take it with you." Whatever money and material possessions we gain in this world will be left behind at the grave.

At the funeral of a rich man, a mourner thought of the deceased's real estate holdings, business interests, and personal fortune and asked a friend, "How much did he leave?"

"How much did he leave?" responded the friend. "All of it."

In Luke 12:15, Jesus said, "A man's life consisteth not in the abundance of the things which he possesseth." Then He told a parable about a rich man who lived like a prince. He was gloating over his gains, over his fields heavy with crops and his barns bursting with goods. He sat up in bed and made plans for bigger and better barns and bigger and better banquets. Then God spoke, "Thou fool," He said, "this night thy soul shall be required of thee: then whose shall those things be, which thou hast provided?" (12:20). Here the parable ended as it had begun—with "things" (12:15, 20).

The Lord went on to describe life lived on a higher plane, free from the tyranny of material things, and gave this piece of advice: "Seek ye the kingdom of God; and all these things shall be added unto you" (Luke 12:31). He advised people to get rid of things and invest instead in the poor and needy and thus secure "treasure in the heavens that faileth not" (12:33). We brought nothing into this world, and we can take nothing out, but we can send something on ahead and be greeted with warmth when at last we reach the other shore (16:9–12). If we want to have treasure in heaven, we should give some money to someone who is going there.

b. A basic formula (6:8)

Paul continued, "Having food and raiment let us be therewith content." The word translated "food" occurs only here in the New Testament and denotes a sufficient supply of food. Paul had been hungry and thirsty often enough to make him not wish actual want on anyone (2 Cor. 11:27). On the other hand, he could not see any sense in stockpiling manna, a pursuit that the Old Testament believers discovered to be impossible (Exod. 16:15–20).

The word translated "raiment" occurs only here in the New Testament. It means "covering, roofing, shelter." Paul used the word to convey the idea of having an adequate place to live and sufficient clothing.

Paul advises us to be "content" if our basic needs are all supplied. The word translated "content" conveys the thought of having enough. It is translated as "is sufficient" in Paul's description of God's wonderful grace in 2 Corinthians 12:9. In 1 Timothy 6:8, Paul says that if we have enough to keep our bodies fed, clothed, and sheltered, that should be sufficient. This formula for contentment was not much in vogue in the world in Paul's day, nor is it in vogue today. But Paul was not living for this world; he was living for the world to come.

Abraham was a very rich man, but he was content to live in a tent. That fact is significant because that's how he proclaimed his attitude toward the world. His pagan neighbors were impressed by his prosperity and power and called him "a mighty prince," but he referred to himself simply as "a stranger and a sojourner." Abraham had his eye on another world. His altar proclaimed his attitude toward the world to come (see Gen. 12:7; 13:2–4). He was a penitent. His tent proclaimed his attitude toward the world in which he lived. He was a pilgrim (see Gen. 12:4, 6; Heb. 11:9–10).

Lot, Abraham's nephew and fellow believer, however, failed to maintain this essential pilgrim character. He pursued the wealth and applause of this world and lost everything. He ended up with a saved soul but a lost life (see Gen. 14; 19; 2 Peter 2:7–8).

Paul had learned the wisdom of the petitioner whose prayer is recorded in Proverbs 30:8–9: "Give me neither poverty nor riches; feed me with food convenient for me: Lest I be full, and deny thee, and say, Who is the Lord? Or lest I be poor, and steal, and take the name of my God in vain." The apostle thus avoided the snare that trapped Solomon, who became rich but very nearly ended up an apostate (2 Chron. 1:12; 1 Kings 11:1–9).

c. A basic folly (6:9)
  (1) The temptation explained (6:9a–b)
    (a) The hidden lure (6:9a)

Riches are deceptive. Paul explained, "They that will be rich fall into temptation and a snare." The word translated "will" here is *boulomai,* which generally refers to deliberate determination. Some people are determined to become rich. Paul was referring to people whose calculated desire to be rich stems not from a passing emotion but from deliberate thought. Their goal might not necessarily be to possess millions; it might simply be to have more than they really need.

Wealth, in and of itself, when acquired in the natural course of events, is neither moral nor immoral. It can be an instrument for good. What Paul criticized is the desire to possess wealth simply for the sake of possessing it. People are tempted to pursue wealth because it gives them influence, power, and things. Money can buy comfort, pleasure, and elegance, but it cannot buy happiness.

Paul condemned the determination to get rich at all costs. Because the desire to get rich can become a consuming passion, it opens the door to temptation. In the pursuit of wealth, many people have pushed aside God, family, and friends alike. Scruples get sacrificed. People stifle their consciences and use and abuse people. As they strive after more and more, they often employ unscrupulous tactics and do mean things in the name of business.

Thus, people who are determined to become rich fall in to a "snare." The word translated "snare" in 6:9 is *pagis,* which means "trap." In this context, *pagis* refers to the allurement with which the Devil traps those who desire to be rich. It is not surprising that such people fall into the trap because the desire to accumulate wealth fixes a person's attention on this world and on himself.

Mirrors are sometimes made of glass backed by silver. One can see others through a clear piece of glass, but he can see only himself when the silver is put on the back of the glass. Once we take our eyes off the Lord and fix them on wealth, we see only ourselves, and we fall into all kinds of sin. The world's pleasures, philosophies, ways, and wisdom become increasingly attractive. And no wonder! This is the world over which Satan presides as prince and god. It is his lair for sinners and his lure for saints. In pursuing wealth, people become more and more attached to this world and increasingly insensitive to God and the world to come.

(b) The harmful lusts (6:9b)

People who are determined to become rich also fall into "many foolish and hurtful lusts." The word *foolish* here describes a person who is thoughtless because he does not apply his mind to what is happening. The Lord used this word to rebuke the unbelieving disciples on the road to Emmaus. "O fools, and slow of heart," he said (Luke 24:25). They had not been thinking properly regarding the death, burial, and resurrection of Christ. Likewise, "they that will be rich" no longer think properly about eternal things.

The word *hurtful* is *blaberos,* which occurs only here in the New Testament and conveys the idea of injuring, marring, and damaging. The emphasis in this verse is on the injury done to a man's soul by his determination to become rich.

The word translated "lusts" here is *epithumia,* which denotes evil desires. Galatians 5:16, 24 refers to the lusts of the flesh. The consuming passion to be rich opens the door to various lusts, all of which are "foolish and hurtful."

(2) The trap exposed (6:9c)

Even worse, these lusts are calculated to "drown men in destruction and perdition." The word translated "destruction" here is *olethros,* which carries the idea of ruin. Paul used the same word when he told the Corinthians to hand the incestuous man over to Satan "for the destruction of the flesh" (1 Cor. 5:5). The apostle also used *olethros* to refer to the "sudden destruction" that will come upon the earth after the rapture of the church (1 Thess. 5:3) and the "everlasting destruction" that awaits the ungodly (2 Thess. 1:9).

The word translated "perdition" in 1 Timothy 6:9 indicates loss of well-being, not loss of being. The word is used to refer to the Antichrist, who is called "the son of perdition" in 2 Thessalonians 2:3, and to Judas, who is similarly described in 17:12. W. E. Vine explains what Paul has in mind here—"the consequences of the indulgence of the flesh" (physical ruin, and possibly that of the whole being) and also "the final, eternal and irrevocable character of that ruin."[20]

Judas furnishes us with a terrible example of what can happen once the illegitimate pursuit of wealth is given reign. He began by dipping into the bag. Then he sold Christ to His enemies for a handful of silver. Finally, he committed suicide.

d. A basic fallacy (6:10)

"The love of money," Paul wrote, "is the root of all evil: which while some coveted after, they have erred from the faith, and pierced themselves through with many sorrows."

Fondness for money led Achan to his downfall. He was a member of the tribe of Judah and a soldier in Joshua's army at the time Jericho was delivered into the hands of Israel. The city was under a curse, and only Rahab and those who sought shelter under her roof were exempt from the approaching doom. The divine

20. Ibid., 1:304.

proclamation regarding the spoils of Jericho was crystal clear: "Keep yourselves from the accursed thing, lest ye make yourselves accursed, when ye take of the accursed thing, and make the camp of Israel a curse, and trouble it. But all the silver, and gold, and vessels of brass and iron, are consecrated unto the LORD: they shall come into the treasury of the LORD" (Josh. 6:18–19).

The battle went according to plan, and Jericho fell. The spoil was collected and put into the treasury of the house of the Lord. Rahab and her relatives were saved. Jericho was burned, and the site was cursed. All seemed to be well—until Achan's sin was exposed.

When the spoil of a fallen city was collected, Achan saw "a goodly Babylonish garment, and two hundred shekels of silver, and a wedge of gold." The love of money took hold of his heart. "I coveted them," he later confessed, "and took them" (Josh. 7:21).

At first, Achan thought that he had pulled off a coup. But things went wrong. The next battle was against the small town of Ai. There the Israelites suffered a disastrous and humiliating defeat. Thirty-six men lost their lives, all because there was sin in the Hebrew camp. Achan had "erred from the faith" because of his fondness for money. Joshua cast lots to determine who was to blame.

Imagine the mounting horror in Achan's soul as the accusing finger pointed more and more in his direction. First, the lot fell on the tribe of Judah, then on the family of the Zarhites, then on the household of Zabdi, and then on Achan, the son of Carmi. Truly, Achan was pierced through with many sorrows. His forced and belated confession did him no good. He was responsible for the death of three dozen soldiers and had brought public shame on himself and his entire family. His ill-gotten gains were displayed before the nation as proof of his guilt, and the terrible sentence was passed. The curse fell on him and his family, who evidently had joined his conspiracy. They were put to death, and a heap of stones was piled over their bodies as a warning to everyone of the high cost of substituting gold for God.

Today, we might not see such dramatic demonstrations of the price to be paid for fondness for money, but those who pursue wealth still "pierce themselves through with many sorrows." The stories of Barbara Hutton (the Woolworth heiress whom the media often called "the poor little rich girl") and Howard Hughes (the billionaire who lived on junk food, was terrified of contracting a disease from casual contact with a passerby, and died a recluse) illustrate Paul's point in 1 Timothy 6:10.

We do not have to look far for proof that "the love of money is the root of all evil." Some people will do anything for money. During the Prohibition Era in the United States, Al Capone and other gangsters committed countless crimes to pile up money. The love of money motivates those who manufacture, smuggle, and sell illegal drugs. The love of money is the driving force behind the Mafia and other crime syndicates. Prostitution, gambling, loan-sharking, and racketeering are their stock in trade. Giant industries have been known to oppress workers and start wars for the sake of bigger profits. Truly, "the love of money is the root of all evil."

4. The pursuit of goodness (6:11–19)
   a. The challenge to Timothy (6:11–12)
      (1) To flee (6:11a)

Paul challenged Timothy, "But thou, O man of God, flee these things." The title "man of God," which is rarely used in the Bible, puts Timothy in some outstanding company. In the Old Testament, the title was usually reserved for a prophet. For example, Moses was called "the man of God" in Deuteronomy 33:1. The mother of Samson saw an angel and described him to her husband as "a man of God" (Judg. 13:6). The prophet who came to denounce Eli, the careless priest, was called "a man of God" (1 Sam. 2:27), as was the prophet who came to Bethel to pronounce God's judgment on Jeroboam and his calf cult (1 Kings 13:1). Elijah was called "man of God" (2 Kings 1:9) and now Timothy was too. He is the last "man of God" in the Bible. The title was intended to vest Timothy with dignity, to add to his authority, and to contrast him with those who were consumed by the love of money. They were not and could not be men of God.

And what did Paul want this "man of God" to do? "Flee!" That is about the last thing we would expect a man of God to do. We would probably have told him to fight. Yet, Elijah once took to his heels. After he single-handedly had taken on all of the power of the enemy and won a resounding victory over the Baal cult on Mount Carmel (1 Kings 18–19), Jezebel threatened to kill him. That, however, was not what Paul was talking about. Not long afterward, God chose Elijah's successor because Elijah ran away from the post of duty and danger.

Paul wanted Timothy to flee from the desire to be rich as if it were the plague. The medieval monks tried to flee by taking vows of poverty; joining mendicant orders; locking themselves up in bleak, prisonlike cells in cold monasteries; and enduring prolonged privations and fasts. But in time the monasteries grew rich and so powerful that they rivaled even kings on their thrones. Paul did not have that kind of flight on his mind either.

The best way to flee the lure of wealth is to seek refuge in the arms of Jesus, who, though He was rich, for our sakes became poor so that we, through His poverty, might become rich (2 Cor. 8:9). The riches that Paul had in mind were not material things but inexhaustible spiritual riches about which he had already written to the Ephesians (Eph. 2:7; 4:7).

(2) To follow (6:11b–g)

(a) The divine character described (6:11b–c)

Paul told Timothy (and us) to "follow after righteousness, godliness." In other words, we are to flee *from* worldliness, as epitomized by the craving for wealth, *to* Christlikeness. The divine character is described by the words *righteousness* and *godliness.* When we become Christlike, "righteousness" describes our *integrity toward man* and "godliness" describes our *integrity toward God.*

The Lord Jesus displayed absolute righteousness. He always did what was right. He "went about doing good" (Acts 10:38). He also exhibited flawless godliness. He could say, "I do always those things that please [the Father]" (John 8:29).

(b) The divine character distilled (6:11d–e)

Paul also told Timothy (and us) to "follow after . . . faith, love." The word *faith* directs our attention to the *Word of God* because "faith cometh by hearing, and hearing by the word of God" (Rom. 10:17). The Lord Jesus lived in accordance with the Word of God at all times. He said, "Lo, I come (in the volume of the book it is written of me) to do thy will, O God" (Heb. 10:7; Ps. 40:7).

The word *love* directs our attention to the *Spirit of God* (2 Tim. 1:7). The Lord Jesus lived His life in the power of the Spirit of God (Matt. 3:16–17; John 3:34).

(c) The divine character displayed (6:11f–g)

Paul told Timothy (and us) to "follow after . . . patience, meekness." The divine character is displayed in patience and meekness. In Revelation 1:9, John, who had known the Lord Jesus so well, reminded us of the "patience of Jesus Christ." How patient He was! He waited from before the foundation of the world to come to earth to consummate the redemptive purposes of God. He waited another thirty years before He moved onto the public stage. He has already been waiting two thousand years for the time when He will come again. And how patiently He dealt with His disciples when they were so slow to believe (Luke 24:25)! He is just as patient with us.

Christ demonstrated meekness by holding His almighty power in check. He spoke of His meekness and offered it to us: "Take my yoke upon you, and learn of me," He said, "for I am meek and lowly in heart" (Matt. 11:29).

The six words that Paul used in 1 Timothy 6:11 to describe the character of Christ—"righteousness, godliness, faith, love, patience, meekness"—should describe the character of every Christian. If we "follow after" all six characteristics, we will find that we have fled effectively from the love of money and all of its attendant evils.

(3) To fight (6:12)

(a) A word of command (6:12a–b)

i. Don't give up! (6:12a)

Paul challenged Timothy to "fight the good fight of faith." The verb *fight* here is one connected with public games. In 6:12, it means "to strive, as in a contest, for the prize." Paul knew all about the Greek games. He came from Tarsus, a Greek city in Asia Minor. Timothy's father was a Greek, and Timothy himself was raised in a Greek city, so we can assume that Timothy understood fully Paul's command to get into the ring and fight. He knew that the contest was not for the timid. According to Kenneth Wuest, "the gloves of the Greek boxer were fur lined on the inside, but made on the outside of ox-hide with lead and iron sewed into it . . . the loser in a wrestling match had his eyes gouged out. . . . Thus, the word 'fight' had a very definite meaning for Timothy."[21]

The noun form of the word *fight* in 6:12 draws attention to the arena where the fight was to take place. Timothy was called upon to fight for the faith, the revealed body of New Testament truth.

ii. Don't let go! (6:12b)

"Lay hold on eternal life," Paul added. The word translated "lay hold on" here can also be rendered "keep your grip on." Paul urged Timothy to appropriate

---

21. Kenneth S. Wuest, *The Pastoral Epistles in the Greek New Testament* (Grand Rapids: Eerdmans, 1952), 97.

practically the benefits, privileges, and responsibilities involved in the possession of eternal life. It is one thing to be saved but quite another to translate that salvation into daily living.

Paul knew what Timothy was up against in Ephesus. He had been up against the same kind of thing in Galatia, Jerusalem, and Corinth, but he was a fighter. Timothy did not have Paul's tough fiber, so Paul sought to infuse a fighting spirit into his more retiring comrade. It was no time to stand on the sidelines. Christianity is for contestants, not spectators.

(b) A word of commendation (6:12c–d)

Paul commended Timothy: "Whereunto thou art also called, and hast professed a good profession before many witnesses." Timothy responded to the call of God when he accepted Christ. That call included a summons to battle because this world is enemy territory, and there can be no neutrality. God will make no compromise with Satan, and Satan will honor no believer's attempt to be neutral. Like it or not, Timothy was already in the ring.

The word *profession* refers to Timothy's confession of faith. Some Bible scholars think that Paul was referring specifically to the confession that Timothy had made at the time of his baptism. Baptism was a bold step for both Jews and Gentiles in those days. The immersion in a river or lake took place in public view, with both believers and unbelievers watching. Some onlookers were merely curious, others were distinctly hostile, and still others scoffed openly. It was no small thing to confess one's faith publicly. Often, such a confession resulted in persecution. Sometimes, however, it led to conversions.

Whether Paul was referring to Timothy's baptism or to his loyalty to Christ and the apostle, his words were commendatory. Timothy might have had a timid disposition, but he was man enough in Christ to overcome it.

b. The charge to Timothy (6:13–19)
(1) The exhortation (6:13a–b)
(a) The presence of God (6:13a)

Paul gave Timothy a fresh charge. There was a job to be done in Ephesus. Paul would like to have been there in person to attend to the work himself, but that was not possible. Timothy would have to do it. Paul could not be with him, but his young colleague would not have to stand alone because God was with him.

His presence would change the picture. "I give thee charge in the sight of God," Paul said, reassuring Timothy.

Just the presence of an angel changed the picture on resurrection morning. "The angel of the Lord descended from heaven, and came and rolled back the stone from the door, and sat upon it. His countenance was like lightning, and his raiment white as snow: And for fear of him the keepers did shake, and became as dead men" (Matt. 28:2–4). If a mere angel had that effect, what difference does the presence of God make? For fear of Him the Devil himself trembles!

(b) The power of God (6:13b)

Paul also reminded Timothy of the power of God. He is the one "who quickeneth all things." The word *quickeneth* here means "to preserve alive" or "to endue with life." Nero's agents even then were killing many Christians in Rome, and Paul counted himself as a "sheep for the slaughter" (Rom. 8:36). But no one could harm Timothy without God's express permission. Even if the enemies of the Cross were to kill him, they would kill only his body—and they could not keep him dead. For a Christian, death simply opens the gates of glory (Phil. 1:23). Timothy had the sure and certain hope of resurrection, so he had nothing to fear.

(2) The example (6:13c–14)
(a) The Lord's confession (6:13c)

Paul charged Timothy "before Christ Jesus, who before Pontius Pilate witnessed a good confession." Paul wanted Timothy to think of Christ's boldness before the man who claimed to have the power to put Him to death. "Thou couldest have no power at all against me," Jesus calmly told him, "except it were given thee from above" (John 19:11). In the end, it was Pilate who retired from the confrontation in fear and shame. Timothy, like the Lord, was to witness boldly to the truth.

The Lord knew all about Timothy's natural fears. He who had faced the worst that men could do was ready to stand by Timothy. Timothy was in the presence of the Lord.

(b) The Lord's coming (6:14)

Paul turned from the past to the future. "Keep this commandment without spot, unrebukeable," he reminded Timothy, "until the appearing of our Lord Jesus

Christ." Apparently, the "commandment" is the one that Paul had just given Timothy in 6:11–12: "Flee . . . follow . . . fight." Timothy needed to ensure that no one would ever be able to accuse him of compromise, carelessness, or cowardice.

The word translated "without spot" here calls upon us to keep ourselves free from all uncleanness, and the word *unrebukable* demands that we live beyond all censure.

A powerful motive for not faltering is the prospect of the Lord's personal return. That hope burned bright in Timothy's days only three decades after Calvary. The word translated "the appearing" in 6:14 is *epiphaneia.* It is one of three words generally used throughout the New Testament to describe the Lord's return.

The first word is *parousia,* which spoke of the arrival of a king. It occurs two dozen times, initially in the introduction to the Lord's prophetic discourse (Matt. 24:3). *Parousia* is commonly used to depict what we call the Rapture, but not always; in 2 Thessalonians 2:8, for example, it refers to the coming of the Lord to destroy the Man of Sin. The word occurs seven times in Paul's two letters to the Thessalonians: it refers to the Lord's coming in 1 Thessalonians 2:19; 3:13; 4:15; 5:23; 2 Thessalonians 2:1, 8; it refers to the coming of the Antichrist in 2 Thessalonians 2:9.

The second word is *apokalupsis,* which means "unveiling" or "revelation." We often speak of the book of Revelation as the Apocalypse because it describes the unveiling of Jesus Christ (Rev. 1:1). The word also occurs, for instance, in 1 Corinthians 1:7; 2 Thessalonians 1:7; 1 Peter 1:7. *Apokalupsis,* which emphasizes the Lord's visible return, is used in connection with both the rapture of the church and the Lord's ultimate return to this planet in power and great glory.

The third word is *epiphaneia,* which, as noted before, Paul used in 1 Timothy 6:14. It means literally "a shining forth." In 2 Thessalonians 2:8, it is used in the description of the Lord's coming to destroy the Antichrist "with the brightness *[epiphaneia]* of his coming *[parousia].*" There Paul is speaking of Christ's coming to earth to reign.

Timothy, of course, was thoroughly at home with Paul's second advent teaching, especially as revealed in the Thessalonian epistles. In writing to Timothy, the apostle did not need to redefine the difference between Christ's coming in the air for the church and His subsequent return to the earth with the church. Timothy knew all about the judgment seat of Christ and the rebukes and rewards to be dispensed. Timothy knew that rewarded believers will reign with the Lord when He displays His glory and returns to the earth with His spotless bride. So Paul could use "the appearing of our Lord Jesus Christ" as a powerful incentive for his young friend to discharge honorably the duties laid on him by the Lord.

(3) The exclamation (6:15–16)

(a) The moment of revelation (6:15a)

Paul's mind soared with the triumphant thought of the Lord's return, "which in his times he shall shew." His day is coming. Today, man is on the throne, and he carries on as if there were no Christ, no God, no revealed truth, and no judgment. But the Lord will come in His own time.

The disciples asked the Lord about the timing of His return as they made their way to the Mount of Olives, where they were to witness His ascension. "Lord, wilt thou at this time restore again the kingdom to Israel?" they asked. He replied, "It is not for you to know the times or the seasons, which the Father hath put in his own power" (Acts 1:6–7). The time appointed for the Rapture is secret (Matt. 24:36), and any attempt to calculate the date is doomed to fail. Paul was content to leave the timing with God, but he had every confidence that the Rapture would take place. The moment of the *epiphaneia* is as certain as was the moment of Christ's birth.

(b) The marvel of revelation (6:15b–16)

i. One who is absolute in power (6:15b–d)

The prospect of the Lord's return gave wings to Paul's meditation. He saw the Lord as *the ruling One* ("the blessed and only Potentate"), *the royal One* ("the King of kings"), and *the reigning One* ("Lord of lords"). Paul thought of Christ in terms of absolute power.

In Rome, a mean and miserable monster of a man named Nero sat on the throne and ruled a great world empire. He used his power to persecute the church with utmost savagery; yet, Paul barely spared him a thought. He knew that a greater King than the Caesar was ruling a greater realm than Rome.

The word translated "potentate" gives us our word *dynasty*. It means "mighty prince." In the New Testament, it is used in reference to the Lord only in this passage. It occurs two other times: to describe earthly rulers in Luke 1:52 and to describe the Ethiopian eunuch in Acts 8:27. The word is akin to *dunamis,* which refers to untrammeled, unequaled power.

Jesus is the "blessed" Potentate in contrast to bestial Nero. The word translated "blessed" here is *makarios,* which means "happy." It is used in reference to God in 1 Timothy 1:11. We have a happy God, a happy Ruler! He stands alone, altogether happy and altogether powerful.

Paul saw Christ as "the King of kings, and Lord of lords;" and Revelation 19 tells us that John did too. John saw Him coming from heaven to "judge and make war. His eyes were as a flame of fire, and on his head were many crowns; . . . he was clothed with a vesture dipped in blood." Calvary was about to be avenged. The armies of heaven streamed forth in His train, and the terrible sword of the Lord was unsheathed. The armies of the earth assembled in vast numbers at Megiddo, and carrion birds flocked to the feast. His name was emblazoned on His vesture and on His thigh: "King of kings, and Lord of lords." The world was soon to discover who was in control.

We can picture the Satan-filled Antichrist, the demonic false prophet, the kings of the earth, and the armies of the world that have "gathered together to make war against him . . . and against his army." As well might a snowflake declare war on an inferno! With a flash of the sword, the war is over. So much for the "battle" of Armageddon! "And the winepress [is] trodden without the city," and blood flows in a crimson tide as high as a horse's bridle for "a thousand and six hundred furlongs" (Rev. 14:20). The Beast and the False Prophet are captured alive and cast into the lake of fire, and the Devil is arrested and locked up in the bottomless pit. Thus, at last, it is proved to the world that Christ is "the blessed and only Potentate, the King of kings, and Lord of lords."

In effect, Paul was saying in 1 Timothy 6:15, "Cheer up, Timothy. Just take another look at Jesus. He's in control. He's coming back."

ii. One who is ageless in person (6:16a)

Continuing his description of the Lord Jesus, Paul wrote, "Who only hath immortality." The word translated "immortality" here is *athanasia,* which means "deathlessness." It is used to describe the immortality of the glorified body of the believer in 1 Corinthians 15:53–54. As used in the New Testament, this word suggests not only endlessness of days but also a remarkable, altogether new quality of life (2 Cor. 5:4).

Jesus conquered death both for Himself and for His own. "I am he that liveth, and was dead," He said, "and, behold, I am alive for evermore, Amen; and have the keys of hell and of death" (Rev. 1:18). It is true that unless the Rapture comes first, we

Christians must die; but, thanks be to Him, "death is swallowed up in victory." Hence, we sing, "O death, where is thy sting? O grave, where is thy victory?" (1 Cor. 15:54–55). We are going to have a body "like unto his glorious body" (Phil. 3:21).

When the Lord rose from the dead, He at once displayed the remarkable properties of His resurrection body. He could pass through a wall and materialize in the Upper Room (John 20:19; Luke 24:36–39); eat a meal (Luke 24:41–43); be touched and seen (John 20:24–28); appear and disappear at will (Luke 24:13–16, 30–31); and, defying the law of gravity, rise to the clouds (Acts 1:9). In His body, He has been seated in heaven for some two thousand years. He does not grow old. He rules the galaxies, watches events on earth, outshines the sun, and lives on and on in "joy unspeakable and full of glory" (1 Peter 1:8). His body is tireless, deathless, and ageless. Cheer up, Timothy!

iii. One who is awesome in presence (6:16b–c)

a. Inaccessible—bathed in fearful light (6:16b)

Paul went on to describe the Lord as "dwelling in the light which no man can approach unto." The apostle was writing from personal experience; when he first met the ascended Christ, He was bathed in blinding light. Paul had been on his way to Damascus to despoil the church there. Known then as Saul of Tarsus, he was armed with letters of authority from the Sanhedrin. Later, he recalled, "As I made my journey . . . suddenly there shone from heaven a great light round about me. And I fell unto the ground" (Acts 22:6–7). In describing the experience to King Agrippa, Paul said, "At midday, O king, I saw in the way a light from heaven, above the brightness of the sun, shining round about me and them which journeyed with me" (Acts 26:13). One and all, they fell to the ground.

Such is the light with which Christ surrounds Himself in glory. Even the shining seraphim, sinless sons of light though they are, cannot bear to gaze on "the brightness of his glory" (Heb. 1:3); they hide their faces in their wings (Isa. 6:1–3).

With such an awesome Lord, Timothy did not have to be intimidated. Neither do we. As the hymn writer reminded us,

> Ye saints of God fresh courage take,
> The clouds ye so much dread
> Are big with mercy, and shall break
> In blessings on your head.[22]

22. From the hymn "God Moves in a Mysterious Way" by William Cowper.

The Lord is inaccessible—but not to His own. For us, death will simply mean that we are "absent from the body . . . present with the Lord" (2 Cor. 5:8).

b. Invisible—beyond all finite sight (6:16c)

Paul also referred to the Lord as the One "whom no man hath seen, nor can see." The thought here seems to be that the Lord conceals His person in dazzling light. Apparently, the primary reference in 6:16c is to the Father. We should remember, however, that the Lord Jesus had the power to make Himself invisible at will (Luke 24:31).

iv. One who is arrayed in praise (6:16d–e)

Paul gives Timothy another encouraging reminder. Our Lord has *everlasting acclaim* and *everlasting authority*: "To whom be honour and power everlasting. Amen." The word translated "power" here is *kratos,* which refers to power put forth with effect and in government.

Caesar had power that seemed to be almost limitless, and he wielded it in terrible ways. Yet, above Roman power was a mightier power wielded by Satan's principalities, powers, rulers of this world's darkness, and wicked spirits in high places (Eph. 6:12). His forces, motivated by dreadful malice and implacable hostility toward humanity, still brood over nations and empires and promote every kind of ill for the children of men. Satan's power is awesome, but even greater than that is Christ's power.

There He sits on His Father's throne in heaven. In His hand is the scepter of universal power and dominion. He pursues His eternal purposes. During this age of grace, He moves mostly unperceived and behind the scenes. We do not know a tithe of His eternal plans, so we often cannot trace the whys and wherefores of His ways. We do know, however, that no power, might, or authority is greater than His. And we do know that He is exercising His authority and power in government. God's will is being done on earth as it is in heaven. "The heavens do rule" (Dan. 4:26). Our problem is with our shortsightedness.

"Cheer up, Timothy!" we can almost hear Paul say. Paul appends a resounding "Amen!" to all of this. Surely Timothy echoed that triumphant word. Surely we can do the same! He could be cheered by the knowledge that he was on the winning side.

(4) The expectation (6:17–19)

(a) The rich man and his goal (6:17)

i. What he must renounce (6:17a–b)

When Paul takes us on such lofty flights, he always brings us back down to earth with a bump. He does that here by returning to the discussion that led to the side excursion into the heavenlies. He now comes back to his discussion of rich men and their gold: "Charge them that are rich in this world, that they be not highminded, nor trust in uncertain riches."

One of the snares of wealth is that it gives rich people a false sense of security and power. Their money can buy most things, shield them from many ills, and smooth their way through life. Poor people tend to turn to God; rich people tend to rely on gold. Money, however, has a way of disappearing. All it takes is a few bad investments, or a disastrous crash on Wall Street, or an encounter with a thief or swindler, and suddenly the rich man is rich no more.

Worse still, money tends to foster a materialistic outlook on life. The person who has plenty of money is in danger of leaving God out of his thoughts. For example, the rich young ruler of Luke 18:18–25 came to Christ but turned away sorrowfully when Jesus bluntly told him that his money stood in the way of his obtaining eternal life. The rich fool of Luke 12:16–21 was counting his money when the sentence of death sounded in his soul. The rich man of Luke 16:19–31 woke up in hell; he discovered too late how his money had blinded him to eternal reality.

Occasionally, a rich man remains untouched by his riches because he has renounced his trust in them. Abraham, Isaac, and Jacob lived above their wealth. Job lost all of his, but his loss strengthened his faith in God.

ii. What he must recognize (6:17c)

The rich man, Paul told Timothy, must trust "in the living God, who giveth us richly all things to enjoy." All good things come from God, but we must put our trust in the Giver, not the gift—whether it be money, good health, happy family life, or anything else.

James reminded us that "every good gift and every perfect gift is from above, and cometh down from the Father of lights, with whom is no variableness, neither shadow of turning" (James 1:17). There is no variation or shadow of inconsistency in God's character. He always does what is right and best—although His point of view is often quite different from ours (Isa. 55:8–9). God is too loving to be unkind, too wise to make any mistakes, and too powerful to be thwarted. He can be trusted absolutely.

(b) The rich man and his goal (6:18–19)

i. His present responsibility (6:18)

Timothy was to charge rich people "that they do good, that they be rich in good works, ready to distribute, willing to communicate." God entrusts some people with riches so that they can use them for the good of mankind. The rich person has a tremendous potential for doing good. Jesus told the rich young ruler, "Sell all that thou hast, and distribute unto the poor, and thou shalt have treasure in heaven" (Luke 18:22). The more wealth we have, the greater is our responsibility to help others.

ii. His prospective reward (6:19)

Wealthy people who fulfill their responsibility are "laying up in store for themselves a good foundation against the time to come, that they may lay hold on eternal life." Happy is the rich person who breaks the bondage of materialism imposed by his wealth and sees beyond time to eternity and beyond earthly riches to eternal rewards.

Many years ago, there lived a rich and highly respected man named Joseph. His reputation for goodness and fair-mindedness was well deserved. He had a seat in the governing body of the country. When the case of the young preacher from Nazareth came up, and the majority agreed with the president of the council that the preacher was a menace and ought to be put out of the way, Joseph cast a dissenting vote.

Years earlier, Joseph had begun to think about his own death and the need he would have for a tomb. He bought a cave near a skull-shaped hill in the environs of Jerusalem and hired workmen to shape the cave into a family sepulcher. He thought fondly of his final resting place in the Holy City where he would await the resurrection.

Joseph likely discussed spiritual things from time to time with one of his colleagues, a man named Nicodemus who had become a secret disciple of Jesus. Joseph himself "waited for the kingdom of God" (Luke 23:51). He was doubtless deeply moved by what Nicodemus told him about his midnight talk with Jesus.

Events moved swiftly after Jesus was arrested. He was falsely accused, condemned, and crucified. Joseph realized that Jesus needed a tomb urgently. He thought of his own sepulcher. He had spent a lot of money preparing it for himself and had long cherished the thought of being buried there. He put all of that on the altar, however, and gave his tomb to Jesus. Joseph counted on his wealth, name, and influence to secure an audience with Pilate and to win permission to bury Jesus—before Caiaphas and his crowd could claim the body and desecrate it. Joseph followed through with his new plan. He would provide the sepulcher; Nicodemus could provide the spices. Together, they would confront the Sanhedrin with a *fait accompli.*

So it was that an ancient prophecy was fulfilled. The Lord's enemies planned for Him a "grave with the wicked," but God saw to it that He was "with the rich in his death" (Isa. 53:9). Joseph and Nicodemus used their wealth to lay up treasure in heaven. Great will be their reward in heaven. Their reward on earth has been great, too, for what they did was recorded in the Word of God. Their story has been told and retold in almost every language under heaven for nearly two thousand years.

The words translated "eternal life" in 1 Timothy 6:19 can perhaps be rendered as "the life that is life indeed." When Joseph gave up the tomb he treasured, he was not a loser. His memory is revered to this day in countless lands. So is that of Nicodemus. After Christ's resurrection, the tomb remained vacant and became sacred to the Lord's memory. No doubt, every time Joseph went past that empty sepulcher, his heart leaped for joy. When he first planned the tomb, he had doubtless been preoccupied with his own death. Now the empty tomb spoke to him of life. We can be sure that thereafter Joseph thought little of where his own bones would rest. He would be with Jesus, enjoying "the life that is life indeed." Likewise, we ought to invest what we have, be it little or much, in the "eternal life" and keep "the time to come" uppermost in our minds.

PART 4

Conclusion

1 Timothy 6:20–21

A. A pleading word (6:20–21a)
   1. A duty recorded (6:20a)

O Timothy," Paul wrote, "keep that which is committed to thy trust." What a wealth of warmth is in that little word *O!* An angel used that word when talking to Daniel: "O Daniel, a man greatly beloved" (Dan. 10:11). David used that word as he wept over his beloved Absalom: "O my son Absalom, my son, my son Absalom! Would God I had died for thee, O Absalom, my son, my son!" (2 Sam. 18:33).

How Paul's great heart yearned over his young colleague! He knew Timothy's strengths and weaknesses. The two men had been together a long time. They had tramped side by side over hill and dale. They had leaned together over many a ship's railing and watched the sun set behind the sea. Together, they had brought the glorious gospel of Christ to city after city—to the Jew first and also to the Gentile.

Paul knew about Timothy's frequent illnesses and retiring disposition; yet, he had sent him on more than one difficult assignment, and each time Timothy had been willing to go. Paul loved him as though he were his son. All of his heart went into that "O Timothy"!

Was Timothy faltering? Was he in danger of surrendering some aspect of doctrinal truth? Was he retreating before the subtle, persistent efforts of a cult? Was he backing down because of the scorn of those who disagreed with Paul's teaching? Was Timothy in danger of being bought by a wealthy member of the Ephesian church? Paul's tone makes us wonder.

"Keep that which is committed to thy trust," Paul continued. The word translated "keep" means "to guard, keep watch, beware." The Greeks used the word in military contexts. A soldier on guard has only one duty: to stay awake and watch over that which has been entrusted to his care. To fulfill his duty, he checks to see if doors are locked, patrols constantly the perimeter of the area for which he is responsible, and ensures that all is well. He looks out for any enemy action and challenges anyone who approaches. He does not allow his attention to wander, even to things in which he might otherwise have a legitimate interest.

This picture of a soldier on guard reminds us of the story that one of the sons of the prophets (in disguise) told to king Ahab: "Thy servant went out into the midst of the battle; and, behold, a man turned aside, and brought a man unto me, and said, Keep this man: if by any means he be missing, then shall thy life be for his life, or else thou shalt pay a talent of silver. And as thy servant was *busy here and there,* he was gone" (1 Kings 20:39–40, italics added).

Ahab responded to the confession at once: "So shall thy judgment be."

The storyteller removed his disguise and said to the king: "Thus saith the LORD, Because thou hast let go out of thy hand a man whom I appointed to utter destruction, therefore thy life shall go for his life" (20:42).

Was Timothy in danger of being 'busy here and there" and consequently allowing the precious truth that he was to guard to be stolen away? It would seem so because Paul admonished him with the warning word *keep* after addressing him with the warm word *O.*

2. A detour recommended (6:20b–21a)
   a. The danger is revealed (6:20b–c)
      (1) Patently silly opinions (6:20b)

Timothy was to be on guard lest he be caught up in "profane and vain babblings." Here we have one of two extremes.

The word translated "profane" means literally "to be trodden" (as a threshold is trodden) or "to be unhallowed." Esau is called "profane" (Heb. 12:16) because he had no interest in the things of God. He sold his spiritual birthright for a bowl of stew. Later, he tried to secure the patriarchal blessing in exchange for well-spiced venison. More! Having displeased his father by marrying a couple of pagan women, Esau tried to make amends by marrying a daughter of Ishmael. These examples are enough. Esau was profane.

The word translated "vain babblings" points to empty discussions. Much talk about nothing.

Taken together, "profane and vain babblings" bring to mind the kind of people whose lack of contact with God leads them to pursue the discussion of useless subjects. The rabbis, for instance, debated endlessly what constituted a violation of the Sabbath. They came up with absurd and burdensome conclusions. More current are the New Age philosophers who surround themselves with trash and trivia—as anyone can see by walking through one of their bookstores. Similarly, leaders of oriental cults invite us to explore the myth of reincarnation and to conjure in our imaginations the lives we supposedly have already lived in our progress toward the ultimate goal of nothingness *(nirvana).* Paul summarized the discussions of all such people as "profane and vain babblings."

(2) Popular "scientific" oppositions (6:20c)

The other extreme is "oppositions of science falsely so called." Such "oppositions," like the "babblings," are a monumental waste of time. The word translated "oppositions" is *antithesis,* which means "a contrary position." The word for "science" means simply "knowledge." The definite article in the Greek implies some special kind of "knowledge" being used to contradict the sound doctrine that Timothy was commissioned to guard. The word translated "falsely so called" is *pseudōnumos,* which occurs only here in the New Testament. In 6:20c, Paul was warning Timothy against primarily the false knowledge touted by the Gnostics. Those false teachers became the church's most dangerous enemies in the second century.

We could well link "oppositions of science falsely called" with the modern theory of evolution, which is possibly the single most dangerous enemy that the church has ever had to face. Opposition to the gospel existed, of course, long before Darwin; but his theory of evolution gave men such as T. H. Huxley the tool they lacked. Huxley seized upon the theory as a working hypothesis for atheism, a way of explaining the universe without God.

After well over a hundred years of research, the theory of evolution remains just that—a theory, and one singularly full of holes. It has prompted countless scientists to engage in a lifelong pursuit of a mirage, and it has undermined the faith of millions. Translated into pragmatic politics, evolution endorses the view that might is right.

"Oppositions of science falsely so called" can be deadly. The temptation is to get sidetracked into fighting them. Paul's word to Timothy was to avoid them. The word for "avoiding" means simply "to turn away." Getting embroiled in discussions with people who want to argue with us over either trivia or false theories is counterproductive. Such involvement turns us aside from our main task. As D. L. Moody used to say, "The main thing is to keep the main thing the main thing."

b. The danger is real (6:21a)

Referring to false doctrines, Paul added, "Which some professing have erred concerning the faith." Some people whom he knew had been taken in by the clever arguments of cultists.

Paul's advice to Timothy to avoid getting involved with cultists was not unusual. The apostle's advice to the Romans was the same: "Mark them which cause divisions and offences contrary to the doctrine which ye have learned; and avoid them. For they that are such serve not our Lord Jesus Christ" (Rom. 16:17–18). Paul knew from his wide experience in dealing with them that they were slippery customers. They still are!

The Devil goes after the mind. In 2 Corinthians 4:3–4, Paul said, "If our gospel be hid, it is hid to them that are lost: In whom the god of this world hath blinded the minds of them which believe not, lest the light of the glorious gospel of Christ, who is the image of God, should shine unto them."

Satan is behind all false teachings, and he is diabolically clever. He bends and warps and twists the minds of men until they believe the most arrant nonsense. The Devil wraps his lies and deceptions in enough truth to make them seem right and reasonable, so it is sometimes difficult to untangle the truth from the error. That is why otherwise clever people embrace satanic sophistries. Demons propagate these falsehoods and energize them with power to hold captive the minds of those who succumb to them. Unless we are especially equipped by the Holy Spirit to deal with Satan's wiles, we are well advised to avoid them.

God does not expect us to win arguments with cultists. He wants us to live in a way that will convict them and to love them in a way that will make them want to be converted. The Holy Spirit goes after the conscience (John 16:7–11) and the heart (2 Cor. 4:6).

B. A parting word (6:21b)

"Grace be with thee. Amen." That is Paul's closing word. John 1:17 tells us that "grace and truth came by Jesus Christ." Timothy had plenty of truth. He was at home in the Old Testament; his mother and grandmother had seen to that. He was also at home in the New Testament (most of it by then had been written); Paul had seen to that. The apostle had instructed Timothy in the doctrines of justification, redemption, reconciliation, sanctification, election, and glorification. He had been well taught in theology, Christology, pneumatology, angelology, ecclesiology, soteriology, bibliology, and eschatology.

Timothy had plenty of truth. What he needed was grace—grace to stand firm in Ephesus as Paul's vice-regent, as God's ambassador, and as the presiding pastor. He needed to stand firm in the face of doctrinal perils from within and dreadful persecutions from without. Timothy needed to stand firm in the all-encompassing, all-enabling, all-sufficient grace of the Lord Jesus Christ.

"Amen," said Paul.

"Amen," echoed all of the watching angels of God.

"Amen," agreed every believing heart in the congregation when Timothy read this letter to them.

"Amen," breathed the Holy Spirit who had guided Paul's pen.

"Amen," says the church in all ages. Amen!

Exploring
TITUS

Author's Note

The biblical order of the Pastoral Epistles is as follows:

- 1 Timothy
- 2 Timothy
- Titus

This commentary, however, follows the chronological order:

- 1 Timothy
- Titus
- 2 Timothy

Using this order of the books enables the reader to observe more closely the flow of events, ending with Paul's pending martyrdom.

Introduction to Titus

Titus, a pagan whom Paul led to Christ, became one of the apostle's most beloved and loyal supporters. Titus likely was a native of either Syria or Crete, a large island in the Mediterranean, lying south of Greece and north of Libya.

Crete loomed for a moment during Paul's fateful voyage to Rome, a voyage that ended in shipwreck on the island of Melita (Malta). As the incident is recorded in Acts 27, the vessel had hugged the eastern coastline of the Mediterranean as far as Cnidus, an important city at the extreme southwestern point of Asia Minor. The seasonal winds, however, were already proving troublesome, so the sailors turned south toward the island of Crete, which promised shelter from the boisterous waves and contrary winds. They managed to make Fair Havens, an anchorage on the island's southern coast that offered some relief from the storm. By then, however, the likelihood of frequent winter storms made further seafaring extremely dangerous. Paul, a seasoned traveler with memories of past shipwrecks (2 Cor. 11:25), urged that the ship remain in Fair Havens until spring. Unfortunately, the bay where the vessel was anchored was not a comfortable refuge, so the centurion sided with the ship's captain, who wanted to make a dash for the more inviting port of Phenice at the western end of Crete. A seductive south wind that "blew softly" (Acts 27:13) seemed to favor the captain's decision, so the attempt was made. The ship failed to make it.

We can picture Paul's standing in the stern of the vessel, watching Fair Havens drop out of sight, and wondering if he would live to see Crete again. Doubtless, his missionary zeal made him long to go ashore and preach the gospel to the Cretans. He did go back later and soon discovered that Crete was not an easy place to labor; the inhabitants were characterized by duplicity, wildness, and sensuality. Cretan Jews who were in Jerusalem on the Day of Pentecost (Acts 2:11) had probably carried Christianity to the island at an early date.

We do not know when or where Paul led Titus to Christ because although he was one of Paul's highly esteemed colaborers, Titus is not mentioned at all in the book of Acts. (He is mentioned in 2 Corinthians, Galatians, and 2 Timothy as well as the epistle to Titus.) Titus appears first in Scripture as Paul's companion in Antioch before the council in Jerusalem. Because Titus was a Gentile, Paul took him to that conference as a test case; Paul wanted to see if the Jewish church would receive a Gentile Christian unconditionally into its fellowship (cf. Gal. 2:3 and Acts 15).

We learn from the epistle to Titus that Paul had either sent Titus to Crete or left him there to deal with disorders that had arisen in the church. Titus had already done well as Paul's emissary to Corinth. No doubt, the experience he gained in dealing with the difficulties in the Corinthian church equipped him for coming to grips with the situation on Crete. He was a loyal friend, capable colleague, wise mediator, and brave warrior.

Both Titus and Timothy were young, gifted, and beloved by Paul; both of them were entrusted with delicate missions on more than one occasion. But there the similarities end. Titus and Timothy are a study in contrasts. Timothy was half Jew and half Gentile; Titus was a full-blooded Gentile. Paul circumcised Timothy because the young man was already half Jewish and making him a full Jew would increase his usefulness in dealing with Jews. Paul did no such thing with Titus. On the contrary, the apostle took advantage of Titus's uncircumcision to face down the Jerusalem church. There were differences in temperament as well. Timothy had a retiring disposition; Titus was made of tougher fiber and was less likely to be intimidated. We also note that Paul often associated Timothy with himself when addressing letters to various churches but never included Titus in his salutation. Also, Timothy appears here and there in the book of Acts; Titus appears nowhere in Acts.

After his release from his first Roman imprisonment, Paul visited Crete. While he was on the island, he doubtless did some evangelizing, pastoring, and teaching. Paul remained there long enough to form a sound opinion of the Cretan character but evidently not long enough to do much about organizing the Cretan churches. He delegated that task to Titus.

Paul's immediate purpose in writing to Titus was to summon him to Nicopolis and to tell him that Artemas or Tychicus would be replacing him on Crete. Paul expanded the letter by including instruction, exhortation, and guidelines for local churches. Although the epistle is brief, it is a veritable miniature manual for ministers and includes several outstanding doctrinal statements (e.g., 1:1–4; 3:11–14). As brief as the letter is, it contains forty-four words that occur nowhere else in the New Testament.

The name *Titus* was a name to be reckoned with in Paul's day. Vespasian, the conquering Roman general and founder of the Flavian dynasty, had a son named Titus. Vespasian was about to be proclaimed emperor (A.D. 69), and Titus was already on the road to fame. It was he who concluded the siege of Jerusalem (begun by Vespasian) and whose soldiers burned the Jewish temple to the ground in A.D. 70. In A.D. 79, Mount Vesuvius erupted and buried Pompeii. Titus became emperor that same year. The next year, he dedicated the coliseum in Rome where so many Christians were to die.

So the world had its Titus. But the church had a Titus too. The world's Titus found his way into history books; the church's Titus found his way into the Book of books. Doubtless, it was a high honor to have one's name written in the roster of the caesars, but it is a far greater honor to have one's name written in the Lamb's Book of Life and in the Word of God.

The Roman Titus had his hour of glory. The triumphal arch built in his honor survives to this day, but he is dead and gone. No one studies his history today hoping to learn lessons on how to live. On the other hand, the biblical Titus will have his triumph in a day to come. Today, people the world over study Paul's brief memo to him; they weigh every word and search out its significance. Titus the Roman will stand at the Great White Throne to answer for his deeds. Titus the Christian will stand at the judgment seat of Christ and hear the Lord's "Well done!" He will "shine as the brightness of the firmament" and "as the stars for ever and ever" (Dan. 12:3)

Complete Outline of Titus

PART 1: INTRODUCTION (1:1–4)

- A. Paul's salutation (1:1a–b)
  - 1. Paul was an available minister (1:1a)
  - 2. Paul was an authorized messenger (1:1b)
- B. Paul's subject (1:1c–3)
  - 1. God's people (1:1c–e)
    - a. They are a chosen people (1:1c)
    - b. They are a challenged people (1:1d)
    - c. They are a changed people (1:1e)
  - 2. God's promise (1:2)
    - a. The substance of our hope (1:2a)
    - b. The security of our hope (1:2b)
  - 3. God's preacher (1:3)
    - a. God's means for making the truth known (1:3a–b)
      - (1) The chosen moment (1:3a)
      - (2) The chosen method (1:3b)
    - b. God's man for making the truth known (1:3c–d)
      - (1) A commitment (1:3c)
      - (2) A commandment (1:3d)
- C. Paul's son (1:4)
  - 1. Titus: beloved of Paul (1:4a–b)
    - a. The unique element in Titus's conversion (1:4a)
    - b. The universal element in Titus's conversion (1:4b)
  - 2. Titus: blessed by Paul (1:4c–f)
    - a. The blessing given (1:4c–e)

- (1) Grace: the provision of God the Son (1:4c)
- (2) Mercy: the protection of God the Father (1:4d)
- (3) Peace: the product of God the Holy Spirit (1:4e)

b. The blessing guaranteed (1:4f)

PART 2: THE NAMING OF ELDERS IN THE LOCAL CHURCH (1:5–9)

A. Elders are to be family men (1:5–6)
1. Paul's authority revealed (1:5)
a. The decision (1:5a)
b. The disorder (1:5b)
c. The deterrent (1:5c)
d. The delegate (1:5d)
2. Parental authority revered (1:6)
a. The prospective elder as a person (1:6a)
b. The prospective elder as a partner (1:6b)
c. The prospective elder as a parent (1:6c–d)
(1) His children not accused of wrong behavior (1:6c)
(2) His children not accustomed to wrong behavior (1:6d)

B. Elders are to be faultless men (1:7)
1. The elder's position (1:7a–b)
a. Its corresponding requirement (1:7a)
b. Its corresponding responsibility (1:7b)
2. The elder's portrait 91:7c–g)
a. Not given to aggression (1:7c)
b. Not given to anger (1:7d)
c. Not given to alcohol (1:7e)
d. Not given to attack (1:7f)
e. Not given to affluence (1:7g)

C. Elders are to be friendly men (1:8)
1. What the elder loves (1:8a–b)
a. His demonstrable friendliness (1:8a)
b. His discriminating friendliness (1:8b)
2. How the elder lives (1:8c–f)
a. His public life (1:8c–d)
(1) He knows how to watch matters (1:8c)
(2) He knows how to weigh matters (1:8d)
b. His personal life (1:8e–f)

- (1) He lives a clean life (1:8e)
- (2) He lives a controlled life (1:8f)

D. Elders are to be faithful men (1:9)
1. Holding fast the Word of God (1:9a–b)
   a. Their trust in God's Word (1:9a)
   b. Their training in God's Word (1:9b)
2. Heralding forth the Word of God (1:9c–e)
   a. Their sound doctrine (1:9c)
   b. Their solemn duty (1:9d–e)
      (1) To exhort (1:9d)
      (2) To expose (1:9e)

PART 3: THE NATURE OF ERROR IN THE LOCAL CHURCH (1:10–16)

A. The motives of false teachers (1:10–11)
1. Facing our foes (1:10)
   a. What they are (1:10a–c)
      (1) They are disorderly (1:10a)
      (2) They are disputers (1:10b)
      (3) They are deceivers (1:10c)
   b. Who they were (1:10d)
2. Fighting our foes (1:11)
   a. The rule (1:11a)
   b. The reason (1:11b)
   c. The revelation (1:11c–d)
      (1) Of their message (1:11c)
      (2) Of their motives (1:11d)

B. The menace of false teachers (1:12–13)
1. Paul quoted a terrible testimony (1:12)
   a. The source of the quotation (1:12a)
   b. The substance of the quotation (1:12b–e)
      (1) The Cretans are liars (1:12b)
      (2) The Cretans are lawless (1:12c)
      (3) The Cretans are lazy (1:12d)
      (4) The Cretans are lustful (1:12e)
2. Paul quoted a true testimony (1:13)
   a. An endorsement of the Cretan character (1:13a)
   b. An enforcement of the Christian character (1:13b)

- C. The message of false teachers (1:14)
  - 1. Its content (1:14a–b)
    - a. Fabulous Jewish tales (1:14a)
    - b. False Jewish traditions (1:14b)
  - 2. Its intent (1:14c)
- D. The morals of false teachers (1:15–16)
  - 1. A contrast (1:15)
    - a. The pure person (1:15a)
    - b. The polluted person (1:15b–d)
      - (1) His polluted outward view (1:15b)
      - (2) His polluted inward values (1:15c–d)
        - (a) He is mentally depraved (1:15c)
        - (b) He is morally depraved (1:15d)
  - 2. A conclusion (1:16)
    - a. What false teachers profess (1:16a)
    - b. What false teachers practice (1:16b–e)
      - (1) A denial of God Himself (1:16b)
      - (2) A denial of goodness itself (1:16c–e)
        - (a) False teachers are repulsive (1:16c)
        - (b) False teachers are rebellious (1:16d)
        - (c) False teachers are reprobate (1:16e)

PART 4: THE NEED FOR EXERCISE IN THE LOCAL CHURCH (2:1–3:11)

- A. Personal exercise (2:1–15)
  - 1. Behavior in the church (2:1–10)
    - a. The sexes and their place (2:1–8)
      - (1) Those with the advantage of years (2:1–3)
        - (a) The men (2:1–2)
          - i. The right doctrine (2:1)
          - ii. The resulting deeds (2:2)
            - *a.* The aged men's solid maturity (2:2a–c)
              - *1.* Sober (2:2a)
              - *2.* Serious (2:2b)
              - *3.* Sagacious (2:2c)
            - *b.* The aged men's spiritual maturity (2:2d–f)
              - *1.* Godward (2:2d)
              - *2.* Manward (2:2e)

3. Selfward (2:2f)

(b) The matrons (2:3)

Noted for their:

i. Sanctity (2:3a)

ii. Sincerity (2:3b)

iii. Sobriety (2:3c)

iv. Sermons (2:3d)

(2) Those with the advantage of youth (2:4–8)

(a) The maidens (2:4–5)

Taught by the matrons to be:

i. Disciplined (2:4a)

ii. Devoted (2:4b–c)

a. In marriage (2:4b)

b. In motherhood (2:4c)

iii. Discreet (2:5a)

iv. Decent (2:5b)

v. Domesticated (2:5c–e)

a. They are to be guardians of the home (2:5c)

b. They are to be good from the heart (2:5d)

c. They are to be guided by their husbands (2:5e)

vi. Defenders (2:5f)

(b) The men (2:6–8)

i. Their sobriety (2:6)

ii. Their service (2:7a)

iii. Their soundness (2:7b)

iv. Their seriousness (2:7c)

v. Their sincerity (2:7d)

vi. Their speech (2:8)

a. Irreproachable (2:8a)

b. Irrefutable (2:8b)

b. The servants and their place (2:9–10)

(1) They are to serve diligently (2:9)

(a) Obeying submissively (2:9a)

(b) Obeying satisfactorily (2:9b)

(c) Obeying silently (2:9c)

(2) They are to serve differently (2:10a)

(3) They are to serve devotedly (2:10b)

- (4) They are to serve demonstrably (2:10c–d)
  - (a) To adorn the doctrine faithfully (2:10c)
  - (b) To adorn the doctrine fully (2:10d)

2. Beliefs in the church (2:11–15)
   - a. Present grace (2:11–12)
     - (1) The appearing of grace (2:11)
       - (a) Sovereign grace (2:11a)
       - (b) Saving grace (2:11b)
       - (c) Sufficient grace (2:11c)
     - (2) The appeal of grace (2:12)
       - (a) What it teaches us to repudiate (2:12a–b)
         - i. Ungodliness (2:12a)
         - ii. Unholiness (2:12b)
       - (b) What it teaches us to reproduce (2:12c–e)
         - i. Gravity (2:12c)
         - ii. Goodness (2:12d)
         - iii. Godliness (2:12e)
   - b. Promised glory (2:13–15)
     - (1) The prophetic aspect (2:13)
       - (a) The glory of our prospect (2:13a)
       - (b) The greatness of our prospect (2:13b)
     - (2) The present aspect (2:14)
       - (a) Who it was (2:14a)
       - (b) What it was (2:14b–c)
         - i. The cost of salvation (2:14b)
         - ii. The completeness of salvation (2:14c)
       - (c) Why it was (2:14d–f)
         - i. To purify us (2:14d)
         - ii. To possess us (2:14e)
         - iii. To perfect us (2:14f)
     - (3) The practical aspect (2:15)
       - (a) Paul's command to Titus (2:15a–b)
         - i. Titus's activity (2:15a)
         - ii. Titus's authority (2:15b)
       - (b) Paul's confidence in Titus (2:15c)

B. Practical exercise (3:1–11)
   1. The behavior of believers as subjects of the land (3:1–2)

- a. We must be submissive (3:1a)
- b. We must be supportive (3:1b–2)
  - (1) By our works (3:1b)
  - (2) By our words (3:2a)
  - (3) By our ways (3:2b–d)
    - (a) Our mildness (3:2b)
    - (b) Our manner (3:2c)
    - (c) Our meekness (3:2d)

2. The behavior of believers as saints of the Lord (3:3–11)
   - a. Remembering what we were (3:3–8)
     - (1) Our conduct (3:3)
       - (a) Our depraved minds (3:3a–c)
         - i. How dumb we were (3:3a)
         - ii. How disobedient we were (3:3b)
         - iii. How deceived we were (3:3c)
       - (b) Our depraved morals (3:3d–e)
         - i. Our wicked passions (3:3d)
         - ii. Our worldly pleasures (3:3e)
       - (c) Our depraved motives (3:3f–h)
         - i. Our evil disposition (3:3f)
         - ii. Our evil desires (3:3g)
         - iii. Our evil dislikes (3:3h)
     - (2) Our conversion (3:4–6)
       - (a) Revelation (3:4)
         - i. Of God's character (3:4a)
         - ii. Of God's compassion (3:4b)
       - (b) Revolution (3:5–6)
         - i. Our works excluded (3:5a)
         - ii. Our washing explained (3:5b–c)
           - *a.* The regeneration of the Holy Spirit (3:5b)
           - *b.* The renewing of the Holy Spirit (3:5c)
         - iii. Our wickedness expunged (3:6)
           - *a.* The measure of this change (3:6a)
           - *b.* The means of this change (3:6b)
     - (3) Our consummation (3:7)
       - (a) Law forever satisfied (3:7a)
       - (b) Life forever ratified (3:7b)

(4) Our confession (3:8)
(a) A great truth (3:8a)
(b) A great test (3:8b)
(c) A great trust (3:8c)
b. Remaining where we are (3:9–11)
(1) A stance to take (3:9)
(a) A requirement (3:9a–c)
i. Avoid foolish questions (3:9a)
ii. Avoid foolish quibbles (3:9b–c)
a. Jewish lists (3:9b)
b. Jewish laws (3:9c)
(b) A reason 93:9d)
(2) A stand to take (3:10–11)
(a) The heretic exposed (3:10a)
(b) The heretic examined (3:10b)
(c) The heretic excommunicated (3:10c–11)
i. His public conviction (3:10c)
ii. His personal condemnation (3:11)

PART 5: CONCLUSION (3:12–15)
A. Guidance for Titus (3:12–14)
1. As to his movements (3:12)
a. What he should do (3:12a)
b. Where he should go (3:12b)
2. As to his ministry (3:13–14)
a. The practical side (3:13)
b. The preaching side (3:14)
(1) The audience (3:14a)
(2) The admonition (3:14b)
B. Greetings for Titus (3:15a–b)
1. Personal greetings (3:15a)
2. Pastoral greetings (3:15b)
C. Grace for Titus (3:15c)

PART 1

Introduction

Titus 1:1–4

A. Paul's salutation (1:1a–b)
   1. Paul was an available minister (1:1a)

As was his custom, Paul authenticated this epistle with his signature. Immediately, he added a twofold description of himself: he was "a servant of God," and he was "an apostle of Jesus Christ." A "servant" of God! The Greek word is the usual word for a slave. Paul called himself here "a slave of God," a description that he uses nowhere else. No one valued his freedom more than Paul. He was born free, a citizen of Rome, and he was proud of it. In Acts 22, when the centurion wrote Paul off as just another troublemaking Jew and commanded him to be scourged, Paul said, "Is it lawful for you to scourge a man that is a Roman, and uncondemned?" The centurion alerted the chief captain, who came and said, "With a great sum obtained I this freedom."

Paul replied, "But I was free born."

Moreover, Paul battled fiercely to keep Jewish shackles off his Gentile converts. He stood up to the formidable James and even scolded Peter when Gentile freedom seemed imperiled. However, when Paul found himself a prisoner in Caesarea, and then later in Rome, he glorified his bonds. He was "the prisoner of Jesus Christ" (Eph. 3:1). He was not Nero's prisoner; he was God's willing slave.

From prison, Paul ruled an empire. His throne was in the affections of God's people, all the way from Rome to Antioch and beyond. Scores of young men waited on him and rushed off to do his will. When he wrote to Titus, however, Paul was free again. He could go where he liked and do what he liked. For the time being, Rome's shackles were shattered, and he was free—to be God's slave! Paul could think of no better thing to be.

It was the same with the Prodigal Son when he finally "came to himself." He could think of no better lot in life than that which the servants of his father enjoyed back at home (Luke 15:17). We picture the prodigal sitting by the pig pail and contemplating sadly the kitchen slops he was supposed to feed to the pigs. He was so hungry that a gnawed piece of bacon rind, a cornhusk, and a sopping crust of bread seemed like treasures. As he stuffed this wretched fare into his mouth, he came to himself. In his mind's eye, he saw the servants' hall in his father's house. Their table was piled high with good food. And he, the son, perished with hunger. "Far better," he said to himself, "to be one of my father's lowliest slaves than to be what I have become—footloose and fancy-free, but friendless and famished in a far-away land." He decided to go home. He would ask to be elevated to the status of a slave in his father's house.

Paul thought that there was no higher calling and no greater joy in life than to be God's slave. As God's slave, he resigned his rank and his rights, his body and his soul. He belonged to God. He would go where God wanted him to go, do what God wanted him to do, and be what God wanted him to be. He had no will of his own, except to do the will of God. In this, he was just like Jesus because the Lord of glory came to earth to do God's will—always, absolutely, and without flaw (Heb. 10:7).

It was his own obedience to the will of God that gave Paul the right to send Timothy here, Titus there, and Tychicus somewhere else. Only a man who has learned to obey is fit to command.

So, as he reminded Titus, Paul was "a servant of God." He would allow no rivals, tolerate no refusals, and contemplate no retreat. He was God's slave, the slave of the Creator of the galaxies, of the God who was served by legions of angels, of the God who was enthroned in glory in absolute power. He, Paul, was the slave of the all-wise, all-loving, all-powerful, and ever-present God. Paul could think of no badge of honor to compare with that. Far better indeed to be God's slave than to be a sin-enslaved Nero on the throne of the Roman world.

2. Paul was an authorized messenger (1:1b)

Paul was "an apostle of Jesus Christ." The title *apostle* occurs a scant nine times in the Gospels. It comes into its own in the book of Acts and the Epistles, where it occurs numerous times. The apostles were a small and exclusive group of men, specially chosen, uniquely gifted, awesomely empowered, and divinely sent to establish God's church.

Titus knew Paul personally as a friend and professionally as an apostle. He had heard Paul preach with anointed, awesome power. He had seen him perform mighty miracles. He had seen him in action and had visited many churches founded by Paul and had talked with his converts. He had read the Spirit-inspired letters that Paul had written. When Titus received his own letter and saw the words *Paul . . . an apostle,* he knew that the scroll he held in his hands was not just a friendly memo. It was a brand-new book of the Bible. He was to be the first man in the world to read this book—but he was not to be the last!

B. Paul's subject (1:1c–3)

After this brief reference to his apostleship, Paul wrote about God's *people* because bringing people into the circle of God's favor was what being an apostle was all about. Then, in verse 2, he wrote about God's *promise* because it was the privilege of an apostle to reveal for all time the matchless and marvelous promises upon which our hope depends. Then, because God's promises are communicated to men through preaching, Paul wrote about God's *preacher;* an apostle, after all, was essentially a preacher.

1. God's people (1:1c–e)

After the salutation, the rest of this first verse is complicated. Paul wrote, "According to the faith of God's elect, and the acknowledging of the truth which is after godliness." Paul does not hesitate to throw us into deep water right at the start. We ought not to expect that every communication from God will be simple. After all, God's thoughts are not our thoughts. They are as far above our thoughts as the stars are above the earth (Isa. 55:8–9). The meaning of Titus 1:1 will be clearer, however, if we think in terms of God's people being chosen, challenged, and changed.

a. They are a chosen people (1:1c)

Paul described God's people here as "God's elect." His own goal as God's slave and Christ's apostle was to further the faith of God's elect, to promote knowledge of the truth, and to produce true godliness.

Truth concerning election is both complex and controversial. Some people envision God's contemplating Adam's ruined race and choosing some to be saved and consigning all others to a lost eternity. What kind of God is that?

Suppose a man's house were to catch on fire and he found himself faced with the fact that he had five children trapped in that house. Suppose that he had the power to save all of them but decided to save only three of them and to let the others burn. What kind of a monster would he be?

Similarly, what kind of a God would He be who behaved in like fashion? One key to the doctrine of election is that it is based on God's foreknowledge (1 Peter 1:2). Another is that election and predestination have to do not with determining who are to be saved but with God's high and holy destiny for all of those who are saved (Rom. 8:29–30).

Extreme Calvinism, when transferred from the pulpit to the pew, sometimes leads to very serious results. The Bible does speak clearly about election and about being chosen. It speaks just as adamantly about human free will, power of choice, and personal accountability. To say that God has endowed us with wills of our own and to say at the same time that we cannot exercise our wills in the matter of our acceptance of Christ is to talk nonsense.

Did I choose Him because He chose me? Or did He choose me because I chose Him? That is the crux of the matter. The question becomes more understandable when we remember that God dwells in the present tense (Exod. 3:14; John 8:38). He is the I Am. So far as God is concerned, His choice of us and our choice of Christ took place simultaneously, in the eternal present tense where He dwells. The past is right now to God; so is the future. We are the ones who live in three dimensions of time. It is when the time element intrudes itself that complications arise.

Election and faith are two parts of the same transaction. Two verbs, two nouns, and one adjective are used in the Greek New Testament to denote faith; each has its own particular emphasis, but each is counterbalanced by its cognate words. The word translated "faith" here is *pistis.* The Holy Spirit uses all words with precision, and *pistis* is no exception. It has to do with faith as the living principle that God has divinely implanted in the human soul.

Everyone has faith, but not everyone has a saving faith. All human transactions are based on faith. We cannot go through a single day without exercising faith. Every time we mail a letter, we exercise faith in the post office. Every time we deposit money in the bank, we exercise faith in the institution. Every time we take some medicine, we exercise faith in the doctor and the pharmacist. Every time we enter a building or cross a bridge, we exercise faith in the architect, the engineer, and the builder. We exercise such faith automatically and instinctively. We rarely think about it. Only when the object of our faith proves unreliable do we realize the need for caution.

Ordinary, everyday faith, the kind that we exercise moment by moment in a thousand ways, becomes *saving* faith when we put our faith and trust in the Lord Jesus Christ. There is nothing intrinsically different about that faith, except that it is exercised in a medium energized and quickened by the Holy Spirit. What is different is the object of our faith—the Lord Jesus Christ!

The Holy Spirit is vitally involved in the transaction that transforms ordinary faith into saving faith. He is the One who convicts us of our sin and our lost estate and prepares us to receive the good news about the Savior. He is the One who enlightens us and directs our attention to Christ. He sends light to everybody (John 1:9).

On a mundane level, a friend might draw our attention to a particular doctor, product, or service that we need. We may be convinced by our friend's sincerity and assurance. That does not help very much—until we go to that doctor, purchase that product, or engage that service. At that point, faith goes to work. So on the spiritual level the Holy Spirit directs our attention to the Word of God and to the Son of God. He removes the obstacles, deals with our objections, and brings us to Christ. The moment we put our faith and trust in Christ, the Holy Spirit indwells us. Our faith grows as it is quickened, energized, and stimulated by the "Spirit of faith" Himself (2 Cor. 4:13) and as we exercise it more and more.

b. They are a challenged people (1:1d)

Truth is imparted to us by means of God's Word. One of the marks of the elect is "the acknowledging of the truth." God's people believe the Bible. The word translated "acknowledging" here indicates "a full or thorough knowledge," "thorough acquaintance." The elect recognize God's Word for what it is and commit themselves to becoming better acquainted with it because "faith cometh by hearing and hearing by the Word of God" (Rom. 10:17). They are challenged to feed their faith on the Word of God.

c. They are a changed people (1:1e)

"Godliness" is the ultimate goal of God's people. The word used here is *eusebeia,* the noun form of the word meaning "to be pious or devout, to act with reverence, respect, and honor." By nature, man is anything but godly; he is ungodly. Enoch preached against ungodliness to a generation ripening fast for judgment (Jude 14–15). Thankfully, people can be changed.

There is all the difference in the world between being religious and being godly. A wicked man can be religious. Members of the Mafia crime syndicate have been known to be religious. One can become godly, however, only by accepting Christ because "the mystery of godliness" is embodied in Him and is imparted to us (1 Tim. 3:16). It is God who gives the believer "all things that pertain unto life and godliness" (2 Peter 1:3).

2. God's promise (1:2)

The believer has a hope that the unsaved person does not have: "hope of eternal life." Eternal life is *the substance of our hope.* Paul says that our eternal life is that "which God, that cannot lie, promised." The trustworthiness of God is *the security of our hope.*

Paul's reference to "eternal" life takes us back to a dateless, timeless past, "before the world began." We picture God the Father, God the Son, and God the Holy Spirit as they commune together and decide to act in creation. In their omniscience, they know that once they act in creation, the time will come when they will have to act in redemption. They foreknew the fall of Satan, the fall of man, and the subsequent ruin of the human race. They pledged themselves to inaugurate a plan of salvation that would offer nothing less than eternal life to fallen mankind.

The plan was made before the world began. Sure enough, Adam and Eve were seduced in the Garden of Eden by the Serpent and fell into sin. In keeping with the divine purpose, God Himself came into the Garden of Eden. The Serpent was summoned and sentenced as the guilty pair stood by awaiting God's pronouncement on them. But wonder of wonders, before God took up their case, He filled their hearts with the hope of eternal life. As He judged the Serpent, He uttered the first great prophecy of Scripture, a prophecy that heralded the coming of a Savior. He said that "the seed of the woman" would one day crush their terrible foe. The actual words that Adam and Eve heard were these: "I will put enmity between thee [the serpent] and the woman, and between thy seed and her seed; it shall bruise thy head, and thou shalt bruise his heel" (Gen. 3:15). The prophecy was the germ promise of eternal life—eternal doom for the Serpent and eternal life for them.

Before the Fall, Adam and Eve had possessed *natural* life. Doubtless, it could have been prolonged indefinitely if they had not sinned, but it still would have been natural life. After the Fall they had the hope of *eternal* life. The concept of eternal life is not merely quantitative (life without end), it is also qualitative (life in a new dimension, life that is life indeed, life as God knows life, the very life of God). The promise includes spiritual life and resurrection life as well as everlasting life. Moreover, along with eternal life comes "an inheritance incorruptible, and undefiled, and that fadeth not away, reserved in heaven" and "joy unspeakable and full of glory" (1 Peter 1:4, 8).

3. God's preacher (1:3)
   a. God's means for making the truth known (1:3a–b)
      (1) The chosen moment (1:3a)

God conveys His purposes and promises to men by divine revelation and He does so "in due times." The expression "due times" is *idios kairos,* which refers to a time or period possessed of certain characteristics. Here it refers to periods in God's dealings with the human race when things come to a head and herald the approach of a new dispensation. At the right moment, God speaks and acts to demonstrate His control over human affairs.

It was thus that God spoke to Adam and Eve after they fell; He made clear to them the new conditions under which they were to live henceforth and, at the same time, He gave them hope of eternal life. God spoke to Noah in the same way—He warned him of the wrath to come, provided a way of escape, acted in the Flood, and subsequently inaugurated a new dispensation of government on earth. God spoke similarly to Abraham; He promised to make him the father of many nations and gave him a son. He pointed him to Christ and made him the father of the nation of Israel. God spoke to David likewise and founded a dynasty that would run for a thousand years until Christ came. Thus time and time again God spoke to the fathers through the prophets, especially during the great crises in the history of the Hebrew people. Finally, God spoke in Christ and through His apostles.

Since the completion of the New Testament, a long unbroken silence has descended on the earth. God has said all that He has to say to us for now. We have His Word, and we must be content with that. "In due time," however, God will speak again. Thoughtful people have wondered at this long, two-thousand-year silence of God and have challenged Him to speak. Some people have become frustrated by it and (like King Saul in his day) have knocked on strange, forbidden, and dangerous doors, hoping to evoke a response from Him. Actually, the silence of God in this age is evidence of His great patience; when He finally speaks, it will be in judgment and wrath.

(2) The chosen method (1:3b)

Normally, God conveys His purposes and promises to men through men. He raises up apostles and prophets to reveal new truth and preachers to spread that truth abroad.

The truths enshrined in the gospel are the most momentous and marvelous concepts ever conceived. Most of the essential facts of the gospel were foretold in the Old Testament type and prophecy. New Testament truths are even more startling; they revolve around the supernatural birth of Jesus—the eternal, uncreated, self-existing second person of the Godhead. He entered human life by being born. He was conceived by the Holy Spirit and born to a virgin, Mary by name. New Testament truths revolve around the sinless life of Jesus; His magnificent, peerless teaching; His countless monumental miracles; His atoning death; His burial and the supernatural preservation of His body in the tomb; His bodily resurrection; His ascension; His present ministry as Great High Priest at the right hand of God in heaven; and His coming again.

These are such startling truths that we might have expected God to use equally startling means to make them known. He could have sent twelve legions of angels to sweep aside all opposition and proclaim the message from the pinnacle of the temple in Jerusalem, from Mars Hill in Athens, from the forum in Rome, and from every other vantage point on earth. He could have issued an ultimatum. God, however, had a different plan—He committed these great eternal truths to a handful of men, most of whom were ignorant and unlearned individuals from a despised province of a downtrodden land. They were to make the truths known "through preaching"!

The word translated "preaching" here emphasizes the substance of what is preached rather than the act of preaching itself. Preaching is a very effective means of conveying truth. Through the preaching of Jonah, Nineveh was brought to its knees. Through the preaching of Peter, three thousand souls were saved in a single day. Mary, Queen of Scots, is said to have been more afraid of the preaching of John Knox than of all of the armies of England. The preaching of John Wesley brought revival to England and saved the country from the horrors of the French Revolution.

God has "manifested his word through preaching." Preaching! Yes, indeed, but preaching in the power of the Holy Spirit. That kind of preaching has a supernatural element to it. The Holy Spirit looks after the results on earth. He does the convicting, the converting, and the consecrating work in the minds, hearts, consciences, and wills of people.

b. God's man for making the truth known (1:3c–d)
(1) A commitment (1:3c)

Paul recognized that God had "committed" the great truths of the New Testament to him. The historical facts of the gospel were quite safe with Matthew, Mark, Luke, and John. The practical aspects of Christianity could be entrusted to Peter, James, John, and Jude. But the theological implications of it all were committed to Paul. This intellectual genius was at once a Jewish rabbi, a Greek scholar, and a Roman citizen. So the gospel, which was for the world, was entrusted to a true cosmopolitan.

Under the inspiration and revelation of the Holy Spirit, Paul hammered out the doctrines of the faith. To him the Holy Spirit revealed the mystery of Christ's cross (see Romans 1; 2 Corinthians, and Galatians), the mystery of Christ's church (see Ephesians, Philippians, and Colossians), and the mystery of Christ's coming (see 1 and 2 Thessalonians). It was all "committed unto me," Paul said—and the "me" is emphatic.

(2) A commandment (1:3d)

Along with the commitment came the "commandment." Paul knew that he was a man under authority. He had his marching orders. Moreover, he had a compulsion to make known, by all means possible, the truths entrusted to him. He said, "Woe is unto me, if I preach not the gospel!" (1 Cor. 9:16).

Paul made demands on Titus, and Titus would be quick to remember that demands had been made on Paul also. He did not make his demands on colleagues such as Timothy and Titus to shirk his own responsibilities. He did so because he could not be in more than one place at a time.

The "commandment," which Paul found so compelling, had been laid on him by "God our Saviour" (Titus 1:3; the same title also occurs in 1 Tim. 1:1; 2:3; Titus 2:10; 3:4; Jude 25). The title, which affirms the deity of Christ, was first used by Mary in her Magnificat ("God my Saviour," Luke 1:47). The word translated "Saviour" is applied here to the Lord Jesus Christ. It is occasionally used of God (1 Tim. 1:1) and often of Christ (Luke 2:11; Titus 1:4). It occurs half a dozen times in this short letter to Titus (1:3–4; 2:10, 13; 3:4, 6).

C. Paul's son (1:4)
  1. Titus: beloved of Paul (1:4a–b)
    a. The unique element in Titus's conversion (1:4a)

Paul addressed this letter to "Titus, mine own son." The expression translated "mine own son" can also be translated "my true son." The Greek word rendered "own/true" means "legitimate."

The apostle Paul had thousands of converts, but few indeed were those whom he called "mine [emphatic] own son." Titus was one, and Timothy was another.

First Timothy 1:2 reads "my [emphatic] own son in the faith." Timothy and Titus were unique; in Paul's mind and heart, they stood apart from all of his other converts. A special bond existed between these two young men and the great apostle. Doubtless, he treasured their love, loyalty, willingness, support, and helpfulness.

b. The universal element in Titus's conversion (1:4b)

However, Titus had been saved the same way anyone is—"after the common faith." The word translated "common" here is *koinos,* which indicates that the faith was one shared with others. We are all saved the same way: "By grace ye are saved through faith; and that not of yourselves: it is the gift of God: Not of works, lest any man should boast" (Eph. 2:8–9).

Doubtless, it was a great honor to have been led to Christ by Paul. Paul, however, had long since warned people against boasting about one's favorite church leaders (1 Cor. 1:10–13). There was and is only one Savior. Our favorite evangelists, pastors, and teachers might hold a place of honor in our hearts, but they all pale, as a candle before the sun, when we think of the One who purchased our common salvation at such infinite cost.

2. Titus: blessed by Paul (1:4c–f)
   a. The blessing given (1:4c–e)

"Grace, mercy, and peace" was the blessing given to Titus. This is the same blessing that Paul bestowed on Timothy (1 Tim. 1:2; 2 Tim. 1:2).

The word *grace* reminds us of *the provision of God the Son.* Paul wrote of "the grace of our Lord Jesus Christ" in 2 Corinthians 8:9: "Though he was rich, yet for your sakes he became poor, that ye through his poverty might be rich."

The word *mercy* reminds us of *the protection of God the Father.* Paul referred to Him as "the Father of mercies" in 2 Corinthians 1:3. Mercy in the Bible is compassion and pity for the guilty and undeserving. God's mercy is revealed in the superlative numerous places ("lovingkindness and tender mercies," Ps. 103:4). All of the power of the Godhead lies behind His *tender* mercies, and all of the pity of the Godhead lies behind His *loving-kindness.*

An eagle hovering over its nest is a picture of God's tender mercy backed by His tremendous, terrible power. An eagle embodies strength in beak and claw, keenness of vision, vast sweep of pinion, and power for rapid and soaring flight.

Moses saw such an eagle in his mind's eye. He saw tenderness displayed, however, instead of terribleness. He saw that the mighty monarch of the sky was busy with its brood, stirring up its nest, fluttering over its young, and spreading its wings to bear them up (Deut. 32:11). The fledglings in the nest looked up at the fierce beak and bright eyes and knew no fear. For them, the great parent eagle, with its power to rend and tear, had nothing but love. So the eagle is a picture of terrible power mingled with tender love; it is a picture of the protection of God the Father.

The word *peace* reminds us of *the product of God the Holy Spirit.* Peace *with* God was purchased for us at Calvary, but the peace *of* God—the peace that "passeth all understanding" (Phil. 4:7), the peace that the world cannot give (John 14:27), the peace that the world cannot take away (John 16:32–33)—is a product of the indwelling Holy Spirit (Gal. 5:22).

Such was the blessing that Paul bestowed on young Titus as he took up his duties on the island of Crete.

b. The blessing guaranteed (1:4f)

Blessings and benedictions are easy to pronounce, so how was Titus to know that Paul's words were more than a pious saying? There was a guarantee: Paul indicated that the blessing did not originate with him; it was "from God the Father and the Lord Jesus Christ our Saviour." Father and Son, seated together on the throne of the universe in high heaven above, with all of the resources of deity at their command, have joined in bestowing this grace, mercy, and peace. This is better than having money in the bank, better than being guarded by angelic hosts, and better than having friends in Caesar's palace. Titus could set his mind at rest.

PART 2

The Naming of Elders in the Local Church

Titus 1:5–9

A. Elders are to be family men (1:5–6)
   1. Paul's authority revealed (1:5)

Paul had much less to say about the subject of elders in his letter to Titus than in his first letter to Timothy. Timothy was up against a well-entrenched establishment and needed more apostolic support of his authority in Ephesus than Titus needed on Crete, where the local church seems to have been somewhat disorganized. Perhaps Timothy, with his retiring disposition, needed more documentation to back up his actions than did the more forceful Titus. In any case, Paul gave Titus only the barest outline of the subject. The apostle began by revealing his authority for laying down the law, as it were, on these matters.

a. The decision (1:5a)

"For this cause," Paul wrote to Titus, "left I thee in Crete." This is the first indication that Paul and Titus had spent time together on the island. During that time, they had evangelized the population and founded churches.

The island of Crete is about 140 miles long and 30 miles wide. The *Encyclopedia Britannica* says it has an area of 3,189 square miles. It lies in the Aegean arm of the Mediterranean Sea. While campaigning on the island, Paul would have been interested in visiting several spots. One such place was the anchorage of Fair Havens, where he had once spent anxious hours. Another was the port of Phenice, which Paul's doomed ship had never reached (Acts 27:7–15).

Very likely Paul had followed his usual policy of starting his missionary work in local synagogues, but it is not likely that he was too successful. By that time, he was too well known by the Jews for him to take a synagogue by storm. He would also have visited all the Christian groups he could find on the island. He would have pursued vigorously a program of house-to-house visitation, and he would have preached wherever he could gather an audience. The outbreak of Neronic persecution in Rome would have alerted him to the shortness of the time he had left and would have given him a new sense of urgency.

It seems that Paul had not stayed on the island as long as he would have liked. Events in Ephesus troubled him, Macedonia beckoned, and he wanted to visit other churches such as Corinth. So he set sail for Miletus and left Titus behind to consolidate his work on Crete.

The word translated "left" suggests leaving someone behind temporarily. We know from 2 Timothy 4:10 that Titus was not left behind permanently. When Paul wrote 2 Timothy 4:10, Titus was on his way to Dalmatia. Paul seems to have left Titus on Crete as a temporary apostolic representative rather than as a permanent resident "bishop." The facts that Paul believed in the autonomy of local churches and that he commissioned Titus to establish elders in the local churches add weight to the view that Paul left Titus on Crete for only the time being.

b. The disorder (1:5b)

Paul continued, "I left thee in Crete, that thou shouldest set in order the things that are wanting." The word for "set in order" appears only here in the New Testament and means "to set right again something that is defective." Medical writers used the term to describe the setting of broken limbs.

When Paul decided to leave Crete, he knew that his work on the island was far from complete and that it would be up to Titus to put things right. That would be no small task. The propensity of churches on the island to fall apart was probably due to the national character of the people as much as anything else.

c. The deterrent (1:5c)

To cure the chaotic conditions in the churches on the island, Titus was to "ordain elders in every city." The word translated "ordain" usually means "to appoint someone to a position of authority."

In a place where people had a natural bent toward turbulence, the churches needed a firm hand, someone, indeed, of Paul's stature, to impose order. The facts that Titus was acting as Paul's delegate and was empowered to supervise the inauguration of elders were probably already well known on the island. This epistle would give Titus added authority. If anyone felt inclined to challenge him, Titus would have a letter bearing Paul's signature as documentary proof that he was the official representative of the great apostle to the Gentiles.

d. The delegate (1:5d)

Turning to his delegate, Paul added the clause "as I [emphatic] had appointed thee." We can picture Titus's going throughout the island, locating the church in each city, and quietly seeking out men with the necessary qualifications to shepherd the congregation. It was no small task for the young man.

2. Parental authority revered (1:6)
   a. The prospective elder as a person (1:6a)

Paul listed a few simple rules to guide Titus in his task. First, he should look for men who were "blameless," men whom no one could call to account. Their integrity had to be impeccable.

When World War II broke out, my father's small automobile business in South Wales was virtually bankrupted. The government commandeered all of the private vehicles on which it could lay its hands and rationed gasoline to the extent that all private cars were, in effect, grounded, except when used for war work. My father paced the floor of his workshop as he prayed and wondered what to do.

About that time, an acquaintance who ran a large automobile rental dealership visited him. He knew that my father was a skilled mechanic. "Len," he said, "we have about two hundred cars. We cannot replace them until the war is over, so we need to keep them in repair. The government will allocate parts since our cars are rented for war work. Can you rebore and rebuild engines for us if we supply the parts?" It was a reprieve.

The next day, an engine was delivered to my father's shop with instructions to strip it down, rebore the block, and rebuild it with the new parts supplied by the dealer. A few days later, the dealer picked up the engine and nothing more happened for about a week.

Then the dealer returned. "Well, Len," he said, "I'll tell you what we did. We took that rebuilt engine into our own shop and stripped it down. We wanted to see if you were honest. We wanted to see if you replaced all the old parts with new parts. We have been ripped off by a number of other small shops, but you have been scrupulously honest. We will bring you two or three engines a week." That is the kind of stuff of which integrity is made. Integrity is the stuff of which all Christians should be made, especially those who are slated for eldership and leadership in the church.

   b. The prospective elder as a partner (1:6b)

An elder should be "the husband of one wife." The word translated "husband" means literally "an adult male" and conveys the idea of an honorable man. When the word is used to signify "husband," it bestows an honorable title.

Paul states here that the ideal elder must be married. There are many lessons in life that a single man cannot learn. He can study married men and their pleasures, problems, and potentials, but all of the information he receives is secondhand. He can buy books, rent videos, attend marriage-counseling seminars, and even lecture on the role of a man in marriage. But if he has never been married, he cannot speak from personal experience.

Some years ago, the dean of a women's school wrote an article on motherhood for a popular magazine. She had observed hundreds of students who had passed through her school, had talked to many of them about their home life, and had corresponded with a number of the graduates even after they were married. Over many years, she had amassed a considerable fund of stories and statistics. Finally, she wrote her article. Its publication caused some local amusement because, although she was a good, able, and efficient dean, she was a spinster. She would have been in a better position to write about motherhood if she had been a mother. Fine theories often break down in practice.

The Holy Spirit requires, then, that an elder be married. Marriage brings disciplines as well as delights. It is an arena where love and loyalty can be practiced, where lessons in personal relationships can be learned, where theories are tested in the crucible of experience, where limits have to be observed, and where laws have to be obeyed. A man who has not learned how to be a good husband—faithful to his wife, a good provider, a spiritual leader, loving his wife as Christ loved the church—does not qualify to be an elder.

Some people inject the divorce issue into the passage. That issue is dealt with elsewhere in the New Testament (e.g., Matt. 19; 1 Tim. 3:2), and it is not touched on here at all. It seems likely that Paul has polygamy in mind here because it was so widely tolerated by God in the Old Testament.

c. The prospective elder as a parent (1:6c–d)

An elder should have "faithful children not accused of riot or unruly." The word translated "faithful" implies that the children have become believers. If an elder has led his children to the Lord, his home has been his training ground for the evangelistic aspects of eldership. A man's testimony and example ought at least to convict his own children.

Noah is a good illustration. He was "a preacher of righteousness" (2 Peter 2:5) for 120 years. Although he never won a convert outside his immediate family, all eight members of his family heeded his warnings and were saved in the ark. No wonder he became the patriarch of a new age.

Lot, on the other hand, failed to win anyone. When judgment was about to fall on Sodom, he was unable to convince his married daughters and their husbands to flee from the wrath to come; they thought that he was joking. Lot's wife and two unmarried daughters practically had to be dragged out of Sodom by angels. Even at that, his wife looked back and perished anyway. Later, his two surviving daughters made him drunk and left him dishonored and the prospective father of Ammon and Moab, whose descendents became historically hostile to Israel. No wonder that, except for a few scattered references, Scripture hardly mentions Lot again after Genesis 19.

In contrast, God said of Abraham, "Shall I hide from Abraham the thing which I do . . . for I know him, that he will command his children and his household after him" (Gen. 18:17–19). The mark of Abraham's domestic circle was *discipline.* When Abraham commanded, the members of his family obeyed. Even such a born rebel as Ishmael submitted to his authority (Gen. 16:11–12; 17:25).

The mark of Isaac's family was *discord.* Doubtless Isaac's favoritism for Esau and Rebekah's favoritism for Jacob were partly responsible, as were Isaac's carnality and Rebekah's conniving. Esau never did turn to God, but Jacob did, and he finished well.

Disorder marked Jacob's family. As his older sons grew to manhood, they manifested the same self-will that he had manifested until God broke him and blessed him at the brook Jabbok. In the end, however, they, too, were judged and blessed (Gen. 42–44; 49).

The principle of a father's being responsible for the spiritual education of his children is spelled out in Psalm 78:1–8. In the church, the rule is that an elder's children ought to be believers. Possibly this is a general rule rather than an absolute rule because Abraham had his Ishmael, and Isaac had his Esau. Similarly in the larger sphere, the Lord had his Judas, and Paul had his Demas. Out of the same family can come both a pervert and a prophet. This is a great mystery. It proves (1) that God has no grandchildren, (2) that my being a child of God is no guarantee that my children will be God's children, and (3) that a parent is not necessarily to blame if one or more of his children grows up to rebel against the Truth.

Astonishingly, few Old Testament fathers had godly sons. Eli's sons were so vile that they died under the judgment of God; God held the aged priest responsible for neglecting the most obvious requirements of discipline. The sons of the prophet Samuel were unworthy of office, and it was partly on their account that the tribes of Israel demanded a king. David's family life was deplorable. Solomon's son, Rehoboam, was a fool. Hezekiah's son was the worst king ever to sit on the throne of David. Josiah's sons were all wicked.

In the church, the ideal is that an elder's children be believers. The ideal might not always be attainable, but at least his children must not be "unruly" or "accused of riot." The word translated "accused" here had to do with judicial procedure. The word translated "riot" here refers to prodigality, profligacy, and wastefulness that points to an abandoned, dissolute life. No such charge ought to be able to be brought against the child of an elder.

The word translated "unruly" describes a person who refuses to be controlled and who defies authority. In the Old Testament, an unruly son who defied parental authority was to be put to death; Deuteronomy 21:18–21 reveals God's hatred of intransigent behavior. The unfortunate father of such a son is automatically disqualified from being an elder.

Paul was not nearly as demanding when he wrote to Timothy. He simply specified that an elder was to be "one that ruleth well his own house, having his children in subjection with all gravity; (For if a man know not how to rule his own house, how shall he take care of the church of God?)" (1 Tim. 3:4–5). Possibly Paul added to the general rule when writing to Titus because of the unruly national character of the Cretans (see Titus 1:10).

B. Elders are to be faultless men (1:7)
   1. The elder's position (1:7a–b)

The position itself elevated a man above the rank and file of church membership and made him more visible. Therefore, Paul mentioned the position's *corresponding requirement:* "A bishop *[episkopos]* must be blameless."

In the early church, the word *episkopos* had none of the connotations that our English word *bishop* has today. A bishop was simply an elder (as in Acts 20:17), and a local church could have as many elders as it needed. As time went on, however, the words *bishop* and *Episcopal* gathered nonbiblical traditions around themselves as a hierarchical structure arose in Christendom. Bishops (who supervised dioceses containing numerous churches) often acquired wealth, power, and influence until they overshadowed and eventually ruled the declining Roman Empire. Our current concept of bishops is derived from the Roman Catholic Church, which does not distinguish the church of God from the kingdom of God.

The word translated "blameless" here is the same word that he had just used in the preceding verse. He reiterated the fact that an elder must be above reproach. He must be the kind of man against whom no charge can be made. That is the requirement.

The position of elder also has a *corresponding responsibility* because the elder is "the steward *[oikonomos]* of God." The word *oikonomos* is used primarily in relation to the management of a household or estate. Paul used it to describe Erastus as the "chamberlain" *(oikonomos)*—that is, treasurer—of the city of Corinth (Rom. 16:23). Paul also used the word when referring to a child's "tutors and governors *[oikonomos]*" (Gal. 4:2). A governor was responsible to the parents for their child's education, discipline, and development.

An elder, as "the steward of God," is responsible to Him for handling the spiritual aspects of the local church. One day, he will be called on to give account to God for the way he discharged his duties.

2. The elder's portrait (1:7c–g)
   a. Not given to aggression (1:7c)

A portrait of an elder begins to emerge as Paul continues. Here a series of required attributes, though expressed in negative phrases, enhances the graphic portrayal.

First, an elder is "not self-willed." In other words, he must not be given to aggression. The word translated "self-willed" here conveys the idea of being arrogant or of being dominated by the desire to please oneself regardless of the cost to others. Once a self-willed person determines his self-interest in a matter, he asserts arrogantly his own will and persists in doing so. Even one such person on a board of elders in a local church can ruin all attempts at progress. A self-willed person is unfit to govern a company of God's people.

   b. Not given to anger (1:7d)

An elder is "not soon angry." The word translated "soon angry" occurs only here in the New Testament and means "irascible, prone to anger." Today we would say that a person who is "soon angry" has a short fuse or is touchy. He has learned to get his way by intimidating other people with his anger.

True, there is a place for anger. For example, Moses, who was noted for his meekness, was angry with Pharaoh for breaking his word so many times and angry with Israel for making the golden calf (Num. 12:3; Exod. 11:8; 32:19). The New Testament principle is stated in Ephesians 4:26: "Be ye angry, and sin not: let not the sun go down upon your wrath." We are told repeatedly in the Bible that the Lord is "slow to anger" (Ps. 103:8; 145:8; Joel 2:13; Jonah 4:2). So a man who becomes angry easily is unfit to be an elder.

c. Not given to alcohol (1:7e)

An elder is "not given to wine." The word translated "given to wine" here and in 1 Timothy 3:3 is *paroinos,* which means "overfond of wine" or "sitting long at wine." The idea behind the word is intoxication that leads to being quarrelsome. The Bible militates against drunkenness.

Noah's drunkenness, the first case of intoxication recorded in the Bible, brought out the worst in his son Ham and brought out the best in his two other sons (Gen. 9:20–29). Mitigating circumstances might have existed in Noah's case. The second example of drunkenness recorded in Scripture is that of Lot, and a sad and sorry tale it is. The utter moral corruption of his two surviving daughters was what led to his inebriation and the dreadful incident recorded in Genesis 19:30–38. The New Testament records the case of some believers who were actually sitting at the Lord's Table in a drunken condition (1 Cor. 11:21). Paul's remedy was for believers to be filled with the Holy Spirit (Eph. 5:18).

God hates drunkenness so much that He lists it as one of the damning sins of the flesh (Gal. 5:19–21) and as an excommunicating sin (1 Cor. 5:11). A man who tarries long over his wine is disqualified from becoming an elder. An elder-to-be should tarry long in the Word of God.

d. Not given to attack (1:7f)

An elder is "no striker." A man who will physically assault another person has no place on the board of elders of a local church. The word translated "striker" here and in 1 Timothy 3:3 paints the picture of a brawler.

A "striker" is a man who is accustomed to bullying his way thorough life and getting what he wants by fighting. Weaker or less forceful men give way to him. The Spirit of God wants no such man to shove and shoulder his way into a position of responsibility in the church. Furthermore, a "railer," a man of similar temperament, is to be excommunicated (1 Cor. 5:11).

e. Not given to affluence (1:7g)

Completing the portrait, Paul said that an elder is "not given to filthy lucre." Being successful in business does not qualify a man to be an elder. The church is not a business. It is a gathering of called-out people whose citizenship is in heaven and who hold lightly to the things of earth.

Abraham was very rich, but he held his earthly possessions lightly (Gen. 13:1–12). When God called him to be a pilgrim and a stranger on the earth, He made him some very great promises: Abraham was to become a great nation, his descendents would be as numerous as the stars, and he would inherit a land that would eventually reach from the Nile to the Euphrates. But these promises were not what impelled Abraham. What motivated him was his vision of a celestial city (Heb. 11:8–10). Abraham was just a migrant passing through this world.

So an elder must not be given to affluence. Being a businessman does not qualify him, but neither does it disqualify him—as long as he is not given to making money. Being given to wealth is as bad as being given to wine.

C. Elders are to be friendly men (1:8)
 1. What the elder loves (1:8a–b)
  a. His demonstrable friendliness (1:8a)

Paul turns now to some positive attributes. He wrote first that an elder should be "a lover of hospitality *[philoxenos]*." *Philoxenos* is a composite word made up of *philos,* which means "loving," and *xenos,* which means "strangers."

I learned hospitality from my parents. Our house always seemed to be full of people. Traveling preachers passing through our town would arrive at my father's workshop at mealtime. They could count on him for an invitation to dinner and a tankful of gas—even when food and gasoline were severely rationed during the war. I don't know how my mother ever managed. She had four hungry children of her own to feed in addition to my father, herself, and her aging mother. But somehow we never missed a meal. When we were short of food, one of my father's customers (some of whom were farmers) would miraculously show up with a dozen eggs, a chicken, or a sack of potatoes. As a result of my parents' hospitality, we children were the auditors of many lively conversations that were spiced by the views of visiting preachers. In those days, children were to be seen and not heard, but there was no law against listening.

An elder is to be addicted, as my father was, to hospitality. Hospitality not only extends a welcoming, friendly hand to the passing stranger but also affords the host an opportunity to minister to the guest's spiritual needs. Doubtless, Aquila and Priscilla invited the eloquent Apollos to their home and treated him to a good home-cooked meal before they attempted to enlarge his understanding of Christian baptism (Acts 18:24–28).

b. His discriminating friendliness (1:8b)

An elder is also to be "a lover of good men." *Philagathos,* the word translated "a lover of good men," is sometimes rendered "a lover of goodness." No greater compliment can be paid to a person than to say that he or she is good. When God appeared to Solomon and challenged him to ask what he would, he did not ask God to make him rich or powerful or to grant him a long life; he asked God to make him wise. He was commended for that, but had he known all that was in his heart, he would have asked instead for God to make him *good.*

Good men are rare. It is easy to find a gifted man, a great man, or even a gracious man. But a good man is much more difficult to find. Nor is his company courted by many men, for his goodness often makes other people feel uncomfortable. Goodness is the sixth fruit of the Spirit (Gal. 5:22–23), but we seldom meet someone who has cultivated this fruit to discernable dimensions. When we do meet a truly good person, we should befriend him at once. That is what an elder who is truly "a lover of good men" would do.

An elder reaches out with love, warmth, and friendliness to all people regardless of color, class, or condition, but he has a special place in his heart and home for good people. He will especially befriend individuals like Joseph of Arimathea and Barnabas, whom the Holy Spirit described as good men (Luke 23:50; Acts 11:24). Goodness is a Christlike characteristic. We are told that Jesus "went about doing good" (Acts 10:38). He was good as God is good. The rich young ruler realized that Jesus was good and addressed Him as such, but he was thinking in terms of comparative goodness. Jesus challenged him to think in terms of absolute goodness (Matt. 19:16–17). Paul says that people are prepared actually to die for a good man (Rom. 5:6–7) in contrast with Christ, who died for sinful people.

2. How the elder lives (1:8c–f)
   a. His public life (1:8c–d)

An elder is to be "sober" and "just." He must know how to *watch* matters and how to *weigh* matters. The word translated "sober" here means "of sound mind." A "sober" person is serious and earnest. The word translated "just," *dikaios,* conveys the idea of doing and being right. The great concern of an elder should be to do what is right. He must not jump to conclusions or act without considering all of the facts. He must look at both sides of an issue because the right course of action is not always obvious.

The classic example of *not* considering all of the facts is found in the case of the woman who was accused of adultery and brought to Christ by the Pharisees (John 8:3–11). On the surface, it was an open-and-shut case. The Mosaic Law decreed death for adultery, and the woman's accusers affirmed that she was caught in the act. Doubtless, the Pharisees were delighted to have a considerable audience to watch them place Christ, as they thought, on the horns of a dilemma.

The Lord Jesus saw through their motive, which was to pit God's law against His love. The Lord brought a sound mind to the problem and a heart that beat with a passion to do what was right. After all, there were mitigating circumstances. If this unhappy woman was taken "in the very act," where was her partner? Was he not caught in the very act as well? Did not the Mosaic Law apply to him too?

Moreover, the Lord knew the Law and its purpose better than the Pharisees did. Two entirely separate Old Testament commandments cover cases of immorality. The command recorded in Deuteronomy 22:22 applied to a *married woman.* The command recorded in Deuteronomy 22:23–24 applied to a *betrothed damsel.* The punishment was death by stoning if the woman was a willing partner in the sin or if she had some measure of control over the circumstances under which she was forced. The command recorded in Numbers 5:11–31 applied to a *married woman* and provided for a special procedure to be followed, a procedure that was invoked under the most solemn conditions and left the punishment with God. The procedure was a ritual that included a test and the utterance of a curse on the woman if the test proved her to be guilty. It might well be that when the Lord stooped down to write with His finger on the ground He wrote the curse required under the law in Numbers.

"The law commanded us, that such should be stoned," the Pharisees had insisted. The Lord's writing apparently revealed that He knew more about the woman than they did, or at least more than they admitted, because it drew their attention to the fact that this case required the procedure of Numbers 5:11–31. When the Pharisees persisted in asserting that He should invoke the Deuteronomic law, the Lord straightened Himself up and faced them. He looked them in the eye and said, "He that is without sin among you, let him first cast a stone to her." Then He stooped down again and wrote on the ground.

This time, maybe, He wrote down names, places, and dates. He knew not only the Law but also them; "being convicted by their own conscience," they "went out one by one, beginning at the eldest, even unto the last." When the woman was left standing there alone, Jesus straightened Himself up again. Then

He looked at her. "Woman," He said, "where are those thine accusers? Hath no man condemned thee?"

She replied, "No man, Lord."

"Neither do I condemn thee," He said, "go, and sin no more." He did not say that He did not condemn her sin; He said that He did not condemn her. He sent her away a saved woman, one who had learned that both grace and truth come by Jesus Christ (John 1:17).

An elder must be just as "sober" and "just." He must be like Jesus and watch and weigh each case.

b. His personal life (1:8e–f)
   (1) He lives a clean life (1:8e)

An elder must be "holy." The word translated "holy" here is *hosiōs,* which is used in Acts 2:27 to describe the Lord Himself: "Thou wilt not . . . suffer thine Holy One *[hosiōs]* to see corruption." Paul chose the same word to describe his own behavior (and that of his coworkers) in 1 Thessalonians 2:10: "Ye are witnesses, and God also, how *holily* and justly and unblameably we behaved ourselves among you that believe."

An elder must be pure from evil conduct and must be observant of God's will. There is no place for even the slightest suspicion of scandal in his life. If he wants to be paid for being an elder, or if he has a lustful heart, or if being an elder feeds a lust for power, his effectiveness is compromised. An elder must "have always a conscience void of offence toward God, and toward men," as Paul testified to Felix (Acts 24:16). Certainly, Felix did not have a clear conscience. While he was sitting in judgment over Paul, he was living in a sinful relationship with Drusilla. Moreover, Felix was noted for his cruelty, treachery, and venality.

The Holy Spirit often put opposites side by side in Scripture so that the contrasts would be instructive, Paul and Felix being a case in point. Another example is found in Genesis 13:12. We read, "Abram dwelled in the land of Canaan, and Lot dwelled in the cities of the plain." In Genesis 38–39, the story of Judah's immorality is followed by an illustration of Joseph's goodness. In 1 Samuel 2:11–18, we read of both the goodness of the boy Samuel and the badness of Eli's sons. Throughout 1 Samuel, the wickedness of King Saul is all the more apparent because of the integrity exhibited by David. The sin of Solomon seems all the worse because the account of it in 1 Kings 11:1–9 follows a description of his glory in 10:23–24. And in the letter to Titus, the holiness of a church elder (1:8) is set against the deplorable Cretan character (1:12).

(2) He lives a controlled life (1:8f)

An elder must be "temperate." The word translated "temperate" occurs only here in the New Testament. A kindred word occurs in Paul's sermon to Felix. Paul, we are told, spoke to him of "righteousness, temperance *[enkrateia]*, and judgment to come" (Acts 24:25). No wonder "Felix trembled"; self-control was glaringly absent from his life and obviously present in Paul's. Paul's self-control, a fruit of the Spirit (Gal. 5:22–23), enabled him to rise above his circumstances.

A man who wants to be an elder must learn how to keep himself in hand. He cannot rule over a local church if he cannot rule over himself.

D. Elders are to be faithful men (1:9)
 1. Holding fast the Word of God (1:9a–b)
  a. Their trust in God's Word (1:9a)

Elders are characterized by their "holding fast the faithful word." God's Word is thoroughly worthy of our trust because it is "the faithful word." It is completely reliable. An elder who does not take God's inspired, inerrant Word at face value is disqualified from holding office. But taking a firm stand for the plenary, verbal inspiration of the Bible is not enough. Elders must also do what Scripture says. They must trust it implicitly to guard them and to guide them through the labyrinths of life.

In this regard, elders are like pilots who fly into thick banks of clouds and lose all sense of direction. Without instruments, they would be in deep trouble. If they were to fly according to their uncertain feelings, they might think that they were on a safe path when they were really heading for a crash. There is only one thing for them to do in the clouds: trust their instruments. Their instruments are objective; their feelings are subjective. Their instruments will keep them on course—at the right altitude, on a level trim, and at the proper speed. The moment they abandon or mistrust their instruments, they are in peril and so are all of their passengers. The navigational aid available to elders is the Word of God. No matter how dense the clouds, or how they obscure the way, they must trust Scripture whenever it speaks to the issue at hand.

Joshua failed to trust God's Word when he was dealing with the Gibeonites

(Josh. 9:3–27). Jericho and Ai had fallen to the Israelites, and Gibeon was next in their line of march. The terrified Gibeonites decided to trick Joshua into signing a peace treaty. First, they concocted a plausible story, then they backed it up with what looked like genuine proof. Joshua was fooled by the moldy food, old wineskins, and worn-out clothes that they exhibited to convince him that they came "from a far country." He signed the peace treaty only to discover that he had been deceived. If Joshua had trusted God's Word, he never would have signed that treaty even if the evidence had been a thousand times more convincing. For God's Word was plain: "Thou shalt make no covenant with them" (Exod. 23:32); "Thou shalt smite them, and utterly destroy them; thou shalt make no covenant with them, nor shew mercy unto them" (Deut. 7:2).

The wisdom of God's Word on this issue of the treaty with the Gibeonites became evident at a later date (Judg. 19–20). Joshua did Israel a great disservice when he trusted in human reasoning rather than the Word of God. He should have been guided by God's Word even though circumstances pointed him in the opposite direction.

Elders must trust God's Word implicitly. Their task is to bring Scripture—not modern psychology, human philosophy, or scientific theories—to bear on a situation. When the Bible tells young women, for instance, to be "keepers at home" (Titus 2:5), that advice is worth more than all of the humanistic arguments for entering the workplace and pursuing careers. When the Bible says that murderers should be put to death (Gen. 9:6; Rom. 13:4), that advice is better than the counsel given by modern sociologists. When the Bible tells believers to separate themselves from all kinds of moral and religious evil (2 Cor. 6:14–18), that advice is better than the opinion of compromisers.

b. Their training in God's Word (1:9b)

An elder is to trust Scripture "as he hath been taught." The word for *teaching* here occurs thirty times in the New Testament and is always translated "doctrine," except in this one place. An elder then must be well taught in the Word of God, and he must be able to impart sound teaching to those entrusted to his care.

Nowadays, it is not uncommon to find elders who are well taught in almost everything except the Bible. Many men are willing to spend years acquiring a mastery of music, mathematics, or medicine but are content to spend less than half an hour a week in Bible study. Paul would require that men spend much more time than that in acquiring knowledge of God's Word before he would allow them to become elders. To be a first-class Bible teacher, a man does not need a degree from a seminary, but he does need to put much time and effort into studying the Bible in depth.

2. Heralding forth the Word of God (1:9c–e)
   a. Their sound doctrine (1:9c)

Paul was reluctant to leave the requirements related to the Word of God. Elders, he emphasized, must be able to teach "sound doctrine." The word translated "doctrine" occurs twenty-one times in the New Testament and fifteen times in the Pastoral Epistles. The idea of action predominates when this word is used, so what Paul had in mind in Titus 1:9c is the act of teaching. An elder must not only be committed to sound doctrine but also teach it.

Any movement that deemphasizes doctrine must be suspect. In a properly functioning local church, the elders place great importance on sound teaching. That was a primary characteristic of the infant church. The new believers "continued steadfastly in the apostles' doctrine" (Acts 2:42). In the last days, Paul warned, people will give heed to "doctrines of devils" and "will not endure sound doctrine" (1 Tim. 4:1; 2 Tim. 4:3). Therefore, we must be sure that those who are chosen to have the rule over us in the Lord are true to the Word of God and zealous in teaching it.

   b. Their solemn duty (1:9d–e)

"By sound doctrine" elders are "to exhort and to convince the gainsayers." Paul was saying that the solemn duty of elders is *to exhort* and *to expose.* The word translated "exhort" here means "to call aside, appeal, beseech, admonish." Exhortation is by nature prospective; it keeps an eye on the future.

The word translated "convince" carries the idea of bringing someone under conviction, which in turn leads to confession. Thus, his sin is exposed. The word translated "gainsayers" means "those who contradict." The first occurrence of this word in the New Testament is found in Luke 2:34, which records old Simeon's prophetic statement, made as he held the infant Christ in his arms: "This child is set . . . for a sign which shall be spoken *against.*" There have always been people who set themselves against Christ. A well-taught elder, ministering the Word of God in the power of the Spirit of God, ought to be able to bring such people under conviction.

The qualifications of New Testament elders listed in these verses set a high standard indeed. If every local church were governed by a body of men meeting that standard, doctrinal error would not dare raise its head, immorality would flee, and unbelievers would stand in awe of the church, an institution that many people now despise. If God's Word were taught in spirit and in truth, multitudes would flock to the meetings, people would be saved, and believers would dwell secure in the knowledge that their shepherds were Christlike. The church would live in a constant state of revival.

PART 3

The Nature of Error in the Local Church

Titus 1:10–16

A. The motives of false teachers (1:10–11)
   1. Facing our foes (1:10)
      a. What they are (1:10a–c)
         (1) They are disorderly (1:10a)

One of the functions of an elder is to deal with people who introduce false teaching into the church. In Titus 1:10, Paul describes such false teachers as "unruly." The word *unruly* here is *anupotaktos,* the same word used in 1:6 to describe disobedient children. False teachers refuse to recognize authority.

Moses had to contend with unruly people when, for instance, he was opposed by Korah, Dathan, and Abiram.[1] They rejected the leadership of Moses and the priesthood of Aaron. Korah was a first cousin of Moses. He and his two rebel companions camped together on the south side of the tabernacle (Num. 2:10; 3:29), but they seem to have collected a widespread following throughout the camp. Twice the Holy Spirit recorded that they were "against Moses and Aaron" (Num. 16:3, 41, 42). In Old Testament times, summary punishment was the reward for such disorderly behavior. The New Testament spirit might be more patient, but it is equally plain: God is against the unruly.

As it was with Israel in the wilderness, so it is with the church in the world. Paul had seen many unruly people rise up and challenge apostolic and pastoral authority.

(2) They are disputers (1:10b)

False teachers are also "vain talkers *[mataiologos].*" The Greek word indicates that they talk nonsense. Certainly, a great deal of nonsense is taught today under the guise of religion, philosophy, and science.

All of the cults talk nonsense. To say, as does Christian Science, that pain is an error of the mortal minds is nonsense—as a vigorous kick on the shins soon proves. To say, as does Mormonism, that we can work our way to becoming gods is nonsense—nonsense as old as the Devil's lie to Eve in the Garden of Eden. To teach—as do Buddhists, Hindus, and New Agers—that we are reincarnated in life after life is nonsense, as is evidenced by people who recall having been Napoleon or Mickey Mouse in some other life.

People who accept such irrational religious delusions are often vocal about their beliefs. They become disputers. Not content with having embraced some

1. Dathan and Abiram were Reubenites. Korah, a first cousin of Moses and Aaron, was a grandson of Kohath.

way-out error for themselves, they continually try to argue their points with those who have more sense than they have. Having abandoned the true faith in favor of one of the Devil's lies, they want to debate those who hold to the truth. Disputers argue that right is wrong, that truth is error, that light is darkness. And frequently they argue with a zeal, passion, and conviction that they never showed for the truth when they were familiar with it.

(3) They are deceivers (1:10c)

False teachers are "deceivers." The Greek word occurs only here in the New Testament. The verb form occurs in Galatians 6:3: "If a man think himself to be something, when he is nothing, he *deceiveth* himself." The verb means "to deceive one's mind, to deceive by fancies."

False teachers are soul deceivers. Peter says that they beguile unstable souls (2 Peter 2:14). Satan beguiled Eve, who showed that she was wavering from the truth by her careless handling of the Word of God. (She misquoted it three times in two verses, twice subtracting from what God had said and once adding to what God said.)

b. Who they were (1:10d)

The false teachers that Paul described were "specially they of the circumcision." The implication is that most of the deceivers and rebels in the early church were Jewish. Judaizing Christians were the most obstinate, difficult, and persistent of Paul's adversaries. They dogged his footsteps, subverted his converts, attacked his apostleship, challenged his authority, undermined his teaching, and distorted the gospel. They insisted that Gentiles become Jews to become Christians and that Gentiles be circumcised, adhere to the Sabbath, abstain from eating nonkosher meat, keep the Mosaic Law, bow to rabbinical teachings, and accept the authority of the "mother" church in Jerusalem. In short, these false teachers wanted to turn Christianity into another Jewish sect.

2. Fighting our foes (1:11)
   a. The rule (1:11a)

Paul was not the kind of man who would stand by while this subversion of his churches was going on. He told Titus to fight the false teachers. Their "mouths must be stopped," he said. In other words, "They must be silenced." The word translated "stopped" means "to muzzle." The noun form refers to the plug for a water pipe.

We are so infatuated by freedom of speech nowadays that we tolerate almost anything. The attitude is "although I may hate what you say, I will die for your right to say it." The Bible—the great champion of all true liberties—knows better than to allow people to say and teach whatever they like without the restraints of truth, morality, and decency. Much of the vileness and violence in modern society stems from the abuse of freedom of speech and from the unrestrained freedom of the press. Paul might have been "un-American" when he said that the mouths of those who teach flagrant error must be stopped, but he was not un-Christian. He was inspired by the Holy Spirit Himself to make the statement.

The mouths of Satan's propagandists can be stopped, at least in any gathering of God's people, in two ways. (1) The false teachers can be refuted and rebuked privately and warned publicly that no further heretical teaching will be tolerated. (2) If the first method fails, they can be excommunicated; expelling them from the church puts them back where they belong—in Satan's camp, where they are exposed to divine discipline. One way or another, their voices must be silenced. That is the rule.

b. The reason (1:11b)

The reason for the rule is that false teachers "subvert whole houses." The word translated "subvert" here means "to overthrow, to destroy." The word translated "houses" is *oikos,* which means "households, families." The favorite method of cultists such as Mormons and Jehovah's Witnesses is to insinuate themselves into homes, take advantage of their hosts' hospitality, and subvert the unwary.

c. The revelation (1:11c–d)

Paul points to the *message* and the *motives* of false teachers: "Teaching things which they ought not, for filthy lucre's sake." To make money, they teach things that they have no right or authority to teach.

Evidently, the Gentile churches were plagued by false itinerant teachers. These subversives traded on their Jewishness, their zeal for the law, their firsthand knowledge of the life and teachings of Jesus, and their personal acquaintance with Peter, James, and the elders of the Jerusalem churches. Some of the Judaizers even carried testimonials and letters from prominent members of the Jerusalem church. They took advantage of Gentile ignorance regarding the Old Testament and its total subordination to the New Testament.

Paul had done battle with such foes all of the way from Galatia to Jerusalem. He had denounced them and their subversive doctrines in half a dozen epistles, especially Galatians, Hebrews, Romans, and 2 Corinthians. These cultists, however, were clever and convincing and were determined to build both a following and a financial base for themselves.

B. The menace of false teachers (1:12–13)

Paul now focused specifically on the Cretans. Jews from Crete had been in Jerusalem on the Day of Pentecost and had heard Peter preach (Acts 2:11). Doubtless, some of them had been converted and had carried the gospel back to their island home. As Jews, they might have been particularly susceptible to the teachings of the Judaizers. Apparently, too, some of them were active in the movement to carry the church back into the Jewish fold.

1. Paul quoted a terrible testimony (1:12)

This verse contains a derogatory description of Cretans in general. All peoples develop national characteristics. Welsh people, for instance, are known for their singing. Germans are known for their thoroughness. The ancient Assyrians were known for their cruelty. Americans are noted for their generosity. Cretans were known for their debasement. Livy, Poybius, and Plutarch all testify to the Cretans' covetousness and dishonesty. "When was there ever an upright Cretan?" asked Leonidas.[2]

To understand Paul's words here, we need to know about the Cretans and their background. Their island was first settled by people from nearby Asia Minor. The first important European civilization (the Minoan) began on the island of Crete. It was named after King Minos, who, according to Greek legend, was the son of Zeus and Europa. Stories depict him as the ruler and lawmaker of a great empire and as a cruel conqueror. He is said to have conquered Athens and demanded an annual toll of seven boys and seven girls to be sacrificed to the Minotaur.

---

2. See H. D. M. Spence and Joseph Exell, eds., "Titus," *The Pulpit Commentary* (Grand Rapids: Eerdmans, n.d.), 4.

The Minotaur was a mythical creature having the body of a man and the head of a bull. According to Greek mythology, King Minos kept the creature in a labyrinth from which no one could escape. Theseus of Athens, however, finally killed the Minotaur and escaped from the maze by following a thread given to him by Minos's daughter Ariadne. The royal palace in Knossos, Crete, had so many passageways that it resembled the legendary labyrinth. Doubtless, Paul was familiar with all of these legends long before he and Titus visited the island.

During the Minoan period, the Cretans made considerable advances in art, architecture, and engineering. They built magnificent palaces surrounded by spacious courtyards, made beautiful pottery and jewelry, developed a system of writing, and made progress in the field of mathematics. However, this progress did not continue.

The Romans invaded Crete in 68 B.C. and two years later made it a province of their growing empire. The Romans dragged the Cretans forcibly into the great Roman world, but the people themselves remained insular. Islanders usually tend to develop strong national characteristics.

a. The source of the quotation (1:12a)

By the time Paul and Titus visited the island, the Cretan character was firmly established and had become the subject of adverse comments by various ancient authors. Their comments corroborate Paul's blunt remark: "One of themselves, even a prophet of their own, said, The Cretians are alway liars, evil beasts, slow bellies" (Titus 1:12). It is generally accepted that the "prophet" (probably a priest of some sort) was Epimenides (born 659 B.C.), a contemporary of Solon and a native of either Phaistos or Knossos.

b. The substance of the quotation (1:12b–e)

(1) The Cretans are liars (1:12b)

The substance of the quotation from Epimenides is fourfold. First, the Cretans were "alway liars." The word translated "alway" in 1:12 means "perpetually, incessantly." Lying was continual among the Cretans. The Cretan addiction to lying even found its way into the Greek vocabulary, for the verb Paul used means literally "to lie like a Cretan."

The Cretans were liars by instinct and practice. At the same time, they were vulnerable to liars and thus easy prey for the Judaizers. The Judaizers "played the

Cretan with the Cretans"—that is, they deceived the deceivers. Paul could appreciate what Titus was up against.

Lying always destroys character, but truth is a great antidote. Nothing reveals the crookedness of lies and liars like the straight edge of divine truth. Titus had Holy Spirit-inspired truth to lay alongside the lies of Cretans and Judaizers alike.

(2) The Cretans are lawless (1:12c)

The Cretans have been described as pirates and wreckers. They were brutal, unreasonable, and rapacious. Their own "prophet" said, "The Cretians are always . . . evil beasts." The word translated "beasts" here means "wild beasts." The word translated "evil" is *kakos,* which means "depraved, bad by nature." It refers to a person's vicious disposition and desires rather than to the active exercise of wickedness. Taken together, the two words "evil beasts" depict the Cretans as thoroughly lawless and ungovernable in their behavior. They behaved like wild animals.

(3) The Cretans are lazy (1:12d)

The Cretans were also "slow." The word translated "slow" here is *argos,* which occurs eight times in the New Testament and is generally rendered "idle" in the King James text. It denotes inactivity and is associated with unfruitfulness and barrenness.

(4) The Cretans are lustful (1:12e)

Paul's quotations make Crete sound like unfruitful soil for the gospel. It was a miracle of grace that there was a church on the island at all. Not surprisingly, Judaizers and other false teachers were able to raise a harvest of sorts on Crete; weeds will grow almost anywhere.

The terrible testimony ends by saying that the Cretans are "slow bellies." The word translated "bellies" is that from which our English words *gastric* and *gastritis* are derived. Here the word is used figuratively *(synecdoche)* to refer to greed or gluttony. In plain words, the Cretans were "idle gluttons." Wuest thought that the Greek word conveyed the idea of gross obesity.[3]

3. Kenneth S. Wuest, *The Pastoral Epistles in the Greek New Testament* (Grand Rapids: Eerdmans, 1952), 187.

From the fourfold description in this passage, the Cretans seem to have been an unlovely crowd and Crete an unpromising mission field. The gospel, however, specializes in changing people. Think, for example, of the unregenerate people in Corinth. In 1 Corinthians 6:9–11, Paul presented a very unflattering description of them and then remarked, "Such were some of you: but ye are washed, but ye are sanctified, but ye are justified in the name of the Lord Jesus, and by the Spirit of our God." Likewise, Ephesians 2:1–6 reveals the great changes in the lives of believers in Ephesus. The God who could redeem and transform the Corinthians and Ephesians could do the same for the Cretans. Titus was up against a tough proposition, but it was by no means hopeless.

2. Paul quoted a true testimony (1:13)
    a. An endorsement of the Cretan character (1:13a)

Paul knew firsthand what the Cretans were like, so he could not argue with Epimenides. "This witness is true," the apostle said. Although Epimenides made the statement hundreds of years earlier, his assessment of the Cretan character proved to be accurate even in Paul's day.

Generation after generation, the Cretan character had run true to form. Greek philosophy had invaded the island but had not changed the Cretans. Roman law had been imposed on this unruly people but had not changed their hearts. Then the gospel came and succeeded where Minoan religion, Greek philosophy, and Roman rule had failed. But now the Judaizers with their rules, rituals, and restrictions were likely to undue what grace had wrought.

b. An enforcement of the Christian character (1:13b)

Because some of the Cretans were falling for the Judaizers' false teaching, Paul told Titus, "Rebuke them sharply, that they may be sound in the faith." The apostle was not doubting the salvation of the Cretan Christians to whom Titus was ministering. Because they were expressing their natural bent toward lying, lawlessness, laziness, and lust, however, Paul realized that a mild protest would not do. A sharp, apostolically backed reprimand was needed. The Cretan Christians were in peril of being bought into the bondage of Jewish legalism and of reverting to the kind of conduct that had characterize them in their unregenerate days.

The word translated "rebuke" here carries the ideas of both reproving and convicting. Titus was to rebuke the Cretans authoritatively in the power of the Holy Spirit to bring about conviction of sin and confession. The word translated "sharply" suggests a curt, abrupt, peremptory rebuke that would cut and hurt.

Many people associate Christianity with mildness—possibly because the popular children's hymn "Gentle Jesus" was often sung by Christian mothers as a lullaby:

> Gentle Jesus,
> *meek* and *mild,*
> Look upon a little child;
> Pity my simplicity,
> Suffer me to come to Thee.
> —Charles Wesley

These words convey an entirely false impression of the Lord Jesus. Meek He most certainly was (Matt. 11:29) because meekness is strength held under leash, but mild He never was. "It is a thousand pities," said J. B. Phillips, "that the word 'child' has so few words that rhyme with it appropriately for a hymn."[4]

The concept of a mild Jesus is entirely false. Scripture reveals that He knew anger (Mark 3:5) and that He took a whip and drove the money changers from the temple (John 2:13–17). He denounced the religious Jewish leaders of His day as hypocrites, children of hell, fools, and a "generation of vipers" (Matt. 12:34), and He said that they were blind, unclean, and full of iniquity. He knew full well that the religious establishment was conspiring to put Him to death, but He continued to be fearless in His denunciations.

There was nothing mild about Paul either. He confronted Peter "before them all" when the need arose (Gal. 2:11–14) and was not intimidated (as Peter was) by the formidable James (Acts 15). Titus knew from personal experience that on doctrinal matters Paul was willing to confront the whole Jerusalem church. He had dared its Judaistic hierarchy to try to make him circumcise Titus, who was a Gentile. The apostles and prophets in Jerusalem had been willing to say that they accepted the principle of Gentiles being free from any obligation to be circumcised; Paul put them to the test. In effect, he said, "Good! Here's my friend and convert, Titus. He is an uncircumcised Gentile. Invite him to sit with you in your homes and at the Lord's Supper."

4. See J. B. Phillips's classic work *Your God Is Too Small* (New York: Macmillan, 1957), 23.

When the high priest Ananias commanded his minions to smite Paul on the mouth, Paul called him a "whited wall" (Acts 23:3). True, when he learned who Ananias was, Paul apologized (although not without a trace of sarcasm), but no one would accuse Paul of being mild.

"Rebuke them sharply," Paul advised Titus. There is no room for mollycoddling people who want to subvert the faith of the people of God—whether the false teachers be the legalists of Paul's day or the so-called liberals of our day.

Paul gave his reason for rebuking those who were listening to the Judaizers: "That they may be sound in the faith." The apostle was not concerned simply with winning an argument with false teachers. He wanted the believers who had been deceived and were in a backslidden condition to be restored to the right path. He wanted them to regain their spiritual health. What was needed was surgery, not a cosmetic or a Band-Aid.

Evidently, Paul thought that Titus had the moral and spiritual fiber to do what he was told. It was no small order. The cultists were a formidable group and very sure of themselves; the Cretans could be awkward customers on their own account. To ask Titus, a young man, to stand up to the false teachers on the one hand and the carnal, contentious Cretans on the other was a tough assignment. Titus would need a high degree of courage, spiritual stamina, and Bible knowledge to do what Paul commanded.

C. The message of false teachers (1:14)
   1. Its content (1:14a–b)
      a. Fabulous Jewish tales (1:14a)

The emissaries from Jerusalem had two items of stock to trade. The first item they tried to peddle to Christians was "Jewish fables." These fairy tales were the kind found in the Apocrypha, the Talmud, and the Cabbala. Paul had been brought up on these fables, and he knew how valueless they were. Some of them could be used to illustrate a moral principle, but they were utterly worthless as a source of spiritual nourishment. To study them was a waste of time. After all, God spoke fully and finally in His Word concerning all pertinent *facts,* so why be taken up with *fables?* The Bible contained enough truth to occupy men's minds and hearts for all eternity, so why should anyone have chased down the blind alley of Jewish fables?

The New Testament shows that the invasion of Paul's churches by Jewish charlatans was widespread. Paul had to confront their false teaching not only on

Crete but also in Galatia, Antioch, Corinth, and Colossae. About the same time that Paul was urging Titus to deal with the problem on Crete, he was writing to Timothy to encourage him to take a stand against Jewish fables in Ephesus (1 Tim. 1:4).

b. False Jewish traditions (1:14b)

The Jerusalem envoys, armed with their useless credentials, peddled a second item: false Jewish traditions, which Paul called "commandments of men." The word translated "commandments" signifies things imposed, injunctions, charges, and moral and religious precepts. The offensive and unreasonable factor in the proclamation of such "commandments" was that they were merely orders issued by men.

The Jews were adept at imposing biblical Old Testament decrees on those for whom they were never intended. The most obvious examples were Mosaic Laws concerning circumcision, the Sabbath, meats, fasts, feasts, and animal sacrifices. The need to observe these ceremonial requirements ended at Calvary. To impose them on Christians was quite out of order because the decrees had no New Testament validity. Because such laws belonged to a past dispensation, they did not even apply to Jewish Christians.

The Jews were also prolific in inventing what they *claimed* were divine decrees. According to the rabbis, God gave Moses two sets of laws at Sinai. There was the written law, which they called the Torah, and there was the oral law that was comprised of ever-burgeoning writings, opinions, rulings, interpretations, discussions, and traditions. This accumulating body of tradition evolved into the Talmud. The Lord Himself repudiated these traditions as being of human origin and worse than useless (Matt. 15:1–12).

The rabbis would argue for months on end over the commandment "Thou shalt not seethe a kid in his mother's milk" (Deut. 14:21). They filled endless pages with their deliberations, came up with a list of rules for everyday work in the kitchen, and made cooking an ordeal. Similarly, the rabbis went on and on discussing what constituted *work* on the Sabbath (Exod. 20:8–11). They made countless petty regulations that, if taken seriously, must have made Sabbath-keeping a nightmare instead of the time of rest, reflection, and relaxation that God intended it to be. The Lord roundly castigated the Jewish religious leaders for fastening such burdens on God's people (Matt. 23:1–4). He refused to be governed by them in His own Sabbath-keeping.

At the Jerusalem conference, convened to decide the status of Gentiles in the church, Peter decried any attempt "to put a yoke upon the neck of the disciples, which neither our fathers nor we were able to bear" (Acts 15:10). The conference affirmed once and for all the principle of freedom from the Law. Emissaries from Jerusalem and Palestine, however, continued to try to fasten this heavy and useless yoke on believers throughout the Gentile world. Paul was indignant and sought to convey to Titus a hearty contempt for all such man-made rules and regulations.

2. Its intent (1:14c)

The intent of these false teachers was all too obvious. Their fairy tales and decrees were intended to "turn from the truth." The word translated "turn from" means "to turn oneself away from." As used here, the word conveys the idea that the false teachers had turned themselves away from the truth. In other words, the fables and commandments came from men who had forsaken the path of truth. There is no more deceitful man alive than one who has deliberately turned away from known and revealed truth.

We have all met people who refuse to accept the truth. They are like the patient who refuses to believe that he has cancer and does not submit to surgery or some other prescribed treatment. The doctor has the X rays and the biopsies to prove the diagnosis, but the patient is not convinced and seeks out quack doctors and phony remedies. People who refuse to accept the truth are also like the man who ignores sound financial advice. His businessman friend urges him not to buy certain shares of stock because the company offering the shares is on the verge of bankruptcy. The company had a good record and reputation, but the businessman has balance sheets and confidential reports to back up his advice. His friend, however, refuses to believe the truth and, preferring to believe the stockbroker's optimistic reports, goes ahead with his investment to his ruin.

The Bible tells us the truth about God, ourselves, and sin and salvation. Because some of its truths are unpalatable to both the natural mind and the carnal mind, some people turn away from them and heed the fables and formulas of men. Having been doubly blinded, they become Satan's emissaries—blind leaders of the blind, deceived and deceiving.

It is a well-known fact that people who are committed to a wrong path like to lead others onto the path they have chosen. Those who have abandoned the path of virtue like to seduce others. The man who drinks alcohol usually likes to have drinking companions. Those who embrace religious error like to lead others down the same wrong road. Jesus said, "Woe unto you, scribes and Pharisees, hypocrites! for ye compass sea and land to make one proselyte, and when he is made, ye make him twofold more the child of hell than yourselves" (Matt. 23:15). Cultists are not content with going astray themselves; they like to lead astray as many others as they can.

D. The morals of false teachers (1:15–16)
   1. A contrast (1:15)
      a. The pure person (1:15a)

Paul now compares the practical results of false teaching with the practical results of true biblical teaching. "Unto the pure," he said, "all things are pure." The word translated "pure" here is *katharos,* which means "pure as the result of cleansing" or "wholesome." To be pure is to be chaste, free from impurity, spotless or without blemish. Ethically, *katharos* has to do with being free from corrupt desire and consequent guilt.

In a sense, pure-minded men and women are insulated from the corruption and vileness of the world by their very purity. Their inner purity repels impurity. They do not allow impure thoughts to linger in their minds and hearts, and they turn away from impure associates, stories, books, movies, and television programs. Because the Holy Spirit rules in their hearts, they recoil from impurity when it intrudes and flee to Calvary for cleansing. Like the sunbeams that pass untouched through dirty panes, they remain as bright and unsullied as the dawn. Their minds dwell on "whatsoever things are pure" (Phil. 4:8).

When an impure person reads the Song of Solomon, he thinks impure thoughts, but when a pure person reads this divinely inspired, God-breathed love poem, he sees Christ. The Song of Solomon presents two contrasting people: the Shulamite woman, whose affections are engaged to her beloved, a shepherd who reminds us of Christ; and Solomon, a prince of this world, panoplied in wealth, wisdom, and splendor. He is determined to seduce the Shulamite.[5]

Armed and protected by her purity, the Shulamite moves uncontaminated through the story. She repels Solomon's most daring and unblushing advances. Indeed, he confesses that he is afraid of her (Song 6:4), and he acknowledges her purity (Song 6:9). Her response to his flatteries and his thinly veiled hints and

---

5. See John Phillips, *Exploring the Love Song of Solomon* (Grand Rapids: Kregel, 2003).

promises is sublime: she reminds him of the one to whom she has already given her heart. "I am my beloved's," she says, "and his desire is toward me" (Song 7:10). And that was the end of it! Solomon was repulsed and had to be content with his other loves. The "one woman among a thousand" (Eccl. 7:26–28), for whom Solomon sought in vain among his thousand wives and concubines, he found too late. Because of his lust, he lost her before he even found her.

b. The polluted person (1:15b–d)
 (1) His polluted outward view (1:15b)

"But unto them that are defiled and unbelieving," wrote Paul, "is nothing pure." Polluted men are cynics. They think that everyone has his price, that everyone is as impure as they are. Their eyes are lecherous, their tongues are filthy, their ears are eager to listen to obscene talk, and their thoughts are depraved. A beautiful young woman they would prostitute. An innocent boy they would contaminate. A little child they would abuse. They applaud pimps, pornographers, and perverts. Their lives are rotten through and through with lust.

Nothing was pure to the people of Sodom. They were foul and filthy beyond words. Lot never really felt at home in Sodom (2 Peter 2:7–8). His protests against the wicked lifestyle of the Sodomites only served to arouse the active enmity of the city. Finally, God resolved to take action and make an example of Sodom for the rest of time.

Just hours before the fiery judgment fell, two angels visited Lot (Gen. 19). They seemed to Lot and the men of Sodom to be fine specimens of manhood. The dragon lusts of the Sodomites were stirred at the sight of them. By midnight, the men of Sodom had collected outside Lot's house. They hammered at his door and demanded that he bring out his visitors and hand them over. Lot was horrified, but his refusal to comply only fanned the flames of their lust. To the decadent men at his door, nothing was pure or sacred. They wanted those two men, and they were prepared to trample on anyone who stood in their way. Two angels of light had just arrived in Sodom from heaven's unsullied shore. The men of Sodom wanted to defile even them. As Paul said, "Unto them that are defiled and unbelieving is nothing pure."

According to the words of Paul, some of the Cretan false teachers had abandoned morality as well as sound doctrine. The professing church today has practicing homosexuals in its midst. Some churches have even ordained them to the ministry.

Solomon is an example of someone who was defiled by lust. No one had ever had a better start in life. He was heir to an empire, he had David for a father, and he had David's great psalms to teach him. When Solomon was visited by God, he asked for and received wisdom from on high. He began well. He built the temple and put Israel on the path to greatness. But, sad to say, he made shipwreck of his life before he was through.

Solomon's lust burned more and more until his harem rivaled that of any pagan king. No woman was safe from his look, which made a pure woman feel contaminated, as the Shulamite discovered. As Solomon pressed his unwanted advances on this spiritually minded country girl, his flatteries and fantasies became shameless. But she was not seduced by his promises and praise. When he rhapsodized on her physical beauty (Song 7:1–9), she sought refuge in thoughts of her absent but soon-coming beloved.

Women were Solomon's downfall. He legalized his lust by marrying hundreds of them. He took an almost prurient interest in the traffic of a local harlot and watched with philosophical but almost criminal interest the way a young man approached her door (see Prov. 7).[6] We might well wonder how Solomon knew so much about that particular harlot, why he did not send someone to intercept the young man, and why he had not brought the full weight of the law to bear on the woman herself. Solomon had become defiled and no longer enthroned pure thoughts. The light that was in him was turned to darkness, and how great was that darkness (Matt. 6:23). With his backsliding, lusts, and idolatries, he practically turned Jerusalem into Babylon before he was through. Paul warned Titus against such men.

(2) His polluted inward values (1:15c–d)

The cultists were depraved both *mentally* and *morally*. "Even their mind and conscience is defiled," Paul said. There is not much hope for a person who, having turned his back on revealed truth, seeks refuge in false teaching and plunges into immoral living. His thoughts and his conscience become warped. He persuades himself that error is truth and that wrong is right. Such a person is in danger of being abandoned by the Holy Spirit to his delusions and fantasies.

---

6. See John Phillips, *Exploring Proverbs,* 2 vols. (Grand Rapids: Kregel, 2002), 1:165–81.

2. A conclusion (1:16)
   a. What false teachers profess (1:16a)

False teachers "profess that they know God." They often occupy important chairs in seminaries and Bible colleges. They fill key pulpits. They sit on mission boards. They become elders, deacons, trustees, and officers of the church and its institutions.

They profess to know God. In fact, however, they become so-called liberals who deny every cardinal doctrine of the faith, legalists who want to substitute Old Testament law for New Testament grace, leftists who want to replace the saving gospel with a social gospel, and libertines who undermine the moral foundations of society by excusing wickedness and encouraging immorality. They profess to know God, but God does not know them (Matt. 7:15–23).

   b. What false teachers practice (1:16b–e)
      (1) A denial of God Himself (1:16b)

They profess to know God, but what they practice amounts to a denial of God. "In works they deny him," wrote Paul. The word translated "deny" here is *arneomai,* which means "to contradict." What false teachers say and do contradicts their profession of faith. If they really knew God, they would take the Bible at face value and seek to implement its precepts and principles.

A young freshman theology student told me about a teacher he had in seminary. The man's opening remarks to his class were blunt and to the point: "The first eleven chapters of Genesis are nothing but myth," he said. (Actually they are the foundation of the whole Bible!)[7] Presumably, he professed to believe in God; otherwise, he would not have been teaching in a seminary. In his first words to that class, he denied the Bible and exposed himself as a charlatan, a wolf in sheep's clothing, a deceiver.

An honest man who held views like that would resign and earn his living some other way. After all, the young men who enroll in his seminary give their time and money to be built up in the faith. They do not expect to have their faith torn to shreds by an unbelieving professor who has earned degrees but knows less about the Word of God than a Spirit-taught errand boy. For such people to continue to teach soul-destroying dogmas to those who are training for the ministry reveals a "defiled" mind and conscience.

---

7. See John Phillips, *Exploring Genesis* (Grand Rapids: Kregel, 2001).

The word translated "defiled" here means "stained, contaminated, polluted" or "diseased." Surely only a person who has a diseased mind and conscience could go on year after year tearing the Bible apart with the outworn and untrue theories of so-called "higher criticism," thus undermining the faith of successive classes of eager young people who have responded to the call to the Christian ministry.

(2) A denial of goodness itself (1:16c–e)

The work of false teachers amounts to a denial of goodness. Paul indicted them on three additional counts. First, they are *repulsive. Abominable [bdeluktos]* is the word that Paul used. *Bdeluktos* can also be translated "obviously vile" and "objects of disgust." Paul looked upon false teachers with a kind of horror. Sins of the flesh are bad enough, but they destroy only the body; sins against God's revealed truth destroy the soul.

Second, false teachers are *rebellious,* or "disobedient." The word translated "disobedient" here suggests an obstinate rejection of God's Word and will. The word also speaks of an unwillingness to be persuaded. There is little point in discussing issues with liberal theologians and cultists. Some of their followers might still be reachable, but the committed teachers of error are usually set on their unbelief (Heb. 6:4–8).

Third, false teachers are *reprobate.* Paul described them as being "unto every good work reprobate." The word translated "reprobate" here is *adokimos,* which is used primarily in connection with the testing of metals. When false teachers are tested as to whether they are doing any real good, they are exposed as frauds. God has put to the test and rejected them.

As we read Paul's description of the error that Titus had to confront on Crete, we realize that there can be no compromise with error and falsehood.

PART 4

The Need for Exercise in the Local Church

Titus 2:1–3:11

A. Personal Exercise (2:1–15)
 1. Behavior in the church (2:1–10)

Having handled doctrinal issues, Paul now turns to practical issues. He deals with varying roles in the local church fellowship and the way people should behave toward each other.

a. The sexes and their place (2:1–8)
 (1) Those with the advantage of years (2:1–3)
 (a) The men (2:1–2)
 i. The right doctrine (2:1)

Paul had thoroughly exposed and demolished false teachers, but they were still in evidence, and their shadow still lay on some hearts and homes. Therefore, Paul urged Titus once more to speak out. "Speak thou the things which become sound doctrine." He wanted Titus to be conspicuous, to stand out as a man opposed to the cultists. He must make his voice heard.

Titus needed to do more than excommunicate the false teachers; he must teach the Cretan Christians what to believe and how to behave. Doubtless, Titus had memorized Paul's teaching as set forth and immortalized in his epistles. Now Titus must teach the Cretans the truths contained in Paul's letters to Rome, Corinth, Galatia, Ephesus, Colossae, and Thessalonica. He must teach the Old Testament as Paul taught it—in the light of Calvary.

ii. The resulting deeds (2:2)
 a. The aged men's solid maturity (2:2a–c)

Christian character and behavior must accompany right doctrine. The older men in the church must take the lead in exhibiting the results of sound teaching. Titus was to teach "that the aged men be sober, grave, temperate."

The word translated "sober" here means literally "free from intoxicants." Nothing will destroy a Christian testimony faster than drunkenness. Years ago, I knew a man who had been a noted believer, a successful businessman, and an honored church leader. After his retirement from business, he became bored and time hung heavy on his hands. One fateful day, he took a drink to cheer himself up; within a year, he was a hopeless alcoholic. He lost his testimony, dropped out of church, abandoned his Bible, and ended his days with a bottle. Paul warned against such insobriety.

The word translated "grave" is *semnos,* which means "serious, august, venerable." Older men, who have seen much of life, have usually tasted its sorrows as well as its joys. Therefore, they are more "grave" than they used to be. When young people come to older people for advice, they want serious advice.

The morning after Ebenezer Scrooge was converted, he skipped around his room and was as giddy as a schoolboy. But he soon learned how to channel his newfound joy for practical purposes. Before the day ended, it was a radiantly transformed but more serious Scrooge who greeted his much abused nephew, poor Bob Cratchit, and Tiny Tim. It was a newly generous, as well as a happy, Scrooge who greeted the two philanthropists whom he had treated rudely a day earlier.[1]

The word translated "temperate" means "right-minded, wise, sagacious, discreet." Such older men can play a key role in steering others away from false teachers.

What a testimony to the power of the gospel to change lives is implied in this passage. Men who had been typical Cretans, accomplished liars, rapacious wild beasts, and lazy gluttons were changed. Now people could see Christ shining through them in their sobriety, seriousness, and godly common sense.

b. The aged men's spiritual maturity (2:2d–f)

1. Godward (2:2d)

Titus was also to teach "that the aged men . . . be sound in faith." The definite article with the Greek word for "faith" shows that Paul was referring to *the* faith, the great body of Christian teaching. If these older men were sound in the faith, that would show their maturity toward God.

Measurable spiritual development should be evident in the lives of older brethren. Young believers ought to be able to look to them for instruction and guidance in the things of God. Mere age is no guarantee of spiritual maturity. That comes from walking daily with God over many years.

2. Manward (2:2e)

Aged men are also to be characterized by "charity" (love). The word points to the highest kind of love, love that is spontaneous irrespective of rights or conditions.

---

1. See Charles Dickens's famous *A Christmas Carol.*

It is God's kind of love. People who show this kind of love have developed spiritual maturity manward.

Love is what Christianity is all about. The greatest revelation concerning God is that "God is love" (1 John 4:8, 16). The Lord Jesus was God incarnate and consequently love incarnate. Paul's great hymn of love, 1 Corinthians 13, can be thought of as a song about the life and person of the Lord Jesus. Substitute the word *Christ* for the word *charity* and then reread that chapter (1 Cor. 13). It sets before us a perfect portrait of Jesus.

Love reaches out to other people. It puts no limit on what it will suffer on another's behalf. It never stops trusting or hoping. It has been called the greatest thing in the world. When all else fails, love still remains. It is more triumphant than all other emotions, more ageless than the stars, and more permanent than the universe. It pours out in a living tide from the heart of God. The measure in which we reflect this love in our lives is the measure of how much we have grown in grace and increased in the knowledge of God.

3. Selfward (2:2f)

Furthermore, older men in the church are to be characterized by "patience." This inner quality is another expression of maturity. The word translated "patience" here means "patient endurance," patience that grows under trial. Youth wants things done now, but age brings the awareness that one must learn to wait.

The first occurrence of this Greek word *patience* in the New Testament is in the story of the parable of the sower (Luke 8:15).The great book of nature repeatedly tells us that God cannot be hurried. It takes time for the seasons to come and go. It takes time for a seed to grow into a flower. It takes time for a plant to bud, blossom, and bear fruit. It takes time for a child to grow up. Old people often wish that time would slow down because the years fly by too fast; children wish time would speed up.

Happy is the maturing believer who has learned patience, because God's most frequent answer to prayer is not yes or no, but wait. The book of Job was inspired by God and included in the canon of Scripture to teach us to wait patiently for God to speak and act.

Abraham's impatience brought Ishmael into the world, and with him problems that have lasted to this day (Gen. 16). Impatience cost Saul his kingdom

(1 Sam. 13). Young David, on the other hand, having learned patience through suffering, refused to take matters into his own hands and waited for God to give him the kingdom (1 Sam. 14–16; 2 Sam. 2:4; 5:3).

How pleasant it is to meet older believers who have learned to possess their soul in patience (James 1:3–4; Luke 21:19)! It must have been a rare and beautiful experience to see, on the turbulent island of Crete, old men full of love, faith, and patience. It is a rare and beautiful experience in today's world too.

(b) The matrons (2:3)
Noted for their:
i. Sanctity (2:3a)

The Holy Spirit desires to develop sanctity in the aging sisters in the church. Paul told Titus to teach "the aged women likewise, that they be in behaviour as becometh holiness." The apostle implies that women ought to mature in spirituality as they mature in years.

The word translated "aged women" is *presbutis,* which occurs only here in the New Testament. The word translated "behavior" occurs only here as well and refers to deportment or demeanor. The way a woman moves, the look on her face, what she says or leaves unsaid, and her habitual attitude of mind and body are all included in "behavior."

And what did Paul expect mature women in the faith to project through their postures and personalities? Holiness! The word translated "as becometh holiness" occurs only here in the New Testament and means "reverent." The deportment of older Christian women must reflect true sanctification of life.

ii. Sincerity (2:3b)

The Holy Spirit also desires to develop sincerity in older women. They are to be "not false accusers." The word translated "false accusers" is *diabolos,* which occurs thirty-eight times in the New Testament and is usually translated "devil." Thirty-four of those times it refers to Satan. Once it refers to the traitor Judas, who became Satan's emissary (John 6:70). Evidently, therefore, slander is the work of the Devil. The word *diabolos* implies a verbal assault. Nothing could be more destructive of harmony in a local church than a few older women hurling slanderous remarks against various people in the fellowship.

iii. Sobriety (2:3c)

Furthermore, the Holy Spirit desires to develop sobriety in older women. Paul said that they should be "not given too much wine." How often Paul mentions the sin of intoxication in his pastoral letters! Evidently, it was all too common a sin in the early church. The Bible does not categorically forbid the use of wine, but it does forbid drunkenness. And it does state as a principle that we must abstain from activities that could cause weaker believers to stumble (Rom. 14:21; 1 Cor. 8:9). That principle alone strictly curtails, or actually forbids, the use of alcohol by believers.

iv. Sermons (2:3d)

Moreover, older women are to be noted for their sermons, that is, they are to be "teachers of good things *[kalodidaskalos]*"—by example as well as by words. There is no hint here of public teaching. Paul most likely had in mind the kind of teaching practiced by Aquila and Priscilla, who instructed Apollos privately (Acts 18:24–28).

This verse does not contradict Paul's teaching elsewhere on the role of women in the church (1 Cor. 11:5; 14:34; 1 Tim. 2:12–15). The situation at Corinth involved "tongues" and total disorder in the church. The conditions under which a woman might teach are spelled out in 1 Corinthians 11:5. The sphere of her teaching ministry is indicated in Titus 2:4–5.

(2) Those with the advantage of youth (2:4–8)
(a) The maidens (2:4–5)
Taught by the matrons to be:
i. Disciplined (2:4a)

The older women come into their own as "teachers of good things" (2:3) as they teach the younger women, by example and exhortation, how to become useful members of the Christian community. The matrons can teach the maidens to be disciplined, for example. As Paul put it, "They may teach the young women to be sober" (2:4). He used a Greek word that means "to make sober minded" or "to recall a person to his senses." It conveys the ideas of chastening, discipline, and moderation.

This instruction was especially necessary for the Cretan girls, given the excesses of their national character. The grace of the Lord Jesus and the indwelling of the Holy Spirit call for a disciplined lifestyle for Christian young women. Of course, the older women have to live disciplined lives themselves if they are to teach the younger women to be "sober."

ii. Devoted (2:4b–c)

The older women in the church should teach the younger women to be devoted to their families. Paul said that young married women should be taught to "love their husbands." The word translated "love husbands" is *philandros,* which occurs only here in the New Testament. *Philandros* conveys the idea of tender affection. Most marriages experience stresses and strains, so we have to work to keep love preeminent in our domestic relationships.

Three little words, *I love you,* can ease a couple through many stormy seas. As someone has said, *"I* is the subject, *you* is the object, and there is nothing between but *love."* Love affects the look, the tone of voice, and the touch of the hand. Love is accompanied by an attitude of willing, joyful service and personal, caring solicitude. Such love is a commodity made in heaven, a balm for all of earth's woes, and a sure remedy when all else fails.

Paul adds that the younger women should be taught "to love their children." Not all mothers love their children, and not all mothers love their children equally and impartially. The temptation is to have a favorite. Sometimes a parent has a less favorite child, especially when the child has a rebellious disposition and tries his mother's patience to the extreme. Paul made no allowance for conflicting temperaments, extenuating circumstances, or human weaknesses. He indicated that mothers who do not love their children are to be taught to love them. Such instruction can often be provided by wise, motherly, spiritually minded, older women. Their knowledge, their experience, and their walk with God equip them to teach the younger women how to cope when things go wrong. We tend to think of love as an emotion, but the Bible commanded it, thereby making it volitional rather than emotional.

iii. Discreet (2:5a)

Moreover, the older women can teach the younger women how "to be discreet." The word translated "discreet" means "sensible, self-controlled."

Most parents do their fair share of foolish things in bringing up their children.

They might overindulge them or overdiscipline them. They might threaten and then fail to do what they say they will do. They might break promises. They might play favorites or take sides. The wonder is that any children survive and become useful members of the community and functioning members of the body of Christ.

The classic example of foolish parents in the Old Testament is found in the story of Isaac and Rebekah. Isaac was placid, pliable, and, in later years, carnal and self-indulgent. His son, Esau, had long since learned how to get what he wanted from his father. Rebekah, on the other hand, was determined and tough-minded. She had been badly betrayed once, and she never forgot it (Gen. 26:6–11). She, too, knew how to trade on Isaac's weaknesses and was not overscrupulous about telling the truth. Moreover, she had a soft spot in her heart for her clever and wily younger son, Jacob.

What Rebekah needed was a wise older woman to counsel and teach her. It is a great pity that she never knew her mother-in-law, for Sarah had traveled through the same troubled domestic waters not once but twice (Gen. 12:10–20; 20:1–18). She did not let that stop her from holding her husband in high honor (1 Peter 3:6). Sarah could have taught Rebekah how to be sensible and self-controlled.

It is a great advantage for young mothers to have wise, saintly older women to teach and counsel them. Preaching and pastoral counseling have their roles, but some problems and pressures are best resolved when women talk to women.

iv. Decent (2:5b)

Paul said, too, that older women can teach younger women to be decent—to be "chaste." The word translated "chaste" here is *hagnos,* which means "pure and immaculate, free from carnality." Chastity has gone out of style these days. We live in the day of the "adult" movie, the marching sodomite, and the demanding feminist. It is the age of "the new morality" based on relativism and humanism. The so-called new morality is just the old immorality but now openly espoused by the media, the schools, the courts, and often the government. Pornographic books, child molestation, syndicated crime, indulgence in drugs, and the senseless pursuit of the demon-haunted occult world characterize our society. Most of the old familiar landmarks of morality and common decency are gone. We have banished the Bible from our classrooms and the Ten Commandments from the courts. The pressure is on to conform to the world's wanton ways.

More than ever, young women need the counterbalancing influence of older women who remember a different, more decent, more disciplined age. Naomi was such a woman. She greatly influenced her young daughter-in-law, Ruth. Ruth was raised as a pagan in Moab, a nation with a very unsavory history and one under the direct curse of God's law (Gen. 19:30–38; Deut. 23:3). Yet, when Boaz first met and talked to Ruth, he exclaimed, "All the city of my people doth know that thou art a virtuous woman" (Ruth 3:11).[2] Ruth is the only woman specifically identified in the Bible as "a virtuous woman." The full measure of all that is implied in that tribute was given later by Solomon (Prov. 31:10–31).

Where did Ruth learn her virtuous ways? She must have been taught virtue by her mother-in-law. Naomi had learned much from the bitter experiences that she had encountered in life. After she was restored to the Lord, her godly counsel played an important part in the events that led to Ruth's subsequent marriage to Boaz.

Happy is the young woman who will heed the counsel of a godly older woman in the matter of dress and deportment, to say the least, and who will espouse chastity in all of its higher and holier implications as a rule of life.

v. Domesticated (2:5c–e)

a. They are to be guardians of the home (2:5c)

The older women can also teach the younger women in the church how to be "keepers at home *[oikourgos]*." The Greek word means literally "workers at home." Some scholars think that the word Paul used was *oikouros,* which refers to watching or keeping the home. In either case, the idea is that the woman's role is in the home.

Our feminist culture urges women to become career women, and enormous pressure is put on them to enter the workforce. Many marriages are wrecked because working wives become discontented with and independent of their husbands. Working mothers face enormous problems, and so do their families. Many children have strayed because their mothers were off to work when they were needed at home. Gone are the days of the extended family when a young wife and mother had the support of her parents, in-laws, brothers, and sisters and when children grew up surrounded by grandparents, uncles, aunts, and cousins who played a supportive role in each other's families.

The pressures of modern life notwithstanding, the Bible ethic is always best

2. The full measure of all that is implied in the words *a virtuous woman* is given in Proverbs 31:10–31.

because it is based on the highest wisdom. Its mandate that wives should be "keepers at home" ought to be the blueprint that Christian wives and mothers follow. Their tasks might not seem as exciting as supervising the production division of a big corporation or as interesting as teaching psychology to young people in college. But, in the light of eternity, the role of "keepers at home" is infinitely more worthwhile

Susannah Wesley might well be considered the patron saint, so to speak, of all of those women who stay at home and raise their children for God. She was the mother of nineteen children. She was well educated and had strong convictions. She homeschooled her children individually and diligently. Her piety, devotion, and Christian character were reproduced in her children. The impact that she made on the world will never be known this side of eternity. As a Moses, an Aaron, and a Miriam came out of the humble home of Amram and Jochabed, so a John and Charles Wesley came out of the home of Susannah Wesley, and with them came the Methodist revival.

According to God's Word, a woman is not to be "busy here and there" (1 Kings 20:40). If she is, she may one day wake up to the fact that her children are gone and that the world has taken them.

b. They are to be good from the heart (2:5d)

Older women can teach younger women to be "good." The word translated "good" here is *agathos,* which has to do with being good in character or constitution and with the beneficial effects of such goodness. It is sometimes used to describe the absolute, essential goodness of God. The idea of kindness is included in the word, as is the concept of being good-natured. Thus, one rendering of *agathos* is "kindhearted."

A woman's role is to make her home a refuge from all of the mean-spiritedness, callousness, cruelty, and wickedness so often encountered in the outside world. Her husband often has to deal with evil in the workaday world. Her children have to battle it at school. When husband and children come home, home should seem to them like a suburb of heaven.

Jochebed—the wife of Amram and the mother of Aaron, Miriam, and Moses—created such a refuge for her family. Her name means "God my glory." She moved around her home like the Shekinah glory-cloud itself. Jochebed transformed the slave hut in which she lived in the Goshen ghetto into a veritable sanctuary.

When Moses, the great emancipator of the Hebrew people, was finishing the writing of the Ninetieth Psalm, he might well have thought of his mother. He wrote, "Let the beauty of the LORD our God be upon us" (90:17). He had seen that beauty in the face of his mother. "God my glory," was her name, and "God my glory" was her nature. The glow of her face and the glory of her grace never left her, and its memory never left Moses. All of the glitter and glamour of Pharaoh's courts and Egypt's schools, and the goals of Moses' royal patron's could not prevail over Jochebed's influence. From the divine standpoint, *that* is the glory of being a wife and mother. Nothing else compares with it.

c. They are to be guided by their husbands (2:5e)

The older women can also teach the younger women to be "obedient to their own husbands." The word translated "obedient" here is a military term that means literally "to be in subjection." God is a God of order. The lines of authority are clearly drawn in the New Testament. Whether in the home, the state, or the church, these lines are not to be tampered with.

"But you don't know my husband," some wives plaintively complain. Maybe we don't, but God does. And that is what matters. These rules are not ours; they are not even the apostle Paul's. They are God's rules and must not be changed.

Come back to the case of Isaac and Rebekah. Rebekah was not in the habit of being guided by her husband, whose appetite had long since replaced her as his first love (Gen. 24:67; 27:4). When she discovered that Isaac was about to do something carnal, worldly, absolutely wrong, and spiritually disastrous, she reacted in a worldly, carnal, wrong, and spiritually disastrous way. Both Isaac and Rebekah knew that the patriarchal blessing had been divinely promised to Jacob (25:23–26). Isaac, however, was determined to give it to Esau. As soon as Rebekah discovered what was brewing, she took matters into her own hands. She coached her favorite son, Jacob, in a course of deception. The results were calamitous.

In the end, Isaac's eyes were opened to his own wrongdoing. He confirmed the fact that the blessing belonged to Jacob and refused to change his mind to please his favorite son, Esau. Esau threatened to murder Jacob, who was thus forced to flee from home. On his mother's advice, Jacob headed to distant Padan-aram to try his "success" with his grasping, squeezing Uncle Laban—and a miserable twenty years he had of it.

"Now therefore, my son," Rebekah said, "obey my voice; and arise, flee thou to Laban my brother to Haran; And tarry with him a few days, until thy brother's fury turn away" (27:43–44). The few days turned out to be a long and unhappy time. As for Rebekah, she never saw her dear son again. Her story would have had a different ending if she had been in subjection to her husband and had presented the matter of the birthright to him in a straightforward way and along spiritual lines.

vi. Defenders (2:5f)

Finally, the older women can teach the younger women how to defend the Word of God against its foes. Women need to obey Scripture "that the word of God be not blasphemed." They, like the men, should not do anything that would give unbelievers an excuse for defaming the Word of God.

When God's Word speaks to an issue—be it spiritual, social, scientific, or secular—it speaks with the highest authority, with unerring wisdom, and with unfailing love. Its principles must be accepted, its precepts obeyed, and its promises believed.

(b) The men (2:6–8)

i. Their sobriety (2:6)

Paul now gives Titus some guidelines for young men. He was to exhort them first of all "to be sober minded." The Greek word means "to exercise self-control, to be of sound mind." Young men are to take life seriously.

David is an example of a "sober-minded" young man. When he brought provisions to his older brothers on the battlefield, he heard about the giant, about Israel's predicament, and about the reward offered by the king to anyone who would go into the valley and kill Goliath. David's eager inquiries met with typical older-brother scorn and contempt. But Eliab's reproofs showed how little he knew his youngest brother, for the next thing he knew David was volunteering to fight the giant.

David was not bragging; he was quite "sober minded" about it. He had already killed a lion and a bear in defense of his flock, and he was already a spiritual giant capable of writing such a poem as Psalm 23. David took life seriously and faced its crises hand in hand with God, as his answer to Goliath's boasts and blasphemies reveals: "Thou comest to me with a sword and with a spear, and with a shield: but I come to thee in the name of the LORD of hosts, the God of the armies of Israel, whom thou hast defied. This day will the LORD deliver thee into mine hand . . . for the battle is the LORD's" (1 Sam. 17:45–47). It was not frivolity but faith that motivated David.

ii. Their service (2:7a)

Young men in the church are to be noted for their service. On the island of Crete, the spiritual temperature was low and the moral climate was bad, so Titus had to set the pace. He was to be "a pattern of good works" in all things. The word translated "pattern" is *tupos,* from which our English word *type* is derived. A type is a divinely planned illustration.

The Old Testament is full of such types. Joseph, for example, was a type of Christ. Joseph was his father's well-beloved son. He was hated by his kinsmen, the children of Israel. He was sold by them for the price of a slave and made to suffer for another person's sins. Eventually, he was exalted to the right hand of the Pharaoh and given a name above every other name and before which all other knees must bow. In all of this, he was a picture, an illustration, a pattern of Christ.[3]

The Old Testament is full of such types. The sacrifices and feasts are types that illustrate New Testament truths. The tabernacle and the temple mirror realities that were not fully revealed in the Old Testament. Abraham and Isaac, David and Jonathan, Ruth and Boaz, Solomon and the queen of Sheba, Moses and Joshua, and Aaron and Melchizedek—all of these pairs are types.

Similarly, Titus was to be a type. Other young men were to be inspired to good works by his tireless devotion to doing good in all things.

iii. Their soundness (2:7b)

Young men are also to be noted for sound doctrine: "In doctrine shewing uncorruptness." The word translated "shewing" here means "to offer, furnish, supply, give." The word translated "uncorruptness" is *adiaphthoria,* which means "free from taint."

Again we note Paul's insistence on sound doctrine. Nothing less than the strictest regard for divinely revealed truth must characterize all teaching. Young men are more likely to be carried away by doctrinal novelties than are older men who have arrived at their convictions after years of study, meditation, and discussion. Truth bought at such a price is more apt to be prized than truth picked up casually in a "sharing" session. "Buy the truth," Proverbs 23:23 says, "and sell it not." Paul urged all young men to get a head start on acquiring a knowledge of sound doctrine.

3. See John Phillips, *Exploring Genesis* (Grand Rapids: Kregel, 2001).

iv. Their seriousness (2:7c)

Furthermore, young men are to be known for their "gravity." The word translated "gravity" here denotes "venerableness, dignity" It is more often associated with age than with youth.

Paul thought that lightness and levity had no place in teaching the Bible. The issues with which Scripture deals—sin and death, time and eternity, heaven and hell, Christ and Calvary—are too serious to be treated with frivolity. We never read that Jesus laughed (although He likely did because He was thoroughly human), but three times we read that He wept.

v. Their sincerity (2:7d)

Young men in the church are also to be noted for their "sincerity." The word translated "sincerity" here is *aphtharsia.* Paul used the same word in Ephesians 6:24, where it is also translated "sincerity," and in Romans 2:7, where it is translated "immorality" but probably means "incorruption." The ideas of glory, honor, and eternal life cluster around *aphtharsia.* It occurs again and again in Paul's great passage on the believer's resurrection body, which is a body of incorruption (1 Cor. 15:42, 50, 53, 54).

Paul expected a great deal from his young men. Their sincerity was to be transparent. While living in a corrupt world, they were to exhibit the characteristics of the world to come. While living in bodies prone to corruption, they were to be incorruptible.

vi. Their speech (2:8)

a. Irreproachable (2:8a)

Concluding his instructions to Titus regarding young men, Paul called for "sound speech, that cannot be condemned." The word translated "sound" here occurs over a dozen times in the New Testament and is usually translated "whole." It is commonly used in reference to physical health. Only here is it applied to what we say. Paul still seems to have teaching on his mind. All speech should be beyond blame, but when teaching the Word of God, the speaker must be particularly careful not to say anything that might be misconstrued.

b. Irrefutable (2:8b)

The words of a teacher must be irrefutable so "that he that is of the contrary part may be ashamed, having no evil thing to say of you [the teacher]." He must ensure that he is so grounded in truth, so based on God's inerrant Word, that people who come to find fault and pick holes in his presentation will be forced to retreat in confusion.

I am reminded of the testimony of a friend of mine, now in heaven, who, before his conversion, was both an atheist and a communist. One day, he noticed that a gospel tent had been erected on some vacant ground near where he lived, and he decided to go to the meeting as a troublemaker. He formulated a plan: he would let the speaker get started, and then he would stand up and contradict him.

The man who was conducting the meetings (whom I also knew) was a courteous gentleman, the kind of person whom one would expect to be the local bank manager or the village doctor. His would-be challenger had a sharp mind and a reputation for being a formidable opponent in debate. Because he was well versed in atheistic arguments against the Bible, he was sure that the preacher would be no match for him. Moreover, he was a tough customer, a prizefighter with a burly body. He would have welcomed any attempt to remove him by force as a chance to start a fight. He was determined to make a fool of that preacher and break up the service.

The townsfolk heard rumors about the atheist's plan and went to the service expecting to see some fun. The preacher, they thought, was in for a surprise. As it turned out, the troublemaker was the one who was in for the surprise!

The message preached that night was well prepared and well presented, and the logic of the gospel arrested the atheist despite himself. He felt himself glued to his seat and unable to jump up and make trouble. His cronies signaled him to get going; instead, he sat and listened—promising himself, however, that he would make mincemeat of the preacher later.

When the service was over, the big man, no longer under the spell of the message, marched forward to pick a fight. He trotted out his infidel rationalizations and the clever arguments that he had found so effective in the past. But to his surprise, the mild-mannered preacher had heard them all and knew how to answer each one. The troublemaker was up against some very "sound speech." He was disarmed by the logic of the Word of God and could find nothing in which to poke holes. Before it was over, the preacher led his adversary to Christ, and the former atheist became one of the ablest teacher-evangelists I have ever known.

Paul wanted his young men to be like that irrefutable preacher. He wanted them to develop exemplary lives, extraordinary competence, and excellence of speech.

b. The servants and their place (2:9–10)
 (1) They are to serve diligently (2:9)
  (a) Obeying submissively (2:9a)

Paul now turns to the place of slaves in the church and spells out some basic characteristics that born-again servants should have. First, they should be submissive. He told Titus to "exhort servants to be obedient unto their own masters." The word translated "servants" here is *doulos,* which means "slave."

Slaves had no civil rights in the Roman Empire. A cruel master could torture and even kill a slave with impunity. Even if a slave had a decent master, who appreciated his talents and liked him, perhaps even loved him, the slave was still a slave. If the kind master died, the slave could be sold. He might be bought by a tyrant. He might be assigned to perform demeaning tasks. He had no recourse. Slavery was deeply entrenched. The only attack on the institution of slavery in the New Testament is the oblique but ultimately overwhelmingly effective one made by Paul in his epistle to Philemon.

A slave (or in our modern world, a servant or employee) must be "obedient" to his master. The word *obedient* is the same word used in 2:5, where Paul mandated a wife's obedience to her husband. In the active voice, it was used to describe a superior officer in the army issuing orders to an inferior. In such a situation, prompt and cheerful obedience is required. Paul expected servants to do what they were told, regardless of whether their masters were good or bad. In this matter, he made no difference between believing and unbelieving masters.

(b) Obeying satisfactorily (2:9b)

Born-again servants should "please [their masters] well in all things." The word translated "please well" is *euarestos,* which describes service that is acceptable or behavior that is well pleasing to God.

Paul's typical attitude toward the servant-master relationship is described in Ephesians 6:5–8 and Colossians 3:22–24. The human master fades from the picture, and the Lord Jesus replaces him as the One who is being served. If we render to Him the kind of service that He deserves, the human master will automatically receive the best service possible. A Christian employee ought to be the most diligent, conscientious, and willing person on the payroll.

Joseph served both Potiphar and the jailer superlatively (Gen. 39:1–6, 21–23). God honored Joseph, just as He will honor all of those who look on their subservient position, not as a form of servility, but as an opportunity for service. Such an outlook is not only spiritual but also sensible.

(c) Obeying silently (2:9c)

Servants should obey, "not answering again." The word translated "answering again" means "to speak against, contradict." Here the word implies overt or covert resistance to the will of the master (or employer or supervisor) and impatience with any rebuke. We see behind this injunction a glimpse of a servant grumbling under his breath when he is told to do something or an employee revealing a surly attitude by his looks or gestures. Such actions are certainly not calculated to win the employer to Christ.

(2) They are to serve differently (2:10a)

A Christian servant should not be guilty of "purloining *[nosphizomai]*." The Greek word means "being light-fingered." It was used in reference to Ananias and Sapphira, who, having sold a piece of property, deliberately gave the impression that they were donating the entire proceeds to the church, when they actually "kept back *[nosphizomai]*" part of the money. In purloining it, they robbed God and died within the day for their wickedness (Acts 5:1–10).

In the Septuagint, *nosphizomai* is used in reference to Achan's theft of a small amount of spoil from the siege and sacking of Jericho (Josh. 7:1). The onward march of the people of God was interrupted by this unconscionable pilfering, and, as was the case with Ananias and Sapphira, it led to Achan's death under the judgment of God. God views purloining seriously because it destroys character and ruins the testimony of the believer when he is caught with his hand in the till.

Today, it is not at all uncommon for employees to pilfer from their employers. Usually, the items stolen are small—stamps, pens, envelopes, stationery—but over a period of a year, the losses from this petty larceny can add up to considerable sums of money. As far as God is concerned, theft is theft. Employees often use all kinds of mental gymnastics to justify taking a bar of soap or a tool or a small amount of change, but God is not impressed with their rationalizations. No Christian should be guilty of such behavior. His conscience should be a tender one.

Stealing was commonplace among the slaves in the Roman Empire of Paul's day. Although slaves had no other way of obtaining some of life's creature comforts, the Bible militated against the practice of pilfering from masters.

We have already noted the quality of Joseph's service in the house of Potiphar. The man soon learned that he could trust Joseph implicitly. "Behold," Joseph could say, "my master wotteth [knoweth] not what is with me in the house, and he hath committed all that he hath to my hand" (Gen. 39:8). Although he was a slave, Joseph was incorruptible. He was different from other slaves. Likewise, the Christian employee should be different from his unbelieving, pilfering coworkers.

(3) They are to serve devotedly (2:10b)

Instead of purloining, the Christian servant should show "all good fidelity." The word translated "fidelity" is *pistis,* which embodies the ideas of faith and faithfulness. A faithful worker will look out for the best interests of his employers and make the best use of his time and talents. His conscientious devotion to duty should be obvious, even behind his employer's back. Again, Joseph is the classic Old Testament example. In the New Testament, we have the example of Onesimus, a runaway slave. Paul won him to Christ and then sent the transformed man back to his master, whom he would now serve with "all good fidelity."

(4) They are to serve demonstrably (2:10c–d)

People on even the lowest rungs of the social ladder can be living testimonials to the gospel. In all areas of life, they can be good advertisements for the Christian message. If they serve demonstrably, they "adorn the doctrine of God our Saviour in all things." The word translated "adorn" means "to ornament." Our English word *cosmetic* is derived from this Greek word. Servants, as much as anyone else, can be ornaments of the gospel.

The Roman system of slavery was pernicious; slaves were treated as pieces of property, so much so that discontent forever seethed beneath the surface of society. Slave owners, in constant fear of a universal slave revolt, used harsh measures to discourage insubordination. When runaway slaves were caught, they were routinely crucified. No restraints were placed on sadistic masters in their choice of tactics for terrorizing their slaves. They used the terrible scourge freely. One slave owner threw slaves who displeased him into a pool, where they were torn to pieces by voracious fish.

Into this scene of injustice and oppression came the gospel. Slaves were won to Christ. Indeed, in Paul's day a high percentage of Christians were slaves. Paul did not urge them to mobilize and march. Instead, he taught them to live as Christ lived, *faithfully* and *fully* adorning "the doctrine of God our Saviour."

2. Beliefs in the church (2:11–15)
   a. Present grace (2:11–12)
      (1) The appearing of grace (2:11)
         (a) Sovereign grace (2:11a)

Paul now expanded his explanation of the doctrine that servants were to adorn. He wrote about three aspects of grace. First, it is sovereign grace, "the grace of God." Because it emanates from God, no power on earth or in hell can frustrate it. It pours out from the heart of the eternal Author of the universe.

Long before time began, long before God stooped down to fashion Adam's clay, grace reigned in the heart of God. When Father, Son, and Holy Spirit, in the council chambers of eternity, decided to create the universe, They knew that if they acted in Creation, the time would come when They would need to act in redemption. Grace would require it.

In time, God's wisdom and power *were* demonstrated in Creation, and His love and grace *were* demonstrated in redemption. An awed universe now marvels at the exceeding riches of God's sovereign grace.

(b) Saving grace (2:11b)

The sovereign grace of God "bringeth salvation." Grace is unmerited favor, getting something we don't deserve. What we deserve is punishment commensurate with our sin. Our sin amounts to rebellion against an all-wise, all-seeing, all-powerful God. His omnipresence places Him on the scene of our misbehaviors. His omniscience makes Him aware of our every thought, word, and deed (and all of their ramifications). His omnipotence can overwhelm all opposition. Instead of simply pouring out His wrath on us, however, God extends His grace toward us. He does not offer to overlook our sin because that would violate His holiness. Nor does He simply offer us forgiveness; He offers us complete justification. He declares us to be righteous. He removes our sins from His memory by an act of mercy and grace.

The plan of salvation proclaimed throughout the Bible is based on the principle of substitution. God passed the maximum sentence demanded by His holiness—eternal banishment from His presence and consignment to the lake of fire—but then He bore the penalty for sin Himself. At Calvary, the Son of God died in our stead and laid down an eternal life as an atonement for our sins. Such is the saving grace of God.

(c) Sufficient grace (2:11c)

God's saving grace is *sufficient* to cover all of our needs because it "hath appeared to all men." No man, woman, boy, or girl ever born of Adam's ruined race is excluded from this "so great salvation" (Heb. 2:3). It becomes *efficient* to cover all of our needs, however, only when it is accepted. Nonetheless, it is available to all people without exception and without distinction.

The universality of God's offer of salvation is confirmed in many Scripture passages. In John 3:16, we read that "God so loved the *world,* that he gave his only begotten Son, that *whosoever* believeth in him should not perish, but have everlasting life" (italics added). And in Romans 10:13, we read that "*whosoever* shall call upon the name of the Lord shall be saved" (italics added).

Moreover, God has sent His Spirit into the world to deal with every human heart in His own way and according to His own wisdom. John mentions the Light that "lighteth every man that cometh into the world" (John 1:9). Not all men *respond* to the Light, but all are *exposed* to it.

(2) The appeal of grace (2:12)
(a) What it teaches us to repudiate (2:12a–b)
i. Ungodliness (2:12a)

Once our hearts have been captured by God's marvelous grace, that grace teaches us to repudiate ungodliness. Paul speaks here of "denying ungodliness." The word translated "denying" is *arneomai,* which occurs thirty-one times in the New Testament. It means "to disown." In other words, the believer is taught to take a stand against the native-born ungodliness of his heart by denying ungodliness the right to express itself and by yielding to the indwelling Spirit of God. Before we are saved, we express our ungodliness (as in Jude 15), but once we are saved, we express godliness. "Denying ungodliness" is the acid test of genuine conversion (2 Cor. 5:17).

John Newton experienced such a conversion. He lived a godless life on the high seas and sank so low that at one time he became the slave of a slave. Ever running away from God, he was ever pursued by the prayers of his loved ones. God caught up with him and saved him on the heaving deck of a ship during a wild storm at sea. He was instantly transformed. He became a blessed and beloved minister of the gospel and never forgot how much he owed to the grace of God. With a thankful heart, he wrote that deathless hymn, "Amazing Grace":

> Amazing grace! How sweet the sound—
> That saved a wretch like me!
> I once was lost but now am found,
> Was blind but now I see.
>
> 'Twas grace that taught my heart to fear,
> And grace my fears relieved;
> How precious did that grace appear
> The hour I first believed.

ii. Unholiness (2:12b)

Saving grace also teaches us to repudiate unholiness. Thus, Paul spoke of denying "worldly lusts." When God's grace catches up with us, it does not at once translate us from here to glory. It leaves us in this world of sin so that we might grow in grace and increase in the knowledge of God (Col. 1:10).

Every area of the believer's life is wrapped in the unfailing favor of God. His grace enables a believer to cope with afflictions that seem overwhelming (2 Cor. 12:7–10). It teaches the redeemed heart to give generously to support the Lord's work (2 Cor. 9:6–7). It colors his conversation (Col. 4:6) and puts a song in his soul (Col. 3:16). It gives him power to serve God (Heb. 12:28).

God's grace also teaches the believer to turn his back on the desires of the world, for this world is an enemy to grace (James 4:4). This world is the Devil's lair for sinners and his lure for saints. This world murdered our beloved Savior, and it has persecuted godly people since the days of Cain. It cannot rob a believer of his salvation, but it can rob him of assurance, peace, and joy; it can also rob him of his testimony and his reward.

(b) What it teaches us to reproduce (2:12c–e)

Saving grace teaches us that "we should live soberly, righteously, and godly, in this present world." In other words, we should reproduce gravity, goodness, and godliness in our lives.

The word translated "soberly" speaks of the *gravity* that should be ours. A call to live "soberly" is a call to exercise self-control over the passions and desires that are native to our hearts so that we might be like Jesus.

The word "righteously" here speaks of a call to *goodness* manward. We are to do what is right at all times at all costs and on all counts. We are to do what we promise to do, even when it becomes irksome and inconvenient—because it is right and proper that we should keep our word. On social, sexual, secular, and spiritual issues, we are to take our stand for what is right—in the home, in the church, and in the world. God's grace teaches us to do so.

The word "godly" speaks of a call to *godliness.* We are to be like Jesus "in this present world." The word translated "world" here means "age." So "this present world" refers to this present age and to the world as the system organized by men in opposition to God, the world as the arena in which the ungodly can express their lusts, their lostness, and their lawlessness. The Old Testament types of the word in this sense include Egypt, the epitome of this world's culture; Assyria, the embodiment of this world's cruelty; and Babylon, the source of this world's creeds. The world—with its pride and prejudices, its pleasures and pastimes, its precepts and principles, its policies, its passions, and its perceptions—challenges the Christian when he tries to live "soberly, righteously, and godly."

What Paul called "this present world" stands in contrast to the world to come, which is the goal and home of the Christian. In this world, we are to be pilgrims and strangers, as Abraham was (Gen. 23:4).

b. Promised glory (2:13–15)

(1) The prophetic aspect (2:13)

(a) The glory of our prospect (2:13a)

When Paul wrote in verse 11 that "the grace of God . . . hath appeared," he was probably referring to the *first* advent of Christ. When Jesus came, God's grace was made incarnate in human flesh. "We behold his glory," John recalled, "the glory as of the only begotten of the Father, full of grace and truth" (John 1:14). Grace, truth, and glory were evident in all that Jesus was, said, and did.

When Paul wrote Titus 2:13, however, he was directing our attention to the Lord's *second* advent. He said that we should be "looking for that blessed hope" and "the glorious appearing," which refer to the two future comings of the Lord Jesus: His coming in the clouds to receive His bride and His coming to the earth to resolve the battle. First, He will come to receive us to Himself, and then He will come to earth to reign for a thousand years. We look forward to both events, particularly the first. It is "the blessed hope" of the church. It is our guarantee that we will escape the time when wrath will be poured out on this rebel planet, as described in both the Olivet discourse (Matt. 24) and the Apocalypse.

The word translated "looking for" in Titus 2:13 is *prosdechomai,* which means "to expect." Luke used it in describing the activity of the aged widow Anna, who, having seen the infant Christ, "spake of him to all them that looked for *[prosdechomai]* their lord, when he will return from the wedding" (Luke 12:36). And Mark used the term in describing the hope that filled the heart of Joseph of Arimathaea, who "waited for *[prosdechomai]* the kingdom of God" (Mark 15:43).

Many Scripture passages encourage us to look eagerly and earnestly for the "blessed hope." The Lord mentioned it to the disciples shortly before He went to Calvary (John 14:1–3). John described the impact that this hope should have on our lives (1 John 3:2–3). Paul gives us a step-by-step preview of the Rapture. He paints in the background, "the times and the seasons," and tells how the Rapture will preserve the church from wrath (1 Thess. 4:15–18; 5:1–9). He also describes the astounding transformation that will take place in our bodies when the Lord returns (1 Cor. 15) and mentions the triumphant duet that will be sung by the resurrected saints and those who are still alive when the great event transpires (15:55).

In Old Testament typology, Enoch prefigures the Christians who will be caught up on that day because he was raptured before God's wrath fell on the godless, antediluvian world. Noah prefigures the sealed believers of Revelation 7 because he went unscathed through the judgment of the Flood to the new world that awaited him on the other side of wrath outpoured.

As soon as the Rapture takes place, the apocalyptic judgments will begin. Crises will continue to mount until the Battle of Armageddon, when the Lord will return in power and glory with the raptured saints and angelic hosts. This will be "the glorious appearing" mentioned by Paul in Titus 2:13 and described in greater detail in Matthew (24:29–31) and Revelation (19:11–20:3).[4]

---

4. See John Phillips, *Exploring the Future,* rev. ed. (Grand Rapids: Kregel, 2001).

(b) The greatness of our prospect (2:13b)

The One who will appear in power and glory is "the great God and our Saviour Jesus Christ." The world does not think of Him as "great"; He is still "despised and rejected of men" (Isa. 53:3). His lovely name is used as a curse word and linked to the foulest words that can be dredged up from the sewage of the unregenerate mind and heart. But to believers He is "the great God and our Saviour," and the names "Jesus Christ" are sweet music to our souls. Both phrases refer to the same individual. Here we have a clear affirmation of the deity of Christ: He Who is "the great God" is also "our Saviour Jesus Christ."

(2) The present aspect (2:14)

(a) Who it was (2:14a)

Jesus Christ, we read, "gave himself for us." The One who is coming back has been here before. Two thousand years ago, He stepped out of eternity into time, descended from His rainbow-circled throne and left the high halls of heaven, to arrive here as the Babe of Bethlehem. He came to die; that fact was foreknown from the foundation of the world.

The most astounding fact in history is that the second person of the Godhead—the One whom angels worshiped, the Creator of the universe—came to die and that He died "for *us.*" That, however, only deepens the mystery. He gave Himself for Adam's ruined race, for sinners of the deepest dye, for creatures of clay, for beings capable of committing all of the heinous sins recorded in tales of horror and blood. Today, if we just look within our own hearts, drag out their secrets, and consider their lustful passions and deceptions, we will realize the startling nature of this truth: *He* gave Himself for *us.*

(b) What it was (2:14b–c)

i. The cost of salvation (2:14b)

Paul wrote that the Lord Jesus died for us "that he might redeem us." The salvation procured for us was costly indeed. The word translated "redeem," reminds us of the cost because it means "to set free by paying a ransom." The Lord Jesus came down into the slave market of this world and purchased us at infinite cost. First Peter 1:18–19 reminds us of the enormous price that was paid: "Ye were not redeemed with corruptible things, as silver and gold . . . but with the precious blood of Christ."

Redemption is a costly business. That is why the kinsman-redeemer Boaz is first introduced in Scripture as "a mighty man of wealth" (Ruth 2:1). And that is why, in both the parable of the hidden treasure and the parable of the pearl, the Lord Jesus is depicted as paying an enormous price to secure the prize—a redeemed Israel in one story and a redeemed church in the other (Matt. 13:44–46).

ii. The completeness of salvation (2:14c)

We are redeemed from "all iniquity." When the Lord Jesus bore our sin on the cross, all of our iniquity was laid on Him. As the hymn writer put it,

> All our sins were laid on Jesus,
> Jesus bore them on the tree;
> God, Who knew them, laid them on Him,
> And believing, I am free!

Some two dozen words are used in the Greek New Testament to describe sin. Various terms in this rich vocabulary are employed to indicate all of the twists and turns of evil in man's fallen nature. The word translated "iniquity" in Titus 2:14, for instance, is *anomia,* which means "lawlessness." It denotes the wickedness and general unrighteousness of the human race. *Anomia* is sometimes translated "transgression" to place the emphasis on lawbreaking. Sin is transgression against God's law (Rom. 7:7).

(c) Why it was (2:14d–f)

i. To purify us (2:14d)

The Savior had a threefold objective. First, the Lord Jesus took our place at Calvary to "purify" us. The word translated "purify" here means "to cleanse." It brings to mind a picture of a goldsmith or a silversmith removing impurities from precious metals, or of a woman removing stains or dirt from a kitchen utensil.

The effectiveness of God's salvation in accomplishing this purification is evident from Peter's words at the Jerusalem conference: "God, which knoweth the hearts, bare [the Gentile believers] witness, giving them the Holy Spirit, even as he did unto us; And put no difference between us and them, *purifying* their hearts by faith" (Acts 15:8–9). This is good news indeed! He has made us clean enough to be with Him and to sit where He sits in the blazing light of God's holy presence.

ii. To possess us (2:14e)

The second part of his threefold objective was to set apart for Himself "a peculiar people." The word translated "peculiar" is *periousios,* which occurs only here. It refers to God's people as an acquisition, as His own possession. Believers, then, are especially and particularly His. We are a people of His own and are set apart from all others.

The church is Christ's unique possession. Each individual believer is, in a sense, His acquisition. We all belong to Him as do no other creatures in the universe. What volumes that should speak to our souls! We are His special, prized possession.

iii. To perfect us (2:14f)

The third part of His objective was to make us a people "zealous of good words." In Paul's day, the Zealots were members of a party that played a fanatical role in the Jewish war with Rome, which had already broken out when Paul wrote to Titus. The Zealots were zealous but for the wrong cause. The Lord Jesus has His own zealots who are zealous in doing good works.

The Greek word translated "zealous" here means literally "a zealot." Paul used the word to describe his devotion to Jewish tradition before his conversion (Gal. 1:14). James, the presiding elder of the Jerusalem church, used this same word, boasting to Paul about the thousands of Jewish believers who were still "zealous of the law" (Acts 21:20). We should be just as sold out to doing good works because of our appreciation for all that the Lord has done for us.

(3) The practical aspect (2:15)

(a) Paul's command to Titus (2:15a–b)

Paul commanded his colleague, "These things speak, and exhort, and rebuke with all authority." In view of the sublime truths connected with both the Lord's first coming and His coming again, Titus could not compromise with the Cretan national character. With all of the power vested in him, he must urge God's people to shun carnality and worldliness and to live Christlike lives. When necessary, he must rebuke them.

We can see young Titus going from house to house with his message. We can picture his walking into a café, sitting across the table from a group of local businessmen, and sharing the gospel with them. We can imagine his standing behind the pulpit and holding up Paul's latest letter. This one is addressed to him! He reads again and again the matchless words concerning the grace of God, the imminence of the "blessed hope," and the subsequent "glorious appearing." Titus would supplement the bare-bones statements in this brief pastoral memo with the expanded teachings of the church epistles. He emphasizes the tremendous truth that every believer—Cretan or Corinthian, Hebrew or Hellenist, Syrian or Samaritan, Philippian or Pamphylian—is Christ's special possession and, as such, must live accordingly. Titus must carry out Paul's command to remind the Cretans and never let them forget "these things."

(b) Paul's confidence in Titus (2:15c)

"Let no man despise thee," Paul added. The word translated "despise" occurs only here in the New Testament and means literally "to think around something" or "to turn over in one's mind." In spite of the facts that Paul had commissioned Titus, that Titus was armed with delegated apostolic authority, and that this epistle provided additional warrant, some people would still ridicule his credentials and regard Titus as a nobody. Titus was not to let people get away with that. He was God's chosen man for that particular place at that special time. Paul wanted him to remember that fact and to ensure that he did not act in a way that would give anyone a basis for despising him.

B. Practical exercise (3:1–11)
   1. The behavior of believers as subjects of the land (3:1–2)
      a. We must be submissive (3:1a)

In the country where they belong, believers should accept the responsibilities that go with their citizenship. They are to be submissive to constituted authority. Paul instructed Titus to tell the believers on Crete that they must be law-abiding. "Put them in mind to be subject to principalities and powers, to obey magistrates," he said. By nature and cultural background, Cretans were rebellious and hostile to authority. Christian Cretans must learn to recognize governmental authority—although at that time the Roman Empire ruled the world and was under the control of Nero, one of the most wicked tyrants of all time.

The word translated "to be subject" is a military word, one that Paul has already used in connection with women and slaves (2:5, 9). The way Paul used the word here suggests that the Cretan Christians were to put themselves in subjection to and under the authority of representatives of the Roman government.

Elsewhere in the New Testament (Eph. 6:12), the words *principalities* and *powers* refer to Satan's ruling authorities in the spirit world, fallen angelic beings who hold this planet in thrall to their terrible overlord. Here, however, the words are used in a different sense. The "principalities" were the heads of state, the legally constituted authorities who represented the Roman government. The "powers" were those to whom authority had been delegated and who therefore had a constitutional right to uphold and administer the law.

As always, Paul insisted that Christians submit to constitutional authority. "What?" the worldly would exclaim. "Submit to a man like Nero? Take persecution lying down?" Well, the church did just that for the three hundred years, and it prospered in spite of its foes. "Submit!" said Paul, in effect. He himself showed how to be in subjection. He always submitted, even in death.

b. We must be supported (3:1b–2)
(1) By our works (3:1b)

As believers, we must support those who rule over us by being "ready to every good work." If Paul seems to be harping on this theme, it is because good works are the discernible outcome of salvation. He and James agreed on this point (James 2:14–26). Christians should support all efforts of those in power to improve the lot of people. Christians should be in the forefront of those who minister to the poor, the sick, the handicapped, the disadvantaged, and the enslaved.

A large segment of the professing church emphasizes good works as a *means* of salvation, but that emphasis is quite contrary to Scripture (Eph. 2:8–9). Some people have gone to absurd lengths in placing value on good works. They teach that the good works of the faithful are added to the good works of Christ to form a spiritual treasury out of which the church can grant indulgences. At one time, indulgences were sold wholesale throughout Europe to enrich the coffers of the papacy. They gave the purchasers license to sin. This godless behavior helped spark the Reformation.

In reaction to the "social gospel" preached by so-called liberals, some evangelicals have de-emphasized good works. We must remember, however, that Jesus "went about doing good" (Acts 10:38). Some Christian institutions have followed in the steps of Jesus. The Salvation Army, for instance, reaches out to the poor and underprivileged. George Müller of Bristol, England, won the admiration of the world with his homes for orphans. Missionaries to uncivilized tribes have traditionally boosted evangelism by accompanying it with hospitals and schools to minister to the body and mind as well as to souls.

(2) By our words (3:2a)

We believers must "speak evil of no man"—especially, in this context, those who rule over them. It is self-evident that Christians should not speak evil of each other or of other people. Christians should shun the widespread tendency of people to attack rulers verbally, even though in a democratic society such outspoken words are generally accepted as normal.

When Paul wrote to Titus, Nero was on the rampage. It would have been natural for persecuted Christians to speak evil of him. Such, however, was not the example of Christ. He did not speak evil of His persecutors. We should follow His example. He was silent when He was abused and falsely accused by both Jews and Gentiles. He ignored the high priest's false witness. He said nothing to Herod. When Jesus spoke to Pilate, He spoke with love in an attempt to reach his conscience. Much the same was true of Paul. Only once did he lash out at a person in authority, and when he discovered whom he had castigated, he apologized, howbeit, not without a trace of sarcasm (Acts 23:2–5).

(3) By our ways (3:2b–d)

(a) Our mildness (3:2b)

In dealing with our fellowmen, especially those in positions of authority, we should display mildness. As Paul said, believers are "to be no brawlers." No doubt, his choice of words is a reflection on the belligerent Cretan character. The word translated "no brawler" is *amachos,* which means "to be gentle" or "not fighting." There is no place for brawling in the church or anywhere else.

Paul was a fighter, but he was not a brawler. He stood up for the truth even when prominent individuals were involved, as Peter and James discovered. But Paul was always the perfect gentleman. When Festus rudely blurted out his opinion that Paul was mad, Paul did not snap back. He courteously answered, "I am not mad, most noble Festus" (Acts 26:25). The apostle taught us by example that when we disagree with someone we do not have to be disagreeable.

(b) Our manner (3:2c)

We are to be "gentle" in our ways. According to James, gentleness is one of the characteristics of spiritual wisdom (James 3:17). The Greek word that Paul uses here has a number of meanings, including "fair" and "moderate." It suggests that we should do what is seemly and fitting, that we should take into consideration extenuating circumstances. We do not know about the pressures that another person might be fighting, the temperamental weaknesses that he has to overcome, or the deficiencies in his background and upbringing, so we ought to make allowances.

Doubtless, extenuating circumstances occurred in the development of the terribly flawed character of Nero. Paul never names him, never runs him down, never even so much as hints at anything negative about him. How could he attack or verbally abuse a man for whom he was praying?

(c) Our meekness (3:2d)

Paul added that we should show "all meekness unto all men." What a sweeping statement! Meekness is not a quality that we much admire, possibly because we confuse it with weakness. But both Moses and the Lord Jesus were meek (Num. 12:3; Matt. 11:29). No one would accuse either of them of being weak! Jesus said that the meek will inherit the earth (Matt. 5:5).

The word translated "meekness" here is one that, according to Trench, refers to "an inwrought grace of the soul."[5] Meekness is like an exotic plant that the Holy Spirit cultivates in the soul of the believer. Meekness is a spiritual disposition that prompts us to bow submissively to the will of God. The same quality of soul enables us to face our fellowmen—including evil men—with patience. The meek person is not easily provoked, even if, like Moses, he has a temper.

To be meek requires great strength. Because of His strength, the Lord Jesus

---

5. Richard C. Trench, *Synonyms of the New Testament* (London: Macmillan, 1876), 147.

could face the enormous provocation of Annas, Caiaphas, Herod, and Pilate and never once raise His voice. He remained calm and courteous; and although He could have called for twelve legions of angels, He hold His peace. As the poet wrote,

> By meekness and defeat,
> He won the robe, the crown;
> Trod all His foes beneath His feet
> By being trodden down.

2. The behavior of believers as saints of the Lord (3:3–11)

As saints of the Lord, we have higher and holier obligations to observe. Paul discussed those obligations but not until after he reminded us of what we were before we met Christ.

a. Remembering what we were (3:3–8)
   (1) Our conduct (3:3)
      (a) Our depraved minds (3:3a–c)
         i. How dumb we were (3:3a)

Including himself, Paul said, "We ourselves also were sometimes foolish." The apostle never forgot what kind of person he had been and how determinedly blind he had been to the truth as it is in Christ.

The word translated "foolish" here is one that the Holy Spirit used in Romans 1:14 to depict the lack of wisdom of the heathen. The Lord used the word when He rebuked the two doubting disciples on the Emmaus road (Luke 24:25). "Senseless" would be a good rendering. The context of Titus 3:3 indicates that the Greek word here describes those who do not rein in their lusts.

Unregenerate people often consider themselves clever in their unbelief. They parade their foolish philosophies, phony theories, and Satan-inspired delusions and congratulate themselves on being clever. God calls them fools.

ii. How disobedient we were (3:3b)

We were also "disobedient *[apeithēs]*" before we met Christ. Paul had already used *apeithēs* in 1:16. "Disobedient" is a good rendering. The word suggests an unwillingness to be persuaded, a condition that ends in obstinacy. Often, a person's rejection of the gospel is nothing more or less than willful and stubborn obstinacy. Thomas exhibited this spirit when, having missed the resurrection appearance of the Lord in the Upper Room, he rejected the united testimony of the other disciples and refused to believe unless some kind of special proof was given specifically to him.

iii. How deceived we were (3:3c)

Paul further reminded us that we had once been "deceived." That is the natural state of the unbeliever. The first sin on this planet was committed by Eve, who was deceived by Satan (1 Tim. 2:14). His strategy was to persuade her to abandon the Word of God, which was her sole protection against his wiles. Satan began by sowing doubt: "Yea, hath God said. . . ?" He continued with a denial: "Ye shall not surely die." He ended with a delusion: "Ye shall be as gods." Eve fell for the Devil's lies. As a result, she was swept headlong into sin.

Deception is Satan's favorite way to keep the unregenerate in their lost condition, and it is his favorite device for turning the redeemed from the truth. He is the father of lies (John 8:44), but he can appear as an angel of light (2 Cor. 11:14). He blinds men's minds to the truth (2 Cor. 3:14; 4:4), as Paul well knew, for he himself had been blinded by Satan before his conversion (Acts 26:9).

(b) Our depraved morals (3:3d–e)

Unsaved people are depraved morally as well as mentally. Reminding us of our former *wicked passions* and *worldly pleasures,* Paul said that we were "serving divers lusts and pleasures." The word translated "serving" here denotes the condition of a slave. Jesus said, "Whosoever committeth sin is the servant [bondslave] of sin" (John 8:34).

The word translated "lusts" in Titus 3:3 is *epithumia,* which signifies strong desire, whether good or bad. In the New Testament, *epithumia* usually refers to desire in a bad sense, and that seems to be the case in this context. The archaic English word *divers* is a translation of the Greek word *poikilos,* which means literally "many-colored, variegated." Here the word denotes "many kinds" of lusts. The Devil has a veritable smorgasbord of evil passions in which we can indulge.

The word translated "pleasures" here is always used in a bad sense in the New Testament. It denotes the gratification of natural, sinful desires. The Lord Jesus likened such worldly pleasure to the thorns that choke out the Word of God in the soul of a professing believer (Luke 8:14). Many a person has been kept from salvation by his love of pleasure. Paul listed the inordinate love of pleasure as one of the outstanding characteristics of the last days (2 Tim. 3:4).

(c) Our depraved motives (3:3f–h)

i. Our evil disposition (3:3f)

Before we accepted Christ, we were "living in malice." The word translated "living" here occurs only here and in 1 Timothy 2:2. It means literally "to pass the time, to spend one's life." The word translated "malice" is *kakia,* which refers to vicious character and conveys the ideas of wickedness, depravity, and malignity. Such is the disposition of the unregenerate human heart, as seen by God.

Malice is the desire to do harm to others. It is a serpent that lies coiled around our hearts, and it does not take much to stir it to swift action.

ii. Our evil desires (3:3g)

Paul reminds us that we also lived in "envy." Envy almost invariably finds its way into Paul's enumerations of sins (Rom. 1:29; Gal. 5:21; 1 Tim. 6:4). The word translated "envy" in Titus 3:3 is *phthonos.* It denotes the terrible feeling of displeasure we are capable of feeling when someone else is preferred, honored, promoted, or extolled. Envy motivated the religious leaders to hand Jesus over to Pilate and to demand that He be executed—and Pilate knew what their motivation was (Matt. 27:18). The viper of envy is malice's twin. They are an evil pair.

iii. Our evil dislikes (3:3h)

In our unregenerate days, we were often "hateful." The word translated "hateful" occurs only here. It conjures a picture of something detestable.

Unregenerate human hearts are full of hatred. As a result, it is not at all uncommon for people to hate each other. A heart full of hatred is capable of any kind of wickedness. No wonder God said that "the heart is deceitful above all things, and desperately wicked" (Jer. 17:9). He alone can measure the wickedness of which it is capable.

(2) Our conversion (3:4–6)
(a) Revelation (3:4)

Scripture says, "But after that the kindness and love of God our Saviour toward man appeared." Oh, that blessed word *but!* How often it comes to our rescue! As in the parable of the Prodigal Son (Luke 15:20, 22), *but* is the small hinge upon which great matters turn. Here it introduces a revelation of God's *character* and *compassion.*

When we were wallowing in the muck and mire of sin and engrossed in the evils just described by Paul, suddenly there He was—"God our Saviour"! Paul's conversion was like that. Before he was saved, he was angry, deceived, malicious, lustful, and full of hatred. We see him heading at a furious pace toward Damascus. He was so eager to get to his destination, to begin wreaking havoc on the church there, that he scorned the usual noontime siesta. Suddenly, he was stopped in his tracks. A light brighter than the noonday sun dazzled him, and a voice from heaven rang in his ears. Paul heard the searching words of the ascended Christ. The kindness and love of God our Savior had appeared. Saul of Tarsus died, and Paul the Apostle rose from his grave.

The history of the Christian church is full of such tales of transformation, but only a few specific conversion stories are recorded in the New Testament. The book of Acts (8–10) chronicles the life-transforming experiences of *Saul,* of the *Ethiopian,* and of *Cornelius*—descendents of Shem, Ham, and Japheth, the three racial heads of humankind. But it does not feed us a steady diet of such accounts. History fills in the gap with countless thousands of stories, as varied as our faces and personalities. Each one is a unique diamond flashing in the sunshine of God's grace to His eternal glory. Our faith, however, is to rest on the Word of God, not on testimonies and choruses.

God reveals Himself in His own time. First, He allows the unregenerate person to run his mile, to do his thing, and have his say. God allows him to discover his utter lostness and brings him to an end of himself. We see this truth illustrated in the case of the Prodigal Son in Luke 15. What a difference there was between the repentant prodigal and his graceless elder brother, who never did come to an end of himself. "After that," to use Paul's phrase in Titus 3:4, God reveals Himself. He was there all the time but unperceived.

The word *appeared* comes from a word that means "to shine." When God reveals Himself, the light breaks through the mists at last! Similarly, in Genesis 1, the sun, moon, and stars were created "in the beginning." Not until the fourth day did they break through in all of their splendor to rule and to reveal (1:14–19). God went to work to dispel the darkness, the disorder, and the desolation that prevailed. Then the sun came out, and the moon and the stars appeared. They were there all along. God's ways with a human soul are equally wise. When God has sovereignly intervened in His own good time and way, He allows events to follow their course. Then, when conditions are right, there comes the full revelation of His goodness and grace.

(b) Revolution (3:5–6)

What happens "after that" is nothing less than a revolution in the soul. "Old things are passed away; behold, all things are become new" (2 Cor. 5:17).

i. Our works excluded (3:5a)

As always, God works to a plan. His plan for conversion excludes all human effort, good works, and supposed merit. We are saved, Paul says, "not by works of righteousness which we have done." This truth rules out all of the world's false religions. Catholic dogma, for instance, is based on human merit. So are all of the works-oriented cults. God will not accept our works for a very simple reason—"there is none that doeth good, no not one" (Rom. 3:10–19).

Sometimes, we think that we are good when we stand alongside people who are immoral, foulmouthed, vile-tempered, or thoroughly dishonest. But that kind of goodness is relative. God's standard is Christ. His transparent goodness could be seen in His every thought and deed. From the moment He first drew breath in that Bethlehem stall until the moment He dismissed His Spirit on Calvary's hill, all that men saw was unsullied goodness. Our imagined righteousness simply does not compare with Christ's blazing holiness. Thus, Isaiah confessed himself to be unclean (Isa. 6:1–5), and Peter confessed himself to be a sinner (Luke 5:8). Through three chapters of his book, Job proclaimed his own righteousness—using the personal pronouns *I, me,* and *my* approximately 195 times—but when he was brought face-to-face with God, he changed his tune. "Behold, I am vile," he said (Job 40:4).

ii. Our washing explained (3:5b–c)

a. The regeneration of the Holy Spirit (3:5b)

We cannot live up to God's standard of absolute perfection, so we desperately need to be cleansed. "According to his mercy [God] saved us," wrote Paul, "by the washing of regeneration." What a wealth of ideas are introduced with these words!

The sin nature we have inherited from Adam is so vile and so entrenched that, apart from God's mercy, there is no hope for us. No one has described God's mercy better than Jonah, who said, "I knew that thou art a gracious God, and merciful, slow to anger, and of great kindness" (Jonah 4:2). At the very time Jonah voiced this marvelous description of God's character, he was angry because God had extended His mercy to Nineveh, instead of destroying the place as Jonah had hoped. The quality of God's mercy is revealed by the fact that He did not punish Jonah for his ugly spirit. Instead, He inspired him to write his book.

The source of our salvation is not in our *morality,* which God writes off as worthless, but in His *mercy.* Our salvation is wrought in us by the Holy Spirit.

In God's sight, we are so vile that a complete bath is required—"the washing of regeneration." The word translated "washing," *loutron,* comes from a word that means "to have a bath." Our bodies were intended to be the temple of the Holy Spirit, and our spirits were intended to be His shrine. When sin entered, however, the Holy Spirit departed, leaving Adam and all of his posterity spiritually dead. Before the Holy Spirit can come back into His temple and sanctuary, there has to be a thorough cleansing. The agent of that cleansing is the blood of Christ (1 John 1:6–2:2).

Once the "washing" has taken place, the "regeneration" can take place. The word translated "regeneration" is *palingenesia,* which is composed of *palin* ("again") and *genesis* ("birth"). So to be regenerated is to be born again. As illustrated in the book of Genesis, the process is one of generation, degeneration, and regeneration. In regeneration, the Holy Spirit comes back into the cleansed believer's body and quickens his spirit because it was always God's intention that He would inhabit man and that the human spirit would act in concord with the indwelling Holy Spirit.

b. The renewing of the Holy Spirit (3:5c)

Paul moves on. He employs a word that is a composite of *kainos* ("new") and *ana* ("again")—renewing! The "renewing of the Holy Ghost" is the continuing operation of the Holy Spirit in the life of the regenerated believer.

In the Old Testament, this process was taught symbolically in the typology of the tabernacle. At one end of the tabernacle stood the sinner in all of his vileness and lostness. At the other end, in the Holy of Holies, God sat enthroned in awesome holiness and glory. Between the sinner and the holy God stood the brazen altar and the brazen laver. As the sinner took his first few steps toward God, he was confronted by the brazen alter and learned that he needed a *radical* cleansing from sin. He must bring a sacrifice and shed its blood. Nothing less than the blood of Christ can radically cleanse us from sin.

Having come to the brazen alter, the man moved on. He comes next to the brazen laver. It was made of polished brazen mirrors, and its function was to reveal the fact that not even a believer can take a step without defilement. The laver contained water so that the revealed uncleanness could be removed. The believer was thus taught that, in addition to his *radical* cleansing from sin, he needed a *recurring* cleansing from sin. The work of Christ secures our radical cleansing, and the Word of God (as inspired, illuminated, and applied by the Holy Spirit) ensures our recurring cleansing from sin (Eph. 5:26).

In another context, Paul reminded the Corinthians that "though our outward man perish, yet the inward man is *renewed* day by day" (2 Cor. 4:16). Although a person's physical frame wears out, the "new man," the new nature, is replenished daily with spiritual power.

iii. Our wickedness expunged (3:6)

The believer is indeed a new person in Christ. Old things have passed away, Paul says, and all things are made new (2 Cor. 5:17). *The measure of this change* is intimated by the word *abundantly. The means of this change* is "Jesus Christ our Saviour." What good would it have done to tell the Cretans, the Corinthians, or the Colossians to be Christlike without giving them the means to be Christlike?

"The washing of regeneration, and renewing of the Holy Ghost" are "shed on us abundantly through Jesus Christ our Saviour" (Titus 3:5–6). The picture suggested by these verses is of water being poured out in abundance. Believers have a vast reservoir of living water in the Holy Spirit; He pours it out in a never-failing stream. The Lord Jesus referred to this resource in John 7:37–39, and it is illustrated in Ezekiel's vision of the river flowing from the temple of God (Ezek. 47:1–12).

The abundant outpouring of the Holy Spirit is ours "through Jesus Christ our Saviour," the One to whom we are indebted for all of this grace (John 14:16–17, 26; 15:26–27; 16:7–15). The Christian life is a supernatural life; the life of Christ is communicated to us by the Holy Spirit, who indwells us, fills us, anoints us, and flows through us.

In the New Testament, the various names and titles attributed to the Spirit of God give us an understanding of what He is like. He is called the Spirit of truth

(John 14:17), the Spirit of holiness (Rom. 1:4), the Spirit of life (Rom. 8:2), the Spirit of faith (2 Cor. 4:13), the Spirit of wisdom (Eph. 1:17), the Spirit of power, the Spirit of love, the Spirit of a sound mind (2 Tim. 1:7), the Spirit of grace (Heb. 10:29), and the Spirit of glory (1 Peter 4:14). Because these characteristics of the Holy Spirit are also characteristics of the Lord Jesus, and because God's great purpose in redemption is to make us like His Son, we are given an abundance of the Holy Spirit through Christ.

(3) Our consummation (3:7)

(a) Law forever satisfied (3:7a)

Now Paul looks to the future. He writes of our "being justified by his grace." The word translated "justified" is a legal term that means "to be declared righteous before the law." The law has no claim against a justified person. Justification is greater than forgiveness. A person who has been proven guilty may be forgiven by the offended party, but the memory of the offense remains. A justified person, on the other hand, has been acquitted; he has no record of being guilty of any wrongdoing. God's great salvation justifies believers. The record of our sins is eternally expunged from God's memory (Jer. 31:34; Heb. 8:12; 10:16–17). The law of God is satisfied. It has no case against it.

(b) Life forever ratified (3:7b)

Furthermore, we are installed in God's favor as "heirs according to the hope of eternal life." The forward-looking word *hope* focuses our attention on "that blessed hope" of which Paul had already reminded Titus (2:13). Because all charges brought against us have been thrown out of court (Rom. 8:33–34), we are heirs of eternal life, the very life of God. No wonder the Holy Spirit tells us in Hebrews 7:25 that we have been saved "to the uttermost" (or as someone has quaintly put it, "from the gutter-most to the uttermost")! We can rejoice in this truth all the more when we think of what has happened to unbelieving Israel: God's displeasure has come upon the Christ-rejecting Jews "to the uttermost" (1 Thess. 2:14–16).

(4) Our confession (3:8)

Paul reminded Titus of *a great truth:* "This is a faithful saying, and these things I will that thou affirm constantly." The "things" to which Paul was referring are the glorious truths just asserted by the apostle about God's changing us fully, freely, and forever.

Sometimes we read our Bibles so carelessly and casually that we allow these monumental verities to slide by us practically unnoticed. What we should do is review them time and again. We should ponder them and appropriate them. These truths are like the stars; we barely notice them. We vaguely accept the fact that they are vast celestial bodies traveling astronomical distances at enormous speeds. But most of the time the stars are "just there." If we were permitted to see them only once in a thousand years, their appearance would be a global event. People would mark the date on their calendars, stay up all night to see them, and never stop talking about them. But because stars are "just there," they go largely unnoticed.

Gospel truths, likewise, are "just there." Suppose that they were not written down in permanent form nor translated into our native tongue and not readily available to us at all times. Suppose that they were accessible to us to read (but not to copy) just once in a lifetime! How eagerly we would await the magic moment! How we would school our memories to lay hold of those truths! How we would treasure them, talk about them, and marvel at them!

Because believers carelessly take these tremendous assertions for granted and fail to appreciate, apprehend, and appropriate them, Paul insisted that they be affirmed constantly. The gospel is not just wishful thinking or some old wives' fable; "these things" are all true. We should never stop talking about them because all around us are people who have never heard them and because we ourselves have such treacherous memories. As the hymn writer put it,

Tell me the story often,
For I forget so soon;
The early dew of morning
Has passed away at noon.[6]

The Greek word translated "affirm constantly" in 3:8 is *diabebaioomai,* which means "affirm strongly, affirm confidently." We are admonished by these definitions to be bold in proclaiming salvation truths in the face of entrenched unbelief. We can assert them with assurance because we are not speaking of scientific theory, debatable philosophy, or religious opinion. We are speaking of truth that is as unchangeable and eternal as God's throne.

6. From the hymn "Tell Me the Old, Old Story" by A. Catherine Hankey.

Paul also reminded Titus of *a great test:* "That they which have believed in God might be careful to maintain good works." We are saved to serve; otherwise, God would have taken us home to heaven the moment we believed. God leaves believers here to do good works.

In Titus 3:5, Paul has just declared that salvation is "not by works." Now we see here that we must be "careful to maintain good works." Paul was not contradicting himself. Good works are invalid as a means of salvation, but they are invaluable as a manifestation of salvation. The instant Saul of Tarsus was saved, he said, "Lord, what wilt thou have me to *do?*" (Acts 9:6, italics added).

There is, of course, a vast difference between the good works of the unregenerate man and the good works of the believer. The good works of an unsaved person are tainted by his sin nature. Many people claim to have done their best. No one has ever done his best. Often his motive is wrong, or he could do more if he tried. Maybe his works are done perfunctorily and are devoid of love. Or his works are done in the flesh to derive inner satisfaction or for some other ulterior motive. Often, too, his works generate complacency, pride, and self-regard. The same is often true of the works of a carnal believer (Rom. 7). People who do good works in the flesh are often harder to reach than self-confessed sinners (Luke 18:9–14).

The good works of a godly believer are quite different. They partake of the character of the Lord's good works. Peter referred to the source of such works when he said, "Jesus of Nazareth, a man approved of God among you by miracles and wonders and signs, *which God did* by him" (Acts 2:22, italics added). Paul was thinking along similar lines when he wrote, "Work out your own salvation with fear and trembling. For it is *God which worketh in you* both to will and to do of his good pleasure" (Phil. 2:12–13, italics added).

Even so, the believer's good works have to be "maintained." The word translated maintain here comes from a word that is usually used in the sense of "preside" or "rule over." Here it indicates that we should give attention to our good works. All too often, we start something and then get tired of it and quit. That is not the way the Holy Spirit works. We may become discouraged because of a lack of results, but the Holy Spirit never gets tired and always gets results.

Paul's third reminder to Titus here is of *a great trust:* "These things are good and profitable unto men," wrote the apostle. Truth has been entrusted to us, and we owe it to those around us to talk about "these things" and to impress others with the practicality of the Christian faith.

b. Remaining where we are (3:9–11)
(1) A stance to take (3:9)
(a) A requirement (3:9a–c)
i. Avoid foolish questions (3:9a)

The first requirement for maintaining our stand is to "avoid foolish questions." Foolish questions are one of the Devil's favorite tricks to get us sidetracked. We get asked such questions as "Where did Cain get his wife?" or "Are the heathen lost?" or "Why does God allow suffering" or "Why doesn't God destroy the Devil?" These can be legitimate questions, but often they are red herrings designed to lead to profitless discussion and away from the uncomfortable truth. The person who brings up such evasive arguments has discovered that the answers to such questions often require considerable preamble before the main issue can be reached. He wants opponents to take a while to get to the issue because he is more interested in confusing the issue than in finding the answer. There are perfectly logical answers for people who ask, "did God create the plague bacillus?" or "Why would a God of love give cats the instinct to play with a mouse before killing it?" But because such questions engender strife, we are to avoid them.

We ought to be "ready always to give an answer to every man that asketh [us] for a reason of the hope that is in [us]" (1 Peter 3:15). We should know what we believe and why we believe it. We should know the answers to the hard questions asked by skeptics and infidels. But we are under no obligation to answer "foolish questions."

ii. Avoid foolish quibbles (3:9b–c)
a. Jewish lists (3:9b)

The second requirement is to avoid pettifogging arguments. Paul particularly had in mind the quibbling of the unbelieving Jews of his day, so he told Titus to avoid "genealogies."

Genealogies certainly have their place. First Chronicles begins with nine chapters of names. The New Testament begins with a genealogy. Several important lists of names in the book of Genesis take us from Adam to Abraham, Isaac, Jacob, and the twelve patriarchs. These genealogies are important, God-breathed parts of the divinely inspired Scriptures.

There are problems connected with these lists at times, but most of the problems have been resolved by diligent Bible scholars. For instance, 1 Chronicles 2:13–17 indicates that Jesse had seven sons and two daughters, but 1 Samuel 16:5–12 indicates that David was Jesse's eighth son. There are several possible explanations for this seeming contradiction. One of Jesse's sons might have died shortly after the anointing of David. One son, perhaps, was the child of a concubine and therefore not counted in the genealogy. One son died without a son of his own and, consequently, was not included in the genealogy. Note also that 1 Samuel recorded *history* and therefore took a different viewpoint from 1 Chronicles, which recorded *genealogies.*

Another apparent problem is that the list of the Lord's ancestors in Matthew has notable omissions: for example, Ahaziah (2 Kings 8:25; 2 Chron. 22:1–9); Joash, who is sometimes called Jehoash (2 Kings 11:2–12, 21; 2 Chron. 24:1–25); Amaziah (2 Kings 14:8–20; 2 Chron. 24:1–25); and Jehoiakim (2 Kings 23:36–24:6; 2 Chron. 36:5–8). The explanation is that the Jews did not always consider it necessary to include the name of every member of the family in a genealogy. In Matthew 1:1, the author accomplished his purpose by listing just three names; his purpose was to link Jesus of Nazareth with David, who was the founder of the Hebrew royal family.

Luke's genealogy is different from Matthew's because it serves a different purpose. Luke wanted to trace the Lord's ancestry through Mary to show Him to be the promised seed of a woman (Gen. 3:15). Luke went back to Adam (Gen. 3:38) to show that Jesus was a member of not only the Hebrew family but also of the human family.

Differences and challenges do confront us when we study the genealogies in Scripture, and it is legitimate for serious Bible students to sort them out. Such activity was not what Paul had in mind when he told Titus to avoid Jewish genealogies. Perhaps he was thinking of Philo's allegorical interpretations of genealogies. (Philo, the father of a radical system of hermeneutics, was much admired by many Jews.) Or Paul might have been thinking of the rabbis who tended to clutter genealogies with fables, or of some Jews who used genealogies to bolster pride of race and religion and feelings of superiority over the Gentiles. Titus was not to waste his time on such futile pursuits.

b. Jewish laws (3:9c)

Titus was also to avoid "contentions, and strivings about the law." The word translated "contentions" here means "strife, quarreling, wrangling." A great deal of quarreling was occurring in the church at Corinth (1 Cor. 1:11) and evidently in the church in Crete.

The word translated "strivings" ("fightings") is always plural in the New Testament. The Jews could be very fierce in defending both the Mosaic Law and the oral law (the endless rabbinical traditions and encrustations that had been added to the Mosaic Law). Perhaps Paul foresaw that, if Jerusalem fell, rabbinical traditions would become more significant than ever to the exiled Jews.

The greatest crisis of their history was approaching the Jews. The Roman army was marching methodically through the Jewish homeland, reducing its cities to ruins. A few more years and Jerusalem would be in Roman hands, and the temple would be a heap of blackened stones. It would no longer be possible for the Jews to practice the ceremonial law. Jews would retreat into the law as interpreted by the rabbis, and the Torah would take second place to the Talmud. The Jewish world would become more and more Jewish—increasingly narrow, ingrown, suspicious, protective, and isolated from the rest of the world. In time, the Talmud would become their home and their very life. Moreover, waves of persecution would fasten rabbinical bonds ever more tightly around embattled Jewish ghettos.

Paul, a trained rabbi himself, was farsighted enough to see what was coming. He told Titus to steer clear of all Jewish wrangling and fighting over the law. Actually, the gospel frees us from the law as a system but not from the law as a standard. Paul recognized this fact and often dealt with the subject in his letters. The Jerusalem apostles also understood this fact (Acts 15), but not as clearly as did Paul.

(b) A reason (3:9d)

Squabbling over Jewish lists and laws should be avoided because "they are unprofitable and vain." The word translated "unprofitable" here means "not beneficial, not serving any useful purpose." The word translated "vain" is *mataios,* which means "void of result." *Mataios* is used in connection with idolatry in Acts 14:15, Greek philosophy in 1 Corinthians 3:20, and liberal theology in 1 Corinthians 15:17.

No one knew better than Paul how worthless such squabbling was. After all, he had been a rabbi himself, and he was a former student of the renowned Gamaliel (Acts 22:3), who was the grandson of the even more famous Hillel, who founded a popular school of thought among the Jews. Paul had once boasted about such things, but not anymore (Phil. 3:1–11). Because love had replaced law, Christ had replaced creed, and New Testament truth had overshadowed Old Testament truth, why argue with Christ-rejecting Jews over their shibboleths?

(2) A stand to take (3:10–11)
(a) The heretic exposed (3:10a)

Paul turned his attention to the case of "a man that is an heretic." The word translated "heretic" is *hairetikos,* which occurs only here in the New Testament. The root of this word conveys the idea of choice or a deliberately chosen opinion. A heretic is a person who rejects sound biblical doctrine to espouse other ideas. Such self-willed opinions lead to factions and divisions in the church.

Paul, Peter, and John were acquainted with heretics. Some of them denied the Resurrection (2 Tim. 2:17–18), others denied the Lord (2 Peter 2:1), and still others were even described as belonging to "the synagogue of Satan" (Rev. 2:9). Church history contains the records of many such men and tells of the incalculable damage they have done. The damage continues because many heretics are in the world today.

(b) The heretic examined (3:10b)

The phrase "after the first and second admonition" refers to the two examinations to be given to a heretic. The word translated "admonition" is *nouthesia.* It has to do with training by word. A person whose mind has been captured by false teaching must be confronted with the truth of God.

Just as a builder uses a plumb line and a level to determine whether a wall is true, the elders of the church must bring the straightedge of God's Word to bear upon the heretical opinions and techniques of a brother who is wrapped in his own perverse, divisive ideas. The elders are to confront him twice while he is still in the church. He is to be given every opportunity to recognize his error and recant his heretical opinions.

(c) The heretic excommunicated (3:10c–11)

Paul told Titus to "reject" a heretic who refuses to repent (3:10). He is to be brought before the church and expelled because of his dangerous, divisive doctrines. That is *his public conviction.*

His personal condemnation follows. That is to what Paul was referring when he wrote, "Knowing that he that is such is subverted, and sinneth, being condemned of himself." The word translated "subverted" is *ekstrephomai,* which occurs only here. It means "to be perverted" or "to change entirely." A heretic has a moral twist to his personality.

The word translated "sinneth" here means "to miss the mark" or "to wander from the right path." It is used in reference to sin against God. A heretic knows that he is sinning, so he is "condemned of himself *[autokatakritos]*." The Greek word, which is used only here, means literally "to be self-condemned because the heretic knows perfectly well that he is doing wrong." Self-condemnation is a heavier condemnation than any inflicted by the law or by the elders of a church. No wonder a heretic is to be excommunicated. A man who has a moral twist and knows it, who embraces a false doctrine and persists in doing so, has no place in the fellowship of the church.

PART 5

Conclusion

Titus 3:12–15

A. Guidance for Titus (3:12–14)
   1. As to his movements (3:12)

Paul's letter was finished, except for some final instructions and greetings. The instructions for Titus in 3:12 involved *what he should do* and *where he should go:* "When I shall send Artemas unto thee, or Tychicus, be diligent to come unto me to Nicopolis: for I have determined there to winter."

Paul was probably writing from Miletus. While he was in Miletus, he sent Timothy to labor in Ephesus until he could go there himself to deal with growing problems in that church. Paul seems to have gone from Miletus to Troas, where he wrote to Timothy to tell him to expect him in Ephesus. But apparently Paul went to Macedonia first. It seems that his trip to Ephesus was further delayed by news of another crisis in Corinth. Evidently, before he went to Corinth, he sent for Timothy and bade him a fond farewell. At this time, the Neronic persecutions were raging, and Paul was full of foreboding. Timothy came and went, and Paul left for Corinth. Corinth was not far from Nicopolis, the city mentioned in this verse.

We do not know for sure whether Paul actually made it to Nicopolis. Some scholars think that he was arrested in Corinth. (He certainly had enough Jewish enemies there who would have been happy to hand over to the Romans the man they hated.) It is possible, however, that Paul did make it to Nicopolis, where he planned to spend the winter. Nicopolis was in Lepirus near Apollonia, the harbor opposite Brundisium. Nicopolis, which was on Paul's route to Rome, was well situated for missionary work in Dalmatia, another area that interested Paul. The name *Nicopolis* means "city of victory." It was built by Caesar Augustus to commemorate his naval victory over Antony and Cleopatra at Actium.

When Paul was still in Miletus writing his final instructions to Titus, he had already decided to hand over the work on Crete to Tychicus or Artemas. Paul had a new assignment for Titus in the neighboring province of Dalmatia (2 Tim. 4:10). Artemas looms up out of the mists of time for one brief mention here and then sinks back into oblivion. However, we can infer that Paul did send Artemas to Crete because he seems to have sent Tychicus on a different errand—to relieve Timothy in Ephesus (2 Tim. 4:12). So although shadows were lengthening and darkness was closing in, Paul was still handing out assignments and planning his strategy. Paul ignored the danger signals and scorned the idea of calling a halt to his mission. He remained true to his resolve to press on until God finally called him home.

As for Titus, he was to leave Crete when his replacement arrived. By then the apostolic letter would have accomplished practically everything that could be accomplished. Someone like Artemas could take over. Titus had to go to Paul.

Titus did leave Crete, but while he was on his way to Nicopolis, Paul was arrested. The apostle's traveling days were over. Indeed, his days on earth were numbered.

2. As to his ministry (3:13–14)
    a. The practical side (3:13)

Paul's letter from Miletus also instructed Titus to "bring Zenas the lawyer and Apollos on their journey diligently, that nothing be wanting unto them." Paul's old friend Apollos was still plowing up and down the Mediterranean, using his influence and oratory to further the cause of Christ. Like Paul, he was dismayed but undeterred by official Roman opposition to the gospel. Evidently, Crete was a stop on Apollos's itinerary.

Zenas, like Artemas, surfaces only once in Scripture. All we know about him is that he was a lawyer. We do not know whether he was a Jew or a Gentile, a Roman advocate or a Jewish scribe. But there he was on the island of Crete, keeping company with the golden-tongued Apollos and evidently being active in spreading the gospel.

It was a common practice in the early church for believers to help visitors and traveling preachers. There were inns on the arterial highways, and travelers always needed suggestions about accommodations, news about local conditions, tips on the best way to get from here to there, names and addresses of Christians who could be contacted along the way. Believers sometimes escorted travelers and probably gave them money, supplies, and letters of introduction. In keeping with this practice, Titus was to ensure that Zenas and Apollos lacked nothing for their journey.

b. The preaching side (3:14)

In attending to the temporal needs of Zenas and Apollos, Titus would be an example to the Cretans. He was not to be secretive concerning his bounty and hospitality. He was to preach once more to the local congregation and explain that members of the body of Christ should minister to one another as he had ministered to Zenas and Apollos. The sermon would be his last before he left on a long journey of his own, during which he, too, would need to be helped by others. The need for Christian contacts along the way was intensifying because political conditions made it increasingly dangerous to be known as a believer and an active Christian worker.

What Paul wanted, of course, was "that [the Cretans] be not unfruitful." He was eager to see all believers become fruit bearers (Rom. 1:13).

B. Greetings for Titus (3:15a–b)

1. Personal greetings (3:15a)

"All that are with me salute thee," wrote Paul to Titus. Titus is not as well known to us as is Timothy, but more likely than not, Titus was well known to the churches in western Asia Minor, Macedonia, and Greece. He was respected as one of Paul's bright young men and trusted envoys.

We do not know who was with Paul at the time he sent these greetings. Word that the apostle was in the area—Miletus was not far from Ephesus—would have spread rapidly and widely, and doubtless visitors were constantly coming and going. And Paul always had a galaxy of young trainees around him.

Greetings from the mainland churches would have cheered Titus's heart. Such salutations were another reminder of the greatness and oneness of the body of Christ. Christianity and interchurch relations were very personal in those days.

2. Pastoral greetings (3:15b)

Paul added his pastoral greetings: "Greet them that love us in the faith." In the short time that Paul had been on Crete, he had made warm, personal friends among the islanders. Doubtless, he had been in their churches, their homes, and their workshops and had visited their farms and gone fishing with them. He had led some of them to Christ. Paul had opened the Scriptures to them and taught them wonderful truths from the Word of God. He sent his greetings to those who loved him. He ignored those who did not love him. Along with his greetings, he sent greetings from those "in the faith." Faith was the unifying factor for those who loved the Lord.

C. Grace for Titus (3:15c)

Paul concluded this epistle with these words: "Grace be with you all. Amen." So much grace was needed—grace to save and sanctify; grace to overcome the lies of the Devil, the lusts of the flesh, and the lure of the world; grace to transform dispositional flaws, temperamental weaknesses, and national characteristics; grace to deal with opposition from without and subversion from within; grace to overcome differences of culture, character, and creed; grace to submit to apostolic authority, the Word of God, and the indwelling Holy Spirit; grace to become more Christlike, less selfish, and more loving; grace to handle advancement and face adversity; grace to face mounting hostility in a pagan world; grace for living and for dying!

"Grace be with you all. Amen!"

Exploring
2 TIMOTHY

Introduction to 2 Timothy

Paul had already written nine church epistles, one general epistle (Hebrews), and three personal epistles. He was now writing his very last one. We see an old man in prison, writing to bid his beloved colleague, Timothy, a fond, faith-filled, and fearless farewell. After a last "Amen" at the end of the letter, the apostle will put away his pen forever.

This letter is now known as 2 Timothy. Its eighty-three verses are Paul's last words to us all. We will never hear from him again until we get to Glory. Meanwhile, we can ponder Paul's teaching—preserved in his epistles—concerning Christ's cross, Christ's church, and Christ's coming again. How perceptive his teaching is! How prophetic! How practical! And how personal! Let us make the most of what Paul has to say to us in these, his famous last words.

When Paul wrote 2 Timothy, he was no longer under comparatively mild house arrest. He was in the condemned cell in Rome, a terrible hole in the ground with a few wisps of stale straw for a mattress and a hard ledge for a bed. It was a dank, dark, rat-infested place. Paul was lonely and cold. He was under sentence of death. He knew that he was soon to die, but he did not know whether his Roman citizenship would protect him from a cross. Paul had seen the face of Nero—hateful, sneering, weak, etched with all of the marks of dissolution and decay. Now he was waiting to see the face of Jesus, beautiful beyond all thought.

Paul's last words were few and weighty. The shadow of the executioner's ax lies on every page. This ominous shadow colors this epistle and makes it superlatively interesting.

The executioner! I am reminded of a game we used to play during recess at school. The game itself had a gruesome rhyme and rhythm of its own. It was a nursery rhyme, but it spelled out terror just the same. Most of the old nursery rhymes are sadistic. Think of Humpty Dumpty's being smashed to smithereens, Jack and Jill falling headlong down the hill, and three blind mice fleeing from the farmer's wife and her carving knife. Or think of "Sing a Song of Sixpence" and the poor maid in the garden running in terror from the blackbird that had escaped from the pie and was trying to peck off her nose.

In the game we played, a boy and a girl stood facing each other with a space between them. They held each other's hands and raised and lowered them in a chopping motion. The rest of the children lined up and, as the nursery rhyme was sung, marched through the space between the boy and girl with the "hatchet hands." As each child entered the space, the "hatchet hands" were lowered and then raised again to allow the child to escape. The accompanying song was about the bells of London—the bells of Old Bailey, the big bell of Bow, the bells of Stepney and Shoreditch. However, as the game progressed, a new note crept into the song:

> Here comes a big candle
> To light you to bed;
> Here comes a great chopper . . .

The children knew what was coming. They scuttled through the space because they didn't want to be caught. As the time of catastrophe drew near, the tramping and stamping of many small feet accelerated, and more words were added to the song:

> Here is a candle
> To light you to bed;
> And here comes a chopper
> To chop off your head.

The "hatchet hands" continued to drop down, momentarily trapping each child, and then went up again, allowing another escape. But then came the final blow:

> Here comes a great chopper
> To chop! Chop! Chop! Chop!
> CHOP OFF YOUR HEAD!

When those words were sung, the "hatchet hands" came down and did not go up. The child who was caught was out of the game.

Now imagine Paul's sitting in his cell with the Devil trying to torment him. Satan whispered, "There comes a great chopper, Paul, to chop! Chop! CHOP OFF YOUR HEAD!" If the Devil wanted to terrify him, he had the wrong man.

The Devil could not frighten Paul. Long ago, Paul had counted himself as a "sheep for the slaughter" (Rom. 8:36). For years, he had been living on resurrection ground (Rom. 6:4). Neither Nero, nor death, nor the Devil himself could frighten Paul. The shadow of the headsman's ax fell upon Paul in that prison, but it did not send cold chills down his spine. Instead, it reminded him that he had a few last words to say. He would write to Timothy.

Paul dipped his pen in the ink. *What should he say?* (What would we have written if we had been in his place?) He decided to try to stiffen Timothy's resolve.

Complete Outline of 2 Timothy

PART 1: INTRODUCTION (1:1–2)

- A. Paul and his status (1:1)
  - 1. His status declared (1:1a)
  - 2. His status described (1:1b)
- B. Paul and his son (1:2)
  - 1. Timothy was dearly beloved (1:2a)
  - 2. Timothy was divinely blessed (1:2b)

PART 2: PRESENT TESTINGS (1:3–2:26)

- A. Timothy's personal responsibilities: the past (1:3–18)
  - 1. To develop his faith (1:3–6)
    - a. In view of Timothy's family connections (1:3–5)
      - (1) What Paul disclosed (1:3)
        - (a) Paul's private life (1:3a–c)
          - i. His communion (1:3a)
          - ii. His consecration (1:3b)
          - iii. His conscience (1:3c)
        - (b) Paul's prayer life (1:3d–f)
          - i. His prayers were perpetual (1:3d)
          - ii. His prayers were personal (1:3e)
          - iii. His prayers were periodical (1:3f)
      - (2) What Paul desired (1:4)
        - (a) The greatness of his desire (1:4a)
        - (b) The goal of his desire (1:4b)

- (3) What Paul described (1:5)
  - (a) The reality of Timothy's faith (1:5a)
  - (b) The roots of Timothy's faith (1:5b)
  - (c) The reinforcement of Timothy's faith (1:5c)
- b. In view of Timothy's formal call (1:6)
  - (1) Something to recall (1:6a)
  - (2) Something to rekindle (1:6b–c)
    - (a) The implanted gift (1:6b)
    - (b) The imparted gift (1:6c)
- 2. To dispel his fears (1:7–18)
  - a. The exhortation (1:7–11)
    - (1) Remember God's Spirit (1:7)
      - (a) The enslaving spirit (1:7a)
      - (b) The emancipating spirit (1:7b–d)
        - i. A will controlled by dynamic power (1:7b)
        - ii. A heart controlled by divine love (1:7c)
        - iii. A mind controlled by disciplined thoughts (1:7d)
    - (2) Remember God's Son (1:8–10)
      - (a) The choice (1:8)
        - i. Don't be ashamed (1:8a–b)
          - *a.* Of the gospel testimony, now imperiled (1:8a)
          - *b.* Of the great teacher, now imprisoned (1:8b)
        - ii. Don't be afraid (1:8c–d)
          - *a.* The apostolic plea (1:8c)
          - *b.* The available power (1:8d)
      - (b) The challenge (1:9–10)
        - i. Our conversion (1:9a)
        - ii. Our calling (1:9b–10)
          - *a.* It is a holy calling (1:9b)
          - *b.* It is a high calling (1:9c–10)
            - *1.* The contrast (1:9c)
            - *2.* The concept (1:9d–10)
              - (i) The great resolution (1:9d–f)
                - *(a)* What has happened (1:9d–e)
                  - *(1)* God's supreme government (1:9d)
                  - *(2)* God's superlative government (1:9e)

- *(b)* When it happened (1:9f)
- (ii) The great revelation (1:10)
  - *(a)* Its focus (1:10a)
  - *(b)* Its features (1:10b–e)
    - *(1)* The foe was absolutely abolished by Christ (1:10b)
    - *(2)* The future is absolutely ablaze through Christ (1:10c–e)
      - *(i)* A new life in Christ (1:10c)
      - *(ii)* A new likeness to Christ (1:10d–e)

(3) Remember God's servant (1:11)

b. The examples (1:12–18)
- (1) The notable example (1:12–14)
  - (a) Paul's persecution (1:12a–b)
    - i. He was not free from it (1:12a)
    - ii. He was not frightened by it (1:12b)
  - (b) Paul's persuasion (1:12c–d)
    - i. His assurance as to the reality of the Lord (1:12c)
    - ii. His assurance as to the reliability of the Lord (1:12d)
  - (c) Paul's persistence (1:13–14)
    - i. Timothy was responsible for the gospel that had been entrusted to him (1:13)
      - *a.* Its Pauline source (1:13a)
      - *b.* Its pristine source (1:13b)
    - ii. Timothy was responsible for the gift that had been entrusted to him (1:14)
      - *a.* It had been given (1:14a)
      - *b.* It had to be guarded (1:14b)
- (2) The negative example (1:15)
  Paul had been abandoned by:
  - (a) One notable province (1:15a)
  - (b) Two named people (1:15b)
- (3) The noble example (1:16–18)

- (a) Onesiphorus was a beloved man (1:16)
  - i. Paul remembered his house (1:16a)
  - ii. Paul remembered his help (1:16b–c)
    - *a.* His material contributions (1:16b)
    - *b.* His moral courage (1:16c)
- (b) Onesiphorus was a brave man (1:17)
  - i. His diligence was remarkable (1:17a)
  - ii. His diligence was rewarded (1:17b)
- (c) Onesiphorus was a blessed man (1:18)
  - i. What Paul requested for him (1:18a)
  - ii. What Paul remembered about him (1:18b)

B. Timothy's pastoral responsibilities: the present (2:1–26)
  1. Timothy was to be a steward (2:1–2)
     - a. What he must resolve (2:1)
     - b. What he must remember (2:2a)
     - c. What he must reproduce (2:2b–c)
       - (1) By extension (2:2b)
       - (2) By example (2:2c)
  2. Timothy was to be a soldier (2:3–4)
     - a. With endurance (2:3)
     - b. Without entanglement (2:4)
       - (1) His duty (2:4a)
       - (2) His detachment (2:4b)
       - (3) His desire (2:4c)
  3. Timothy was to be a success (2:5–7)
     - a. The test of success—the fighter (2:5)
       - (1) The contest (2:5a)
       - (2) The crown (2:5b)
       - (3) The criterion (2:5c)
     - b. The taste of success—the farmer (2:6–7)
       - (1) Truth perceived (2:6)
         - (a) The husbandman's toil (2:6a)
         - (b) The husbandman's triumph (2:6b)
       - (2) Truth pondered (2:7)
         - (a) Paul's plea (2:7a)
         - (b) Paul's prayer (2:7b)
  4. Timothy was to be a sufferer (2:8–13)

a. The triumph of the Christ (2:8)
   (1) His royalty (2:8a)
   (2) His resurrection (2:8b)
b. The tribulation of the Christian (2:9–13)
   (1) Paul's fearful sufferings (2:9–10)
      (a) How he described them (2:9)
         i. The sting (2:9a)
         ii. The stigma (2:9b)
         iii. The song (2:9c)
      (b) How he dismissed them (2:10)
         i. What he suffered (2:10a)
         ii. Why he suffered (2:10b–c)
            a. To shield God's people (2:10b)
            b. To show God's people (2:10c)
   (2) Paul's faithful saying (2:11–13)
      (a) Our decisions (2:11–12)
         i. Death in the balance (2:11)
         ii. Duress in the balance (2:12a)
         iii. Denial in the balance (2:12b)
      (b) Our doubts (2:13)

5. Timothy was to be a student (2:14–19)
   a. The framework (2:14)
      (1) Who should be aroused (2:14a)
      (2) What should be avoided (2:14b)
   b. The focus (2:15)
      (1) Diligence in the study (2:15a)
      (2) Discipline by the student (2:15b)
      (3) Division of the Scriptures (2:15c)
   c. The falsehoods (2:16–18)
      (1) The portrait (2:16–17a)
         (a) The advent of error (2:16a)
         (b) The advance of error (2:16b–17a)
            i. It was mobile (2:16b)
            ii. It was malignant (2:17a)
      (2) The propagandists (2:17b–18)
         (a) The principal leaders (2:17b–18a)
         (b) The principal lie (2:18b)

d. The foundation (2:19)
(1) The foundation was secure (2:19a)
(2) The foundation was Scripture (2:19b–c)
(a) The truth revealed (2:19b)
(b) The test revealed (2:19c)

6. Timothy was to be a servant (2:20–26)
a. The criteria of service (2:20)
(1) Vessels and their worth (2:20a–b)
(a) Some are costly (2:20a)
(b) Some are common (2:20b)
(2) Vessels and their work (2:20c–d)
(a) Some serve distinguished purposes (2:20c)
(b) Some serve dishonorable purposes (2:20d)
b. The condition of service (2:21–23)
(1) A must (2:21)
(a) God wants a clean vessel (2:21a)
(b) God wants a consecrated vessel (2:21b)
(c) God wants a compliant vessel (2:21c)
(2) A method (2:22a)
(3) A move (2:22b–c)
(a) In the right path (2:22b)
(b) With the right people (2:22c)
(4) A mandate (2:23)
(a) An exclamation (2:23a)
(b) An explanation (2:23b)
c. The character of service (2:24–26)
(1) Dealing with the opposition (2:24–25b)
(a) What must be excluded from Christian service (2:24a)
(b) What must be exuded in Christian service (2:24b–25b)
i. The right attitude (2:24b–d)
a. The Lord's servant must not be harsh (2:24b)
b. The Lord's servant must not be hesitant (2:24c)
c. The Lord's servant must not be hasty (2:24d)
ii. The right attempt (2:25a–b)
a. The Lord's servant must speak meekly (2:25a)
b. The Lord's servant must speak meaningfully (2:25b)

(2) Dealing with the opportunity (2:25c–26)
(a) The need of the unbeliever to be repentant (2:25c)
(b) The need of the unbeliever to be rescued (2:26)

PART 3: PREDICTED TESTINGS (3:1–4:18)
A. Approaching the day of the great apostasy (3:1–4:5)
1. Some deadly roots exposed (3:1–3a)
a. The last days indicated (3:1)
b. The last days illustrated (3:2–3a)
(1) Dismal facts about the last days (3:2a–b)
(a) Love of self (3:2a)
(b) Lust for wealth (3:2b)
(2) Dreadful follies in the last days (3:2c–e)
(a) Inflated egos selfward (3:2c)
(b) Inflated egos manward (3:2d)
(c) Inflated egos godward (3:2e)
(3) Disrupted families in the last days (3:2f)
(4) Distinctive features in the last days (3:2g–h)
(a) Ungrateful (3:2g)
(b) Unholy (3:2h)
(5) Dead feelings in the last days (3:3a)
2. Some deadly fruits exposed (3:3b–4:5)
a. The morality of the last days (3:3b–4a)
(1) The deceitfulness of people (3:3b–c)
(2) The disposition of people (3:3d–e)
(a) Incontinent (3:3d)
(b) Intolerant (3:3e)
(3) The disdain of people (3:3f)
(4) The duplicity of people (3:4a)
b. The mentality of the last days (3:4b–9)
(1) There will be scornful maniacs (3:4b–c)
(a) Heady (3:4b)
(b) High-minded (3:4c)
(2) There will be secular materialists (3:4d)
(3) There will be sanctimonious moralists (3:5)
(a) What is revealed (3:5a)
(b) What is required (3:5b)

- (4) There will be seducing marauders (3:6)
  - (a) Their prowl (3:6a)
  - (b) Their prey (3:6b)
- (5) There will be sophisticated morons (3:7–9)
  - (a) Their futile quest for the truth (3:7)
  - (b) Their fatal quarrel with the truth (3:8–9)
    - i. An example (3:8a)
    - ii. An explanation (3:8b–c)
      - *a.* Their blindness to the facts (3:8b)
      - *b.* Their blindness to the faith (3:8c)
    - iii. An exposure (3:9)
      - *a.* They will be stopped in their path (3:9a)
      - *b.* They will be stripped of their power (3:9b)

c. The malice of the last days (3:10–13)
- (1) Paul's world (3:10–11)
  - (a) His teaching (3:10a)
  - (b) His testimony (3:10b–g)
    - i. The pattern of Paul's life (3:10b)
    - ii. The purpose of Paul's life (3:10c)
    - iii. The priorities of Paul's life (3:10d–f)
      - *a.* Godward (3:10d)
      - *b.* Selfward (3:10e)
      - *c.* Manward (3:10f)
    - iv. The patience of Paul's life (3:10g)
  - (c) His troubles (3:11a)
  - (d) His triumph (3:11b)
- (2) Paul's warning (3:12–13)
  - (a) The great dislike of the world (3:12)
  - (b) The growing decadence of the world (3:13)

d. The message for the last days (3:14–17)
- (1) A word of exhortation (3:14–15)
  - (a) Resolve (3:14)
    - i. Continuance in the Scriptures urged (3:14a)
    - ii. Confidence in the Scriptures urged (3:14b)
  - (b) Remembrance (3:15)
    - i. Timothy's boyhood (3:15a)
    - ii. Timothy's Bible (3:15b)

(2) A word of explanation (3:16–17)
(a) The Bible and its inspiration (3:16a)
(b) The Bible and its information (3:16b)
(c) The Bible and its instruction (3:16c)
(d) The Bible and its intention (3:17)
e. The man for the last days (4:1–5)
(1) The charge to Timothy (4:1–4)
(a) The witness (4:1)
i. The living God (4:1a)
ii. The Lord Christ (4:1b)
(b) The work (4:2)
i. To preach (4:2a)
ii. To persevere (4:2b)
iii. To probe (4:2c–d)
a. By reproving (4:2c)
b. By rebuking (4:2d)
iv. To plead (4:2e–f)
a. Lovingly (4:2e)
b. Loyally (4:2f)
(c) The warning (4:3–4)
i. The time approaching (4:3a)
ii. The truth abandoned (4:3b–4)
a. The lusts people will have (4:3b)
b. The lies people will heed (4:4)
(2) The challenge to Timothy (4:5)
(a) Be vigilant (4:5a)
(b) Be valiant (4:5b)
(c) Be versatile (4:5c)
(d) Be victorious (4:5d)
B. Approaching the death of the great apostle (4:6–18)
1. Paul's hope (4:6–8)
a. With death before him (4:6–7)
(1) The last jeopardy (4:6a)
(2) The last journey (4:6b)
(3) The last judgment (4:7)
(a) Well won, Paul! (4:7a)
(b) Well run, Paul! (4:7b)

(c) Well done, Paul! (4:7c)
b. With death behind him (4:8)
(1) A crowning day for Paul (4:8a)
(2) A critical day for all (4:8b)
2. Paul's hardships (4:9–15)
a. His plea (4:9)
b. His plight (4:10–15)
(1) His friends (4:10–13)
(a) The deserter—Demas (4:10a)
(b) The departed—Crescens and Titus (4:10b–c)
i. Paul's named friend—Crescens (4:10b)
ii. Paul's famed friend—Titus (4:10c)
(c) The doctor—Luke (4:11a)
(d) The disciple—Mark (4:11b)
(e) The dispatched—Tychicus (4:12)
(f) The dependable—Carpus (4:13)
i. Paul's assumption (4:13a)
ii. Paul's assertion (4:13b)
(2) His foe—Alexander (4:14–15)
(a) A devilish man (4:14a)
(b) A doomed man (4:14b)
(c) A dangerous man (4:15)
3. Paul's heroism (4:16–18)
a. Paul's loneliness (4:16)
(1) His abandonment by his friends (4:16a)
(2) His absolution of his friends (4:16b)
b. Paul's Lord (4:17–18)
(1) The Lord's conscious presence (4:17a)
(2) The Lord's conquering presence (4:17b)
(3) The Lord's confirming presence (4:17c)
(4) The Lord's controlling presence (4:17d)
(5) The Lord's continuing presence (4:18)
(a) To protect Paul from the king (4:18a)
(b) To preserve Paul for the kingdom (4:18b–c)
i. A crowning blessing (4:18b)
ii. A closing benediction (4:18c)

Part 4: Conclusion (4:19–22)

- A. A salutation (4:19–20)
  - 1. Notes (4:19)
    - a. Some remembered helpers (4:19a)
    - b. A remembered household (4:19b)
  - 2. News (4:20)
    - a. The abode of Erastus (4:20a)
    - b. The ailment of Trophimus (4:20b)
- B. A supplication (4:21a)
- C. A supplement (4:21b–22)
  - 1. A final greeting (4:21b)
  - 2. A fitting good-bye (4:22a)
  - 3. A farewell gift (4:22b)

PART 1

Introduction

2 Timothy 1:1–2

A. Paul and his status (1:1)

Many of us have favorite authors. We ask the publishers to keep our names on file and send us new titles as soon as they come off the press. Similarly, the believers in the early church must have eagerly awaited the appearance of another inspired letter autographed by Paul, and they must have been delighted with the publication of 2 Timothy. Little did they realize that this masterpiece was to be his last. They would never again see Paul's signature heading another canonical letter.

Luke was probably the one who had handed Paul the pen with which to sign his name to the letter. It was probably Luke, too, who had acted as Paul's secretary, taking down verbatim the words that dictated but that were inspired by the Holy Spirit.

1. His status declared (1:1a)

Paul began by declaring his status: "Paul, an apostle of Jesus Christ." Timothy did not need to be reminded about Paul's apostolic authority, but others might well need the warning that went along with the title *apostle*. The letter would be read to the church at Ephesus, and copies would be sent without delay to the churches at Smyrna, Pergamos, Laodicea, Colossae, and all of the other churches in the area. The Christians in these churches undoubtedly were terrified of Nero. Paul, however, as an apostle of Jesus Christ, wielded power greater than that of any caesar. Paul, as Christ's "ambassador in bonds," awaited calmly the execution of the unjust sentence of death that had been passed upon him. Churches and believers, no matter when or where they lived, should remember that Paul was "an apostle of Jesus Christ."

Paul would remember that Christ, too, had suffered under an unjust sentence. Rome did its worst to Him. Pilate, the Roman governor, trembled before Jesus but went along with the case concocted by the Jews. The trumped-up charges, the accusations motivated by envy—Pilate listened to them all and pronounced Him innocent. Then he callously ordered his soldiers to scourge and crucify Him. Rome's seal endorsed the closing of the tomb. Thus, Pilate closed the case. Jesus was dead, and that was that—except for one thing: three days later, He arose from the dead!

2. His status described (1:1b)

Paul described himself as an apostle "by the will of God, according to the promise of life which is in Christ Jesus." Nero's signature might well have been on Paul's death warrant because Nero was the one who sent him to his death. *Good riddance to him*, Nero thought. But he was mistaken! All he really did was promote the grand old apostle to Glory! The ax of the executioner dismissed Paul from this world and ushered him into the presence of the Lord. Moreover, Paul's name would live on in cherished memories, whereas Nero's name would live on in infamy.

Some thirty years earlier, the risen Christ had invaded Paul's life when they met face-to-face on the Damascus road. That life, the very life of God, that poured into Paul's soul still coursed through every fiber of his being. New life in Christ! That new life had transformed him. It had made it possible for Paul, as one born out of due season, to become an apostle. Nero could not change that fact.

Paul became an apostle "by the will of God." It was not Peter, James, or John who bestowed apostleship on Paul. It was neither the Jerusalem church nor the Antioch church, neither dear Barnabas nor beloved Silas who had made Paul an apostle. He had been made an apostle by the risen Christ! God's will was that this man, who had so cruelly persecuted the infant church, be ordained an apostle. The word translated "will" here emphasizes the *desire* rather than the determination. God's will always achieves its end! So Saul became Paul; the great enemy became the great ambassador.

B. Paul and his son (1:2)
   1. Timothy was dearly beloved (1:2a)

Paul addressed the letter "to Timothy, my dearly beloved son." As far as we know, Paul did not have a son of his own. He had adopted Timothy as his own son in the faith.

Timothy's mother, Eunice, was a Jewess, and his father was a Greek. Eunice and Timothy's grandmother, Lois, both godly women, guided his early studies in the Word of God.

Paul and Timothy first met in Lystra (Acts 16:1). Timothy joined Paul's team when the apostle revisited Galatia during his second missionary journey. The young man came highly recommended by the church elders in the area (Acts 16:2).

He accompanied Paul to Troas, Philippi, Thessalonica, and Berea. When Paul was forced to leave Berea, Timothy stayed on until the apostle summoned him to Athens (Acts 17:14–15). Paul then dispatched him to Thessalonica to help the infant church there (1 Thess. 3:1–2). Timothy rejoined Paul in Corinth (Acts 18:1, 5; 1 Thess. 3:6).

The next place where we find Timothy is Ephesus. Paul sent him from Ephesus to Corinth when trouble in the Corinthian church called for the presence of an apostolic envoy. Later, Timothy joined Paul in Macedonia. The tidings that Timothy brought with him from Corinth prompted Paul to write 2 Corinthians. Timothy went part of the way with Paul to Jerusalem at the end of Paul's third missionary journey and later joined Paul in Rome during the apostle's first imprisonment. Timothy and Luke were Paul's most constant companions. We learn from Hebrews 13:23 that Timothy himself suffered a period of imprisonment.

After Paul was released from prison, he sent Timothy back to Ephesus. Timothy was still there when 2 Timothy was written. According to tradition, Timothy returned to Ephesus after Paul's death and was martyred there under Nerva or Domitian. If this view is true, Timothy, in his later years, could have been a colleague of the apostle John, who also made Ephesus his home.

As Paul wrote 2 Timothy, he doubtless thought of the many experiences that he and Timothy had shared on the highways and byways of the Roman world and of the many other adventures they had shared aboard ship. They had invaded city after city with the gospel. They had shared perils, joys, and triumphs. Paul conjured Timothy's face—the face of his son, his beloved son, his dearly beloved son.

2. Timothy was divinely blessed (1:2b)

Once again, Paul used the special trilogy he reserved for letters to personal friends: "Grace, mercy, and peace, from God the Father and Christ Jesus our Lord."

"Grace," flowing from the wisdom of God, reminds us that God has "devised a means" to deal with all of our sins. In His wisdom, He conceived salvation's plan. He found a way to make His salvation work for people who are totally under the sway of sin and helpless to do anything to save themselves. Salvation could not hinge on human effort because sin taints even the best of our works. Salvation could not hinge on human cleverness because sinful men are often fools when it comes to thinking about God. Salvation could not hinge on human resourcefulness because man is incapable of producing perfect righteousness. God's wisdom solved the problem by making salvation dependent on His grace. Grace is the key.

"Mercy," which flows from the love of God, reminds us that God can still all of our fears. Stark terror was abroad in the Christian community when Paul wrote to Timothy. News of what was happening in Rome chilled every heart. Christians were being torn to shreds and eaten by ravenous wild beasts in the arena. Believers were being dipped in tar and ignited to provide light for midnight revels in Nero's garden. Christians were being cut down like corn. They were being scourged, mocked, and crucified. Nero had no mercy, but God was full of mercy and tempered the wind to the shorn lamb. No matter what happened to those tormented Christians of Nero's Rome, God could and would provide the strength necessary to face each trial. He promised a way to escape (1 Cor. 10:13; Rom. 8:35–39).

"Peace" flows from the power of God. The word reminds us that God can put down all of our foes. It is He who draws the line in the sand, and not even a Nero can defy Him when He does so. When Paul wrote 2 Timothy, the Neronic persecution was at white-hot heat, and Christians were in terror. It was very dangerous to be a Christian, one of those people who were accused publicly of setting fire to Rome. They needed the perspective of eternity, the perspective from which all Scripture was written.

Significantly, the Bible ignores Nero. It mentions neither the man nor his deeds. It was left to the Roman historian Tacitus to relate Nero's diabolical wickedness. However, there is a kind of poetic justice in the fact that Nero cut his own throat the same month that Paul was executed (June A.D. 68).

So Paul wrapped his dear son in the grace, mercy, and peace that emanate "from God the Father and Christ Jesus our Lord."

PART 2

Present Testings

2 Timothy 1:3–2:26

A. Timothy's personal responsibilities: the past (1:3–18)
  1. To develop his faith (1:3–6)
    a. In view of Timothy's family connections (1:3–5)
      (1) What Paul disclosed (1:3)
        (a) Paul's private life (1:3a–c)
          i. His communion (1:3a)

To encourage Timothy to develop his faith, Paul gave him some glimpses into his own personal situation in life. First, he wrote about his personal communion with God. Paul was victorious in spite of the fact that he was chained in his cold, malodorous cell and abandoned by almost everyone. He does not even hint at his circumstances here. Instead, he said, "I thank God."

Paul was in touch with the living God—the Creator and Sustainer of the universe, the One who had invaded time in the person of the Lord Jesus; who had conquered death and all of its powers; and who controls all of the factors of matter, space, and time. All of the regiments of the Roman army could not hinder Paul's communion with such a One as that. No wonder he could say, "I thank God!"

ii. His consecration (1:3b)

Paul continues, "I thank God, whom I serve from my forefathers." He could trace his spiritual roots back to a period before the time he first met Christ on the Damascus road because he had been chosen in Christ "before the foundation of the world" (Eph. 1:4). When God commissioned Ananias to visit the newly converted Saul, and Ananias objected, God told him that this his former foe was "a chosen vessel" (Acts 9:15). Paul knew he had been separated unto the gospel from his mother's womb (Gal. 1:15).

God chose the particular family into which Paul was to be born. It was an influential Jewish family in which both Hellenism and old-fashioned Hebraism found a comfortable balance. Like Timothy, Paul had been reared on the Scriptures. Many generations of believers were in his ancestry; he could trace his roots to Benjamin, the father of the tribe, and, through him, to Abraham and hence to Noah and to Adam himself.

Paul acknowledged his Jewish heritage in 2 Timothy 1:3. He was thankful for it because it had helped prepare him for the time when he would become the great theologian of the church. During the early days of the church, Paul was the one man who had the background, training, and ability to think through the Old Testament Scriptures in light of Calvary and then, guided by the Spirit of God, distill from the Old Testament Scriptures the mighty truths of Christ, Calvary, and the church that fill his epistles. As a result, the world is indebted to him.

Caesar's soldiers, dark prisons, and iron chains could not diminish for one moment Paul's high sense of calling and commitment. It had roots in his encounter with Christ on the Damascus road. His commitment had been instant and irrevocable—"Lord! What wilt thou have me to do?" For the next thirty years or so, it had continued unabated. He had seen active Christian service as an apostle, prophet, evangelist, pastor, and teacher. His consecration would be maintained until the headsman's ax severed Paul's head from his body and sent the great apostle on to serve his Lord on the everlasting hills throughout ages yet to be.

iii. His conscience (1:3c)

Paul gave Timothy a further glimpse of his personal life. He had served God "with pure conscience," he said. Paul had testified just as honestly to Felix, Festus, and Agrippa as he had to anyone else. He had been bold and truthful even when called to stand before Nero.

He could say to the Ephesian elders (Acts 20:26, 31) that his conscience was clear: "I take you to record this day, that I am pure from the blood of all men. . . . By the space of three years I ceased not to warn every one night and day with tears." He added, "I have coveted no man's silver, or gold, or apparel. Yea, ye yourselves know, that these hands have ministered unto my necessities, and to them that were with me" (Acts 20:33–34). When Timothy read this verse to the Ephesian church, the elders no doubt nodded their heads. They knew what Paul meant when he talked about a "pure conscience."

(b) Paul's prayer life (1:3d–f)

i. His prayers were perpetual (1:3d)

Paul was "a man subject to like passions as we are," as James wrote of Elijah. And, like Elijah, Paul prayed (James 5:17). He knew how to pray. When Paul told the Thessalonians to "pray without ceasing" (2 Tim. 1:3), he was only challenging them to do something that he did himself (1 Thess. 5:17). At times, his thoughts would soar upward to the courts of bliss. He would find himself in spirit in the audience chamber of the universe. There, he would pour out his heart in praise and adoration. At other times, some news, a passing incident, or the mention of a need or a name prompted Paul to pray.

Everything was grist for his mill when it came to prayer. When there was a change of soldiers in his cell, he prayed. When a crust of bread and some unsavory water were handed to him with a growl, he prayed. When Luke departed on an errand, Paul prayed. During the night watches, he could recall the cities, churches, and individuals on the pages of his copious prayer book, and he would pray for them. Nor would he forget to pray for Nero and his Jewish wife, for the members of the Roman senate, and for the executioner who was sharpening his ax. After all, Paul had once told Timothy to offer up "supplications, prayers, intercessions, and giving of thanks . . . for all men; for kings, and for all that are in authority" (1 Tim. 2:1–2).

ii. His prayers were personal (1:3e)

Paul told Timothy, "I have remembrance of thee in my prayers." How often he must have mentioned that name *Timothy* to the Lord! It was the name of his dearly beloved son. We can hear the apostle say, "And now, Lord, let me talk to You about my friend, Timothy." In prayer, Paul reviewed Timothy's personality, his gifts, his ministry, his need for support, his weakness, his strengths, his fidelity, and his love. No doubt, Timothy's name was at the top of every prayer list Paul made.

iii. His prayers were periodical (1:3f)

Paul prayed for Timothy "night and day." Probably Paul had designated times during the night and during the day when he paused to engage in concentrated prayer. Perhaps, like Daniel, Paul prayed three times a day and, like Daniel, he would not have been secretive about it (Dan. 6:10).

Or perhaps Paul made his times for periodic prayer coincide with the times of the daily offerings in the temple. Day after day, the priests offered their sacrifices like clockwork. They began at six o'clock in the morning with the burnt offering. At nine o'clock, there was the meal offering; at noon, the peace offering; at three o'clock in the afternoon, the sin offering; and at six o'clock in the evening, the trespass offering.

We do not know how Paul regulated his prayer times, but we do know that he kept in constant touch with the throne of God.

(2) What Paul desired (1:4)

One of Paul's constant prayer requests was that he might see Timothy again. "Greatly desiring to see thee," the apostle wrote, "being mindful of thy tears, that I may be filled with joy." People, not things, moved Paul's heart.

When Paul left Titus on Crete, he went to Miletus and then to Troas, intending to go from there to Ephesus to visit Timothy. Instead, Paul wrote Timothy a letter and went on over to Macedonia. There, Paul paused to decide whether he should go to Corinth to deal with a fresh crisis in the church there. It seems likely that he summoned Timothy from Ephesus to Macedonia and that this verse refers to their meeting there. When Timothy returned to Ephesus, and Paul went on to Corinth, their parting was tearful. Both men must have realized that Paul's days were numbered. After all, how long would Nero leave such a dynamic leader free to pursue activities on behalf of the "criminals" who were accused of burning Rome? Timothy especially seems to have been brokenhearted at the prospect of losing the man who had been in every way more than a father to him.

What they feared did take place. Nero's spies tracked Paul down. Roman officials seized him and doubtless charged him with being a ringleader of the Christian cult, regarded by the officials as arsonists. His Roman citizenship was not much help to him anymore. He was hustled back to Rome and tried swiftly, probably before Nero. Paul was well known to be *the* outstanding leader of Gentile Christianity. Nero would have at least been curious to see him, if only to mock and bully him.

Now Paul was in the condemned cell, and, by the time he wrote this letter, he was certain that his days were numbered. He longed to see his dear Timothy one more time.

(3) What Paul described (1:5)

(a) The reality of Timothy's faith (1:5a)

Throughout 2 Timothy, Paul makes every effort to stiffen Timothy's resolve in the face of mounting peril. The church was entering a new phase of its history. The postapostolic years (Rev. 2:1–7) were giving way to the persecution years (Rev. 2:8–11). For the next three centuries, Christians would face savage outbursts of persecution under ten different caesars. The age of tolerance was over, and the age of tribulation had begun. Drastic changes and terrible dangers faced the Christian community throughout the Roman world.

Timothy would now have to stand on his own two feet in the midst of persecution. Paul kept urging him to play the man. He paid tribute to the reality of Timothy's faith: "I call to remembrance the unfeigned faith that is in thee" (1:5). Timothy's faith filled Paul with joy (1:4).

The word translated "unfeigned" in 1:5 is the negative, adjectival form of *hupokrisis,* which means "hypocrisy." Timothy was not pretending or playacting. Paul was too old and too wise a believer to be fooled by something put on for his benefit. He was glad that Timothy had real faith because only genuine faith, anchored inside the veil (Heb. 6:19), would withstand the storm that was breaking on the church.

Defining Old Testament law, Paul wrote, "The end of the commandment is charity [love] out of a pure heart, and of a good conscience, and of faith unfeigned." Love is the root of all of the commandments, and a good conscience is the fruit. In between is "faith unfeigned," which recognizes the authority, inerrancy, and inspiration of the Word of God as expressed in the commandments of God. Faith places its confidence in the wisdom, love, and power of God and remembers that His commands are His enablings.

(b) The roots of Timothy's faith (1:5b)

Paul reminded Timothy, "The unfeigned faith that is in thee . . . dwelt first in thy grandmother Lois, and thy mother Eunice." The word translated "dwelt" here means "to live in a place as one lives in a home." Unfeigned faith had found its abode in the hearts of Timothy's mother and grandmother. It felt at home there.

The word *grandfather* does not occur in the New Testament, although the idea certainly is found in the Bible. For example, Abraham was Jacob's grandfather, and Ahithophel was Bathsheba's grandfather. The word translated "grandmother" occurs only here.

The institution of grandmothers is a marvelous invention of God, an idea born of heaven for the well-being of the human race. The example of Lois shows us that a grandmother ought to be the kind of person who prepares the hearts of her children and her children's children so that genuine faith finds itself at home in their hearts too.

Both Lois and Eunice had Gentile names, but they were Jewesses and among the first to believe in Christ in Asia. All that we know about Timothy's father is that he was a Gentile (Acts 16:1). That fact probably explains why Timothy was not circumcised. As Hellenistic Jews, Lois and Eunice were more open-minded about such things than were the Hebrew purists of Judea and Jerusalem. Timothy's father was a Gentile, but he must have been fairly open-minded because he did not hinder his wife and mother-in-law from instructing Timothy in the Holy Scriptures. Or perhaps Timothy's father died while the boy was still young. In any case, Paul became a father figure to him.

The mention of Lois and Eunice would have given wings to Timothy's thoughts. In his mind, the years would be stripped away. He would be back in his boyhood home in Lystra. He would see again, in thought, Paul and Barnabas marching into town with considerable fanfare and flourish. He would recall the healing of the lame man, the cheers of the crowd, and the attempt to deify the missionaries. He would remember, too, the subsequent attempt to murder Paul. Timothy would remember how people were saved under the preaching of Paul—he and his mother and grandmother among them. He would remember that Paul was no stranger to persecution. He had dared danger and death from the first day that Timothy had known him.

Timothy's thoughts would come back to the letter that he held in his hand. By referring to Timothy's roots, Paul was trying to fortify Timothy's faith to face the mounting persecution. Meanwhile, in that dismal dungeon in Rome, Paul's own faith blazed out. If he was going to die, he would die like a man—yes, like a martyr. He would make an exodus worthy of an apostle of God.

(c) The reinforcement of Timothy's faith (1:5c)

Paul added, "I am persuaded that [faith dwells] in thee also." Timothy's mother's and grandmother's faith was Timothy's faith too. After the attack on Paul, it probably had not been easy for that faithful trio in Lystra to unite publicly with the infant church and other new believers. Jews and Gentiles alike must have eyed the fledgling church with suspicion. Their smoldering hostility could have been disarmed by only the testimony, faith, and good works of the Christians. In any case, Timothy had grown in the faith. By the time Paul returned to Lystra on his second missionary journey, the elders of the church could recommend Timothy to Paul as one of their most promising young men. Paul needed a replacement for John Mark but was no doubt cautious lest he make a second mistake. However, he soon agreed with the elders; Timothy was ready for the mission field.

b. In view of Timothy's formal call (1:6)

To encourage Timothy to develop his faith, Paul reminded him of his formal call: "Wherefore I put thee in remembrance that thou stir up the gift of God, which is in thee by the putting on of my hands."

Paul and Barnabas had been officially ordained to the work of world evangelism by "the laying on of hands" (Acts 13:1–3). The act symbolized the fellowship and endorsement of the church in Antioch in the enterprise. John Mark had not been thus formally connected to the work (Acts 13:5). Paul had made sure that, when Timothy joined the missionary party, he was formally identified with it in the sight of both God and man by the laying on of hands. Apparently, at the same time the Holy Spirit, the giver of spiritual gifts (1 Cor. 12:7–11), bestowed a special spiritual gift on the young man. From what we know of the assignments that Paul gave to him, Timothy's gift seems to have been that of a pastor-teacher (Eph. 4:11–12).

Paul seems to have been concerned that Timothy might neglect his gift, so he urged him to "stir up the gift of God." Spiritual gifts, in this respect, do not differ from other gifts. They have to be developed, exercised, and used. A person with a talent for playing a musical instrument must study the mechanics of music and practice constantly. A person who is a "natural" at sports still has to master the rules of the game. He still has to go into training. Likewise, a person with a spiritual gift has to hone and sharpen it in the school of experience.

The word translated "stir up" occurs only here in the New Testament and means literally "to stir into flame." Anyone who has a fireplace knows that a fire needs attention. After the first flames diminish, the logs or coals need to be stirred up so that air can get to them and the flames leap up again. The Greek form of this word is found in the Septuagint, where the despondent spirit of old Jacob is described as *reviving* once he was convinced that Joseph was alive (Gen. 45:27). Timothy likely was so depressed over Paul's arrest and the terrible dangers that overshadowed the whole church that he was neglecting his duties and the exercise of his gift. Second Timothy 1:7 adds credence to this possibility.

2. To dispel his fears (1:7–18)
   a. The exhortation (1:7–11)
      (1) Remember God's Spirit (1:7)

Paul called upon Timothy to dispel his fears and to develop his faith. He exhorted him to remember the ever present Spirit of God as a healthy counterbalance to his brooding anxieties.

(a) The enslaving spirit (1:7a)

Paul recognized that "God hath not given us the spirit of fear." Satan and his emissaries are the ones who seek to paralyze Christians with fear. Peter was thus paralyzed by fear when he stood around in the high priest's garden and repeatedly denied all knowledge of the Lord, who even then was on trial for his life (Luke 22:54–62). In the Old Testament, King Saul was paralyzed by fear at the sight of Goliath (1 Sam. 17:4–11), and Abraham was motivated by fear when he denied his wife (Gen. 12:11–13).

Such apprehension does not come from God. It is a powerful weapon in the hand of the enemy, but it can be overcome. Terror stalked the Christian world when Paul wrote this letter, but the long and growing roll call of martyrs showed that fear can be conquered. The enslaving spirit can be overcome by the emancipating Spirit.

(b) The emancipating spirit (1:7b–d)

i. A will controlled by dynamic power (1:7b)

In the recipe for overcoming fear, the first ingredient listed is power. We have been given the spirit of "power, and of love, and of a sound mind." God cannot be unkind. The word translated "power" here refers to the absolute, untrammeled power of God.

Jesus told Pilate, "Thou couldest have no power at all against me, except that it were given thee from above" (John 19:11). Pilate had no power, none at all, to do anything apart from what he was permitted to do by God, who was working out all things according to His will. Why God permits tyrants like Nero and Hitler to wreak havoc on earth is a mystery that will be fully resolved only in heaven when the books are opened and the full story is told. God is still sovereign, even though men like the Pharaoh defy Him to the end.

ii. A heart controlled by divine love (1:7c)

The second ingredient in the recipe for overcoming fear is love. In the heart that is controlled by divine love is a conscious enjoyment of God's love—"the greatest thing in the world"—and a conscious love for our enemies. Jesus said, "Love your enemies, bless them that curse you, do good to them that hate you, and pray for them which despitefully use you, and persecute you" (Matt. 5:44). Such is the "perfect love" that "casteth out fear" (1 John 4:18). Because He had perfect love, the Lord Jesus could face Satan and Golgotha without fear. He loved Annas and Caiaphas. He loved Herod Antipas and Pontius Pilate. He loved the soldier who scourged Him and the man who nailed Him to the tree. He loved poor, lost Judas and the dying thief who cursed Him. Jesus loved His Father in heaven and knew that His Father loved Him, even when, in the awful extremity of Calvary, the curse of the Law came upon Him. The Lord knew that God's love would see Him through and that all was well, even when it did not seem to be so.

iii. A mind controlled by disciplined thoughts (1:7d)

The third ingredient in the recipe for overcoming fear is "a sound mind." The Greek word occurs only here in the Scripture and conveys the idea of discipline and self-control.

The mind of every believer needs to be brought under the control of the Holy Spirit and under the authority of the Word of God. Wild, wayward, and wicked thoughts must be curbed. In Paul's day, when news of Nero's savageries terrorized the minds of Christians, their fearful thoughts needed to be countered by the thought that God cannot make any mistakes.

So Timothy needed to get hold of himself, to bring his fears to the cross, where they could be crucified. That would enable the power, love, and wisdom of God to rule in his heart and mind. That was how Geoffrey Bull, who was subjected to daily brainwashing and terror in a Communist Chinese prison camp, overcame his fears. When he was forced to sit absolutely motionless on a hard floor hour after hour, under the constant gaze of a prison guard who spied on his slightest move, Bull retreated mentally to a place of quiet rest deep in his soul, where he rested in the goodness, faithfulness, wisdom, love, and power of the One who had died for him and who is now seated at the right hand of God.

(2) Remember God's Son (1:8–10)

(a) The choice (1:8)

i. Don't be ashamed (1:8a–b)

a. Of the gospel testimony, now imperiled (1:8a)

Paul urged Timothy, "Be not thou therefore ashamed of the testimony of our Lord." That testimony was imperiled because Satan was hurling his own hellish hosts into battle. The Neronic persecution was only the opening salvo. Later, Domitian launched an attack, as did Commodus, Decius, Severus, and Diocletian. Christians were slaughtered in the arena and burned alive in front of the statue of the sun god at the arena's entrance. Diocletian's persecution eclipsed that of all of his predecessors. Every effort was made to stamp out Christians and to find and burn every existing copy of the Scriptures.

When Paul wrote, Christians had no peace; there would be no real peace for them for some three hundred years. This was no time for Timothy and the other believers to be ashamed of the testimony of the Lord, no time to hide their light under a bushel. This was the time to dare, like Daniel, to blaze abroad the truth that Jesus is Lord.

Timothy needed to be constrained by the spirit of love. His backbone needed to be stiffened by the spirit of power. Timothy must face unflinchingly the hardships and afflictions that lay ahead. Of course, he would be exposed to terror! As a church leader, he was certainly already a marked man. Paul urged him to nail his colors to the mast and be strong in the Lord and in the power of His might (see Eph. 6:10). Legions of angels were encamped around him. He was immortal until his work for God was done.

b. Of the great teacher, now imprisoned (1:8b)

Neither was Timothy to be ashamed of Paul. Doubtless, Caesar's spies knew that Timothy was a close friend of Paul. Any friend of Paul would soon have his name written in Caesar's black book. Some believers, hoping to save their own skins, were already distancing themselves from the apostle. Surely Timothy would not be such a coward. No! Timothy was Paul's friend. Let him wear that as a badge of honor. More than that, Timothy was Paul's dear son.

Timothy should arm himself with the same mind as Nehemiah, who hurled this defiance into the faces of his foes: "Should such a man as I flee?" (Neh. 6:11). Never!

ii. Don't be afraid (1:8c–d)

Note *the apostolic plea:* "Be thou partaker of the afflictions of the gospel." No one in Bible times preached what, in our pampered age, is called the prosperity gospel. This false gospel espouses the "name-it-claim-it" philosophy. It says that health and wealth are the birthright of every believer. The whole concept is foreign to the New Testament, to personal experience, and to church history. The prosperity gospel is based on a total failure to distinguish between the Old Testament blessing and the New Testament blessing, between the nation of Israel and the church of God, and between God's earthly people and His heavenly people. The New Testament promises tribulation in this world (John 16:33). The hymn writer understood this truth when he asked,

> Must I be carried to the skies
> On flow'ry beds of ease,
> While others fought to win the prize
> And sailed through stormy seas?[1]

From the time he met Christ until the time he penned this letter to Timothy, Paul faced hardships: poverty, danger, strife, flogging, stoning, imprisonment, persecution, ill health, and narrow escapes. His poor body was a register, engraved by chains and scourges, of the sufferings that a person might expect if he lived for Christ in a Christ-hating world. Doubtless, Timothy had often seen the scars and welts on Paul's back—potent advertisement of what might be involved in being a "partaker of the afflictions of the gospel."

To relieve Timothy's fears, Paul reminded him of *the available power.* Timothy was not called to stand against the power of the enemy in his own strength, and neither are we. When Satan, "as a roaring lion walketh about, seeking whom he may devour" (1 Peter 5:8), we can withstand him "according to the power of God" (2 Tim. 1:8).

Again, the word for "power" is *dunamis.* Here it refers to the inherent power of our God, who can hurl galaxies into space and pack into an atom's sphere enough energy to explode an island. That power might not always be made available to deliver us from the enemy because God often has other purposes in mind at the moment. God's power, however, is always available to keep us from falling, even in the midst of terror. His power might not save us from the tempest, but it will bring us through and strengthen us in the process (Heb. 11:33–40).

Paul's words about affliction in 2 Timothy 1:8 were not the words of a man who sat safely and securely in an ivory tower in some distant haven. It was a word from Paul, writing from a fearful and filthy cell. The rattle of his chain chimed in with the sound of his voice as he dictated these words. Paul was not

1. From the hymn "Am I a Soldier of the Cross?" by Isaac Watts.

theorizing. He was writing out of a glorious, triumphant, personal knowledge of the truth.

(b) The challenge (1:9–10)

i. Our conversion (1:9a)

Paul broadened the base of his appeal. He reminded Timothy of his conversion and his call. The God who controls all of the factors of space and time is the God "who hath saved us."

Jesus once asked the scribes whether it was easier to say "Thy sins be forgiven thee" or to say "Arise, and walk?" (Matt. 9:5). They had just seen people bring to Jesus "a man sick of the palsy, lying on a bed." The Lord's first words to the sick man had been, "Son, be of good cheer; thy sins be forgiven thee." The scribes' immediate response had been to say, "This man blasphemeth." So Jesus asked His question. Then to prove that He could both forgive sins and heal the sick, He instantly healed the sick man, who was lying right there at His feet.

The question remains, which is easier? To heal sickness, Jesus had only to speak; to forgive sins, He had to suffer. To cleanse the leper, raise the dead, and still the storm, He needed only to give a word of command; to forgive sins, He had to go to Calvary. The ability to heal was simply a matter of power; the ability to forgive was a matter of pain—the terrible agony of death by crucifixion and the even greater, more terrible agony of being abandoned by God during those dark hours when He "became sin" for us.

Paul said to Timothy, in effect, "God has already done the harder thing; He has saved you! Why worry about the lesser things, the hatred and cruelty of Nero and his kind? If God does not save you from martyrdom, it is not because He cannot do so; it is because He has a higher purpose in taking you home in a chariot of fire." Paul simply put things in perspective.

ii. Our calling (1:9b–10)

a. It is a holy calling (1:9b)

Paul reminded Timothy that God has "called us with an holy calling." We are to be holy! "Be ye holy," God said, "for I am holy" (1 Peter 1:16).

Picture Paul, a man with a holy calling, standing face-to-face with Nero. What a scene for an artist to paint! The emperor is lolling on his throne, surrounded by sycophantic courtiers, who imitate and applaud him. Soldiers with masklike faces stand as still as statues, their faces expressionless and grim, their weapons sheathed but ready. Marks of decadence are written into Nero's face, and a sneer is on his lips. An olive circlet rests upon his brow, and, scepter in hand, he points derisively at Paul.

Nero is laden with sins. He is known to have murdered his mother. His bestial vices are the subject of gossip all over Rome, and his hands are red with the blood of countless Christians. And there stands Paul, surrounded by the rich trappings of the room. His eyes have looked into the face of Jesus. Now he looks at Nero. Paul's life, ennobled by suffering, "adorns the doctrine" still (Titus 2:10). Respectful, earnest, and unafraid, he is just as prepared to appeal to Caesar's soul as he once appealed to King Agrippa's soul—just let Nero give him half a chance. How different are these two men, Nero and Paul.

Christians are called to be different from unsaved people. They are called with a holy calling. Timothy had been called, just as Paul had been called. Paul called on Timothy to expose the wickedness of the world simply by being different. He was to emanate holiness. In his small corner, he was to be as distinctive as Paul was standing there, robed in goodness and silently condemning badness. He did not need to say a word; holiness emanated from him, and we can be sure that Nero hated and feared it.

b. It is a high calling (1:9c–10)

1. The contrast (1:9c)

God has called us to holiness, but "not according to our works." Our holy calling is not based on our efforts. Paul was not urging Timothy to grit his teeth, set his jaw, and take a stand for God in a wicked world. Paul was not urging Timothy to be holy in his own strength or as a result of his own resolve.

The world has had more than enough hermits, monks, weird ascetics, and Oriental holy men. The case of Simeon Stylites (A.D. 390–459), who was noted for his incredible feats of asceticism, comes to mind. He devised various means of self-torture, and his feats of fasting were almost beyond belief. Once he had himself walled up in a monastery for the entire period of Lent. Eventually, he moved to a hillside not far from the monastery and sat on a pillar. He put a heavy iron collar around his neck and chained himself to the pillar. At first, the pillar was six feet high, but as time went on, he gradually increased its height until it was far higher than that. His disciples had to climb a ladder to bring him what scraps of food he would deign to eat. Throughout the bitter cold of thirty Syrian winters and the burning heat of thirty Syrian summers, without shelter from wind or rain or sun or frost, Simeon perched on his pillar. And the Roman Church canonized him.

That is certainly not the kind of "holiness" to which God has called us. Simeon's pillar was simply a monument to self-discipline, fanaticism, and a mistaken concept of holiness. Such asceticism is all self-effort carried to extraordinary lengths. The monk Martin Luther was well on his way down the same path when God met him and sent him forth to preach the true gospel.

2. The concept (1:9d–10)

(i) The great resolution (1:9d–f)

(a) What has happened (1:9d–e)

God has a better plan for making us holy. He transfers to each believer the holiness of the Lord Himself. God calls us to be holy "according to his own purpose and grace, which was given us in Christ Jesus." The word translated "purpose" is *prothesis,* which means literally "that which is put before someone." The Latin equivalent is *propositum,* from which our English word "proposition" is derived. God proposes to make believers holy. The means of accomplishment is His remarkable grace. So we do not become holy, in spite of the vileness of our Adamic nature, through our own self-effort and resolve. We become holy because God, having proposed to make us holy, washes us in the blood of Christ and indwells us by His Holy Spirit.

(b) When it happened (1:9f)

God's grace "was given us in Christ Jesus before the world began." The fall of man did not take God by surprise. The decision to redeem us, reconcile us, and regenerate us was no afterthought, no desperate attempt by God to reverse the effects of the Fall. The need for grace was foreseen and taken into account even before Adam fell.

Before the worlds were hurled into space, God decided to act on a certain planet in space and at a certain moment in time to accomplish the divine purpose of making salvation available to Adam's ruined race. They, themselves, would have to make people holy.

Timothy had a holy calling. God had proposed to make him holy. God had called; Timothy had come. There was no way to reverse the process, no way for

Timothy to back out of his holy calling. That knowledge should stiffen his backbone! Timothy need not be afraid. He had become part of something much bigger than the Roman Empire or any other worldly power. And so have we.

(ii) The great revelation (1:10)
(a) Its focus (1:10a)

After explaining that God's proposal in eternity past was to do something permanent and spectacular regarding man's fallen state, Paul told Timothy that God's purpose was "now made manifest by the appearing of our Saviour Jesus Christ." Hints of God's plan are evident throughout the Old Testament, but Christ's advent brought it into focus.

The arrival of Christ on earth changed things forever. Our planet was invaded from outer space by the Son of God, who became the Son of Man. Satan's hold on the world was torn loose, or "spoiled." His power was broken (Col. 2:15). Calvary spelled utter defeat for him. Now his ability to act is limited severely, made subject to God's permissive will—just as it was in the case of Job. Indeed, the book of Job casts a great deal of light on the mystery of Satan's activities against God's people (Job 1:6–12; 2:1–8).

When Christ appeared on earth, Satan was allowed to stir up hatred and opposition, even to the extent of orchestrating His crucifixion. Since then, Satan has been allowed to oppose and harass the church and create havoc in the world, but only to the degree that his activities coincide with God's ultimate purposes of bringing grace to the lost and glory to His own blessed name. The second coming of Christ will deal with Satan once and for all. Well he knows and dreads that day.

(b) Its features (1:10b–e)
(1) The foe was absolutely abolished by Christ (1:10b)

Satan's most terrifying weapon in his war against mankind is death. Jesus, however, has "abolished death." Hebrews 2:14–15 explains, "As the children are partakers of flesh and blood, [Christ] also himself likewise took part of the same; that through death he might destroy him that had the power of death, that is, the devil; And deliver them who through fear of death were all their lifetime subject to bondage." Death is the last enemy. "Leave him to last!" That is sound advice. God gives dying grace when the time comes.

When Christ returned victorious from the tomb, He declared, "I am he that liveth, and was dead; and, behold, I am alive for evermore, Amen; and have the keys of hell and of death" (Rev. 1:18). For Christians, the grave has been robbed of its terror. Death has become the door to life; we are suddenly "absent from the body" and "present with the Lord" (2 Cor. 5:8). We depart "to be with Christ; which is far better" (Phil. 1:23).

What was Paul doing? He was stiffening Timothy's resolve. In light of such truths, Nero and his ilk become totally insignificant.

(2) The future is absolutely ablaze through Christ (1:10c–e)

Jesus not only abolished death but also "brought life and immortality to light through the gospel." He effected a permanent change in the way we view the time of our death. Darkness has been replaced with light, and death has been replaced with life. All that is terrible about death must be viewed in the light of His triumph over the tomb. Even in the hour of death, we can be aglow with the shining realities of the life that is eternal.

Martyrs have even been able to sing triumphantly in the flames. Stephen, the first martyr, saw heaven opened and Jesus standing to welcome him home (Acts 7:56). Many other dying saints have testified to the light and loveliness that filled their vision as they crossed over to heaven's shore. D. L. Moody had a wonderful time dying. He spoke to those around his deathbed of what he could see. "It is beautiful," he said. "God is calling me, and I must go." He caught a glimpse of two grandchildren who had died in infancy and called out their names: "I can see Irene and Dwight," he said. Shortly afterward, he passed on joyfully to the other side.[2]

(3) Remember God's servant (1:11)

In a deliberate attempt to dispel Timothy's fears by means of exhortation, Paul reminded him of God's Spirit and God's Son. Now comes a closing reminder. Paul urges Timothy to remember *him.* If Timothy needed a visible, tangible source of encouragement, then let him think of his own beloved father in the faith, who had taught him about the Lord's triumph over death.

---

2. W. R. Moody and A. P. Fitt, *Life of D. L. Moody* (London: Morgan and Scott, n.d.), 121.

He referred Timothy to the great truths of the faith. He said, "Whereunto I am appointed a preacher, and an apostle, and a teacher of the Gentiles." Precisely because he was a preacher, an apostle, and a teacher, Paul found himself in a cell of the condemned in Rome. With his gifts and talents, he could have gone into business. He could have made a fortune. He could have been safe and sound in a villa on some Mediterranean isle. Instead, he remained true to his calling to reach Gentiles for Christ. He would remain true even when face-to-face with Nero. More! He would try fearlessly to win that tormented man to Christ just as he had tried so many years ago to win Timothy's own soul to Christ.

Paul would seek to win every soldier who did guard duty in his cell. He would even try to reach the executioner assigned to cut off his head. He would continue to be a preacher, apostle, and teacher of the Gentiles, down to the door of death itself, because God had appointed him and because the truths that he had to preach and teach were the greatest truths in the world.

Now let Timothy do the same. There is no discharge in this war. Once we enlist, we are enlisted until death. Sooner or later, death will come anyway. What is important is that we be at our posts when it comes. For us, death means life, immortality, and light!

b. The examples (1:12–18)
  (1) The notable example (1:12–14)
    (a) Paul's persecution (1:12a–b)

Exhortation now gives way to example. Having just mentioned himself as an example, Paul continued to speak of himself because he had suffered persecution.

He was not free from it as an apostle, and he was not frightened by it. "I also suffer these things," he wrote. "Nevertheless I am not ashamed." These words pointedly remind Timothy that Paul was far worse off than he was. Timothy was free and was not suffering, whereas Paul was under arrest and under sentence of death.

Paul could have been troubled by his circumstances. He could have asked, "Is this the reward and thanks I get for my faithfulness as a preacher, apostle, and teacher of the Gentiles? Is this how God rewards those who are faithful in His service? Does He let them be abandoned to the lions?" No! Paul said he was "not ashamed."

The word translated "ashamed" here is *epaischunomai,* the same strong word that Paul used when he told the Romans that he was "not ashamed of the gospel of Christ" (Rom. 1:16). In 2 Timothy 1:12, *epaischunomai* can be rendered "disappointed in my hope." Paul was not disappointed. He knew that God's rewards were not handed out on earth. If he was martyred—and it certainly seemed that he would be—that would simply add a martyr's crown to the other rewards that he expected to receive. He was not disturbed by the way things had turned out; he had not expected anything better down here (Rom. 8:36; 2 Cor. 11:23–33). He knew that the Lord had not let him down.

(b) Paul's persuasion (1:12c–d)

i. His assurance as to the reality of the Lord (1:12c)

"I know whom I have believed," Paul told Timothy. His first glimpse of Jesus was dramatic enough for any man! On the Damascus road, he saw "the Lord from heaven" and thereafter always thought of Him in those terms (1 Cor. 15:47). Paul had seen the prints of the nails in His hands, and he had heard His voice saying, "I am Jesus" (Acts 22:8). Soon after Paul's first arrest, the Lord appeared to him again. "Be of good cheer, Paul," He said, "for as thou hast testified of me in Jerusalem, so must thou bear witness also at Rome" (Acts 23:11).

Paul knew the reality of the truths that he preached. There was never any doubt about them in Paul's mind because he had met Jesus—the altogether lovely One, the chief among ten thousand, the One whom the angels worship, the "King of Glory." It was the memory of this first, life-transforming encounter with the ascended Lord that upheld him in the midst of the fiercest opposition.

ii. His assurance as to the reliability of the Lord (1:12d)

Paul added, "[I] am persuaded that he is able to keep that which I have committed unto him against that day." The word translated "that which I have committed unto him" conveys the idea of a deposit as, for instance, a deposit made in a bank. Paul was laying up treasure in the bank of heaven.

Paul never lost sight of "that day." At all times, he kept in mind the coming day when believers will stand before the judgment seat of Christ to receive rewards for deeds done in the body (1 Cor. 3:12–15). God gives unmerited salvation, and we can be thankful that He does; otherwise, no one would get to heaven. But He does not give unmerited rewards. Rewards have to be earned.

However, it was not just the idea of being rewarded for faithful service that motivated Paul. It was the thought of being rewarded by *Jesus,* of hearing *His* "Well done!" Paul was also motivated by his memory of Stephen's triumphant death. What a thrill it must have been for Stephen to see the Lord of glory, surrounded by angelic hosts, actually standing to cheer him down the last lap, over the line, and on into heaven! We can almost hear Him saying, "Well done, Stephen!" Paul wanted the same abundant entrance into heaven. Nero's hellhounds were baying at his heels, but they only sped him on. At the end of the way, the gates would open wide, and a great cloud of witnesses would beckon him on. Jesus would be waiting for him with his well-earned rewards.

(c) Paul's persistence (1:13–14)

i. Timothy was responsible for the gospel that had been entrusted to him (1:13)

a. Its Pauline source (1:13a)

Paul wanted Timothy to keep making deposits in the bank of heaven so that when the time came, he, too, would receive a good reward. Therefore, the apostle told him to "hold fast the form of sound words, which thou hast heard of me."

The word translated "form" here means "outline, sketch, pattern." An outline, for instance, is a guide, a framework upon which a message is built. Timothy had been around Paul long enough to have grasped the points and perimeters of all of the apostle's teaching. Doubtless, Timothy knew most of Paul's outlines by heart.

b. Its pristine source (1:13b)

The gospel in its barest outline is about Christ Jesus, faith, and love. In other words, it is about a person, a persuasion, and a passion. The *person* is the most wonderful person in all of human history, the most wonderful person in the universe. The gospel is about His coming, His character, His career, His cross, His conquest, His coronation, and His coming again. The *persuasion* is the kind that Paul has just mentioned (1:12). It is a conviction that all of the great truths centered in Christ are absolutely dependable. Faith like that calls for total, unswerving commitment. Then, too, there is a *passion,* "so amazing, so divine" that it sweeps us up in its embrace and bears us on its tidal wave toward the golden shore, spilling over in love for others on the way. Such was the gospel that had been entrusted to Timothy. He must not let frowning circumstances cast their shadows on his faith.

ii. Timothy was responsible for the gift that had been entrusted to him (1:14)

Paul comes now to Timothy's gift. *It had been given to him,* and *it had to be guarded by him:* "That good thing which was committed unto thee keep by the Holy Ghost which dwelleth in us." The word translated "that good thing which was committed unto thee" means "deposit." The same word is used in 1:12, where it is translated "that which I have committed unto him." The word translated "keep" is also the same in both verse 12 here and in verse 14.

Paul had made his investments in a place where they would be kept safely. Timothy needed to do the same and to remember as well that the One to whom Paul had made a commitment had made a commitment to Timothy. The deposit that Timothy had received in trust was truth. He was called upon to "keep" this valuable, sacred deposit, but he was not expected to guard it in his own strength. He had the Holy Spirit to keep him true to this trust. In a day when safety from persecution could often be purchased by denying the truth, as it is in Christ Jesus, Timothy was not to allow even the thought of such a betrayal to cross his mind.

(2) The negative example (1:15)

To dispel Timothy's fears, Paul referred to himself as an example. To provide a contrast, Paul presented the negative example of his own abandonment.

He had been abandoned in his hour of peril by *one notable province.* "All they which are in Asia be turned away from me," he said. The reference here is to proconsular Asia, which included the districts of Mysia, Lydia, much of Phrygia, Caria, all of the districts that bordered the Aegean Sea, and the islands off the coast. Ephesus, the cities mentioned by John in the Apocalypse (Rev. 1–2), along with Colossae and Hierapolis, would all have been embraced by the word *Asia.* Thus, the abandonment of the great apostle was wholesale and widespread. It must have broken his heart.

We are reminded of Mark Antony's famous speech at Caesar's funeral in Shakespeare's *Julius Caesar.* Antony pointed to the dead body of the great Roman and to the stab wounds that various conspirators had inflicted. He said,

> Look! In this place ran Cassius' dagger through:
> See what a rent the envious Casca made.

Then, pointing to the wound made by Brutus, Caesar's closest friend, Mark Antony continued,

> Thro this the well-beloved Brutus stabb'd
> And, as he pluck'd his cursed steel away,
> Mark how the blood of Caesar follow'd it,
> As rushing out of doors, to be resolv'd
> If Brutus so unkindly knocked or no;
> For Brutus, as you know, was Caesar's angel:
> Judge, O you gods, how dearly Caesar loved him!
> This was the most unkindest cut of all.[3]

"All they which are in Asia be turned away from me," wrote Paul. Surely for him this was "the most unkindest cut of all." We can almost hear the pathos in his voice as he dictated this letter. He had done some of his best work in Asia Minor, despite the fact that for years doctrinal disturbances had occurred among the churches there. The Jews had done all they could do to subvert his converts. Incipient Gnosticism had been spreading in the area, and Paul's ministry in that part of the world was being undermined. Even as Paul wrote, Timothy was trying to stem the tide in Ephesus.

Of course, not everyone had "turned away," but there were defections in all of the area churches and in ever increasing numbers. Doubtless, Paul's imprisonment had emboldened his enemies to mount a growing offensive against him and his teachings. Doubtless, too, his imminent execution as a criminal at the hands of Nero put panic in the hearts of some believers. For their own safety, they decided to put some distance between themselves and Paul. Such cowardice did not surprise the apostle, but it saddened him. He reminded Timothy gently of these things. His goal was to add weight to the arguments intended to secure his young friend's loyalty.

Two named people, "Phygellus and Hermogenes," were among those who had abandoned Paul. Of all of the thousands of people who were turning tail, these two men stood out. Evidently, they were well known to Timothy, but we know nothing about them. Paul in mercy and love drew a veil over their case. It seems, however, that he was particularly hurt by their disloyalty. Maybe at one time they had been especially solicitous of Paul. Maybe, like Peter before he denied the Lord, they had vowed that, even if everyone else forsook him, they never would.

---

3. Shakespeare, *Julius Caesar,* 3.2.

Or perhaps they were leaders of a faction that took many other people away with them. We do not know, but Paul knew, the Lord knew, and Timothy knew. We can read between the lines of 2 Timothy 1:15. In effect, Paul said to Timothy, "Surely you don't want to be put in the same camp as Phygellus and Hermogenes."

(3) The noble example (1:16–18)

(a) Onesiphorus was a beloved man (1:16)

Paul now devotes a few verses to Onesiphorus, a man who had risked all for him. "The Lord give mercy unto the house of Onesiphorus," the apostle wrote. The reference to the "house" of Onesiphorus, rather than to Onesiphorus himself, suggests that he had already become a victim of the persecution.

"He oft refreshed me," Paul said. Many times, it would seem, this brave soldier of the cross visited the market to pick up supplies for Paul and then looked for a chance to bring them into the prison. The word translated "refreshed" means literally "to make cool again." Probably Onesiphorus brought the apostle some refreshing fruit and drink.

Paul added, "He . . . was not ashamed of my chain." The word translated "chain" is *halusis,* which means "handcuff." Paul doubtless had in mind the manacle that shackled him to a Roman soldier twenty-four hours a day. Onesiphorus was brave to bring supplies to Paul's cell because not all of the soldiers chained to Paul were friendly. Risk was involved, too, because it was a tedious, tiring occupation to be chained to a prisoner and to have to make every move in concert with him. Some of the soldiers probably believed Nero's lie that the Christians, of whom Paul was chief, had torched Rome—perhaps a number of them had lost loved ones in the conflagration. Likely, some of the guards doubled as spies and reported Paul's conversations and the names of his visitors to the authorities. Onesiphorus had refused to be intimidated by such considerations. Paul prayed that the Lord would "give mercy" and protect "the house of Onesiphorus."

(b) Onesiphorus was a brave man (1:17)

"When he was in Rome," Paul wrote, "he sought me out very diligently, and found me." It was a risky business to travel all over Rome—to the market, to the forum, to the barracks, to the wealthy residential areas, to the courthouse, to the squalid slave quarters—asking for information regarding the whereabouts of Paul. Evidently, the authorities were hushing up the arrest, trial, and imprisonment of this notable prisoner; possibly they feared that Paul or his followers might instigate a riot. Yet, Onesiphorus boldly, "very diligently," sought for Paul.

The word translated "very diligently" comes from *spoudaios* ("zealous"), signifies "with haste," and suggests exertion beyond the call of duty. Anyone less determined than Onesiphorus would have given up and said, "Well, at least I tried!" But he kept looking, and his diligence was rewarded. "He found me," Paul said. What a meeting that must have been! Then, one day Onesiphorus did not come. He had paid, so it seems, the ultimate price for his boldness and love.

(c) Onesiphorus was a blessed man (1:18)

Note Paul's request for Onesiphorus: "The Lord grant unto him that he may find mercy of the Lord in that day." He wanted to see Onesiphorus as he received his reward in heaven. Paul remembered his friend's generous and consistent support. He said to Timothy, "In how many things he ministered unto me at Ephesus, thou knowest very well." Evidently, Onesiphorus had lived in Ephesus, where Timothy was now pastoring. The word translated "very well" is *beltion,* which means "better." In effect, Paul was saying to Timothy, "You know better than I do all that this dear brother did for me in Ephesus."

"Now then," Paul adds, "either you are going to be like Phygellus and Hermogenes and be intimidated by my chain, or you are going to be like Onesiphorus."

B. Timothy's pastoral responsibilities: the present (2:1–26)
   1. Timothy was to be a steward (2:1–2)

Paul reminded Timothy of his great responsibilities as a pastor. Much was expected of him. One day, the books in heaven are to be opened, and he, along with the rest of us, will be held accountable for what he had done with his gifts, opportunities, and responsibilities.

When I was a young man, I worked at a branch of a large Canadian bank. During banking hours, while the other employees and I were busy with customers, paperwork piled up on our desks. When the last customer left, there was an almost audible sigh of relief. We took off our jackets and loosened our ties. The aroma of coffee filled the air, and we began to work on the logjam of piled-up matters needing attention. Cash had to be counted, books had to be sorted, volumes of correspondence had to be handled, and securities had to be put in the vault.

About once a year, this routine would be interrupted abruptly. We would hear a knock at the door, and someone would make a caustic remark about a tardy customer who thought he could transact business after hours. Then we would hear another knock. Someone would go to the door—to be greeted by half a dozen bank examiners! They would descend like vultures on the tellers, dive into the vault, and demand keys to its inner compartments. For the next week or so, the examiners would poke and pry into everything. They would count all of the cash, go through all of the deeds and securities, inspect every transaction made during the past year, and write voluminous reports. Their one purpose was to remind us that we were stewards of other people's money, and we were accountable for what we did with it.

Timothy was a steward. He would be held accountable one day for his stewardship.

a. What he must resolve (2:1)

Stewardship requires resolve, so Paul wrote to Timothy, "My son, be strong in the grace that is in Christ Jesus." The word translated "be strong" here means literally "to be strong within." It conveys the idea of strength of soul and purpose. The same word is used in Acts 9:22 to describe Paul himself. There we read that soon after his remarkable conversion, "Saul increased the more in *strength,* and confounded the Jews which dwelt at Damascus, proving that this is very Christ." Paul's resolve was so strong that "the Jews took counsel to kill him" (9:23). Now Paul looked for similar resolve in his "son." Timothy needed to be strong. It was no time for weakness. He had all of the resources of God's boundless grace upon which to draw.

The word translated "son" in 2 Timothy 2:1 is *teknon,* which has tender overtones. It means "child" and, unlike the synonym *huios,* which emphasizes the character of a relationship, *teknon* emphasizes the fact of birth. The apostle wanted Timothy to recall the moment when he was saved and became Paul's "child" in the faith.

b. What he must remember (2:2a)

Timothy needed to remember what Paul had taught him: "the things that thou hast heard of me among many witnesses." The "things" included the theology of the entire New Testament. Timothy had heard most of the monumental truths of the gospel from Paul's own lips. There were "many witnesses" to the fact that Paul had discipled Timothy zealously. If the young man backed down now, Paul would be disgraced publicly.

Paul had been taught, led, and inspired by the Holy Spirit. He had seen the risen Christ for himself. During several visits to Jerusalem, he had questioned Peter, John, and the other notables regarding details of the life of Christ. Paul had filtered his comprehensive knowledge of the Old Testament through the fine mesh of the death of Christ on the cross of Calvary and had refined his beliefs. He had poured liberally into Timothy's mind his knowledge, understanding, and wisdom. Timothy, in turn, had soaked it all in. Paul was so satisfied with his student's grasp of his teaching that on several occasions, when Paul wrote an inspired epistle, he turned to his young colleague and invited him to sign the letter with him.

What Timothy had learned from Paul was not mere theology. Paul had incarnated the truth in his life. He had been "strong in the grace that is in Christ Jesus." Timothy had been with Paul in Philippi when both Paul and Silas had been beaten, thrown into prison, flung into the security cell, and fastened in the stocks. Paul easily could have purchased immunity from such barbarous treatment by proclaiming his Roman citizenship, but then the mob would have vented its rage on Timothy. By shielding Timothy from that danger, Paul demonstrated strength. The same strength enabled Paul and Silas to sing in their cell and to win the jailer and his family to Christ (Acts 16:16–34).

Now Paul was in a prison that was far worse than the Philippian jail. He faced a far more serious charge and a far more terrible judge. Yet, he remained strong. His one fear was that his young disciple, into whom he had poured so much of his life, would buckle under pressure and persecution.

c. What he must reproduce (2:2b–c)

Just as Paul had poured himself into Timothy, Timothy was to pour himself into others. They, in turn, could pour themselves into ever-multiplying generations of disciples. He would thus reproduce *by extension* ("the same commit thou to faithful men"). He would also reproduce *by example* ("who shall be able to teach others also"). What Paul had been to him, Timothy was to be to others.

In this verse we have the Holy Spirit's formula for church growth—the formula that Paul followed. Paul used no clever tricks. He had no need to promote contests that offered incentives and prizes to the one who brought in the most visitors. He did not give away free trips to Jerusalem or arrange conducted tours of Rome. He did not give away camels or curios. He did not try to encourage one church to compete with another church in reporting conversions and baptisms. He would have scorned such expedients. Paul added people to the church one convert at a time. His method was like Christ's. The Lord poured Himself into a dozen men who, when filled with the Holy Spirit, poured themselves into others.

2. Timothy was to be a soldier (2:3–4)
    a. With endurance (2:3)

Paul continued, "Thou therefore endure hardness, as a good soldier of Jesus Christ."

When I was eighteen, I was drafted into the British army. In boot camp, we raw recruits were turned into soldiers by being taught to "endure hardness." The officers instilled into us the army's concepts of discipline and obedience. We endured hours of drilling, endless parades, long-route marches, constant pressure, tasteless food, guard duty, bullying sergeants, lectures, and exposure to inclement weather. The whole procedure was designed to toughen us up.

The Roman soldiers of Paul's day were the toughest, most disciplined, and most efficient soldiers in the world. Paul had known many of them, and their example was in his mind when he reminded Timothy that he was a "soldier of Jesus Christ." He had been enlisted the moment he had accepted Christ. He needed to learn to "endure hardness." A good soldier does not quit just because he faces a difficult task or a dangerous situation. He knows that his life is expendable, and he must be prepared to lay it down when required.

The word translated "endure hardness" means literally "to suffer evil, to suffer trouble, to endure affliction." God does not hand out brochures offering all kinds of fringe benefits to those who become Christians. On the contrary, He enlists them as soldiers and calls upon them to engage in a battle that will not end until their death or until the Lord returns. Even as Paul wrote, he was an embattled warrior, a prisoner of war who was sentenced to death. He would remain faithful to the end, and he wanted Timothy to have as much endurance as he did.

b. Without entanglement (2:4)
    (1) His duty (2:4a)

Timothy was on active service, manning a strategic outpost of the Christian world. Ephesus was located on an important highway, and the church in that city was a key center for evangelism. It was a post of honor, and Timothy was there as Paul's handpicked representative. There could be no thought of compromise or surrender for the "man that warreth."

(2) His detachment (2:4b)

Paul made clear to Timothy that no soldier "entangleth himself with the affairs of this life."

I am reminded again of my service in the British army. When I was enlisted, I was issued a uniform, a mess kit, and a gun. The day after my induction, I was given a cardboard box for my civilian clothes, which were to be packed up and shipped home. I was in the army! I had to surrender many of the rights and freedoms of my civilian life. I could no longer pursue my career in banking, attend my home church, live at home, engage in my favorite hobbies, or come and go as I pleased. I could take only a peripheral interest in politics. I was a soldier, and, as such, I had to keep myself free from anything that would interfere with my being available to obey the commands of those in authority.

An ordinary citizen is a free agent. He can make his own decisions; tie up his time as he wills; and become involved in sports, education, business, or politics. A soldier, on the other hand, cannot entangle himself in anything that might interfere with his duty. He cannot say to his commanding officer, "I'm sorry, sir, but I cannot board the boat tomorrow. I have a big business deal I'm working on, and that comes first."

The officer would respond, "You're in the army now, soldier. You be on that boat tomorrow, or I'll see to it that you will wish that you were!"

General Douglas McArthur faced the consequences of entanglement. He was an American war hero and is remembered for many things, especially for his ringing pledge to the people of the Philippines when the Japanese overran their country: "I shall return!" At the end of World War II, he accepted the surrender of the Japanese aboard the American flagship. He is also remembered as the commander of the United Nations troops in the Korean War. He is best remembered for being fired by President Truman when he entangled himself in politics and attempted to defy Truman's foreign policy.

Timothy was to steer clear of entanglements. He was not expected to organize marches and demonstrations to mobilize public opinion against slavery, persecution, and other social ills. God's purposes in this world in this age are spiritual rather than social. If enough people are saved from their sins, social reforms will follow as a matter of course. God has worked this way in history for the last two thousand years.

Think, for instance, of the deplorable social conditions in England in the eighteenth century. Corruption and crime in high places went hand in hand with vice and violence at all other levels of society. The church was materialistic and spiritually dead. It was the butt of jokes and was devoid of authority and power. A high-handed aristocracy rode roughshod over the rights and ambitions of the common people. Conditions in France were very similar. France exploded in a revolution that produced the guillotine and the Reign of Terror. England, too, was taken by storm, not by revolution but by revival; the Wesleys and the Methodist awakening led to a widespread cleanup of society. Throughout history, genuine spiritual awakenings have resulted in social change.

(3) His desire (2:4c)

A soldier should avoid entanglements so that "he may please him who hath chosen him to be a soldier." The word translated "chosen to be a soldier" means simply "enlisted." The Lord saw certain great qualities in Timothy. He had enlisted him. Timothy needed to strive to please Him who had placed him in a position of trust.

The word translated "please" here is used in Genesis 5:22 in the Septuagint to describe the translation of Enoch. It reads, "Enoch *pleased* God." A similar word occurs in the New Testament comment about Enoch: "Enoch . . . *pleased* God" (Heb. 11:5). So Timothy was challenged to join with the Enochs of this world. Enoch, who stood for God in a pagan and pornographic society, was rewarded by rapture. If Timothy did the same, he could be sure that he would be rewarded at *the* Rapture.

3. Timothy was to be a success (2:5–7)
   a. The test of success—the fighter (2:5)

Paul now changes the setting from the barracks to the arena. He wrote, "If a man also strive for masteries, yet is he not crowned, except he strive lawfully." He had the public games in mind, in which contestants competed with all of their might to be victors in the various athletic events. The word translated "strive for masteries" comes from a Greek word that gives us our English word *athlete.* Paul probably had in mind the wrestling and boxing events conspicuous in Greek arenas. Comparing Timothy to a fighter, Paul pictured *the contest, the crown,* and *the criterion.*

In Paul's day, the goal of the athlete was to win a crown, a circlet of wild olive or laurel (or sometimes oak, ivy, parsley, or myrtle) leaves. The word translated "crowned" here refers to the crown that was given as a token of honor for public service, as a recognition of military achievement, or as the symbol of nuptial bliss or triumph in the Olympic games. The same word is used for the crown of thorns that the soldiers pressed blasphemously on the Savior's brow and also of the crown that Paul expected to receive when his days on earth were done.

Timothy was already in the ring. It was too late to back out. He had to fight or be covered with shame, so he might as well go all out to win. Athletes went all out to win their laurels. Training for the Olympic games was serious business. The athletes went into training ten months before the actual contest. They were segregated from everyday life, went on a rigid diet, and exercised strenuously to build up their strength.

Above all, the athletes had to go by the rules. Otherwise, in spite of all of their efforts, they would be disqualified. Timothy, too, must "strive lawfully." He must abide by all of the rules of Christian conduct mandated in the New Testament. He must be Christlike. He must strive in the power of the Holy Spirit, not in the energy of the flesh.

b. The taste of success—the farmer (2:6–7)
   (1) Truth perceived (2:6)

Just as the athlete has to abide by the rules of the various games, so, too, the farmer must go about his business according to the laws of nature. He has to plow, plant, cultivate, and reap in due season if he wants to taste the fruit of his labors.

The husbandman's toil comes first. The chores on a farm or in a vineyard are endless, and a farmer's hours are long.

Doubtless Paul had visited many a farm in his travels. We tend to think of him in an urban setting because his strategy was to evangelize the population centers of the Roman world—places like Tarsus, Antioch, Corinth, Athens, Ephesus, Rome, and Jerusalem. His missionary journeys took him to the great cities of his day. However, he must have spent plenty of time in small market towns too. Many of his converts were likely to have been farmers. Paul would have taken a keen interest in their work, just as he would have taken an interest in the work of goldsmiths, weavers, and sailors. Some of Paul's farmer friends doubtless hosted him when he was in their area, and, true to form, Paul would have joined his hosts at dawn and gone to the fields with them to plow, hoe, and pull a rake along with the best of them. Paul was never afraid of hard work.

So Paul knew what he was talking about when he used the illustration of "the husbandman that laboureth" in 2:6. The word translated "husbandman" here means "tiller of the ground." The word translated "laboureth" conveys the ideas of toiling and becoming weary. We can be sure that many times Paul was utterly worn out at the end of a day's work in the fields.

The believer is like the farmer in that his work is never done. Fields must be plowed and harrowed, seed must be sown, soil must be fertilized and kept free from weeds, plants must be protected from harmful pests and watered, and fences must be kept in good repair. At harvesttime, crops must be cut, threshed, and gathered into barns. In Paul's day this hard work was done by hand; they had no tractors, no mechanized harvesters, and no other modern laborsaving devices. The farmer had to be up at cock crow, and he saw no end to his labor until after sunset. Paul reminded his young friend that he had put his hand to the plow, and there could be no looking back.

But after the toil comes *the husbandman's triumph:* he "must be first partaker of the fruits." The taste repays the toil. The principle introduced here is taught throughout Scripture. It is the principle of labor and reward. The soul winner tastes the fruit when a person accepts Christ under his ministry. The pastor tastes the fruit when a young person whom he has been cultivating dedicates his life to full-time Christian service at home or abroad. The full feast will be spread out at "the crowning day that's coming by and by."[4]

(2) Truth pondered (2:7)

"Consider what I say," Paul pleaded, "and the Lord give thee understanding in all things." The word *consider* means "to perceive with the mind." Paul was challenging Timothy to think about the illustrations in 2:1–6, ponder them, and work out in his mind all of their implications. Paul's prayer was that the Lord would help Timothy to do that.

Timothy needed to ponder first what it meant to be a steward. God had entrusted him with talents, truth, and tremendous opportunities. Not many people in the history of the church could say that they had been discipled by the greatest of

4. From the hymn "The Crowning Day" by D. W. Whittle.

all of the apostles. Timothy must not—dare not—squander the enormous investment of time, teaching, and training that Paul had made in him. He must not throw away his training, as did Demas. Timothy needed to be *a dutiful steward.*

Timothy also needed to be *a disciplined soldier* because the empire had declared war on the church. The roll call of casualties was already long. Rome itself was the fiercest theater of the conflict. The Lord's people were called on daily to face the most dreadful deaths imaginable. Paul himself was a prisoner of war. He had already been interrogated, and he fully expected to be executed. He rattled his chain and challenged Timothy, "Don't be a coward. Don't flinch in the hour of battle. You have your orders. If an ordinary soldier can leave family and friends, place and prospect, to endure hardship on the front lines, surely you, Timothy, as a soldier of the Christ, dare not shirk your duty."

Paul was also challenging Timothy to be *a determined fighter.* An Olympic boxer or wrestler subordinated everything to his one goal: achieving mastery in the ring. He curbed his appetites, put his body under subjection, studied the stamina and style of his opponents, gave up many legitimate pleasures and pastimes, and hardened himself for the critical hour when he would be alone with his adversary. Behind all of this vigorous training was a driving determination to win a crown. How could Timothy do less? Did he not have Paul's own fearless example to spur him on? Had not Paul told the Corinthians, "I keep under my body, and bring it into subjection: lest that by any means, when I have preached to others, I myself should be a castaway" (1 Cor. 9:27). In the face of every danger, difficulty, and discouragement, Timothy must be determined to win.

The final challenge in this passage was for Timothy to be *a diligent farmer.* The farmer is dedicated to the long haul; he does not expect rapid results. Timothy needed to ponder the husbandman's patience and hard work.

4. Timothy was to be a sufferer (2:8–13)
   a. The triumph of Christ (2:8)
      (1) His royalty (2:8a)

Paul could have given Timothy many such illustrations. Instead, he simply pointed him to the greatest of all examples: the person and work of the Lord Jesus. "Remember . . . Jesus Christ of the seed of David," Paul wrote.

Commentators have wondered why Paul mentioned David here. Perhaps it was because David had been *a superlative steward.* Toward the end of his life, David devoted himself to amassing an enormous fortune (1 Chron. 22); he became a faithful steward of incalculable wealth and eventually handed it all over to Solomon for the building of the temple. David had been a famous soldier and *a splendid fighter.* He slew single-handedly the Philistine giant. He led the armies of Israel from victory to victory and subdued all of the nation's foes, including the formidable Philistines. Moreover, David had been *a successful farmer*—as a shepherd he hazarded life and limb to defend his flock against both a lion and a bear. Moreover, he became the great shepherd of Israel. He carried the concept of being a shepherd to the throne itself so that succeeding generations would understand that God's ideal king must always be a pastor of his people.

The Lord Jesus, being "of the seed of David," took these characteristics of David and lifted them to the spiritual realm. What an amazing steward He was of the grace, goodness, and glory of God! In Christ, we see a perfect demonstration of stewardship. What God said, Jesus said. What God did, Jesus did. What God was, Jesus was. He was a perfect custodian of the greatness of God.

What a magnificent warrior the Lord Jesus was! He came to shake Satan's kingdom to its foundations, shatter his power, and destroy his works. Demons fled before Him. Disease and death met their match in Him. Satan failed to deflect Him, even for an instant, from His purpose. Finally, Christ, on the cross, triumphed over all of the power of the enemy—at the very moment when Satan thought that he had won (Col. 2:15)!

Christ was more patient than any farmer. He was never in a hurry and never impatient. When His friends said or did foolish things, He corrected them gently and patiently. Right from the start, He knew that He was plowing and planting for a harvest that would take thousands of years to ripen. Through the centuries, He has been sitting on His Father's throne, "expecting till his enemies be made his footstool" (Heb. 10:13). Slowly, a seed germinates in the soil. Slowly, the first tender shoots appear. Slowly, the stem rises and the leaves unfold. Slowly, flowers appear. Slowly, the budding fruit develops. With the sublime patience and assurance of a farmer, the Lord Jesus waits for the ripening of God's purposes, all of which take time to mature.

Paul was right on target. Jesus embodied perfectly the characteristics once illustrated in David. Timothy was to ponder these things, and so must we.

(2) His resurrection (2:8b)

Jesus Christ "was raised from the dead according to my gospel," added Paul. Here Paul seems to be fortifying Timothy further against his natural fears that apparently threatened to fill his soul: the fear of being arrested, arraigned, and marched off to face a terrible death.

The Lord Jesus had paid such a price. Terrible things happened to Him. He was betrayed by a friend, falsely accused, and wrongfully condemned. He was mocked and mauled, scourged to the bone, hounded to Calvary's hill, and crucified. But—and this was Paul's main point—Christ was "raised from the dead." He is alive! He has ascended into heaven, and He is seated at God's right hand on the highest seat of power. He ministers to us now as our Great High Priest. Death is not by any means the end. Timothy should remember that.

Paul wrote of the people who were propagating a false gospel. Paul's gospel—the true gospel, the only real gospel—is wedded eternally to the truth of the Lord's resurrection. When Paul preached his gospel in Jerusalem, he was mobbed. When he preached it in Athens, he was mocked. When he preached it in Rome, he was martyred. But he was not the least bit ashamed of it (Rom. 1:14–1). He was just as prepared to preach it to Nero as to Caiaphas, Felix, Festus, Agrippa, or anyone else. Paul could call it "my gospel" because in all of its glorious fullness it had been revealed and entrusted to him (Gal. 1:15–17). It finds its greatest expression in the Roman epistle. We may well call that theological masterpiece "The Gospel According to Paul."

b. The tribulation of the Christian (2:9–13)
   (1) Paul's fearful sufferings (2:9–10)
      (a) How he described them (2:9)
         i. The sting (2:9a)

Timothy knew very well that Paul was no coward. When Paul challenged him to face tribulation, he was only asking him to do what he himself was prepared to do. Paul described his own sufferings: "I suffer trouble," he said. He used the same word in verse 3 where he urged Timothy to "endure hardness." Paul was incarcerated under the most rigorous conditions and was in such dire circumstances simply because he preached the gospel.

He expected to be executed. He had no protection against the malice of Nero, who was capable of any wickedness and who had a vested interest in making a public example of Paul. Nero hated Christians for their godly lives, their uncompromising doctrine, and their boldness in the hour of death. Nero regarded them as the scum of the earth. Paul had no hope of release. He might have to face torture, exposure in the arena, crucifixion, or dismemberment. As far as Paul knew, his sufferings had just begun; yet, he faced his "trouble" boldly and unflinchingly.

ii. The stigma (2:9b)

Paul endured hardship "as an evildoer, even unto bonds." The word that he used for "evildoer" is ***kakourgos,*** which means "malefactor." It is used only here and in Luke 23, where it describes the men who were crucified with Christ.

Kakourgos is composed of ***kakos*** ("evil") and ***ergon*** ("work"). *Kakos* conveys the idea of being depraved, bad to the very core of one's being.

Paul felt the shame of being "numbered with the transgressors," but he knew that the world had done the same to Jesus (Isa. 53:12). Paul was one of the most godly men who ever lived. He must have shrunk in horror at being paraded through Rome to the prison as a man addicted to acts of depravity. His bonds must have chafed not only his wrists but also his soul. He rose above these dark circumstances, however, and mentioned them here merely as proof that he was demanding of Timothy only what he demanded of himself.

iii. The song (2:9c)

Although Paul was suffering the sting and stigma of "trouble," he could add triumphantly, "But the word of God is not bound." His thoughts could soar on the wings of song because, no matter what happened to him, God's Word had been turned loose on the world. All of the decrees of all of the Neros in the world could never change that.

No power on earth or in hell can shackle the Word of God. Sometimes God's servants are stifled, or even silenced in death, but God's Word still rings out. Diocletian made a mighty effort to destroy every Bible in the empire, but he failed. Voltaire once declared that he would bury the Bible. Not long afterward, Voltaire died and was buried, and his house was purchased by the Geneva Bible Society and used as a place for storing Bibles. Through centuries, the papacy fought fiercely to keep the Bible from the people. The early translators and Reformers paid a high price for their courage in printing and promoting the Scriptures; they were imprisoned, maligned, persecuted, and burned at the stake. However, Rome fought in vain; the Word of God triumphed. The Bible is the world's best-seller and is now published in thousands of tongues and in all kinds of versions.

"The word of God is not bound." It is the living Word! It is "quick, and powerful, and sharper than any twoedged sword, piercing even to the dividing asunder of soul and spirit, and of the joints and marrow, and is a discerner [*kritokos,* "critic"] of the thoughts and intents of the heart" (Heb. 4:12). Men may deny the Word of God. They may doubt it, despise it, defame it, and distort it, but it still pierces their innermost beings, where it awakens conviction of sin, of righteousness, and of judgment to come. The Word of God is incorruptible seed. It possesses divine life (1 Peter 1:23). Once lodged in a human soul, the seed remains there until the first flicker of faith germinates it and quickens it to life.

(b) How he dismissed them (2:10)

i. What he suffered (2:10a)

Paul considered his sufferings as being hardly worth mentioning in the light of eternity, but he did mention them in passing. "Therefore I endure all things," he wrote. He recognized the direct link between his sufferings and the fact that he was God's instrument to turn the Word of God loose on the world—even to the point of being the author of half of the New Testament. The Devil had desired to have Peter to sift him as wheat (Luke 22:31). How much more the Devil must have wanted to get his hands on Paul (2 Cor. 12:7)! Now Satan had Paul where he wanted him: in the most dreadful of Nero's dungeons, facing the death sentence, and awaiting only the time and manner of his execution. Paul was equal to the occasion, however. "No matter what," he said in effect, "I can endure it."

ii. Why he suffered (2:10b–c)

Speaking more specifically of reasons, Paul explained that he suffered "for the elect's sakes, that they may also obtain the salvation which is in Christ Jesus with eternal glory." The knowledge that people were being saved through his ministry and strengthened through his example helped to fortify Paul in his dreadful circumstances. He was "a man subject to like passions as we are" (James 5:17) and was not exempt from fear. He well knew the terror and torment of torture. He bore the marks of many lashings on his back. And he had a lively enough imagination to picture the horrors that could yet be ahead for him.

But out there, all across the pagan Roman world, were God's elect, His called-out ones. They were set apart by God to be instruments in the salvation of more and more people. Satan could do nothing to stop this onward march. If Christians were murdered by the millions, more and more would rise up to take their places. God in heaven already knew their names. In a sense, they had been handpicked, and Timothy was one of them. He had his own converts and disciples, too, and they in turn had theirs (2 Tim. 2:1–2). The ranks of the redeemed were multiplying, and the faith was spreading.

It was "for the elect's sake" as much as for Christ's sake that Paul held his head high. The whole Christian and pagan world would be watching to see how he, the great Apostle to the Gentiles, stood up under trial. Paul was determined to finish well.

(2) Paul's faithful saying (2:11–13)

(a) Our decisions (2:11–12)

i. Death in the balance (2:11)

Five "faithful" or "true" sayings are in the Pastoral Epistles (1 Tim. 1:15; 3:1; 4:9; 2 Tim. 2:11–13; Titus 3:8). The one here begins, "It is a faithful saying: For *if* we be dead with him, we shall also live with him" (italics added). This is no hypothetical *if.* This is the *if* of a fulfilled condition. The hypothesis is assumed to be an actual fact. Thus, the clause can be translated, "*Because* we have died with him." The aorist tense speaks here of a past fact, not of a present condition.

This verse helps to explain why Paul could look death in the face so calmly—he was already "dead" (see Rom. 6:1–11)! The Lord Jesus died not only *for* us but also *as* us. In God's sight, when Jesus died, we died. When He was buried, we were buried. When He arose, we arose. In Him, each believer has already passed through death and burial and now stands on resurrection ground. The occasion of one's physical death is simply an incident of momentary concern.

Paul, we can be sure, had taught Timothy this truth before. Now he reminded him that the believer has nothing to fear from death. The worst is already over. Paul wanted Timothy to remember the principle contained in Romans 8:35–37:

> Who shall separate us from the love of Christ? shall tribulation, or distress, or persecution, or famine, or nakedness, or peril, or sword? As it is written, "For thy sake we are killed all the day long; we are accounted as sheep for the slaughter." Nay, in all these things we are more than conquerors through him that loved us.

Paul had written those words to the Christians in Rome. Now Roman Christians themselves feared Nero and all of the terrifying apparatus of persecution. The words apply to us as well. Our decisions should be influenced by the fact that death has been dealt its deathblow by Christ.

ii. Duress in the balance (2:12a)

Paul continued, "*If* we suffer, we shall also reign with him" (italics added). This is the same kind of *if* as the one in the preceding verse. Undoubtedly, Christians are called on to suffer in this world. We are not exempt from the ordinary ills and disasters that overtake people down here. In addition, we suffer from the active malice of Satan (as we learn from the book of Job) and the hatred of the world system that despises the Christian ethic and view.

The word translated "suffer" here is translated "endure" in 2:10. It means "to endure, to persevere" and conveys the idea of bearing up courageously under suffering.

To fix our eyes on the reward God promises for suffering, Paul reminds us that we will "reign." The Greek word means "to reign as a king." Paul was looking forward to the day when he would reign himself (4:8)—and Nero would be dead.

Behind the teaching of this verse, we can discern the shadow of the judgment seat of Christ, where all of God's people will face the consequences of their lives (Rom. 14:10). Then, beyond the judgment seat of Christ, we can discern the form of the millennial kingdom, in which all believers will reign with Christ in the heavenlies.

Rewards have to be earned. Faithfulness to Christ, our love for Him, submission to the Father's will, and cooperation with the indwelling Holy Spirit are all factors that will determine what our rebukes and rewards will be at the judgment seat. Our position, power, and prominence in the millennial kingdom are all to be decided there. We should look at our sufferings in the light of the judgment seat.

iii. Denial in the balance (2:12b)

There will be tears as well as cheers at the judgment seat of Christ because "if we deny him, he will also deny us." In view here is not the Great White Throne. That is where *sinners* are to be arraigned, exposed, condemned, and banished to the lake of fire (Rev. 20:11–15). The reference here is to the judgment seat of Christ, where *God's people* are reviewed, rebuked, and rewarded.[5] Those whose souls have been saved, but whose lives have been wasted, will suffer loss in the millennial kingdom (1 Cor. 3:12–15).

Second Timothy 2:12 does not imply an absolute denial of us as God's children. Peter denied the Lord with oaths and curses; yet, the Lord sought him out, restored him, and used him (Matt. 26:69–75; Luke 24:34; Acts 2). The denial, here, relates to rewards, not salvation, and salvation and rewards are not the same.

Our decisions should not be influenced by our circumstances, whether threatening or thrilling, but by the promise of the Lord's return, by the certainty of the judgment seat of Christ, and by the fact that spiritually we are already on the other side of death.

(b) Our doubts (2:13)

Paul continued, "If we believe not, yet he abideth faithful: he cannot deny himself." The word translated "believe not" refers to a believer's unfaithfulness. The sad fact is that believers are often unfaithful; Paul cites the example of Demas in 4:10. Paul did not want Timothy to become unfaithful.

Even when we disappoint the Lord, He remains true to His Word and His character and is faithful in His dealings with us. Note, for instance, His dealings with John Mark, who disappointed the Lord at Perga (Acts 13:13). Paul felt Mark's defection keenly (15:36–41), but the Lord did not write Mark off. He used Barnabas, Peter, and other believers to bring Mark back into useful ministry (2 Tim. 4:11). Timothy was quite familiar with this case history.

5. Timothy was to be a student (2:14–19)
   a. The framework (2:14)

Paul refers directly to Timothy's own case. He reminded him that he needed to confront some unruly believers in Ephesus. Attending to his duties would help Timothy take his mind off his fears. Paul wrote, "Of these things put them in remembrance, charging them before the Lord that they strive not about words to no profit, but to the subverting of the hearers."

5. We must not confuse things that differ. See John Phillips, *Exploring the Future,* rev. ed. (Grand Rapids: Kregel, 2001).

In spite of all of the dangers to the church from outside, "wordy battles" were being fought inside the church. Satan was busy without and within. Surely the church should close ranks in the face of a common foe like Nero. Instead, members of the church were at loggerheads over trivia, wrangling over unimportant issues. They needed to concentrate on matters of life and death, time and eternity, judgment and reward—the "things" about which Paul had just been writing—instead of striving over words. The word translated "strive about words" conveys the ideas of fighting, quarreling, and disputing.

The fierce arguments at Ephesus served no good purpose. The wrangling helped no one. Paul said it was to "no profit." Furthermore, it was subversive. To express this thought, Paul used the word from which our word *catastrophe* comes. It signifies "to overthrow." It is a picturesque word in the original. It paints the picture of a plow turning the soil over and over. Some believers were being plowed under as a result of squabbles over nonessentials. Paul urged Timothy to address this situation.

b. The focus (2:15)
   (1) Diligence in the study (2:15a)

Paul now spurred Timothy on to more diligent, systematic, and thorough Bible study. He began, "Study to shew thyself approved unto God." The word translated "study" here means "be diligent." It conveys the ideal of hurrying to do something and of exerting oneself.

Sometimes people who have heard a sermon or two, or read a few articles in a Christian magazine, or answered a few questions in a Sunday school manual, or taken a correspondence course imagine themselves to be authorities on the Scriptures. Often, individuals who have been overindoctrinated in an aspect of Bible truth will challenge seasoned Bible teachers over points in a sermon on which they disagree. The Bible is about the only book on which people deem themselves to be authorities when, in reality, their acquaintance with its teachings is meager indeed.

It takes seven years of intensive training to become a medical doctor and three or four additional years to become proficient in some highly specialized field of medicine. Thereafter, it takes a lifetime of continuous study for the doctor to stay abreast of developments in his field. The mysteries of medicine are much less profound than the eternal themes that are woven into the fabric of the Word of God. The educated Ethiopian chancellor was able to read the Scriptures, but he frankly admitted his inability to understand what he read and readily confessed his need for someone to teach him its significance (Acts 8:30–31).

The Bible is a big book with many themes. It was written over a period of some fifteen hundred years. It was written by some forty men from various backgrounds, cultures, and walks of life, men who were divinely inspired to write down its immortal truths. They wrote in places as far apart as Babylon in the East and Rome in the West. The geography, history, and languages alone of the Bible supply subject matter for years of intensive study. Hermeneutics, the interpretation of biblical truths, is a science of its own. Its rules and principles cannot be violated with impunity. No wonder Paul called on Timothy to study!

A person does not become a master car mechanic by reading an automobile operator's manual. One does not become a mathematician, astronomer, nuclear physicist, biochemist, historian, or performing artist by taking a course or two at a junior college. A person must study if he is to become an authority in any subject, much more so if he is to speak with authority about Scripture.

Diligent study requires time, commitment, and hard work. Only by that kind of study can the student of Scripture "shew [himself] approved unto God." The word translated "shew" means "to present." Here the idea is that of being in a position where one's quality or worth as a diligent student of Scripture is displayed. Possibly, Paul had in mind the judgment seat of Christ. The word translated "approved" here is *dokimos,* which was used of coins and metals that are tested in the fire to prove their worth.

(2) Discipline by the student (2:15b)

Paul wanted Timothy to be able to present himself to the Lord as "a workman that needeth not to be ashamed." The word translated "workman," often rendered "laborer," is used to describe a farm laborer. Bible study, properly done, entails a great deal of hard labor because the field is vast, the issues are profound, and the disagreements are many and varied.

Doctrinal studies are divided, for the sake of convenience, into a number of branches. The first and foremost branch is *theology,* which is the study of the nature, attributes, character, and names of God. Next is *Christology,* which is the study of the deity, preexistence, attributes, incarnation, life, teachings, crucifixion, burial, resurrection, ascension, and second coming of Christ. Then there is *pneumatology,* which is the study of the person and work of the Holy Spirit and the relationships He sustains with saved and unsaved people. Of equal importance is *bibliology,* the study of the divine and human authorship of the Bible, its inspiration, its inerrancy, its infallibility, its authority, its composition, and its preservation.

There is also *angelology,* the study of angels. Subjects included in this branch are Satan and his domains, the realm of demons, and the relationship of the spirit world to the human race. Still another branch of doctrinal study is *soteriology,* the study of salvation as revealed throughout the Scriptures. Also of great interest is *eschatology,* the study of the end times, the second coming of Christ, and God's eternal purposes. So the field is vast, and the student must be a "workman."

The difficulty of the work is increased by the fact that each of the branches of doctrinal study has become a battleground for differing views and dogmas. For example, the ultra-Calvinist and the Arminian lock horns in the debate over the sovereignty of God versus the free will of man and in the debate over eternal security versus the possibility that a child of God might lose his salvation.

The student of prophecy finds disagreement everywhere. Will the second coming of Christ take place before the Great Tribulation, in the middle of it, or after it? Is the reign of Christ premillennial, postmillennial, or amillennial (no millennium at all)? Should we interpret the book of Revelation literally or symbolically? Is the Antichrist a Jew or a Gentile?

Similarly, areas of disagreement also exist in pneumatology. The so-called "charismatics" believe that all the gifts of the Spirit are for today, whereas other people make a distinction between temporary sign gifts and permanent spiritual gifts. Wide differences exist over the baptizing work of the Holy Spirit.

Muddying the waters beyond all common sense are the liberal theologians who chop and change the Scriptures. They deny the supernatural, especially the divine inspiration and inerrancy of Scripture. They would like to reduce the Bible to the level of a merely human book, Christ to equality with Buddha, the gospel of salvation to a social gospel of good works, and Christianity to just another religion on common ground with Hinduism and Islam.

Added to all of this confusion is Catholicism, which adds its dogmas to the Bible, and the cults that systematically deny and distort the truth of Scripture in all sorts of ways.

No wonder the Bible student is called upon to be a "workman." He has his work cut out for him if he is to think his way through the maze of dead-end roads that block his path to a clear understanding of the truth.

(3) Division of the Scriptures (2:15c)

The phrase *rightly dividing the word of truth* calls for a proper division of the Scriptures. What did Paul have in mind here? One suggestion is that he was thinking of a stonemason who knows how to cut the stone straight and true so that it will fit into its proper place in a building. Another suggestion is that he had in mind the need to hold a straight course when presenting God's truth and not to deviate from it to suit one person or another. Doubtless, he meant that we must handle God's truth honestly, fully, and straightforwardly. We must plow a straight furrow in exploring and expounding the Scriptures.

To divide the word of truth rightly, we must have a consistent hermeneutic. We must interpret the Bible not allegorically but literally, taking into account the Hebrew and Greek languages of its birth and making allowances for the cultural, historical, and geographical backgrounds against which it arose. We must take into account the obvious differences between the dispensations, the various kinds of judgments that people will face, the two different resurrections, our standing and our state, Israel and the church, the church and the kingdom, and the kingdom of God and the kingdom of heaven. In other words, we must make a difference where God made a difference. We must pay attention to figures of speech, types and symbols, the chronology of events, the structure of each book, the harmony of Scripture, and the significance of names and places. If we follow these guidelines, an adequate, comprehensive, consistent, and correct exegesis of the text should emerge from our study.

In all of this work of "rightly dividing," we should not scorn the help of other people. God has given the gift of teachers to His church. The preaching and writings of gifted, godly men can be invaluable—as long as we listen to them and read them with Berean caution (Acts 17:10–11).

The diligent student will build an ever growing library of useful books, including commentaries, dictionaries, encyclopedias, atlases, histories, biographies, systematic theologies, works on comparative religion and the cults, word studies, and even good fiction. He will extend his study into a score of disciplines, including archaeology, geography, history, astronomy, apologetics, and languages. He will fill file drawers with illustrative material culled from extensive reading of magazines, journals, newspapers, and books. He will join libraries, subscribe to a variety of periodicals, attend lectures, and consult experts. In short, the diligent student will work. He will fill his notebooks as he steeps his mind in "the word of truth."

When the drums of World War II were stilled and men turned hopefully to the pursuits of peace, they soon discovered that their dreams were turned into a nightmare. The Soviet Union launched a global effort to communize the world. The Iron Curtain came down, and Eastern Europe was swallowed up. The Cold War began.

Sir Winston Churchill was appalled. It occurred to him that the Bible had prophecies that might shed light on his path as he sought to guide his people along the perilous paths of peace. But who could he get to shed light on these things?

After diligent inquiries, he chose a former missionary named Harold St. John, a gifted Bible teacher and one who was at home in the prophetic Word. Arrangements were made for the two to meet. For the better part of a day, the great statesman sat at the feet of one of God's choicest saints as the great Bible teacher took him through the Scriptures.

As the two men parted at the end of the day, Churchill said to his new friend, "Mr. St. John, I would give half the world for your knowledge of the Bible." Mr. St. John acknowledged the compliment and quietly said, "Sir, I gave *all* the world to get it."

c. The falsehoods (2:16–18)
   (1) The portrait (2:16–17a)
      (a) The advent of error (2:16a)

One reason Timothy needed to press on with his Bible study was that "grievous wolves" had come to Ephesus, as Paul had known they would (Acts 20:17, 29–31). These people were given to "profane and vain babblings." The word translated "profane" refers to a threshold over which everyone treads. It speaks of that which is unhallowed and common. It describes those who have no feeling for God. The word translated "vain babblings" means "discussion of useless things." It refers to words that, being empty, lend themselves to actual evil. Paul had used both of these words in his earlier letter (1 Tim. 1:9; 6:20), so it seems that Timothy either had done little or nothing about the problem or had been unsuccessful in dealing with it.

Paul wanted Timothy to "shun" those who participated in this dangerous talk. The word translated "shun" also occurs in Acts 25:7, where it is translated "stood round about" and refers to people who hung around the court of Festus and made all kinds of false accusations against Paul. In John 11:42, the word is used in reference to the people who were standing around the tomb of Lazarus. As Paul used the word here, it means "to turn around in order to avoid someone." The apostle told Timothy bluntly to turn his back deliberately on people who were given to "profane and vain babblings."

(b) The advance of error (2:16b–17a)

Paul warned Timothy that such people "will increase unto more ungodliness. And their word will eat as doth a canker." Paul clearly foresaw that they would enlarge their sphere of influence. He knew from the Lord's mystery parables (Matt. 13) that Christianity (contrary to the optimistic theology of some people) was not going to convert the entire world. The word translated "increase" pictures a blacksmith hammering a red-hot piece of metal to spread it, thin it, or lengthen it. Paul knew that these false teachers would lead people farther and farther from the truth and thus bring in more and more ungodliness. Because Timothy could not shut them up, he had better show them up.

The word translated "canker" is *gangraina,* from which our English word *gangrene* is derived. A "canker" is a spreading sore that produces mortification that, if not dealt with drastically by amputation, will end in death. Paul was saying that some people in Ephesus were like gangrene in the body of the local church.

(2) The propagandists (2:17b–18)

Paul named the two leading cultists in Ephesus: Hymenaeus and Philetus. We know nothing about Philetus, but we have met Hymenaeus before. He is one of the men whom Paul handed over to Satan so that he might learn not to blaspheme (1 Tim. 1:20). Evidently, Hymenaeus had not learned his lesson because now he and Philetus were teaching false doctrine about the resurrection of believers. Their principal lie was that "the resurrection is past already" (2 Tim. 2:18).

We are not told how these heretics were able to convince people that wrong was right, that error was truth, and that the Resurrection (a future event) was already a past event. Most likely, they spiritualized the Resurrection by distorting Paul's teaching in such verses as Romans 6:4 and Ephesians 2:1. In any case, Hymenaeus and Philetus were robbing believers of vital truth (as those who allegorize the Old Testament still do). In Paul's day, they had already succeeded in overthrowing the faith of some.

d. The foundation (2:19)

"Nevertheless," Paul wrote, "the foundation of God standeth sure." Paul himself remained unshaken, in spite of the defection of some people, because *the foundation was secure.*

The church, solidly founded on the work of Christ, the Word of God, and the witness of the Spirit, could no more be overthrown by its enemies within than it could be overthrown by its enemies without. The Lord Jesus had said so: "Upon this rock I will build my church; and the gates of hell shall not prevail against it" (Matt. 16:18). The church is built on solid Rock, so let the storms come! Let the winds howl! Let the tides roar (see Matt. 7:24–27)!

To a casual observer, it might have seemed that Paul had labored in vain. The mightiest empire on earth had mobilized its might to destroy the church; an assault that would last three hundred years had commenced. Paul himself was a prisoner under sentence of death. Many of his friends, converts, and disciples were abandoning him. Entire provinces where he had planted numerous churches were turning against him. Even trusted Timothy seemed to need constant prodding. Yet, Paul was unperturbed because he was looking ahead to the end times. He knew that God was still on the throne and that the foundation was secure. It was secure because it was founded on Scripture.

So Paul took Timothy back to his Bible. He told him, "The Lord knoweth them that are his" (2 Tim. 2:19). He was alluding possibly to Numbers 16 and the story of Korah, Dathan, and Abiram. When these Old Testament apostates were judged for seeking to overthrow the authority of Moses and Aaron, the Lord first segregated the culprits from those who were truly His—the Lord knew His own (Num. 16:1–40)—and then He put forth His might in judgment.

The Lord Himself had predicted that tares would grow among the wheat (Matt. 13:24–30). It is not our task to try to root out the tares. That will be done by the angels in the last days. The Lord knows the true wheat, knows each of His own just as Joseph knew each of his brothers (Gen. 42:7). Our task is to ensure that we "depart from iniquity."

6. Timothy was to be a servant (2:20–26)
   a. The criteria of service (2:20)

The universal church, composed of "them that are his," is impeccable and impregnable. The local church, however, is far from perfect. Both are described by the Lord in Matthew's gospel. He mentioned the universal church in Matthew 16, where it is presented as being founded on the Rock and invincible. He mentioned the local church and its functions in Matthew 18. The functions include *the reception of believers* as little children, *the restoration of backsliders* who are like sheep going astray, and *the reconciliation of brethren.* The chapter portrays the local church as being in need of corrective ministry. Some members needed to be restored, and others needed to be expelled. Both the universal church and the local church were yet future when the Lord spoke, but He introduced the subject quite adequately in these two initial references.

In 2 Timothy 2:20, Paul sees the local church as a "great house" containing a variety of utensils. It gathers into its fellowship a mixture of saved and unsaved people. Some of them have grown up in the church and have learned to speak "the language of Canaan." They have knowledge in their heads but nothing in their hearts. They have been baptized, received into membership, and entrusted with avenues of service, but they have never been saved at all. Others have professed conversion, perhaps in response to an overzealous soul winner's efforts or a high-pressure evangelist's emotional appeal, but they have never shown any evidence of new life in Christ.

One way or another, such people come into the church and even find their way into the pulpit or accept the office of a deacon. In their hearts, however, they remain strangers to Christ. Their thinking is worldly, their responses are those of the natural man, and their service is blemished. They might be educated, polished, capable, and successful members of the community, but in the church they are counted by God as vessels of "dishonor" because they do not know the Lord (see Matt. 7:21–23).

Some vessels in a household are *costly* and some are *common.* Just so in the church. Some members are pure gold. They render the highest possible kind of service, and their character and faithfulness are of great *worth.* Other believers are silver vessels. They are made of genuine metal, but it does not come up to the excellence of gold. Unregenerate church members are made of common clay; they are earthen vessels. Other unsaved people are wooden vessels. Earthen vessels, or vessels of clay, suggest service rendered by unregenerate people. Wooden vessels suggest service that is of man-made workmanship. Human nature and human effort characterize such service.

The *work* accomplished by spiritual believers is of the highest order. The work accomplished by well-meaning but unregenerate church members, on the other hand, has little to commend it. Just as an earthen pot can crack and break, and just as a wooden container can become chipped and damaged, the service rendered by the unsaved soon shows its flaws. Hymenaeus, Alexander, and Philetus are examples of earthen and wooden vessels. Timothy and Titus are prime examples of gold and silver vessels.

The "mixed multitude" that accompanied God's redeemed people out of Egypt were a constant source of confusion, conflict, and complaint (Exod. 12:38; Num. 11:4). Likewise, unsaved church members are a constant source of trouble in the church. Think of the damage done to the church at large by liberal theologians or by arrogant and worldly professional priests and ministers. No matter how much praise and applause they receive from their peers, they are vessels of "dishonor" and will eventually be exposed as such.

b. The condition of service (2:21–23)
   (1) A must (2:21)
      (a) God wants a clean vessel (2:21a)

Timothy was to separate himself from "the vessels of dishonor" who were members of the church in Ephesus. Paul had already told him to "shun" such men as Hymenaeus and Philetus and all of those whose jangling words were upsetting the church (2:16–17). Now the apostle told Timothy to "purge himself from these." The word translated "purge" occurs in only two places in the New Testament, here and in 1 Corinthians 5:7. Only by disassociating himself totally from such men could Timothy himself be a clean vessel.

(b) God wants a consecrated vessel (2:21b)

A Christian should be "a vessel unto honour, sanctified, and meet for the master's use." Much that goes on in the local church in the name of service is carnal and worldly because it is performed by unsaved church members or by carnal Christians. We should not be surprised. The mystery parables in Matthew 13 predict seeming failure everywhere. God, however, always has His gold and silver vessels, just as in the Old Testament there was always a faithful remnant in Israel. Consider Boaz, for example, who was Ruth's kinsman-redeemer, or the seven thousand people in Elijah's day who had not bowed to Baal, or that illustrious company who made up the ranks of the prophets.

The word translated "honour" in 2 Timothy 2:21 is testimony to the value of God's gold and silver vessels in the church. The word for "sanctified" here signifies that they have been set apart for God. The word translated "meet for use" means "useful, profitable." Paul used the word to describe Onesimus after his conversion (Philem. 11).

(c) God wants a compliant vessel (2:21c)

A compliant vessel is one "prepared unto every good work." God's work is vast and varied. It is being carried on by compliant vessels in every nation under heaven and in countless languages and dialects around the world. The work of God includes spiritual ministries, which call for the exercise of spiritual gifts. It also embraces social ministries, ministries of kindness and compassion, such as those of missionaries who have organized leper colonies, founded schools, established orphanages, helped the poor and weak, built hospitals and asylums, and reached out to derelicts, drunkards, and drug addicts. All of these ministries are part of the work of the church (Matt. 5:16).

(2) A method (2:22a)

To be a useful vessel, we must "flee also youthful lusts." That is how God's servants can keep free from contamination in a pornographic society. We can either foster our carnal desires or flee them. We are told to "resist the devil" (James 4:7) but to *run* from youthful lusts. Joseph, the classical biblical example, fled from Potiphar's wife when she turned her charms upon him (Gen. 39:7–12). Two who did not flee were David, who played with temptation when he was attracted to Bathsheba (2 Sam. 11:1–5), and Samson, who played with temptation when he was enticed by Delilah (Judg. 16:4–21). Both stories detailed at length in the Bible to warn us against indulging our lusts. We are to put as much distance as possible between ourselves and anything that could fan our lusts into flame. That is God's method. It cannot be improved.

(3) A move (2:22b–c)

(a) In the right path (2:22b)

We are not only to flee but also to "follow righteousness, faith, charity, peace." These are God's great standard bearers. With banners flying, they march ahead of us, and we are to follow them.

"Righteousness" evidences itself *manward.* It has to do with being right and doing right. "Faith" is *godward.* It has to do with trust in God, His Word, His will, and, above all, Him. "Charity" (love) reaches *outward.* It is what caused God to reach out from heaven to a lost and ruined world. Love is also what causes the believer to reach out to people who desperately need the Savior. "Peace" is *inward.* Peace means that the war is over. The peace of God reigns within the believer's heart, enabling him to meet the circumstances of life with equanimity.

(b) With the right people (2:22c)

Believers are to move in the right path "with them that call on the Lord out of a pure heart." We are not alone. Countless millions of people from all parts of the world and from all ranks of society have called on the Lord with a pure heart. They, too, are fleeing the lusts of the flesh. They, too, have overcome the lure of the world and have seen through the lies of the Devil. And as we all march heavenward and homeward, we are guarded by "an innumerable company of angels" and cheered on by members of "the general assembly and church of the firstborn, which are written in heaven" (Heb. 12:22–23).

Paul's soul must have soared in song as he thought of those who were true gold and silver vessels, believers whose hearts were pure. His heart must have been moved as he thought of the brave Christians in Rome who would rather die terrible deaths than deny the faith. Obliquely, he reminded Timothy that he was in good company despite those who had joined the unholy fellowship of Hymenaeus and Philetus.

(4) A mandate (2:23)

Presenting one more condition of service, Paul wrote, "Foolish and unlearned questions avoid, knowing that they do gender strifes." The word translated "foolish" means "dull, stupid." It stems from a root that means "to be silly." The word translated "unlearned" describes a person who is untaught or uninstructed. Timothy was not to avoid inquiries of thoughtful people; he was to avoid answering people who liked to deal in trivia and ask stupid questions. The word translated "avoid" here means "to decline." Timothy was to decline to answer silly questions because they led to strife. To become involved in such quarrels is not part of our ministry either.

c. The character of service (2:24–26)
(1) Dealing with the opposition (2:24–25b)
(a) What must be excluded from Christian service (2:24a)

Paul continued, "The servant of the Lord must not strive." This rule follows naturally with the reference to people who ask foolish questions because cognate words are used in verses 23 and 24; the word translated "strifes" speaks of quarreling and fighting, and the word translated "strive" means "to fight."

The words that follow perfectly describe Christ, God's unique Servant, whose coming was prophesied of old. Hundreds of years before the Lord Jesus came to earth, the prophet Isaiah described Him as God's Servant (see Isa. 42:1–3; Matt. 12:17–21). God declared, "Behold my servant . . . He shall not strive." The quotation in Matthew (with Holy Spirit-inspired additions) comes after the account of the healing of the man with a withered hand. When the Pharisees saw the Lord perform this miracle on the Sabbath, they immediately went out and held a meeting to plot His destruction. The Lord Jesus quietly withdrew. Large crowds followed Him, and He healed all of the sick people among them. Far from capitalizing on His popularity and success, He charged the people not to advertise His presence or what He had done. The Lord Jesus, God's perfect Servant, avoided quarrels. He had not come to strive with people but to love them and save them.

(b) What must be exuded in Christian service (2:24b–25b)
i. The right attitude (2:24b–d)
a. The Lord's servant must not be harsh (2:24b)

Instead of striving, the servant of the Lord must "be gentle unto all men." The word translated "gentle" means "mild, affable." It was used to describe a nurse dealing with difficult children or a teacher dealing with rebellious students.

Isaiah 42:3 says of God's perfect Servant that "a bruised reed shall he not break, and the smoking flax shall he not quench." A bruised reed represents something that never was any good; a smoking flax represents something that is no longer any good. The Lord Jesus fulfilled Isaiah's prophecy because He dealt gently with everyone. Think of how kind He was to the woman at the well, to Martha and Mary, to His disciples, and to Pilate. The servant of the Lord must cultivate this kind of gentleness; he must not be harsh.

b. The Lord's servant must not be hesitant (2:24c)

Instead of being hesitant, the servant of the Lord should be "apt to teach *[didaktikos]*." He should "be ready always to give an answer to every man that asketh" (1 Peter 3:15), just as Ezra was "a ready scribe in the law of Moses."

Didaktikos means "skilled in teaching." The Lord Jesus was the greatest Teacher of all. Matthew, commenting on the teaching in the Lord's Sermon on the Mount, wrote, "The people were astonished at his doctrine: For he taught them as one having authority, and not as the scribes" (Matt. 7:28–29). The Lord's servant, taught by the Spirit of God, should be just as apt to teach.

c. The Lord's servant must not be hasty (2:24d)

Instead of acting hastily, the servant of the Lord must be "patient." The Lord Jesus was never in a hurry. This unhurried attitude of His was clearly illustrated in an incident at the time of the annual Jewish Feast of tabernacles (John 7:2–10). The Lord's unbelieving brothers offered Him some advice—"Go on to Judea. Show yourself there. Show yourself to the world." He replied pointedly, "My time is not yet come." Then He added, "Go ye up." The word translated "go up" is a technical term. It indicated that they should go up with the others in a caravan. After His interfering brothers were well on their way, the Lord went up quietly by Himself.

Another example of the Lord's patience is found in John 11:6. When He learned that Lazarus was sick, He "abode two days still in the same place where he was." Jesus had in mind a much greater miracle than the mere healing of Lazarus, so He did not proceed hastily but tarried where He was until after Lazarus was dead.

Besides being patient, the Lord had a flawless sense of timing. When His mother urged Him to do something about a problem that had arisen at the wedding in Cana, He said, "Mine hour is not yet come" (John 2:4). John mentioned that mysterious "hour" on other occasions (John 7:30; 8:20). Then John recorded that, as the Lord's last Passover drew near, "Jesus knew that his hour was come" (John 13:1). Christ lived on the principle of waiting on God.

The Lord's servant needs this same awareness that God's timing is perfect. The believer cannot afford to be impatient. He should say with David, "My times are in thy hand" (Ps. 31:15). Because David waited on God, he was able to refrain from taking matters into his own hands (1 Sam. 26).

ii. The right attempt (2:25a–b)

The servant of the Lord should attempt to deal with the opposition by speaking "in meekness, instructing those that oppose themselves." As we read the continuing dialogue that the Lord had with His enemies as recorded throughout the gospel of John, we cannot help being impressed with the Lord's meekness. He heeded His own dictum well: "Blessed are the meek: for they shall inherit the earth" (Matt. 5:5; also see 11:29). He never argued, never raised His voice in anger, never lost His temper.

At the same time, He never let His enemies get away with their terrible attitudes and scandalous accusations. They were often malicious, and He rebuked their insolence, but He did so calmly and rationally. He never ridiculed them or reviled them. He answered their loaded questions honestly and fearlessly. He taught them unpalatable truth boldly, but He was always quiet, self-controlled, and polite. The Lord's servant should seek to do the same.

(2) Dealing with the opportunity (2:25c–26)

(a) The need of the unbeliever to be repentant (2:25c)

Paul concluded this passage by emphasizing the work of the Lord's servant in dealing patiently with souls in the hope that "God peradventure will give them repentance to the acknowledging of the truth." Paul probably still had in mind Hymenaeus, Philetus, and those who were siding with them. They were in serious spiritual peril.

Repentance has to do with a change of mind. Regeneration has to do with a change of heart. Reconciliation has to do with a change of will. Repentance toward God and faith in the Lord Jesus Christ are two sides of the same transaction (Acts 20:21).

In the New Testament, two main words are used for repentance. One means "to regret." It has to do with the annoyance we feel when we are found out in a sinful act. We are more concerned with the unpleasant consequences that result from our exposure than we are with the need for deep remorse. It is used in connection with Judas (Matt. 27:3).

The other word means to change one's mind for the better. It results in our forsaking our sin. It denotes genuine repentance toward God. As it is used here, the word points to the work of the Holy Spirit in bringing about repentance. After all, the first great work of the Holy Spirit in a human heart is to convict of sin, righteousness, and judgment to come (John 16:8–11). Thus, the Holy Spirit quickens, awakens the conscience, and creates the condition that makes repentance possible and effective. When the Holy Spirit is at work bringing a person to repentance, an "acknowledging of the truth" will follow naturally. The word translated "acknowledging" signifies precise, experiential knowledge. The repentant person will obtain that kind of knowledge of the truth.

(b) The need of the unbeliever to be rescued (2:26)

Repentance is necessary "that they may recover themselves out of the snares of the devil, who are taken captive by him at his will." Bible scholars agree that this verse is difficult because the antecedents of *him* and *his* at the end are unclear. There is no difficulty, however, with the rest of the verse. Sinners are the Devil's captives, and they have been snared by him. They need to be recovered, and this recovery hinges, to some extent, upon themselves. Repentance has its roots in man's free will and moral accountability. The preceding verse gives the balancing truth: God gives repentance. That is the divine side of the transaction.

The word translated "they may recover themselves" can be rendered "they may come to their senses [and so be rescued]." That is exactly what happened to the Prodigal Son. "When he came to himself, he said, . . . I will arise and go to my father, and will say unto him, Father, I have sinned against heaven and before thee. And am no more worthy to be called thy son" (Luke 15:17–19). He came to himself; then he came to the father. The son was his own voluntary agent. The father ran to meet him, but he did not run after him.

The literal meaning of the word is "they may become sober again." The implication is that a sinner acts like a drunkard, a man bereft of his senses. The cause of his behavior, according to the Bible, is spiritual, not psychological; therefore, the cure also must be spiritual rather than psychological. Psychology deals with symptoms; the Bible deals with causes. No system of therapy, however sophisticated it might be, ultimately can be successful if it ignores "the law of sin and death" (Rom. 8:2). One reason modern man is unable to alleviate the ever growing problems of violence and crime is that he has been persuaded that these problems have a psycho-sociological cause and cure. The cause goes far deeper, and the cure is far better when the sin question is dealt with and the sinner is brought by God's grace into a knowledge of salvation through Christ.

Those who have not recovered themselves are in the "snare of the devil." The word translated "snare" means "a trap" and refers to the allurements that the

Devil uses to catch people. Hymenaeus and Philetus were prime examples of people who had been snared by the Devil into propagating false doctrine and thus disrupting the church, and overthrowing the faith of some. Hymenaeus and a man named Alexander (probably the coppersmith of 2 Tim. 4:14) had not only been snared by the Devil but had also been formally handed over to him so that they would learn not to blaspheme (1 Tim. 1:20). So far, the excommunication of these men apparently had only put a sharper edge on their rebellion.

Now we must consider the difficult part of 2 Timothy 2:26: "Who are taken captive by him at his will." One view is that the pronouns *him* and *his* do not refer to the same person—the *him* refers to the servant, and the *his* refers to God. According to this interpretation, the Devil stirs up those whom he has ensnared and those who are in authority in the local church lest God should give them repentance and lest, having been taken captive by God's servant, they should escape the snare and do the will of God.

Another view is that the *him* and the *his* refer to the same person, namely, the Devil. According to this interpretation, those who have been captured and enslaved by the Devil are led captive at his (Satan's) will. One commentator wrote, "Paul was at the moment emphasizing the fact of these captives being deprived of their own will, and made subservient to the will of another [Satan]." This expositor comes to the conclusion that God may give such captives repentance so that they will recover the knowledge of truth so that they can then recover themselves out of the snare of the Devil—after having been led captive by him and made subservient to his will.[6]

Whichever view is correct, the fact remains that the captives need to be rescued.

6. This view militates against "the wholly unjustifiable intrusion into the text [in the revised version] of the words 'the Lord's servant' and of 'God,' producing altogether a sentence of unparalleled awkwardness, grotesqueness, and utter improbability." See H. D. M. Spence and Joseph Exell, eds., "2 Timothy," *The Pulpit Commentary* (Grand Rapids: Eerdmans, n.d.), 24.

PART 3

Predicted Testings

2 Timothy 3:1–4:18

The fearful persecution that was raging as Paul wrote his epistle turned his thoughts inevitably to end-times events. He foresaw that the defection in the ranks of church members in his day would be nothing compared with the wholesale apostasy that would characterize the church in the last days.

A. Approaching the day of the great apostasy (3:1–4:5)
   1. Some deadly roots exposed (3:1–3a)
      a. The last days indicated (3:1)

"This know also," Paul told Timothy, "that in the last days perilous times shall come." To many of their contemporaries, it must have seemed that the last days had already come, that there could be no more perilous times than those that gripped the world as Nero raved and stormed. Paul, however, knew his Bible better than that.

True, the Lord had said, "In the world ye shall have tribulation" (John 16:33), but He had also spoken of a great tribulation (Matt. 24:15–22), and the present outbreak of persecution bore no resemblance to that. Moreover, the Great Tribulation was to be "the time of Jacob's trouble" (Jer. 30:7), and Nero was persecuting Christians, not Jews.

Paul also knew that the church is to be raptured before the Antichrist comes (1 Thess. 4:15–5:11; 2 Thess. 2:3–12). When the Antichrist comes, he will sign a seven-year treaty with the Jews, break it after three and a half years, seize the rebuilt Jewish temple, put his image in that temple, and then launch a massive economic and political campaign of terror against the Jews (Dan. 9:24–27; 11:31; 12:11). At the same time, Gentiles, saved as a result of the preaching of the 144,000 witnesses, will be massacred by the millions (Rev. 7).

Persecution is one thing; the Great Tribulation will be something else. The times when Paul was writing indeed were perilous, but they were not the end times.

      b. The last days illustrated (3:2–3a)
         (1) Dismal facts about the last days (3:2a–b)
            (a) Love of self (3:2a)

In the last days, "men shall be lovers of their own selves." Love of self will be unbridled.

Children are born with self-love firmly enthroned in their hearts. One of their earliest words is *my*—"My ball!" "My spoon!" "My doll!" A healthy society puts a curb on self-love and self-will. Parents teach children to obey, share, take turns, and think of others. Schools should reinforce parental authority and discipline, and government ought further to restrain rebellion by means of the law.

However, much of the discipline practiced in former times has been abandoned in our day. Psychologists and social workers, backed by massive powers of intervention and intrusion, intimidate parents who apply old-fashioned ways and means. In many regions, it is a crime to apply corporal punishment. In some circles, it is considered wrong to restrain temper tantrums—restraint might cause children to develop inhibitions! So a child is allowed to grow up with his every wish gratified, believing that his will should be law and that the world owes him a living. A generation raised without being taught self-discipline demands indulgence of all of its lusts and scoffs at everything once held sacred.

(b) Lust for wealth (3:2b)

In the last days, men will also be "covetous." Benjamin Franklin's dictum "It is better to go to bed supperless than to run into debt for breakfast" sounds silly to most people today. Some people carry credit cards and use them as if they were an endless supply of cash. Americans owe billions of dollars to creditors, and the country's national debt and trade imbalance are astronomical.

One survey revealed that college students are fatalistic about the future of this country but are determined that if they are going to sink, they are going to sink in style. The phenomenon was likened to being aboard the sinking *Titanic* and fighting for a first-class cabin. The old idea of working, saving, and paying cash is rarely considered a sensible option. Many young people coming out of college expect to start off with a large house, a fancy car, a high salary, a seaside cottage, and a boat. They are quite willing to go head over heels into debt to acquire these symbols of wealth.

(2) Dreadful follies in the last days (3:2c–e)

(a) Inflated egos selfward (3:2c)

Paul foresaw that in the last days people would have enormously inflated egos. They would be "boasters," he said. The word translated "boasters" means "a wanderer about the country." It can be rendered "a vagabond" or "one who swaggers."

The Beatles, high on the list of society's heroes, were a group of wandering minstrels who paved the way for our present godless culture. They once boasted that they were more popular than Jesus Christ. The Beatles were mild in contrast to their musical heirs, who glorify sex and sodomy; promote lust and rebellion; praise drunkenness, profanity, immorality, and the use of drugs; and sing of hatred, murder, and violence.

The inflated egos that Paul foresaw as an important ingredient in the end-times recipe for ruin are already in evidence today.

(b) Inflated egos manward (3:2d)

Men will be "proud," Paul said. The word translated "proud" here describes those who imagine themselves to be above other people. In the Bible, the word is always used derogatorily to mean "haughty, arrogant, disdainful."

People in high places often display a lofty contempt for divine things and for other people. Hitler is an example. Once he acquired absolute power, no one in Germany dared to contradict him. The allied armies were closing in, Germany was being reduced systematically to rubble, and total defeat stared him in the face, but Hitler continued to rant and rave in his bunker, bullying his generals and scorning everyone else. Woe betide anyone who said or did anything that Hitler considered to be an affront to his genius. His ego was grossly inflamed.

Men like Hitler and Stalin, intoxicated with grandiose ideas of their own importance, will wax worse and worse as time goes on. What else can we expect? Regardless of whether our children make the grade, we pass them through our school systems, graduate them, and turn them loose on society full of a sense of their own importance. (We dare not give the young things a failing grade; they might develop some kind of complex!) When they try to enter the workforce, they expect to start at the top.

What happens to those who cannot make the grade when, finally, they encounter the real world? They are shocked when they discover that their inability to spell, speak proper English, do simple mental arithmetic, submit to discipline, take orders, and be diligent is not tolerated. The rejection hurts their pride, so some of them turn to drugs and drink and seek acceptance in the murky underworld of crime. Others seek acceptance in a sphere where alternate lifestyles are accepted and where their vaunted pride can be fanned into a swaggering contempt of others.

(c) Inflated egos godward (3:2e)

In the last days, men will also be "blasphemers." The Greek word refers to all kinds of slanderous, reviling, and abusive speech, especially evil speaking against God and sacred things.

Today the Judeo-Christian ethic is increasingly under attack in the Western world. People do not hesitate to say or write the most terrible things against Christ. Much of the fare on television is tainted by profanity. The lovely names of the Lord Jesus Christ are used frequently as swear words in best-selling books and popular movies. The name of God is linked with the vilest words that can be dredged up from the sewer of an unregenerate mind. There was a time when even the mildest swear words were not acceptable in books, television shows, or movies. Now writers seem to delight in plastering page after page of their books and scripts with offensive words.

All of this wickedness is preparatory. It is paving the way for the coming of the Antichrist, about whom we read, "There was given unto him a mouth speaking great things and blasphemies; and power was given unto him to continue forty and two months. And he opened his mouth in blasphemy against God, to blaspheme his name, and his tabernacle, and them that dwell in heaven" (Rev. 13:5–6).

(3) Disrupted families in the last days (3:2f)

In the last days, children will be "disobedient to parents." Paul foresaw a total breakdown of parental authority as an end-of-the-age phenomenon. It looks as though we are approaching the last days because defiance of parental authority has become epidemic. Such defiance is fostered by the humanistic and libertarian doctrines espoused by many people in high places. In many instances, the breakdown of parental authority is aggravated by the sinful and indulgent lifestyle of the parents. Many of them have long since ceased to be an example to their children.

It is no wonder that children are disobedient to parents. By the time he is eighteen, the average child will have spent twenty-two thousand hours watching television—many more hours than he has spent in school. Through television, he has been exposed to a steady, systematic diet of fantasy, violence, sex, drunkenness, and pornography. Increasingly, comedies ridicule parental authority and routinely depict the father of the family as some kind of clown. Schools, too, have encouraged defiance by challenging the home's age-old standards on sex, morality, and discipline.

Time magazine, in analyzing the youthful crime wave that has inundated our country, described the widespread mayhem and declared, "A new, remorseless, mutant juvenile seems to have been born, and there is no more terrifying figure in America today."[1] The courts bear much of the blame. Some judges act as if there were no such thing as a bad child. Parental rights have been so eroded by the courts that children can now sue their own parents. Schools routinely hand out contraceptives to youngsters and arrange abortions for them without their parents' knowledge. Many states uphold a teenager's right to run away from home. Some lawmakers advocate that children be given the rights to live where they please and do what they please and that they be provided with legal aid to protect those rights if their parents protest. We seem to have arrived at those "perilous times" of which Paul wrote. In some states, parents suspected of using corporal punishment suddenly find their homes invaded by police and social workers and their children snatched from them and put into foster homes.

(4) Distinctive features of the last days (3:2g–h)

(a) Ungrateful (3:2g)

In the last days, people will also be "unthankful *[acharistos]*." The Greek word, which means "thankless," occurs in the New Testament only here and in Luke 6:35, where the Lord says that God is "kind unto the unthankful and to the evil."

The fact that *unthankful* is placed next to *disobedient to parents* in 2 Timothy 3:2 suggests that ingratitude takes root in the home. At one time, children were taught to say "please" and "thank you" as a matter of course, but today's youngsters are rarely heard expressing thanks voluntarily.

Paul listed ingratitude as one of the damning sins in his great treatise on sin in Romans (1:21). His own attitude of thankfulness stands in vivid contrast (1:8). Ingratitude to God for His revelation of Himself is what leads to idolatry, lust, and lawlessness. In the end, those terrible sins cause God to give people up to pornography, perversion, and consequent judgment (1:21–28).

1. "The Youth Crime Plague," *Time*, 11 July 1977, 18.

(b) Unholy (3:2h)

Another distinctive feature of the last days is that people will be "unholy." *Anosios,* the Greek word translated "unholy" here, means "profane."

After World War II, we witnessed the erosion of traditional moral and religious values and the profanation of almost everything. The collapse was sudden, violent, unexpected, and widespread. This dramatic loss of values coincided with a massive, sustained, and well-financed attack of everything moral, decent, and Christian in the Western world. Much of the attack was inspired by the Soviet Communists who, to carry out their plans for global conquest, sought to bring about the rot of Western society. And the attack was aided and abetted by a subculture dedicated to rock music, a drug-sex-occult lifestyle, militant pacifism, and the overthrow of the establishment. This subculture was able to mobilize enormous numbers of people, especially college students and young people, who were willing to march and chant, participate in mass demonstrations, attend giant rallies, and engage in general lawlessness. The authorities seemed unable or unwilling to deal with the movement and largely capitulated to it. Now the unkempt, foulmouthed, bearded, longhaired hippies have put on business suits and invaded the halls of government. They are just as determined to pursue their agenda (gay rights, abortion on demand, and freedom to promote pornography and moral decadence) by means of Congress and the courts.

Widespread profanation is seen in art galleries and museums, where "artists" display works that are really nothing more than temper tantrums on canvas. Shapeless blobs of stone are exhibited as "sculpture," as are tangled and twisted steel contortions that look like they were salvaged from a bomb explosion in an ironmonger's yard.

The National Endowment for the Arts gives taxpayers' money to artists who paint pornographic abominations depicting Christ as a pervert. The movie industry has adopted violence, vice, explicit sex, masochism, perversion, and child pornography as favorite modes of expression and has produced such blasphemous movies as *The Last Temptation of Christ,* which depicts God's beloved Son as a womanizer and Judas Iscariot as a hero. Society is becoming increasingly unholy as we approach the last days.

(5) Dead feelings in the last days (3:3a)

Exposing another deadly root of the great apostasy, Paul said that in the last days men will be "without natural affection." The phrase is a translation of *astorgos,* which is the negative form of the usual Greek word for affection. Love between parents and their children is natural, but the last days will see the total disintegration of family life. Paul envisioned a generation that will not know the joys of mutual sharing of normal family life.

In our society, no-fault divorce laws foster a high divorce rate. Until the cultural revolution of the 1960s, most families stayed together in spite of stresses and strains, but now marriages are fragile and easily dissolved. Many couples dispense with marriage altogether and cohabit with no regard for the laws of God or the norms of a healthy society.

Children suffer the most from divorce. They are often shunted back and forth between the parents, dumped on grandparents, or largely left alone. The children are sometimes left to their own devices when the mother is forced to go to work to support them or the father has to take another job to meet his alimony payments. Sometimes, youngsters find themselves in the center of a power struggle between their parents. When parents remarry or take up with live-in partners, the offspring of the first marriage may easily find themselves unwanted, exploited, or abused.

Another example of the disintegration of family life is found in Brazil, where many people live in abject poverty in shantytowns attached to great cities. Young children in these shantytowns are frequently abandoned by their parents and turned lose to roam the city streets and fend for themselves. Such children are often terribly abused in the cities. They either succumb to an early death or become members of gangs that prey on the society that has abused them.

Many inner cities in our own country are haunted by hoodlum gangs. Sometimes, bands of juvenile delinquents beat up old men and women and rob, maim, and kill. Some gangs will not accept a new member until the applicant has proven himself by murdering someone. Such youth are "without natural affection." They resemble the generation that Paul foresaw.

2. Some deadly fruits exposed (3:3b–4:5)
   a. The morality of the last days (3:3b–4a)
      (1) The deceitfulness of people (3:3b–c)

In the last days, men will be "trucebreakers *[aspondos]*." The Greek word is composed of a negative prefix and a word that means "libation." A libation, or sacrifice to the gods, often accompanied the making of a formal truce. The negative form of the word referred to people who refused to make a truce or be placated. The word is rendered "implacable" in Romans 1:31. Implacable people are relentless; they will not give in. *Aspondos* may also refer to people who are untrue to their promises.

Hitler was such a man, absolutely relentless in his hatreds. Even as Germany was going up in flames and Soviet tanks were entering the outskirts of Berlin, he continued reviling his enemies, railing against the Jews, ranting against his generals and the German people, and sending young boys to the front to fight the Russians.

Throughout his career as Führer, Hitler was surrounded by implacable men who backed his determination to exterminate the Jews of Europe and to conquer the world. Goebbels and Streicher preached the inferiority of the Jewish race day and night to the German people. Himmler remorselessly kept the boxcars moving to the concentration camps.

Hans Frank, governor-general of occupied Poland, wrote in his diary of the treatment of Jews at Treblinka, Auschwitz, and other extermination camps. (The diary was used against him at the Nuremberg trial.) While victims were being processed, they were forced to strip off their clothes and shoes. Then they were herded into the death chambers, women and children first. Small children were simply flung inside. Frank revealed his mind-set when he wrote, "That we sentenced 1,200,000 Jews to die of hunger should be noted only marginally. It is a matter of course. . . . The Jews for us also represent extraordinarily malignant questions."[2]

The Antichrist will be like that—relentless, remorseless, and implacable—a truce-breaker.

Further describing the deceitfulness of people in the last days, Paul wrote that they would be "false accusers *[diabolos].*" *Diabolos,* the Greek name for the Devil, means "slanderer, adversary, or scurrilous."

The Antichrist will imbibe the deceitful spirit and philosophy of Machiavelli. When Machiavelli's book *The Prince* was published, Pope Clement VII applauded it as though it were inspired, which doubtless it was—by the rulers of this world's darkness (see Eph. 6:12). Thomas Cromwell, Henry VIII's unscrupulous servant, made *The Prince* his Bible. Catherine de Medicis, who was responsible for the St. Bartholomew's Day Massacre, drew her inspiration from the same book. Phillip II read it, and it inspired him to intrigue the murder of England's Queen Elizabeth. The duplicities of Louis XVI were also inspired by the book. It was Napoleon's constant companion and his chief political advisor.

2. G. M. Gilbert, *Nuremberg Diary* (New York: Farrar, Straus, 1947), 67–68.

Adolf Hitler, another deceiver, admired Machiavelli. He also admired Nietzsche, who called for the superman, the antichrist. In *Mein Kampf,* Hitler wrote that the greater a lie is, the greater its chance of being believed. The communists likewise became masters of deceit. Slander was, and is, one of their favorite weapons.

Years ago, the *Intelligence Digest* warned of the existence of a crime organization that is bigger than many governments. The *Digest* claimed that the organization's tentacles are in every major city, that it is the secret power behind the world's drug and vice traffic, and that some of its leaders are highly placed, outwardly attractive, and polished members of society. The organization used slander and innuendo to destroy those who discover its secrets.[3]

When the Antichrist comes, he will "cause craft to prosper" (Dan. 8:25). His coming will be "with all deceivableness" (2 Thess. 2:10)—that is, with every form of deceit. He will speak, as one native born, the language of Satan, the father of lies. Using the idiom of that language (the lie), the Antichrist will deceive, slander, and accuse falsely and will make "craft to prosper" (Dan. 8:25).

(2) The disposition of people (3:3d–e)

(a) Incontinent (3:3d)

In the last days, people will be incontinent and intolerant. The word translated "incontinent" here means literally "without power" and, by extension, "having no power over one's self." Its Latin counterpart is *impotens,* from which our English word *impotent* is derived. Thus, the word *incontinent* conveys the idea of being without command over one's passions.

We see many illustrations in modern society of every form of vice being given free rein. People who used to slink down back alleys, hide their shame, and indulge their dragon lusts in secret now flaunt their shame openly. Shouting slogans and waving banners, they march down Main Street, cheered by onlookers and supported by governments.

Paul clearly foresaw a day when people would no longer make any pretense at restraining their passions. The Antichrist will make his appeal to these unregenerate people in his guise as the "man of sin" (2 Thess. 2:3). He will be lenient on sin, encourage it, and indeed incarnate it. He will tell people to do what comes naturally, to indulge their desires, to express themselves, and to throw away their inhibitions and the repressive dictums and dogmas of the Judeo-Christian ethic. The Antichrist will "liberate" people from their consciences and moral restraints.

---

3. *Intelligence Digest,* May, June, July, 1963.

Already our society is paving the way for the coming of the Antichrist. Abortion and sodomy have champions in high places. Euthanasia is battling for legality. People who love pornography, who encourage prostitution and free love, and who are in favor of legalizing unrestrained use of drugs can find powerful and eloquent voices to speak for them. Only the presence of the Holy Spirit and the living church, acting as a divinely imposed check, hold back the full flood tide of wickedness (2 Thess. 2:6–7).

(b) Intolerant (3:3e)

The word translated "fierce" occurs only here in the New Testament and means "untamed, savage, wild." It brings to mind a vast, ruthless crime cartel that deals in drugs and vice, knows no pity, tolerates no rivals, respects no laws, and fears no government. The term also brings to mind Daniel's vision of Gentile rule (Dan. 7:11–8:12).

We think, too, of the terrorist network that from time to time unleashes mayhem on us. Unrestrained by conscience, terrorists bomb cars and buildings, blow up passenger planes, and hold innocent victims hostage. In Japan, terrorists have used nerve gas to attack commuters at train stations during the rush hour. For years, the Soviets sponsored, financed, and benefited from the operations of such international bandits. The Soviet regime methodically trained them, supplied them with sophisticated weapons, sheltered them, and encouraged them. Since the breakup of the Soviet Union, there has been a growth of fear that terrorists might be able to acquire Russian nuclear weapons. Countries such as Iran, Syria, Libya, and the Sudan still encourage terrorism.

Time magazine once estimated that at least 140 terrorists groups are active in the world.[4] These groups include factions of the Palestine Liberation Organization, Hamas, and other anti-Semitic, anti-Israel parties, and also the Irish Republican Army. The September 11, 2001, attacks on the United States by Islamic fundamentalists has opened a new chapter on terror. The United States has declared war on terrorism, but the Al-Qaeda operatives have been extremely elusive. In the Middle East, new heights of horror have become almost a daily occurrence with the advent of the suicide bomber. Weapons of mass destruction are also available to rogue nations and might well become weapons for terrorists to use.

4. "The Tightening Links of Terrorism," *Time,* 31 October 1977, 45.

Such fierce, wild, untamed, and savage people remind us that the end times are here. They are ready tools for the coming Antichrist.

(3) The disdain of people (3:3f)

In the last days, men will be "despisers of those that are good." Christians were despised in Paul's day, and they are looked upon with disdain by many people today too.

For three hundred years, the early church endured the world's scorn, slander, hatred, and persecution. Christians were despised because they were good. They took their stand on the words of Jesus: "Blessed are ye, when men shall revile you, and persecute you, and shall say all manner of evil against you falsely, for my sake. Rejoice, and be exceedingly glad: for great is your reward in heaven: for so persecuted they the prophets which were before you" (Matt. 5:11–12). As one persecuting caesar after another came and went, and the church was purged of its dross again and again, people began to take note. Pagans in ever increasing numbers were won to Christ when—in spite of the world's propaganda, slanders, and lies—they saw that Christians were good and that the God of the Christians was good, not vile and vengeful like the pagan gods of Rome.

Persecution kept the church pure. For three hundred years, the church was invincible. Although they were despised, rejected, and persecuted, Christians remained true to Christ. The church was in the world, a bitterly hostile world, but Christians were, to put it quite simply, good. They were submissive to even the most tyrannical authority.

Then the world came into the church. What ten persecuting caesars had not been able to accomplish in three centuries, the patronizing Constantine accomplished in one reign. Under his rule, the church traded spiritual power for secular power. It became political, accommodated itself to the world's philosophies, and acquired a taste for worldly pomp and power. The doctrines of the church were debased, and new dogmas were invented. Paganism was baptized as the gods of the pagans were given new names and incorporated into the church's pantheon of saints. Idolatry took root. Taking hold of the world's hand, the church forgot that that hand was stained with Jesus' blood and the blood of countless martyrs.[5] The church became a kingdom and ruled over the nations of earth.

---

5. Satan's stroke of genius was to marry the church to the world. Some people in the so-called religious right today would have us do the same thing: compromise, tone down our distinctive doctrines, and make common cause with Catholics and Mormons to

Today's world is just as disdainful and pagan as was Paul's world. The Lord warned that the last days would be like the days of Noah. Noah lived in a pornographic society in which "every imagination of the thoughts of [man's] heart was only evil continually" (Gen. 6:5). The Lord also warned that the last days would be like the days of Lot, who lived in a perverted society (see Gen. 19). The vile people of Sodom despised Lot. Even as fire and brimstone were being readied to destroy them, they demonstrated before that righteous man's house and demanded their "rights."

There are other kinds of moral rot at work in the world. Hundreds of thousands of couples are living together out of wedlock. A cartoon in *New Yorker* magazine depicts how lax our society has become. Two women of the older generation are depicted sitting on a living room couch. One says to the other, "No, no, it's Frank and Gloria who are married but not living together. George and Judy are living together but not married."

Divorce is so common that nearly half of the babies born today can expect to spend a significant part of their childhood in one-parent families. Our courts continue to ban the Bible from America's public school classrooms. Posting the Ten Commandments (the time-honored basis of morality in our society) on the walls of public buildings is prohibited. Prayer in schools and at public events is under constant attack. Manger scenes cannot be erected on public property. At the same time, however, a federal court ruling upheld an exhibitor's right to show a film depicting brutality, prostitution, delinquency, and sodomy.

Whatever happened to the idea of being good? The idea is simply ludicrous to many people. We have raised a generation of "despisers of those that are good."

(4) The duplicity of people (3:4a)

In the last days, men will be "traitors." The word used here is used almost as a title in connection with Judas Iscariot (Luke 6:16). There have always been traitors. Jesus had His Judas, and David had his Ahithophel. But in our times, treachery has become epidemic. Political systems such as fascism and communism have

---

achieve a common political and social agenda. God's way is best, however. His way is to send revival and to bring people to Christ to make them good. When people are made good, they no longer want abortions. They no longer want to practice sodomy or indulge in pornography or weird sex. If we Christians are going to be despised by an increasingly foul and wicked world, it would be better for us to be despised because we are good than because we try to wield the world's weapons.

learned how to mobilize millions of people to riot and demand change and to sell out their native lands to foreign powers.

During the Spanish Civil War, General Mola announced that he would capture Madrid because he had four columns of troops outside the city and a "fifth column" of sympathizers inside the city. The world pounced on that phrase "fifth column" because it helped express the unprecedented dimensions of treason that were becoming common in society. In World War II, a Norwegian named Quisling sold out his country to Germany. Thereafter, traitors were often called "quislings." Similarly, Hitler was able to ride triumphantly into Austria because thousands of Nazi sympathizers in that country had paved his way.

Fascist-style treachery was eclipsed by the treachery sponsored by the Soviet Communists. After World War II, American traitors handed atomic secrets to Russia. A French spy ring gave the Russians information about advanced Mirage-2000 fighter planes and NATO defense strategies. American industrial techniques were stolen to help the Soviets run their war machine. A secretary in the office of the German chancellor turned out to be an East German spy. A Swiss general admitted giving defense secrets to Moscow agents. Britain expelled at one time more than one hundred Soviet diplomats for spying. A former CIA agent sold an important technical manual to Russia. These are only random samples of the treachery that has become commonplace in our time.

b. The mentality of the last days (3:4b–9)
   (1) There will be scornful maniacs (3:4b–c)

In the last days, men will be "heady, highminded." The word translated "heady" means literally "to fall forward, to fall headlong." It signifies precipitous, rash, and reckless behavior. The word was used by the town clerk in Ephesus when he urged the rioters to do nothing "rashly" because they had already done enough to warrant an official inquiry (Acts 19:36). The word translated "highminded" in 2 Timothy 3:4 is *tuphoō,* which means literally "to raise a smoke." It can also be rendered "to wrap in a fog." To be "highminded" is to be insolent.

Perhaps nowhere in our modern world are these Greek words illustrated better than in the reckless, headlong rush of millions of people to smoke pot and plunge into the drug culture. Americans now spend more on marijuana than they do on cigarettes. Millions of Americans smoke pot regularly in spite of increasing medical evidence that the drug attacks the body's infection-fighting white blood cells, the lungs, the reproductive system, and the brain. Some varieties now being marketed (such as cannabis or Indian hemp) are seven times stronger than those used when marijuana first became popular.

Not content with pot, the addict rushes on to try a variety of other highly dangerous drugs. PCP, often referred to as "angel dust," causes disorientation and a spaced-out feeling. Cocaine is subtle. It is fast acting and produces intense, vivid, sensational experiences, but it slowly changes the user's personality. Acting on the central nervous system as a powerful stimulant, cocaine causes delusions, but they can be followed by depression and hallucinations. Heroin, probably the most deadly of all drugs, is a morphine derivative. It offers a feeling of joy and release, and the high it produces can last up to ten hours. It is highly addictive, and withdrawal symptoms are severe. Just the same, users frequently turn to crime to support their habit rather than quit. People who surrender themselves, body and soul, to drugs, truly are wrapped in a fog.

(2) There will be secular materialists (3:4d)

In the last days, men will be "lovers of pleasures more than lovers of God." Even today, the things of God are neglected. There was once a time when Sunday was known as the Sabbath or, more correctly, the Lord's day, and it was set aside for worship. Stores closed, public transportation operated on a reduced schedule, and places of amusement and entertainment were closed. But those days are gone. Sunday is now a day for sports and outings.

We have become a nation of pleasure seekers. There has indeed been a pleasure explosion in America. The pleasure business keeps on growing in this country. Increasing sums are spent on recreation, sports equipment, sporting events, vacations, travel abroad, beach cottages, country homes, swimming pools, boats, campers, snowmobiles, radios, televisions, and so on.

According to one estimate, Americans drive more than 350 billion miles a year in pursuit of pleasure. Spectator sports draw enormous crowds. Gambling casinos snare millions. National parks attract millions. Theme parks such as Disney World and Six Flags pull in enormous crowds. They climb aboard "scream machines" and "mind benders" to experience the thrill of riding gravity-defying roller coasters that hurl their riders around one loop after another and plunge them through underground tunnels. One such roller coaster circles more than eighty feet in the air; it races almost straight up for ten stories and then orbits its riders upside down at a force of six Gs.

Video games almost rival television as a popular pastime. Annually, people spend billions of dollars and thousands of man-years on such games outside the home.

Meanwhile, people neglect the things of God. Most Americans stood by silently as the Supreme Court banned the Bible and prayer from their country's classrooms. Many Americans have turned a deaf ear to the cry of millions upon millions of unborn babies being slaughtered in government-approved abortion clinics. Many Americans acquiesced as a president of the United States threw the weight of his influence on the side of gross immorality and shrugged their shoulders at his sexual antics in the White House and elsewhere. People watch movies and TV shows that portray preachers as wimps or fools; fathers as clods or clowns; pornography, perversion, and prostitution as alternate lifestyles; and violence as a way of achieving success.

In America, many people still consider going to church on Sunday as the thing to do. America has many fine churches, including a considerable number of megachurches. However, commitment usually does not go much beyond church attendance. A large segment of the professing church is liberal in its theology, lifeless in its performance, and deadly in its influence. Televangelists still draw followers in spite of scandals, but much of what these evangelists offer the viewing public is shallow, materialistic, and doctrinally unsound. People in general simply ignore the church or refer to it angrily as "the religious right" when it speaks to the issues of the day. They are more likely to accept the liberal agenda because it endorses a humanistic view of life, and the church to a large extent has long since compromised its right to speak with spiritual authority on matters of faith.

People shrug their shoulders, ignore God, and pursue wealth and pleasure. The Puritan founders of America seem to have belonged to some other planet. They came to this country determined to build a nation based on the Bible. They stamped their faith in God onto the coins of the realm and wrote it into the Constitution of the country. Their great educational institutions were based solidly on the Bible. These founders of America's liberties are totally irrelevant in many people's minds. Instead, the heroes of today are the latest baseball heroes, football stars, movie queens, and rock artists.

(3) There will be sanctimonious moralists (3:5)

(a) What is revealed (3:5a)

In the last days, there will be moralists "having a form of godliness, but denying the power thereof." The word translated "form" here means "an outward semblance." The word translated "godliness" here is *eusebeia,* which means "being devout, reverent." The people whom Paul has in mind here have only a façade of religion.

The word translated "power" here is *dunamis,* which refers to the power inherent in the gospel to transform lives, the kind of power that the Lord demonstrated when He rose from the dead (Rom. 1:4, 16). The outwardly religious people whom Paul introduces here have never been transformed by the power of God. They will attend church and go through the motions of religion, but they do not practice what they profess. Their conduct puts the lie to their pretense.

(b) What is required (3:5b)

Paul told Timothy, "From such turn away." We should steer clear of such sanctimonious moralists because their case is hopeless. All of this rings counter to modern thinking, which favors compromise. We are urged to make common cause with anyone who professes to be religious. The emphasis is on ecumenical unity. Paul foresaw that ecumenism would be a characteristic of the end times and warned against it. Christians who know the power of God in their lives should distance themselves from people who don't, no matter what they profess and regardless of the fact that the biblical doctrine of separation is out of vogue.

(4) There will be seducing marauders (3:6)

In the last days, seducing marauders will be on the *prowl* looking for their *prey,* namely, immature women. Paul warned that these men will "creep into houses, and lead captive silly women laden with sins, led away with divers lusts." The word translated "creep" here means "to insinuate oneself." It conjures a picture of people worming their way into the houses of the unsuspecting; they get in by trickery and stealth and under false pretenses. The word translated "silly women" is *gunaikarion,* which means literally "little women." It is a diminutive form used in a sense of contempt. Immature women will be easy targets for cunning teachers.

The word translated "lead captive" here signifies a blind surrender of the will and conscience to such teachers. A kindred word can be translated "to be a prisoner of war." Paul paints a picture of passive helplessness. The word translated "laden" conveys the idea of heaping one thing upon another. The victims of these prowlers will be laden down with a sense of guilt, perhaps because they will be "led away with divers lusts." The word translated "led" here means "to move, impel." The word translated "divers" is *poikilos,* which means "variegated, many-colored." The word translated "lusts" is *epithumia,* which means "strong desires, passions." In other words, the seducers will appeal to the lusts and cravings common to all.

What a picture! Unscrupulous, devious teachers worm their way into the homes of immature women who, driven by their cravings, become easy prey. Preachers and teachers abuse the trust given to them to seduce members of their own congregations! Paul saw this kind of activity becoming epidemic in the church in the last days. It has already become endemic. In many cases, the seducer is not judged and excommunicated. Instead, his wicked behavior is hushed up because of his personality, popularity, or power. Even if the guilty man is forced to resign, he either splits the church and starts a new one down the street or is passed on to another church where he repeats his performance.

(5) There will be sophisticated morons (3:7–9)
(a) Their futile quest for the truth (3:7)

The victims of these ministerial predators will be "ever learning, and never able to come to the knowledge of the truth." To lure women into their clutches, these seducers will exploit their craving for more knowledge. These women do not really want knowledge of the truth because that would lead to conviction of sin and call for repentance. What they want is, at best, more head knowledge of truth and, at worst, titillating bits of information. Paul was describing the kind of women whose thoughts are easily captivated by "religion" (especially of the more exotic sort), whose consciences are burdened with real or imaginary sins, whose capacity is limited by their "littleness," and whose weakness allows them to become easy victims of seducing church leaders.

Church history gives many examples of the victims of men who pretended to be holy. The Russian priest, Rasputin, was a wholesale seducer of women. Joseph Smith founded a religion based on polygamy, although present-day Mormons try to deny it; Brigham Young had scores of wives, and *Time* magazine declared that Mormons still practice polygamy.[6] David Koresh, former leader of the Branch Davidians, was able to persuade the married men in his congregation that he alone had the right to be the husband of their wives. The sad list of ministerial miscreants and their sorry victims could go on and on.

---

6. "The Whispered Faith," *Time,* 11 October 1971.

(b) Their fatal quarrel with the truth (3:8–9)

i. An example (3:8a)

Paul viewed the false teachers as veritable ministers of Satan and compared them with "Jannes and Jambres." Paul probably took these names from the Jews' oral or written traditions, with which he, as a trained rabbi, was doubtless very familiar. Or perhaps, by direct illumination of the Holy Spirit, the apostle named these two Egyptian magicians who took the lead in opposing Moses and deceiving the pharaoh.[7] In any case, they "withstood Moses." The word translated "withstood" means "to set oneself against, resist." The same word is used in the account of Paul and Barnabas's encounter with Elymas the sorcerer, who "withstood them, seeking to turn away the deputy [Sergius Paulus] from the faith" (Acts 13:8). Elymas was promptly and spectacularly judged by the apostle.

When Moses first appeared before the pharaoh, he stated God's demand that Pharaoh release his Hebrew slaves. Moses presented his credentials; he told Aaron to cast his rod on the ground. When he did so, the rod became a serpent. The magicians of Egypt were able to duplicate this miracle by satanic power and by their secret arts. Aaron's serpent immediately swallowed up the Egyptians' serpents. That result only hardened Pharaoh's heart (Exod. 7:9–13).

The next day, Moses confronted Pharaoh again, this time by the banks of the Nile. Moses turned the water to blood, and again the magicians duplicated the miracle with their enchantments. Once again, Pharaoh's heart was hardened (Exod. 7:14–24).

In the next confrontation, Moses smote the land of Egypt with frogs. The magicians did the same. The Lord gave "respite," but Pharaoh hardened his heart once more (Exod. 7:25–8:15).

The next plague fell without warning. The dust of the land became lice, which swarmed everywhere. This time, the magicians were unable to duplicate the miracle and confessed to Pharaoh that they detected "the finger of God" in it. By now, however, the damage had been done; Pharaoh was wedded to a hardened heart (Exod. 8:16–19).

Paul used this historical account as an illustration. The two Egyptian sorcerers symbolized the determination of end-times false teachers to resist God. The souls of their followers will be hardened as was Pharaoh's heart. These false teachers will be the heralds of the final apostasy, which will be led by the Beast. He and his

7. Jannes and Jambres are mentioned in the Targum of Jonathan.

fellow deceiver, the False Prophet, will seduce the world with lying miracles (Rev. 13; 2 Thess. 2:9).

ii. An explanation (3:8b–c)

The false teachers of the end times will be blind to *the facts* and *the faith.* They will "resist the truth: men of corrupt minds, reprobate concerning the faith."

Today, many pulpits in Christendom and many seminary classrooms are occupied by men of this caliber. They pride themselves in being liberal or "moderate," but, in actual fact, they are blind to the truth of God and devote their time to denying the faith. They deny the inerrancy of Scripture, the deity of Christ, and all of the other cardinal doctrines of the church. They set out to destroy whatever faith the people entrusted to their care might have. The victims of these false teachers leave seminary with a Bible torn to shreds by the false theories of the so-called "higher critics." They preach a social gospel devoid of all power to convict of sin. They are wholly unable to lead people to a life-transforming faith in Christ. People come to their churches for bread and they are given a *stone.* When they ask for an egg, they are given a *scorpion.* When they ask for a fish, they are given a *serpent* (Matt. 7:9–10).

In the last days, the minds of the false teachers will be distorted and utterly corrupted. The word translated "corrupt" occurs only here and in 2 Peter 2:12. There, in his description of end-times apostates, Peter says that they "shall utterly perish."

The word for "reprobate" is *adokimos,* which means "not standing the test." The word *adokimos* was used primarily of spurious metals, but here it refers to men whose moral sense is perverted and whose minds are beclouded with their own speculations.[8] They are traitors to the faith. They juggle with biblical truths and terms. Although some of these false teachers have been raised in Christian homes, they have rejected the truth.

One famous modern occultist called himself the Great Beast, or Beast 666, and described himself as "the wickedest man on earth." He was an Englishman but believed himself to be the incarnation of Alexander VI, the infamous Borgia pope. During World War I, this man spent time in the United States, where he produced anti-British propaganda. He was a grossly immoral man. He was also

8. W. E. Vine, *An Expository Dictionary of New Testament Words,* 4 vols. (London: Oliphants, 1963), 3:283.

deeply involved in the activities of a German occult society. He had a wide following and remarkable powers. A cult leader and a thoroughly evil man, this man was a forerunner of the Antichrist. At his funeral in 1947, an orgiastic poem of his was recited, one in which he described himself as a god.

This false teacher came from a Christian home! He was reared among a group of believers who were committed to the inspiration of Scripture, the deity of Christ, the great redemptive truths of the Bible, and salvation by faith. This evil man was taught the truth, but he rejected it. His mind was corrupt, and he was "reprobate concerning the faith."

iii. An exposure (3:9)

In the last days, false teachers will be *stopped in their path* and *stripped of their power.* Paul wrote, "They shall proceed no further; for their folly shall be manifest unto all men, as theirs also was." In other words, they will be exposed as frauds, just as were Jannes and Jambres. Those Egyptian magicians were allowed to succeed up to a certain point, but then they were stopped dead in their tracks.

The tides of apostasy are rising today. Perilous times are upon us, and they will get worse. Soon, the river will be in full flood and will overflow its banks as the various tributaries of delusion and deception join the parent stream. The flow of events is now carrying all before it to the coming of the Man of Sin.

c. The malice of the last days (3:10–13)
(1) Paul's world (3:10–11)

The anti-Christian forces that will eventually usher in the last days were already arrayed against the church in apostolic times.

Satan threw everything he had at the early church. He tried warping and twisting Christian doctrine only to be countered by a string of apostolic epistles that gave the lie to his deceptions. He has no new deceptions. Modern cults are simply old heresies in new guises.

Satan tried moral seduction of believers, but, apart from the defection of Judas (foretold in Ps. 41:9), he got nowhere. As for everyday excesses of lust for money and power and ordinary immorality, the early church simply exhorted offenders and excommunicated those who would not repent.

Satan tried persecution, threats, and terror, but the church triumphant laughed in his face. As clever, as powerful, and as persistent as he was, the Devil was no match for the Holy Spirit.

He keeps on trying; he has no other option, but the Holy Spirit counters his every move. We do not always see how or when the Holy Spirit acts, but He does. When we get to heaven, however, and learn the other side of the story, we will wonder with great admiration (as John did in Rev. 17:6). When the last days are fully come, the church will be removed, and the Holy Spirit will cease to restrain evil. Satan will seize his opportunity and will think that he has won. He will soon find out, however, that he has lost forever.

In Paul's day, Satan's opposition to the church was violent. Indeed, violence had been practiced against the church from the beginning (Acts 5:33–42). Paul himself (in his unconverted days) had once been a strong advocate of violence (Acts 8:1–3). The persecution of Christians had now become the official policy of the empire.

(a) His teaching (3:10a)

Paul now resumed attempts to stiffen his younger colleague's resolve. He reminded Timothy of his teaching: "Thou hast fully known my doctrine." The word translated "hast fully know" means "to follow fully." It conveys the idea of discipleship, of conforming fully to someone else's example. Paul had every right to appeal to Timothy's loyalty because he had poured himself into Timothy's life from the earliest days.

The pronoun *thou* is emphatic. Barnabas had come and gone. Demas had come and gone. Timothy remained. He had been special, right from the beginning. Paul loved him as a son and had taught him and trained him. Soon Paul would be gone too. It would be up to Timothy then to hold the gospel banner high.

Ephesus was a good place to do it. The church there was one of Paul's best. He had written one of his greatest epistles to the Christians in Ephesus. Their God-appointed elders had been mightily challenged by Paul (Acts 20), and the apostle John would join the fellowship of the Ephesian church. Satan, fully aware of the potential of that strategically located church, was attacking it. Timothy must not—dare not—waver. As the depository of all of Paul's teaching, Timothy needed to uphold that teaching in defiance of the impostors who were trying to teach other doctrines. Paul's anxiety was but thinly veiled.

(b) His testimony (3:10b–g)

Timothy knew Paul's "manner of life, purpose, faith, longsuffering, charity, patience" as well as his teaching. The young man was aware that Paul practiced what he preached.

i. The pattern of Paul's life (3:10b)

Timothy knew the pattern or "manner" of Paul's life firsthand. The word translated "manner of life" occurs only here in the New Testament. A good rendering would be "my lifestyle." Strictly speaking, the word denotes a teaching. Paul modeled his teaching. What he preached was incarnate in what he practiced.

ii. The purpose of Paul's life (3:10c)

Timothy knew Paul's purpose. The word translated "purpose" is *prothesis.* Paul had already used this word in 1:9 to describe God's eternal purpose in saving us and calling us, a purpose rooted in the mind of God before the world began. Paul's purpose marched in step with God's purpose. From the moment he met Christ on the Damascus road, he had a single-minded determination to do the will of God. We can trace Paul's steps to Damascus, to the wilderness, back to Damascus, to Cilicia, back and forth to Jerusalem, to Antioch, to Galatia, to Europe, and to Rome. We see no wavering of his will, no mental reservations, and no conflicting desires. Paul's unflagging resolve was to allow God to accomplish His good, acceptable, and perfect will in his life (Rom. 12:2).

Timothy needed to have a purpose too. He had to make up his mind, as Daniel did, not to waver from his obvious duty (Dan. 1:8).

iii. The priorities of Paul's life (3:10d–f)

Paul's priorities were threefold, and Timothy was well aware of them. The first, "faith," was *godward.* Paul's trust in the living Lord, whom he had met so dramatically on the Damascus road, was total. After his conversion, he had scoured his Old Testament from end to end. His faith had been confirmed. The Christ, foretold in direct prophecy and portrayed in type and shadow in the Old Testament, was the Christ of Calvary.

He was Christ of recent history. He had been conceived of the Holy Spirit and born of the Virgin Mary in Bethlehem. He had been reared in Nazareth. He had made Himself known throughout the Promised Land from Dan to Beersheba. He had been crucified and raised and was now enthroned on high. He was the Christ of God. He was the Son of God. He was the Son of Man. He was Prophet, Priest, and King. Altogether lovely, He was the chief among ten thousand. He was the seed of the woman, the seed of Abraham, and the seed of David. He was Eternal, uncreated and self-existing, the second person of the Godhead, the Alpha and Omega. The Jehovah of the Old Testament was the Jesus of the New Testament! Paul's faith in Him never faltered for a moment.

Paul's personal priority godward was to enthrone this Jesus in his heart as Lord and to place his unquestioning trust in Him. The apostle's faith must have left its mark on Timothy.

Paul's second priority, "longsuffering," was *selfward.* The word translated "longsuffering" is *makrothumia,* which means "forbearance, endurance." It is composed of *makros* ("long") and *thumos* ("temper"). Paul was not short-tempered because he exercised long-suffering and learned patience.

Paul could put up with things. He was not hasty, as his dealings with the church in Corinth illustrate. The opposition party in that church was radical, organized, and fierce. The attacks of his enemies in Corinth were scornful, abusive, and personal, and some of their doctrines were subversive and heretical. Paul's long-suffering was astounding. He wrote again and again to the Corinthians. He visited them, sent Timothy and Titus to them, prayed for them, and pleaded with them. Paul had at his disposal the miracle-working power of an apostle. He could strike a man with blindness, as in Acts 13:6–12. He could hand people over to Satan. He could have gone to Corinth and dealt death to his enemies. He did nothing of the kind.

Paul's third priority, "charity," was *manward.* The word translated "charity" refers to God's kind of love, now shed abroad in Paul's heart by the Holy Spirit. It was love that held back Paul's hand of judgment from smiting his enemies.

Each stanza of Paul's poem of love in 1 Corinthians 13 was echoed in his own heart and life. His love for lost souls drove him over river, sea, and shore to seek them in many lands. The Ephesian elders knew of his deathless passion for the souls of men (Acts 20:20–26). His love for the Lord's people also abounded. He longed that all might come into the fullness of the blessing of Christ. And above Paul's love manward was his love for the Man, Christ Jesus, who had translated him from the kingdom of darkness to the kingdom of light and filled his soul with joy.

Timothy was familiar with the testimony of Paul's life because he had tramped with the apostle over many miles, shared his hardships, and been the recipient of his bounty. No doubt, Paul had told him countless stories of experiences that were never recorded down here but will receive recognition over there on the crowning day that's coming.

iv. The patience of Paul's life (3:10g)

Certainly, Timothy would have observed Paul's "patience." The Greek word means "abiding under." Patience is a plant that is difficult to cultivate; it develops slowly, and it grows best under trial (James 1:3). When Paul wrote about patience in 2 Timothy, he was enduring the most severe trial of his life.

Paul's world had been reduced to a dark, dank cell. He had been in many tight corners before, but this time he knew that his days were numbered. He was bereft of life's smallest amenities, but he did not fret and fume. He accepted his lot in quiet confidence that God was still on the throne. He took life one day at a time, as from the Lord's pierced hand. Now the Holy Spirit ministered patience to his soul (Col. 1:11).

Paul's patience was a mark of his growth in grace and the perfecting of his character. As we read through 2 Timothy, his last letter, we sense that patience in the way he wrote to Timothy and exhorted him. We find no hasty words or high-pressure appeals—just quiet insistence that Timothy stir up his gift and shoulder his responsibilities as God's soldier, student, and saint.

(c) His troubles (3:11a)

Paul wrote to Timothy, "Thou hast fully known my . . . persecutions, afflictions, which came unto me at Antioch, at Iconium, at Lystra; what persecutions I endured." Actually, he was reminding Timothy of the circumstances of his first missionary journey and his first visit to Timothy's hometown. The word translated "afflictions" denotes suffering.

On that first journey, Paul had arrived at Pisidian Antioch after a successful tour of the island of Cyprus. John Mark had defected from the missionary enterprise. Perhaps he was irritated because Paul, rather than Barnabas, was now definitely in charge, or perhaps John Mark was fearful of the proposed daring march through the wild, brigand-infested Taurus mountains.

In Antioch, Paul was given a hearing in the synagogue on the Sabbath. The following Sabbath, huge crowds of Gentiles turned up to hear Paul. The Jews, filled with envy and resentment, "contradicting and blaspheming," turned against him, whereupon Paul turned wholeheartedly to the Gentiles. Many of them were saved, and a church was formed. The Jews responded by whipping up public sentiment against Paul; they "raised persecution," Luke says. Paul responded by shaking the dust of the synagogue off his shoes (Acts 13:14–52).

Paul had moved on to Iconium, where a great multitude of Jews and Gentiles believed. Again, "unbelieving Jews stirred up the Gentiles" and poisoned their minds. This time, Paul rode out the storm. For a long time he remained, preaching and performing miracles. However, opposition grew, culminating in a combined Gentile-Jewish assault, instigated by the Jewish rulers for the purpose of insulting and stoning Paul and Barnabas. The missionaries escaped to Lystra and Derbe (see Acts 14:1–6).

How well Timothy must have remembered Paul's arrival in the twin cities. At Lystra, Paul healed a lifelong cripple. The astonished multitude decided that he and Barnabas were gods and prepared to worship them. Paul dissuaded the crowd and attempted to turn their minds toward the true God. Soon, Jews from Antioch and Iconium showed up; bent on mischief, they persuaded the people to stone Paul. He was left for dead but recovered and went on to Derbe, where he preached the gospel to many people. At the end of the crusade, he returned to Lystra, Iconium, and Antioch—the cities in which he had been so bitterly persecuted—to strengthen the new believers and organize the churches (see Acts 14:7–23).

Timothy would have known from his subsequent travels with Paul that the apostle viewed persecutions and afflictions as occupational hazards; he took them in his stride. Paul endured persecution in Philippi (Acts 16:15–24) and in Thessalonica and Berea (Acts 17:1–14). He endured mocking in Athens (Acts 17:32) and opposition and persecution in Corinth (Acts 18:1–12). In Ephesus, he was at the center of a riot (Acts 19:24–41). In the temple at Jerusalem, Jews beat him and attempted to kill him (Acts 21:26–31). Subsequently, he was arrested and became the center of another riot (Acts 22:22–30; 23:10). When news of a serious plot to kill Paul surfaced, he was whisked out of the city by the Roman believers (Acts 23:12–24). He was imprisoned for two years in Caesarea (Acts 23:33–35). Surviving yet another plot to kill him, Paul finally appealed to Caesar (Acts 25:1–11) and was shipped off to Rome, where he was imprisoned on trumped-up charges (28:16).

Now back in prison for the last time, Paul reviewed all of these troubles, summarizing them in a few words, not because he wanted to dwell on them but because he wanted Timothy to take persecutions in stride as well.

(d) His triumph (3:11b)

Paul assured Timothy, "But out of them all the Lord delivered me." Although he had been beaten and battered and his body was crisscrossed with the marks of whippings that he had endured (his poor plowed and beaten back was a veritable encyclopedia of his pain and suffering), he was still alive. He was invincible until his work was done. But with every word that he wrote Paul drew closer to the end of that work and closer to the headsman's ax.

(2) Paul's warning (3:12–13)

(a) The great dislike of the world (3:12)

Knowing what kind of place his world was, Paul warned Timothy, "All that will live godly in Christ Jesus shall suffer persecution." Satan's end-times machinations began early in the church's history, and Paul knew that they would continue. The world gave our Lord a cattle shed in which to be born and a cross on which to die. Not surprisingly, the true church has also suffered from the world. All of the apostles were persecuted, and most of them were martyred. Timothy himself had already had a taste of suffering (Heb. 13:23).

This awareness of the world's dislike is a far cry from the thinking of many people in our pampered church age. Some preachers promise wealth and health for those who follow their religious teachings and subscribe to their causes. Such teachers urge people to learn the power of positive thinking and assure us that it is not God's will that we be sick or poor or unhappy. The voice of Jesus cuts through these honeyed calls: "In the world ye shall have tribulation," He says, "but be of good cheer; I have overcome the world" (John 16:33).

(b) The growing decadence of the world (3:13)

Paul continued his warning: "Evil men and seducers shall wax worse and worse, deceiving, and being deceived." The word translated "evil" here means "full of labors and pains" in working wickedness, and it conveys the idea of malignant evil. The noun form, translated "evil one," is used of Satan (1 John 2:13). The word translated "seducers" occurs only here. The primary meaning of the word is "wailer." In classical Greek, it referred to a juggler, a cheat, or an enchanter.

There have always been evil people on earth who labor like a woman in travail to bring wickedness to birth. They are liars and cheats like their father, the Devil.

Paul lived in a world of such people, and Nero was their head. Morally, it is but a short step from then to now, from the world of Nero to the world of the coming Antichrist, from the evil men and seducers of Paul's day to the evil men and seducers of our day.

Bible prophecies often have a twofold fulfillment—a partial, initial fulfillment at the time they are given and a later, complete fulfillment at some distant time—usually in relation to the Lord's first and second comings. Often, the Holy Spirit uses a current situation to inspire a vision of a future situation. The immediate, local situation is real to those who are experiencing it, but in the vision it is simply a type or shadow of a much later event. The prophecy of the Virgin Birth is a case in point (Isa. 7:13–18; Matt. 1:22–25). Isaiah used the coming birth of a child to foretell the dissolution of the Syro-Ephraimitic alliance in the days of King Ahaz, and the Holy Spirit used it to foretell the Virgin Birth, which would take place about six centuries later.

Daniel's prophecy regarding Antiochus Ephiphanes is another example. The Syrian king's nefarious reign and his dealings with the Jews were an immediate fulfillment of prophecy. They were also a type of the career of the Antichrist of the last days (Dan. 8:8–27; 11:21–45). The near, partial, and illustrative fulfillment of the prophecy was enacted in history by Antiochus, and the later, end-times fulfillment will be enacted by the Antichrist.

Just as Isaiah's and Daniel's prophecies had immediate and future fulfillments, Paul's comment about "evil men and seducers" applied to two time periods. It was a graphic statement about the moral decadence and continuing deterioration of the pagan Roman world of his day, and it was a prophecy of the moral corruption of the world at the end times.

The increasing decadence of our age is a fulfillment of prophecy, and it is preparing the world for the coming of the Antichrist (2 Thess. 2:3). Evil people, such as Paul envisioned, are hard at work chipping away at our society's historic Judeo-Christian foundations. Pornography and perversion are accepted by more and more people. Vice and violence are tolerated, and many crimes go unpunished. Family values are being eroded by "no-fault" divorce and the promotion of promiscuity and abortion.

The educational system is failing in many ways. Schools are used as instruments of radical social change, and some of them have become playgrounds for violence and drug addiction. The church, riddled with scandals, is losing its voice. Politicians are often despised as self-seeking opportunists. The courts and media, along with the schools, are largely controlled by liberals, libertarians, and secular humanists who hate Christianity. The influence of feminism with its anti-Bible agenda is increasing. Under the banner of the New Age movement, satanism and occult societies eat away at the soul of the Western world.

The Bible and prayer are outlawed in public schools. Vile, incurable illnesses are running rampant as governments and health officials resort to platitudes to hide the true seriousness of new opportunistic diseases that they cannot control. Pagan lifestyles are approved and often applauded. Truly, the world is getting ready for the coming of the Man of Sin. Evil men and deceivers are indeed waxing worse and worse. What, then, is a Christian to do?

d. The message for the last days (3:14–17)
(1) A word of exhortation (3:14–15)
(a) Resolve (3:14)
i. Continuance in the Scriptures urged (3:14a)

Paul's challenge to Timothy is the Holy Spirit's challenge to us: "Continue thou in the things which thou hast learned." In other words, we are to hold fast to our Bible. When the old landmarks are removed, when rot and decay are everywhere, "when the enemy comes in like a flood" (Isa. 59:19), the Bible is the only sure anchor. The world's signposts will blow down in the storm. Human psychology and philosophy are full of uncertainties. Only God's Word is authoritative, eternal, and changeless.

"Continue," urged Paul. The word means "to abide, dwell, remain." (It occurs more than one hundred times in the New Testament and more than fifty times in the writings of the apostle John.) Timothy was to abide, to make himself at home, in the Word of God. It was a safe refuge from the windblown heresies of his day, a secure retreat from the fear of being blown to gale force by the hatred of the world.

ii. Confidence in the Scriptures urged (3:14b)

Paul expanded his challenge: "Continue thou in the things which thou . . . hast been assured of, knowing of whom thou hast *learned* them." The word means "to increase one's knowledge" by study, observation, and asking questions.

Timothy knew that he had learned his Bible from the best of teachers. Paul had been his greatest and most gifted instructor. Having just a casual conversation with a man like Paul would have been educational. What long and interesting talks he and Timothy must have had! Paul doubtless told Timothy how once he had studied to be a rabbi under the renowned Jewish scholar Gamaliel. He had tried Judaism but found it wanting. Doubtless, too, Paul told Timothy how, as a new convert of the risen Christ, he had spent years in the desert. There, he had reexamined the Old Testament in the light of Calvary.

Probably from time to time the apostle threw out a question for Timothy to consider, or elucidated a point of doctrine, or exposed the fundamental error in a false teaching. Perhaps Paul taught him some Hebrew and explained why he used a certain Greek word in one context and a different Greek word in another. No doubt, he rounded out Timothy's general knowledge of Old Testament history, poetry, and prophecy with his own profound insights.

Yes, Timothy had been blessed with the best of teachers, but he needed to "continue." Much land still remained to be possessed through personal Bible study.

(b) Remembrance (3:15)

Again Paul drew Timothy's attention to his Bible and his boyhood: "From a child thou hast known the holy scriptures, which are able to make thee wise unto salvation through faith which is in Christ Jesus."

Timothy's father was a Greek (Acts 16:1). Likely enough, he had told his little boy stories about the greatness of Greece and her gods and how Mount Olympus was their home. There were many gods such as Zeus, the father of the gods; Hermes, the messenger of the gods; and Neptune, god of the sea. Timothy's mother told him that the imaginary lawless, lustful gods of Greek mythology were really imaginary gods made in the image of fallen man.

Timothy's father probably told his boy Homer's tales about Ulysses, Helen of Troy, Circe, the Cyclops, the Sirens, Medusa, and the Minotaur—once-upon-a-time stories full of adventure, excitement, and narrow escapes. He also told him of historical accounts of Philip of Macedon and Alexander; of Thermopylae, Salamis, the Spartans, and the wars with Persia; of Athens and Mars Hill; of the golden age of Greece; and of Plato, Pythagoras, Aristotle, Archimedes, and Herodotus. And little Timothy no doubt listened with wide-eyed wonder.

But Timothy's mother and grandmother were Jewish, and they had other tales to tell Timothy. They told Timothy about Adam and Eve; Cain and Abel; Abraham and Isaac and Jacob; David and Goliath; Samson and Delilah; Moses and Pharaoh; and Joseph, Jonathan, Jeremiah, Jonah, and Job. These were the stories that captured the mind and heart of Timothy.

After all, what was Mount Olympus compared with Mount Moriah, Mount Sinai, or Mount Zion? What was Hercules compared with Samson? What were the gods of Greece compared with the Elohim-Jehovah-Adonai of the Jewish people? Who could settle for human reasoning when he could have divine revelation? So young Timothy's heart turned toward the Scriptures. In the battle for his soul, the fairy stories of Greek religion lost out to the truths of Scripture. The Greek philosophers met with the same fate.

"From a child" Timothy was rooted and grounded in God's Word. The word translated "child" here is *brephos,* which means literally "embryo," or "newly born babe." So Timothy imbibed the Scriptures with his mother's milk. Her lullabies were the Psalms. The songs she sang around the house were Hebrew hymns. She taught him to read from the Bible and to respect it as the foremost and final authority on all matters. And when his mother wasn't teaching him, his grandmother was. Timothy's father must have been a very tolerant man, or perhaps he died when Timothy was still young.

From boyhood, Timothy knew about Moses in the bulrushes, Moses at the burning bush, Daniel in the lions' den, and Elijah on Mount Carmel. Timothy was taught about the Mosaic Law and God's righteous demands; about the moral law and the ceremonial law; about the sacrifices, the offerings, the tabernacle, and the temple; about Hebrew history from Abraham to the theocracy to the monarchy to the dependency to the worldwide dispersion of the Jewish people. Timothy read the prophets and learned about the Hebrew hope of a coming Messiah.

Timothy knew "the holy scriptures" well. The word translated "scriptures" in 2 Timothy 3:15 is the plural *gramma,* which refers to the letters of the alphabet. Timothy not only learned his ABCs from the Scriptures; he was a man of letters, as we would say today. The same was true of the Lord. People marveled at Him and His authoritative teaching. They said, "How knoweth this man letters *[gramma],* having never learned?" (John 7:15). It is far better to be "lettered" in the Scriptures than to have a string of letters after one's name from a galaxy of Ivy League colleges but no understanding of the Bible.

By the time Paul came to his hometown, Timothy's heart and mind had been well prepared. He responded at once to the message of "salvation through faith which is in Christ Jesus." Thereafter, Paul was not only Timothy's spiritual father but also his mentor. Under Paul's instruction, Timothy's learning went beyond anything that his godly mother and grandmother could teach him.

Now he was about to lose his beloved teacher. So Paul continued in his attempt to strengthen Timothy's resolve by reminding him of his deep roots in the Word of God. Of him to whom much had been given, much was expected.

(2) A word of explanation (3:16–17)

(a) The Bible and its inspiration (3:16a)

Paul went on to make important statements about the Holy Scriptures. First, he wrote about the inspiration of the Bible: "All scripture is given by inspiration of God." The phrase translated "all scripture" here refers to the written Scriptures. In this context, the reference is to the Old Testament Scriptures that the Jews considered to be canonical and to the New Testament writings that Christians would ultimately regard as canonical and authoritative. These books are distinguished from the Apocrypha and from various forged epistles and religious writings that would clamor in vain for acceptance.

The description of the Scriptures as "written" ruled out, once and for all, the so-called Jewish oral law. The oral law consisted of vain human traditions beloved by the rabbis. Paul had been trained in those traditions and knew them to be valueless. The Lord Himself had rejected and denounced them (Matt. 15; Mark 7).

Paul's statement in 2 Timothy 3:16 is clear: "All scripture is given by inspiration of God." Yet, we have today many modern versions of the Bible that read, "Every Scripture inspired of God." This modern rendering weakens Paul's statement. Dr. Ralph Keiper of the Evangelical Foundation, Inc. in Philadelphia, Pennsylvania, addressed this subject at the 1964 annual Founder's Week Conference of the Moody Bible Institute in Chicago. He said,

> If you are familiar with some of the other translations, you will realize they are different from the Authorized Version. Some read: "Every scripture inspired of God." This immediately raised the question, Does this indicate that some of the Scriptures are inspired and others are not? Why is there the difference in translation? It is interesting to note that the Revised Standard Version restores the truth of the Authorized. Those of you who are familiar with the Greek text will be able to understand the obscurity that the English text gives us. The Greek reads: "Every scripture is God inspired."
>
> Where the difficulty comes is first of all in the use of the word *scripture.* As you know, in English we have nouns that are of several grades.

Some nouns are singular, such as house, boat, horse. Some nouns, on the other hand, are collective, as when we speak of fish or fruit. We may mean fruit or fruits. The word *scripture* is such a word. Here it is used in its collective sense.

To be a little technical again, if we had here a present participle in the adjective form, the American translation might be correct, which reads, "Every scripture inspired of God." And naturally a question would arise in our minds as to whether or not all the Scripture is inspired. But the Greek is very, very clear. It does not use a participle, nor does it use the adjective in the attributive position. It literally says, "All scripture is inspired" or technically speaking, "Every scripture is inspired by God." . . .

The word *inspired* is also very interesting because it comes from the Greek word *Theopneustos,* which means literally God-breathed. *Theos,* God . . . The "pneu" part is the word *to breathe.* For example, you have it in the pneumatic tires and pneumatic drills. . . . "All scripture is God-breathed."

In II Peter 1:21 we discover that the means of this breath which inspired the Word is none other than the Holy Spirit Himself. "For the prophecy came not in old time by the will of man: but holy men of God spake as they were moved by the Holy Ghost." Here the Scriptures flatly say that human initiative did not play a part in the inspiration of the Scriptures as far as original ideas and original words are concerned: "For the prophecy came not in old time by the will of man." Again permit me to refer to the Greek. The words *came* and *moved* in our English text are the same words in the Greek text. Thus if I may translate it consistently we might well read: "For the prophecy was not carried along in old time by the will of men, they were but the agents or the channels; they were not the creator of the Word of God, but were the instruments." The creator, if you will, is none other than the Holy Spirit.

"For the prophecy came not in old time by the will of man: but holy men of God spake"—not thought—"spake as they were moved by the Holy Ghost." We have a very interesting illustration of this in Acts 1:16. Peter . . . says: "Men and brethren, this scripture must needs have been fulfilled, which the Holy Ghost by the mouth of David spake before concerning Judas, which was guide to them that took Jesus." The method of inspiration is shown in the clause "which the Holy Ghost spake by the

> mouth of," indicating that the mouth of David was used as the instrument of the Holy Spirit to declare the truth of God.[9]

So the Word of God is God-breathed. Just as a pneumatic drill is an air-driven, air-empowered, air-activated drill, Scripture is God-breathed, God-inspired, God-empowered, and God-activated. Literally, it is "God in-breathed." Just as God breathed the breath of life into Adam's body (Gen. 2:7), He breathed His own divine life into the very words of Scripture—not just some Scripture but *all* Scripture. *Pasa graphē* signifies one single whole. Every word—every jot and tittle (Matt. 5:18)—is inspired. That is what we mean when we speak of the plenary, verbal inspiration of Scripture. It is all verbally inspired; it is all divinely inspired.

More could be said concerning this crucial subject. The rendering of 2 Timothy 3:16 in the Revised Version and a number of other modern versions is (as Alford, one of the champions of the rendering, admits) awkward, harsh, and without the support of a single parallel usage in the whole New Testament. The King James rendering is both sound and simple as well as sublime. Furthermore, it is in complete harmony with its context. In 3:15, Paul extolled the Scriptures as having the power to make a person "wise unto salvation"; in 3:17, he showed the effectiveness of Scripture in the life of "the man of God."

(b) The Bible and its information (3:16b)

The next statement Paul made about the Bible is that it is "profitable for doctrine, for reproof, for correction." The Word of God is a down-to-earth document. It meets us where we are and tells us what to do. This practical Book is designed to help us deal with the realities of our everyday lives.

The word translated "profitable" in 3:16 means "useful." The word translated "doctrine" is *didaskalia,* which indicates that the function of the Bible is to teach. *Didaskalia,* which is primarily a Pauline word, occurs fifteen times in the Pastoral Epistles. The word translated "reproof" is *elenchos,* which indicates that God's Word has the power to convict. The Bible is the instrument that the Holy Spirit uses to quicken our consciences. It rebukes us. The word translated "correction" occurs only here in the New Testament and has to do with the redirection of a person's life. It means literally "restoration to an upright state."

Paul's epistles to the churches illustrate these "profitable" functions of the Word

9. Ralph L. Keiper, "The Inspiration of the Scriptures," in *1964 Founder's Week Message Book* (Chicago: Moody Bible Institute), 198–200. Used by permission.

of God. The letters addressed to the Romans, Ephesians, and Thessalonian churches are key epistles. All three are concerned with the *doctrine.* Romans deals with the doctrine of Christ's *cross,* Ephesians deals with the doctrine of Christ's *church,* and 1 and 2 Thessalonians deal with the doctrine of Christ's *coming.*

Romans is followed by 1 and 2 Corinthians, which are concerned with *reproof.* Paul reproved the believers in Corinth because they were not living up to the practical teaching of the epistle to the Romans. The Corinthians failed to apply the teachings of the cross to their lives.

The Corinthian letters are followed by the book of Galatians, which is concerned with *correction.* Paul corrected the believers of Galatia because they were not entering into the doctrinal teaching of the epistle to the Romans. The Galatians were moving away from the simple teaching of the cross to "another gospel" (Gal. 1:6).

Like Romans, Ephesians is followed by an epistle that is concerned with *reproof:* the letter to the Philippians. In it, Paul reproved Euodias and Syntyche, whose squabbling had destroyed, on a practical level, the teaching in Ephesians about the oneness of the body of Christ.

Following the pattern, Philippians is followed by Colossians, which is concerned with *correction.* Paul corrected the Colossians because of a doctrinal departure from the teaching in the book of Ephesians. A dangerous cult that attacked the headship and lordship of Christ had spring up in Colossae.

According to the pattern, the doctrinal letters to the Thessalonians come next, but they are not followed by epistles of reproof and correction. Although they were probably written first, the Thessalonian letters are the last of the church epistles in the New Testament. All truth climaxes in them, for no higher truth can be taught than the second coming of Christ. Those who are seen as dead and risen in Christ in the epistle to Romans, and as seated in the heavenlies in Christ in the epistle to the Ephesians, are seen as caught up with Christ in the epistles to the Thessalonians. In Romans, we are seen as *justified* in Christ; in Ephesians, we are seen as *sanctified* in Christ; and in Thessalonians, we are seen as *glorified with* Christ. Once we are in heaven, there will be no more need for reproof and correction.[10]

(c) The Bible and its instruction (3:16c)

Paul further stated that Scripture is useful for "instruction in righteousness." The word translated "instruction" is *paideia,* which refers to the education and

10. See E. W. Bullinger, *The Companion Bible* (reprint, Grand Rapids: Kregel, 1990), 1660.

training of children or the cultivation of heart and mind. When used in connection with the Word of God, *paideia* also conveys the idea of chastening. Thus, "instruction" suggests Christian discipline and development of Christian character. The Holy Spirit uses the Bible to train us in righteousness. It commands us. It convicts, corrects, and counsels us. It curbs us, commends us, and comforts us.

(d) The Bible and its intention (3:17)

Paul makes one more statement here about the Bible. He wrote of its intention: "That the man of God may be perfect, thoroughly furnished unto all good works." God is not content simply with our knowing our Bibles. He wants us to incarnate its truths in our lives as well. Just as the Lord Jesus was the Word "made flesh" (John 1:14), we should be living epistles "known and read of all men" (2 Cor. 3:2).

Paul had called Timothy a "man of God" in 1 Timothy 6:11. Now he reminded him that being a man of God involved modeling the Holy Scriptures in his daily life. The goal is to be "perfect *[artios]*." The Greek word means "complete, fitted." The Word of God fully fits us, as it did Timothy, to accomplish God's will. The Scriptures enable us to be "thoroughly furnished." The Greek word can be rendered "fitted out." We could say, then, that the Holy Scriptures provide us with a complete outfit, with all of the equipment we need to live lives that are characterized by good works. The Bible, the living Word of the living God, enlightens us and enables us. It directs our paths and energizes us to do the will and work of God in an alien world.

e. The man for the last days (4:1–5)

As Paul continued his letter, the shadow of the executioner's ax lengthened and grew darker. The apostle's work on earth was almost done. His busy pen would soon be still forever. All that remained for him to do was to charge and challenge his young colleague. In 2 Timothy 4, we sense a new urgency in Paul's words. He was laying siege to Timothy's heart and pressing the attack on all fronts.

(1) The charge to Timothy (4:1–4)

(a) The witnesses (4:1)

In his closing charge to Timothy, Paul summoned two witnesses, *the living God* and *the Lord Christ.* "I charge thee therefore," he wrote, "before God, and the Lord Jesus Christ, who shall judge the quick and the dead at his appearing and his kingdom." The word translated "charge," *diamarturomai,* is a strong word, so the beginning of the verse could be rendered, "I solemnly charge you!" The word translated "before" is a compound word, at the heart of which is the Greek word for the eye. Paul used this word because he wanted Timothy to know that this charge was being made in the presence of and in the sight of the living God and the Lord Christ.

It is a serious matter to be brought into a human court and sworn in. Timothy, however, was charged before the supreme court of the universe; he was put on notice that the proceedings were being watched closely by God, and he was reminded that in a coming day he would be called to account by the Lord Jesus Christ. Paul referred to these Divine Witnesses because he could think of no better way to impress Timothy's heart, mind, will, and conscience with the importance of the charge. The apostle used Christ's full title to add even more solemnity to his words.

Timothy needed to bear in mind the Lord's *return*—His "appearing" *[epiphaneia].* The verb form of the Greek word means "to shine forth, to appear, to become visible." Here, *epiphaneia* refers to the Lord's coming at the end of the tribulation age to destroy the Man of Sin. "Then shall that Wicked [one] be revealed, whom the Lord shall consume with the spirit of his mouth, and shall destroy with the brightness *[epiphaneia]* of his coming" (2 Thess. 2:8).

Before that return the church will have been raptured at the *parousia* (1 Cor. 15:23; 1 Thess. 4:14–17). While end-times events come to a head on earth, the believers from the church age will appear at the judgment seat of Christ (Rom. 14:10) to be rebuked or rewarded according to their faithfulness (1 Cor. 3:12–15). One purpose of this arraignment will be to evaluate the life and ministry of each believer and apportion each his appropriate place in the millennial kingdom (Matt. 25:14–30). When this judgment is over, the blood-bought saints of God will return with Christ to share in His glorious appearing on earth. What a strong incentive to holy and practical Christian living! By referring to the "appearing" in 2 Timothy 4:1, Paul reminded his young colleague of these other matters, which are intimately connected with the *epiphaneia.* Timothy would understand, for he was fully conversant with Paul's eschatology (3:10).

Closely related to the Lord's return is His *reign.* His "kingdom" here refers to His millennial reign on earth, which is the subject of many glowing Old Testament prophecies. Not all believers will reign with Christ. Our individual spheres of service are being determined here and now by our cooperation, or lack of it, with the Holy Spirit. This fact is another powerful incentive to holy and practical Christian living.[11]

(b) The work (4:2)

i. To preach (4:2a)

In a series of short, stabbing clauses, Paul called on Timothy to do four things. First, he was to "preach the word." The word translated "preach" here means "to proclaim as a herald." According to *The Companion Bible,* the word is "without reference to the *matter* proclaimed . . . and without including the idea of *teaching.*"[12] It simply suggests a picture of an imperial herald, trumpet in hand, standing at attention in a public place and conveying a mandatory proclamation in the emperor's name. There is no room for discussion or debate. The herald is not there to argue the pros and cons of the demand; he is there to proclaim it and call for instant obedience.

The Spirit-anointed preacher has a message to proclaim, a summary demand of the living God that sinners of Adam's ruined race repent and receive Christ. The teacher gives all of the whys and wherefores, but the preacher simply hands down a mandatory requirement that people ignore or reject at their peril.

Before the Athenian court on Mars Hill, Paul, as a preacher, handed down the divine ultimatum. "God," he said, "now commandeth all men every where to repent: Because he hath appointed a day, in the which he will judge the world in righteousness by that man whom he hath ordained; whereof he hath given assurance unto all men, in that he hath raised him from the dead" (Acts 17:30–31). The response was typical: some mocked, some procrastinated, and some believed.

Timothy was not in Ephesus to pat people on the back. One of the foulest cults of antiquity was housed in that vile city. Timothy was there to stand as a herald in the public thoroughfares and hand down heaven's ultimatum. He might well have shrunk from the task because Paul had been the one to do the preaching in the past. But now, like it or not, the mantle was Timothy's. He was so charged before God.

---

11. Psalm 24 sheds considerable light on all of this. See John Phillips, *Exploring the Psalms,* 2 vols. (Grand Rapids: Kregel, 2002), 1:180–85.
12. Bullinger, *The Companion Bible,* app. 121:1.

ii. To persevere (4:2b)

The second thing on which Timothy was called to do here was to "be instant in season, out of season." Solomon had said, "To every thing there is a season, and a time" (Eccl. 3:1), but Paul swept that maxim aside. The day was too far spent for that comfortable philosophy. The world was too full of wickedness and woe; life was too short; heaven and hell were too real; the needs were too great; the opportunity was too fleeting. It was now or never.

The word translated "in season" and the word translated "out of season" are companion words. The word for "in season" occurs here and in Mark 14:11 in connection with Judas. After Judas made his nefarious deal with the priests, he tried to find a convenient time to hand Jesus over to His enemies: "He sought how he might conveniently betray him."

Timothy was not to wait for convenient times to preach. He was to pay no heed to the weather. He was to take no notice of the curious or hostile stares of the crowd. He was not to stay home because he had a cold, because a thousand other things clamored for his attention, or because the times were too dangerous for public proclamation of the gospel. He needed to be like Paul, who wrote to the Romans, "I am ready to preach the gospel to you that are at Rome also. For I am not ashamed of the gospel" (Rom. 1:15–16). Timothy needed to let words like these burn into his soul: "Woe is unto me, if I preach not the gospel!" (1 Cor. 9:16).

iii. To probe (4:2c–d)

The third task listed here for Timothy is "reprove, rebuke." Timothy's preaching must bring people under conviction for their sin. The word translated "reprove" here is used in connection with the account of the scribes and Pharisees who tried to embarrass and ensnare the Lord. They brought to Him a woman taken in adultery (John 8:3–11). The Lord's response was to stoop down and write something on the ground. Then He said to them, "He that is without sin among you, let him first cast a stone at her." He wrote on the ground again. As He did so, all of the accusers, "convicted" by their own consciences, slunk away. The same word was used in John 16:8 to describe the convicting work of the Holy Spirit in a human heart: He will "reprove" the world of sin.

The word translated "rebuke" here is used in connection with preaching that, for one reason or another, does not result in conviction. Yet, it is a strong word, implying the possibility of a penalty. Paul wanted Timothy to know that even when Timothy's preaching failed to secure conviction, he was to continue making the proclamation, sternly warning of judgment to come. He was called not to be popular but to state the truth of God without fear or favor.

iv. To plead (4:2e–f)

Timothy's fourth task was to plead *lovingly* and *loyally*—to "exhort with all longsuffering and doctrine." He had already been reminded of Paul's doctrine and long-suffering in 3:10.

The word translated "exhort" conveys the idea of calling someone aside to appeal to him, entreat him, instruct him, or beg him. Thus, the preacher's responsibility is taken a step beyond the proclamation.

The exhorting must be done in a spirit of "longsuffering *[makrothumia]*." The meaning of the Greek word embraces the love that will not let us go, the love that "many waters cannot quench" (Song 8:7), the love that "suffereth long, and is kind" (1 Cor. 13:4).

Timothy was to be long-suffering, but he was not to compromise "doctrine" to win someone to Christ. The word translated "doctrine" simply means "instruction." There is sometimes an element of teaching in preaching, although preaching is usually directed to the conscience, the heart, and the will. Teaching is primarily directed to the mind. People need to be given a reason for responding to the divine demands (Isa. 1:18).

(c) The warning (4:3–4)

i. The time approaching (4:3a)

In Paul's day, a rising tide of defection from the church and dissent against revealed truth was developing. This tide will rise and become a major factor in the scenario of the last days (2 Thess. 2:3). Paul warned Timothy, "The time will come when they will not endure sound doctrine" (2 Tim. 4:3).

The word translated "endure" means "to hold." Paul envisioned people in the last days not holding themselves upright regarding sound doctrine. He had in mind primarily his own teaching, which is the backbone of all New Testament theology.

In Timothy's day, Gnostic heresy was on the rise. Today, liberal theology has taken over many seminaries and churches that were founded by men of conviction who believed the Bible and stood solidly on its great doctrines. Many pulpits and classrooms are occupied by men who deny the inerrancy, authority, and inspiration of Scripture. They also deny the deity of Christ; His incarnation, miracles, infallibility, immaculacy, resurrection, and ascension; and His personal, literal coming again. They deny the fall of man, the blood atonement, the doctrine of hell, and the need for the new birth. They are apostates, wolves in sheep's clothing, blind leaders of the blind. "They will not endure sound doctrine."

The phenomenon of unsound doctrine is not limited to liberal circles. For example, many people who profess to be believers and claim to uphold the cardinal teachings of the faith are uniting on the basis of "charismatic" experience. They disparage doctrine and say that it is divisive. A charismatic Baptist can join hands with a charismatic Roman Catholic. They sidestep their glaring differences in doctrine.

ii. The truth abandoned (4:3b–4)

a. The lusts people will have (4:3b)

Referring to people of unsound doctrine, Paul wrote, "After their own lusts shall they heap to themselves teachers, having itching ears." Paul had in mind the insatiable lust of the mind for exotic teachings. In the last days, people will ride fantastic theological hobbyhorses. The word translated "itching" means "to scratch, to tickle." It suggests the craving that people will have to hear sensational news, to see miracles, to explore occult mysteries, to indulge in unsound hermeneutic systems of interpretation, to espouse fanciful theories on the fulfillment of prophecy, and to spawn weird cults.

b. The lies people will heed (4:4)

Paul added, "They shall turn away their ears from the truth, and shall be turned unto fables." The word translated "fables" is *muthos,* which refers to fiction as opposed to fact. People will turn, for instance, to Mormonism, much of which is based on fiction. Or they will turn to other "fables" such as those spun by liberal theologians to explain away revealed truth, especially Bible accounts of miracles. These can be considered fiction because they rest on the unsound and disproved speculations of so-called "higher criticism."

The expression *they shall turn away their ears* can be rendered "they will no longer listen." The people whom Paul envisioned will do more than turn their ears away from the truth; they will deliberately close them.

The word translated "shall be turned" means "to turn, to twist." It has a medical connotation and is used, for instance, to describe the dislocation of a limb. A dislocated arm or leg has no freedom of action. Similarly, people who are twisted away from the truth to receive a lie become the helpless victims of the delusions they embrace. They refuse to receive the love of the truth and take pleasure in unrighteousness (2 Thess. 2:10–12). In the last days, these gullible people will easily become victims of the Antichrist's propaganda.

(2) The challenge to Timothy (4:5)

(a) Be vigilant (4:5a)

Paul's challenge to Timothy here is fourfold. First, he wrote, "Watch thou in all things." The word translated "watch" actually means "to abstain from wine, to be sober." Here it is used to mean "to be alert." Timothy was to keep his eyes open. Paul had told the Ephesian elders much the same thing: "Take heed therefore unto yourselves, and to all the flock, over the which the Holy Ghost hath made you overseers. . . . For I know this, that after my departing shall grievous wolves enter in among you, not sparing the flock. Also of your own selves shall men arise, speaking perverse things, to draw away disciples after them" (Acts 20:28–30). The wolves were already on the prowl, and Timothy was warned to keep alert.

(b) Be valiant (4:5b)

The next part of Paul's challenge was to "endure afflictions." Timothy needed to be prepared to suffer hardship. Paul was under no illusions as to the increasing cost of being a Christian in a world that was increasingly hostile to Christ. The apostle had already told Timothy to be a good soldier and endure hardship (2:3). Now Paul seems to be rattling his chain and casting an eye at the shadow of the ax. Time was running out.

(c) Be versatile (4:5c)

Timothy, by virtue of his gifts and calling, was a pastor (1:6). However, Paul challenged him to "do the work of an evangelist." The gifts of pastor and evangelist are quite distinct (Eph. 4:11). The pastor is essentially a shepherd. His task is to feed, protect, and care for the flock entrusted to his care. The evangelist, on the other hand, is essentially a soul winner. When he preaches, people come under conviction and turn to Christ, sometimes in great numbers. Timothy did not have that *gift* of the evangelist; he was to "do the *work* of an evangelist" (italics added). He was to preach the gospel and extend the invitation; he was to talk to people about Christ; he was to be a witness and seek to lead people to Christ.

(d) Be victorious (4:5d)

Paul further challenged Timothy, "Make full proof of thy ministry." Timothy was to carry out the commission that God had given him. The word translated "make full proof" means "to bring in a full measure." It paints a picture of a ship moving along with all sails set. Timothy needed to set his sails and make an all-out effort because there was still a fair wind in Ephesus. A storm might well be coming, but no sails needed to be shortened. Timothy was to keep moving forward, whether under full sail with a favorable wind or with sails furled because of the howling tempest.

Thus, urging Timothy to be victorious, Paul completed this fourfold challenge to his "son." The rest of the letter would be a series of miscellaneous remarks, requests, remembrances, and resolves.

The rest of 2 Timothy is one of the most interesting passages in the Bible because those short verses close the great apostle's life, ministry, and epistles. After his last "Amen," silence descended. These verses were Paul's last written words, and, as such, they stir an interest that is out of proportion to their content and size. However, what a man says when he knows that his days—and perhaps even his hours—are few is always noteworthy because last words often best reveal the man as he really is.

B. Approaching the death of the great apostle (4:6–18)
   1. Paul's hope (4:6–8)
      a. With death before him (4:6–7)
         (1) The last jeopardy (4:6a)

The shadow of the executioner's ax was moving ever closer. Paul's death was imminent. When my grandfather knew that he was dying, he said to my father, "There's nothing to dying, Leonard. It's the living that counts!" Paul said much the same thing. Having lived well, he was ready to face the last jeopardy.

"I am now ready to be offered," the apostle wrote to Timothy. Paul was always ready. Years ago, he had written to the believers in the city where he was now imprisoned, "I am ready to preach the gospel to you that are at Rome also" (Rom. 1:15). And so he had. Now he was paying for it, but the Christians in Rome were giving him a wide berth. With Nero using them as human torches, most of them did not want to add to their dangers by associating with Nero's most notable prisoner.

The word translated "am ready to be offered" is *spendomai,* which means "to be poured out as a drink offering or libation." Thus, another rendering might be, "I am already being poured out." If Paul were decapitated, the blow of the ax would indeed pour out his blood as a libation. It would be his last service to his beloved Lord.

Although he did not know what the unpredictable Nero would command, Paul hoped that his Roman citizenship would save him from torture and crucifixion. Decapitation seemed the most likely form of execution to expect. The Roman Catholic Church preserves a strong tradition that Paul was indeed beheaded at the site of the Church of the Three Fountains. According to this tradition, when his head rolled, it touched the earth three times, and each time a fresh fountain of water sprang up.

In any case, Paul was not deterred by the thought of death. He expected to die as a martyr; he thought of his death as an offering. If his head rested on the executioner's block, it would transform that grim piece of state furniture into an altar.

(2) The last journey (4:6b)

Paul added, "The time of my departure is at hand." The word translated "departure" is *analusis,* which occurs only here in the Scripture. However, the verb form occurs elsewhere. Paul used it when telling his Philippian friends about his "desire to depart, and to be with Christ; which is far better" (Phil. 1:23). The word, which means literally "to unloose," is picturesque. It is used in speaking of taking down the tent in preparation for a march, or weighing anchor before setting sail, or unyoking a beast of burden. The same word is used to mean "return" in Luke 12:36, which refers to men who "wait for their lord, when he will *return* from the wedding."

When Paul wrote to the Philippians about his "desire to depart, and to be with Christ," he was in prison in Rome for the first time. That imprisonment was comparatively benign. The trumped-up charges were not likely to stand up in court, and Nero had not yet embarked on a course of open brutality toward Christians. Paul was uncertain then about what his sentence would be, but he was optimistic that he would be released. However, he had come to grips with the possibility of death. The word translated "desire" in Philippians 1:23 is *epithumia,* the common New Testament word for lust. Paul was lusting to go to heaven. He was longing to weigh anchor and set sail for yonder heavenly shore, to attend the wedding and return with the groom!

Now he was back in prison, this time facing imminent death. Paul picked up his old word *analuō.* He hadn't changed his mind. Soon the anchor would be weighed, or, to put it more accurately, the anchor rope would be severed by the executioner's ax, and he would be gone! In Paul's mind, nothing about this prospect was grim or gloomy. It was the logical end of a life poured out in service to the king.

The journey after the anticipated departure would not be long. The distance between earth and heaven is not measured in miles. Paul had long since thought through what was involved. In one of the most interesting chapters in the New Testament, Paul explained how the transition worked: "Absent from the body . . . present with the Lord" (2 Cor. 5:8). The journey would be over just like that!

(3) The last judgment (4:7)

The last judgment for the Christian will be at the judgment seat of Christ (Rom. 14:10; 1 Cor. 3:10–15). Paul was mindful of it, but it held no terrors for him. "I have fought a good fight," he said. "I have finished my course, I have kept the faith." This loved and oft-quoted statement shows that Paul anticipated the judgment with eagerness; he longed to hear his Lord's resounding words of praise. The apostle never forgot Stephen's triumphant entry into glory (Acts 6:15; 7:53–60).

(a) Well won, Paul! (4:7a)

Paul could say, "I have fought a good fight." The word translated "fought" here means literally "to engage in conflict." The reference might be to competing in the Olympic games or engaging in military conflict. Paul possibly had in mind a comparison between himself and *a Roman soldier.* The apostle would not have had to look far for this figure of speech because he was chained to one! He had known many Roman soldiers and during his first imprisonment had won a number of them to Christ, some of them members of the Praetorian guard (Phil. 1:13).

Paul had often acknowledged the fact that the Christian is at war. He had told the Ephesians to don the armor of God and engage the foe on all fronts in the battle against Satan's principalities and powers, against the rulers of this world's darkness, and against wicked spirits in high places (Eph. 6:11–18). Paul had just finished reminding Timothy to "endure hardness, as a good soldier of Jesus Christ" (2 Tim. 2:3).

Paul had practiced what he preached. He had waged war day and night against all of the power of the enemy. Now he was a battle-scarred prisoner of war; but even so, the Devil did not know what to do with him. If Satan turned Paul loose, he would turn the world upside down. If Satan locked Paul up in prison, he would win his jailers to Christ, engage in prayer that would shake the Devil's strongholds to their foundation, and write deathless letters that would arm multitudes of believers in ages yet unborn to fight as the apostle had fought. If Satan killed Paul, he would simply be promoted to glory, where he longed to be.

"I have fought a good fight," Paul wrote. The verb, being in the perfect tense here, speaks of past action and implies continuing results. The apostle looked forward to the moment when he would hear the Lord say, "Well won, Paul!"

(b) Well run, Paul! (4:7b)

Paul could also claim, "I have finished my course." The word translated "course" here is *dromos,* which refers to a racecourse. The apostle now saw himself as *a Greek athlete.*

When preaching to the Jews in the synagogue in Pisidian Antioch during his first missionary journey, Paul had used the same word in speaking of John the Baptist. "John fulfilled his course *[dromos],*" he said. Paul quoted John's words: "Whom think ye that I am? I am not he. But, behold, there cometh one after me, whose shoes of his feet I am not worthy to loose" (Acts 13:25). Shortly after John made that statement, Herod murdered him. More recently, Paul had used the word in his farewell challenge to the Ephesian elders in Miletus: "Bonds and afflictions abide me. But none of these things move me, neither count I my life dear unto myself, so that I might finish my course *[dromos]* with joy" (Acts 20:23–24). Many of the believers at Ephesus would be reminded of that farewell when they read what Paul wrote to Timothy.

Now Paul had crossed the finish line. The word *finished* awakens a score of memories. It takes us straight to Calvary, where we see the Lord on the tree (John 19:28–30). He knew that "all things were now accomplished (finished)." As He hung on the cross, we can picture the Lord as His omniscient mind reviewed all of the promises, prophecies, types, and shadows in the Old Testament Scripture that had any bearing on His first coming to ensure that each of them had been fulfilled. Only one prediction remained unfulfilled: "In my thirst they gave me vinegar to drink" (Ps. 69:21). So "that the scripture might be fulfilled," Jesus said, "I thirst." Nearby was "a vessel full of vinegar." In response to the Lord's exclamation, the bystanders "filled a sponge with vinegar, and put it upon hyssop, and put it to his mouth. When Jesus therefore had received the vinegar, he said, It is *finished:* and bowed his head, and gave up the ghost." The word means "to bring to an end, to complete, to perfect," so when the Lord cried triumphantly, "It is finished," He meant that His sufferings were over. His great work of redemption was done.

In a lesser sense, Paul's situation was similar. His mind was running back over the years since he had first met Christ. He thought of Damascus, Arabia, Cilicia, Antioch, Galatia, Europe, and Asia Minor, and he realized that his work was finished. Some of it had been finished a long time ago. He wrote from Corinth to the church at Rome, "From Jerusalem, and round about unto Illyricum, I have fully preached the gospel of Christ" (Rom. 15:19). He had cut a wide swath extending some fifteen hundred miles from Jerusalem to what we now call Yugoslavia. He had indeed finished his work in those parts. "Having no more place in these parts, and having a great desire these many years to come unto you," he told the Romans, "whensoever I take my journey into Spain, I will come to you" (Rom. 15:23). Later, he could say the same thing about Ephesus. The Ephesian elders had left him in tears, "sorrowing most of all for the words which he spake, that they should see his face no more" (Acts 20:38). Since then, he had traveled to Spain and Rome.

Paul's work was done. He had traveled his last mile, preached his last sermon, written his last book—finished his course. Now he looked forward to the moment when he would hear the Lord say, "Well run, Paul!"

(c) Well done, Paul! (4:7c)

"I have kept the faith," Paul continued. Possibly, he now had in mind a comparison between himself and *a Hebrew prophet* standing fearlessly for God in an apostate age. A host of such heroes of the faith parades across the stages of our minds. We see Elijah confronting weak Ahab and wicked Jezebel, brandishing miracles. We see Elisha fearless in an apostate age. We see Isaiah scolding Ahaz and strengthening Hezekiah, only to be sawn asunder by Manasseh. We see Jeremiah and Ezekiel warning or weeping as the times required and braving the wrath of their countrymen. We see Daniel keeping the faith and preaching boldly to such tyrants as Nebuchadnezzar, Belshazzar, and Darius. And we see the twelve so-called minor prophets, stars of lesser magnitude, perhaps, but stars just the same, braving death to reach the conscience of their times.

Like the prophets, Paul had "kept the faith." The word translated "kept" means "to keep by guarding, to watch over." The word translated "faith" is *pistis,* a word that has to do with a conviction based on hearing (Rom. 10:17). Paul had never wavered in his implicit trust in the Lord. His faith was as firm and steady under the shadow of the executioner's ax as it had been the moment he first believed on the Damascus road.

Moreover, Paul had guarded with his life the body of truth entrusted to him. He had stood firm in the faith before the rage of the Jews and the violence of the mob. He had stood uncompromising before Felix, Festus, and King Agrippa. Nor had Paul wavered before the savage Nero.

Fearless before the apostles and elders in the Jerusalem church, Paul had defended the right of Gentile believers to be emancipated from all of the trappings of Judaism (Acts 15). He had boldly confronted Peter face-to-face, rebuking even that outstanding apostle when he showed signs of compromising vital truth (Gal. 2:11–16).

Satan had sought to undermine Paul's teaching by opposing him. There had been Galatian legalists, Jewish ritualists, and Colossian Gnostics. There had been forged letters (2 Thess. 2:2). There had been vicious attacks on his integrity, his personal appearance, and his unpolished speech (2 Cor. 10:10; 11:6). Paul's stand against Satan was simple: "I know whom I have believed, and am persuaded that he is able to keep that which I have committed unto him against that day" (2 Tim. 1:12). What God committed to Paul, Paul committed back to God. Now Paul looked forward to the moment when he would hear the Lord say, *"Well done, Paul!"* With death before him, Paul could rejoice that he was not going to end up as a "castaway" after all (1 Cor. 9:27).

How Timothy's heart must have been stirred as he read the words. He knew them to be true.

b. With death behind him (4:8)

(1) A crowning day for Paul (4:8a)

Paul anticipated the moment when, with death behind him, he would stand at the judgment seat of Christ. He said, "Henceforth there is laid up for me a crown of righteousness, which the Lord, the righteous judge, shall give me at that day." With this statement, Paul endorsed the fact that although salvation is free rewards have to be earned. He had no doubt whatsoever that he had earned a crown. The word translated "crown" here is *stephanos,* which refers to the victor's crown of oak leaves or ivy that was given to the winners of Greek athletic events.

Paul expected to receive a "crown of righteousness." Scripture mentions other kinds of crowns as well: 1 Peter 5:4 mentions the crown of glory; James 1:12 mentions the crown of life; Philippians 4:1 refers to the soul winner's crown; Revelation 2:10 refers to the martyr's crown. Doubtless, Paul will receive all of them, but the one of which he was sure was the crown of righteousness. It would be his reward for having lived a righteous life.

In his epistle to the Romans, Paul developed at length the whole subject of righteousness—how it is *required,* how it is *received,* and how it is *reproduced.* He knew well the difference between the "righteousness of Christ" that is *imputed* to us by God and the "righteousness of saints" that is *implemented* in us by the Holy Spirit (1 John 3:7; Rev. 19:8). The former has to do with our *standing,* which is perfect; the latter has to do with our *state,* which is imperfect. As far as was humanly possible in a body of the flesh, Paul had allowed the indwelling Holy Spirit to make him like Jesus. Paul had lived with an ungrieved Holy Spirit. The righteous Judge would see that he received the appropriate reward.

(2) A critical day for all (4:8b)

We, too, will stand before that judgment seat. As Paul said, the crown will be given "not to me only, but unto all them also that love his appearing." He linked the rewards that believers will receive "at that day" with the measure of their love of His appearing. A steady focus on the Lord's return to the air to take home His bride is a powerful motive for righteous living. The apostle John said the same thing in 1 John 3:1–3. It is possible, however, for us to lose our crowns if we fail to live a Spirit-filled life.

It is never too late to start living righteously. Think of the dying thief. With only hours left to him, he trusted Christ and witnessed so triumphantly that his testimony became part of the living Word of God (Luke 23:39–43). Many people will be in glory as a result of that man's words.

2. Paul's hardship (4:9–15)
   a. His plea (4:9)

Paul begins his closing remarks with a plea: "Do thy diligence to come shortly unto me." He longed to see his dear Timothy one more time. He urged him to come to Rome, to visit him in prison, to dare the dangers, and to prove the measure of his manhood in Christ. It was no small plea, for Rome was about the last place on earth that any Christian would want to be at that time. Many Christians were scrambling to get out of that town because Nero was on the warpath.

Nero Claudius Caesar Germanicus was brought up by his mother Agrippina the Younger, a great-granddaughter of the emperor Augustus. She was a sister of the wicked Emperor Caligula, who tortured and killed hundreds of people just for the pleasure of watching them die in agony. Agrippina poisoned her second husband, then married her uncle, the emperor Claudius. Nero married Octavia, the daughter of Claudius. Claudius made Nero his heir, and Agrippina murdered Claudius before he had time to change his mind. Such was the climate in which history's most notorious villain grew up.

Nero became emperor when he was seventeen years old. He showed some promise during the first few years of his reign. Under the guidance of Seneca and Burrus, it seemed that Nero would justify the people's high hopes of him. Even then, however, the seeds of decay could be seen. Salvius Otho and Ofonius Tigellinus influenced Nero to jettison any belief in the gods. He and his friends would disguise themselves and roam the streets molesting women and giving themselves over to debauchery and vice.

Once on the throne, Nero murdered Britannicus, the fourteen-year-old son of Claudius, to ensure that the teenager could not be used to challenge his right to the throne. Nero tried to drown his own mother; and when his plot failed, he sent a band of thugs to stab her to death. Nero loathed his wife, so he banished her and then had her killed. Then he married one of his mistresses, a Jewess named Poppaea Sabina, whom he had stolen from the senator Otho. Later, Nero kicked Poppaea to death. He then married Messalina after having her husband murdered. To excite Nero's dislike or suspicion was as good as writing one's own death warrant.

In A.D. 64, fire broke out in the poor section of Rome where most of the slum tenements were built of wood. The fire burned fiercely for more than a week. Stories circulated that Nero fiddled while Rome burned, and it was widely believed that he had started the fire himself, or at least ordered someone to do it. He wanted to reconstruct the city in the Greek style and build a fabulous golden house for himself. Suddenly, he needed a scapegoat, so he blamed the new sect of Christians. He charged them with the crime of arson and launched a fierce, widespread, demonic reign of terror against Christianity. Christians were hunted down and savagely executed. They were burned alive as torches to light Nero's midnight orgies; they were sewn up in skins and thrown to wild beasts in the arena.

Terror hovered over Rome. In A.D. 65, a widespread conspiracy involving some of the most prominent people in Rome was uncovered. Their rank did not spare them from Nero's wrath. The poet Lucan, Nero's old tutor, was killed, and the philosopher Seneca was forced to commit suicide. Nero was in full stride as the bloodthirsty, suspicious tyrant that history remembers him to have been. Guilty or innocent, senators, leading citizens, and officers of the guard who aroused suspicion were killed.

Then Roman legions in Spain, Gaul, and Africa revolted against Nero and made Galba emperor. The senate, aroused at last, condemned Nero to die a slave's death on a cross and under the whip. His personal troops, the prestigious Praetorian guard, joined his enemies.

Nero heard of the revolts brewing abroad. He simply laughed. After all, he was the emperor! He was god! But one night in A.D. 68, he awoke to an ominously silent palace. His guards were gone; the place was deserted. Nero threw an old cloak over his tunic, climbed on a horse, and rode through the night to the house of Phaon, a former slave. There, Nero received word that the senate had sentenced him to die as a public enemy. According to Suetonius, at dawn, when Nero heard horses approaching, he committed suicide by cutting his own throat.

While Nero was still in power, Paul asked Timothy to come to Rome. The apostle wrote, "Do thy diligence to come." The word translated "do thy diligence" means "do your best" or "make haste" or "make every effort." In 2:15, the same word is rendered "study." So Paul's plea was that Timothy study ways to get to Paul while there was still time.

Paul had taught Timothy that a good soldier does not shrink from danger, but he wanted Timothy to be fully aware of the dangers that he would face when he came. Paul spelled out the situation in Rome clearly enough for Timothy to make an intelligent decision. The apostle did not want his young friend to let his heart run away with his head. If he came, he needed to come with his eyes wide open.

b. His plight (4:10–15)
(1) His friends (4:10–13)
(a) The deserter—Demas (4:10a)

As Paul pondered the situation in Rome, a string of names came to his mind. First, he thought of Demas. "Demas hath forsaken me," Paul said, "having loved this present world, and is departed unto Thessalonica." Demas was given honorable mention in letters written during Paul's first Roman imprisonment (Col. 4:14; Philem. 24), but during that time the danger was minimal. But now Demas left a nasty stain on his character; he forsook the great apostle.

The word translated "hath forsaken" in 2 Timothy 4:10 means "to leave one in the lurch, to let one down, to desert, to abandon." The Lord used the same word to describe His feelings of utter abandonment on the cross (Matt. 27:46).

Paul attributed the defection of Demas to a love of this world. "This present world" is a danger that we all face. We have to decide for which world we are going to live—this world or the world to come. This world is our enemy. The word *world* is used in the Bible to symbolize human life and society with God left out. It is the Devil's lair for sinners and his lure for saints. Paul attributed Demas's defection to crass worldliness. If Demas had cultivated a love for the world to come, he would not have shrunk from martyrdom. Evidently, Demas did not know the Lord as Paul knew the Lord or "love his appearing" as Paul did.

We do not know why Demas went to Thessalonica. Perhaps that was his hometown. Perhaps he had a job offer there. Perhaps he simply wanted to put the distance of Italy, the Adriatic, and much of Macedonia between him and the madman who was running Rome. Paul did not brand Demas as an apostate. Demas just did what John Mark had done when he abandoned Paul and Barnabas (Acts 13:13).

(b) The departed—Crescens and Titus (4:10b–c)

Two more friends came to the apostle's mind. Crescens *(Paul's named friend)* had departed for Galatia, and Titus *(Paul's famed friend)* had departed for Dalmatia. None of the stigma attached to Demas is attached to their names.

We know nothing about Crescens. He seems to have set out for Galatia on his own initiative but with Paul's consent. He did not sneak away like Demas. Galatia, of course, was far away from the center of the maelstrom, but really no place anywhere in the Roman world was safe for a Christian. Nero had agents, spies, and soldiers everywhere. Because of the mercuric Galatian character, Paul might have recognized the value of allowing Crescens to go to Galatia with his blessing, but it was yet another good-bye. Perhaps Titus went to Dalmatia on the same basis.

We know about Titus. Paul had used him in connection with the Corinthian crisis years earlier and had left him on the island of Crete to bring order and discipline to the churches there. About the same time that Paul wrote his first letter to Timothy, he wrote a similar letter of instruction to Titus. Titus was made of tough fiber. We cannot imagine his leaving Paul in the lurch.

The circumstances surrounding Paul's last movements and the actual place of his arrest are uncertain. We know, however, that he intended to winter at Nocopolis near Corinth. He summoned Titus to meet him at Nocopolis and sent Artemas to relieve Titus from his duties on Crete. When Titus arrived at Nocopolis, he likely found that Paul had already been arrested and was now a prisoner in Rome. It is also likely that he followed Paul to Rome and went from there to Dalmatia at Paul's command. It is possible, of course, that Titus found Paul at Nicopolis and from there went to Dalmatia, which was not very far from Rome. Dalmatia, just across the Adriatic, ran parallel with Italy's eastern coastline.

(c) The doctor—Luke (4:11a)

Demas, Crescens, and Titus had departed. Only Luke remained with Paul. Luke and Paul had journeyed together from time to time after they met in Troas during Paul's second missionary journey. Luke was very likely a Greek; Paul might have known him during his student days in Tarsus. Luke might have been the "man of Macedonia" whom Paul met the moment he awoke from his epochal vision (Acts 16:9).

Luke always modestly keeps himself out of sight in Scripture. His presence with Paul in the Acts story is indicated by the use of the personal pronoun *we*. Luke accompanied Paul on the eventful voyage to Rome that he described so vividly in Acts 27, and he seems to have remained with Paul during his first, two-year Roman imprisonment. During that time, Luke likely wrote the book of Acts. He was with Paul when the apostle wrote the epistles to the Colossians and Philemon from prison in Rome (Col. 4:14; Philem. 24). Possibly, Luke remained with Paul during the period between his release from prison and his rearrest. Paul had severe infirmities, some of which had been brought on by the beatings and other hardships that he had suffered in the cause of Christ. He needed a personal physician.

Dear Dr. Luke was "the beloved physician" indeed. Paul was virtually forsaken and incarcerated under terrible circumstances, and he thanked God for brave Luke, who still stood beside him. Evidences of Nero's atrocities were everywhere, and the ax was drawing nearer. How can we ever measure the pathos of the words *only Luke is with me*? Of all of the thousands of people whom Paul had led to Christ and to whom he had ministered, only Luke remained a close, daily companion. On the other hand, how can we ever measure the praise and thanksgiving of the words *Luke is with me*? Great will be Luke's reward in heaven!

(d) The disciple—Mark (4:11b)

Paul continued, "Take Mark, and bring him with thee: for he is profitable for me for the ministry." Paul and Mark had a stormy history. When Paul and Barnabas embarked on their first missionary journey, Mark tagged along as their "minister" (servant) (Acts 12:25–13:5). Mark, however, deserted them when faced with the perils that loomed ahead. Paul had decided to go to Galatia, and the road through the Taurus Mountains and the Cilician gates was notoriously infested with brigands. Mark quit. Later, when Paul and Barnabas were planning their second missionary journey, they quarreled over Mark. Barnabas wanted to give Mark, who was his nephew, a second chance and take him along. Paul said, "No!" A disagreement followed that resulted in a parting of the ways (Acts 15:36–41).

Apparently, Mark was reconciled to Paul before the apostle wrote to the Colossians and Philemon during his first imprisonment in Rome (Col. 4:10; Philem. 24). Likely, Mark was with or near Timothy when Paul wrote asking Timothy to bring Mark. Something must have happened to renew Paul's confidence in Mark. Barnabas and Peter seem to have taken Mark in hand and given him another chance.

Then one day, perhaps, someone handed Paul a manuscript and said, "You should read this. It is a gospel of the life and ministry of Christ. It bears the hallmark of Peter, but he didn't write it. It is fast paced and has a Gentile, possibly Roman, audience in mind. It emphasizes the Lord Jesus as the servant of Jehovah. One might call it the Gospel of the Servant."

Paul read the manuscript with ever growing interest. "Who wrote this?" he asked.

"Mark!"

"Well, Barnabas was right. I didn't know the boy had it in him!"

We don't know for sure, but that is what could have happened. In any case, something happened because Mark, who had failed as a servant and had fled from danger, was now an asset to the ministry and quite willing to court danger. Paul wanted to see him. Besides, it would be better for Timothy to have company when walking into the lions' den than to come to Rome alone.

(e) The dispatched—Tychicus (4:12)

Because Timothy would be leaving for Rome, it would be good for someone to take his place in Ephesus. So Paul dispatched his friend Tychicus. Ephesus seems to have been his hometown. He had been a member of the delegation of Gentiles who had accompanied Paul to Jerusalem to deliver the cash collection for the poor (Acts 20:4). Tychicus had also been with Paul in Rome when he wrote to the Colossians (Col. 4:7). It must have been another wrench in the apostle's heart to see Tychicus go because he was one of Paul's bright young men. "Tychicus have I sent to Ephesus," he said.

(f) The dependable—Carpus (4:13)

Paul seems to have had no doubt that Timothy would come to Rome. He was dependable, as was Carpus. Carpus surfaces here for a moment, just long enough to get his name written into the Bible and long enough for us to gather that he was one of Paul's countless friends. The apostle wrote, "The cloak that I left at Troas with Carpus, when thou comest, bring with thee, and the books, but especially the parchments." This is a weighty verse because it suggests the dire straits in which Paul now found himself and about which he wrote nothing at all.

Paul, we can assume, was in the Mamertine prison. We can picture the Romans as they took him along its northeastern flank, up the so-called "steps of groaning," and into the gloomy interior, where he was handed over to the public executioner. He was stripped of his outer garments and left naked, except for his tunic. He was a notable prisoner, the acknowledged and self-confessed leader of the detested Christians; the jailer would not dare to be lenient. Paul was then taken over to a trapdoor in the floor. The door was lifted, ropes were passed under his armpits, and he was lowered into the terrible Tullianum dungeon. Paul's feet touched the floor, the ropes were drawn up, and the trapdoor was slammed into place. He was now in the dark.

In Paul's day, the name of that dungeon was spoken in whispers. It was a black pit, a hole in the ground. It was damp and chilly. The bed was a clump of stale, damp straw, and the floor was heaped with filth. There was a spring, at least, but the air was foul. Food was lowered to prisoners from time to time—rough fare to keep body and soul together—and perhaps a kidskin of thin, sour wine. Prisoners had been known to be eaten by the rats in that dreadful hole.

Such was Paul's last prison. No wonder he wanted Timothy to bring his coat. No wonder he valued Luke, who stood by him in his need and found a way to penetrate the tight security that surrounded Nero's most important prison. Perhaps the rigors of Paul's confinement were relieved a little after a while because he somehow found a way to write this last letter. Maybe he was allowed a candle. Perhaps Paul's Roman citizenship afforded him some relief. Maybe Luke voluntarily shared his confinement. Nero doubtless wanted to get some political capital out of Paul's execution and did not want him to die of hunger, disease, or neglect in the Tullianum—although the caesar would have gotten malicious satisfaction from knowing that Paul was there.

In the chill of his prison, Paul remembered "the cloak that I left at Troas." Troas was the place where Paul received the Macedonian call to invade Europe with the gospel. The word translated "cloak" refers to a heavy mantle used by travelers to protect themselves against stormy weather. The garment, often made of goat's hair, apparently was stiff and cumbersome and certainly not needed in the hot Mediterranean summer months. When Paul left the mantle with Carpus, he could not have known that he would later need it.

William Tyndale had a similar experience. The father of the English Bible, Tyndale translated the Scriptures from the Hebrew and Greek (unlike Wycliffe, who translated them from the Latin). Tyndale's goal was to "cause a boy that driveth the plough to know more of the Scripture than the clergy." About 90 percent of his finished work passed directly into the King James Version. Tyndale, however, was hated by the clergy. Not wanted in England, he fled to the Continent, where his enemies continued to plot against him. Betrayed at last by a man who had wormed his way into his confidence, Tyndale was tried as a heretic by special commissioners of the Holy Roman Empire. While awaiting trial, he languished for months in a comfortless prison. He was burned at the stake in Vilvorde, Belgium, on Friday, October 6, 1536.

One of Tyndale's letters from prison has survived. Written in Latin by his own hand during the winter of 1535, it was addressed to the governor of the castle. In the letter, Tyndale begged that the commissary might be permitted to send him, from his personal effects, a warmer cap and also a warmer coat, because the one he had was very thin. In addition, he asked for a piece of cloth with which to patch his leggings. "My overcoat is worn out," he wrote. "But most of all," he continued, "I beg and beseech your clemency to be urgent with the commissary, that he will kindly allow me to have the Hebrew Bible, Hebrew grammar, and Hebrew dictionary, that I may pass the time in that study." Doubtless, Tyndale was familiar with the way his situation paralleled that of Paul.

Paul urged Timothy, "Bring with thee . . . the books . . . the parchments." The word for "books" is *biblion,* a common enough word in the New Testament. We derive from it both our English word *bibliography* and our monumental word *Bible.* The original word refers to the inner part of the papyrus plant. It came to describe the paper that the Egyptians made from this bark and, hence, to a written book. The books to which Paul refers here were papyrus rolls.

The word for "parchments" is *membrana* and occurs only here in the New Testament. This writing product was prepared from the skin of sheep and goats, the quality product being made from the skin of calves or kids. Paul's parchments were probably treasured copies of Old Testament Scriptures. His "books" were collections of other writings.

In any case, Paul wanted to read and study his books and his Bible while the countdown to his execution continued. Perhaps he wanted to leave them as his legacy to Timothy and Luke. That and his cloak were all that he had to leave to anyone. The Lord had even less to leave, just his clothes and his cloak.

As Spurgeon once said, Paul was an inspired apostle; yet, he wanted his books. He had been preaching for at least thirty years; yet, he wanted his books. He had seen the Lord; yet, he wanted his books. He had been caught up into the third heaven; yet, he wanted his books. He had heard things untranslatable; yet, he wanted his books. He had written a major part of the New Testament; yet, he wanted his books.[13] "Bring . . . the books," he said.

(2) His foe—Alexander (4:14–15)

Paul shared with Timothy a reminiscence and a warning concerning *a devilish man:* "Alexander the coppersmith did me much evil" (4:14). Very likely, this Alexander is the same person mentioned in 1 Timothy 1:20; Paul had handed him over to Satan so that he would learn not to blaspheme. Some scholars think that he is the same Alexander whom Luke mentioned in connection with the Ephesian riot instigated by Demetrius the silversmith (Acts 19:33). The crowd in

13. Charles H. Spurgeon, *Metropolitan Tabernacle Pulpit* (n.p., 1863).

Ephesus was out of control when the Jews tried to put forth a man named Alexander as their spokesman. Presumably, they wanted to disassociate the Jewish community from the Christians. However, as soon as he tried to speak, the mob recognized him as a Jew and howled him down. If he was the same Alexander mentioned in 1 Timothy, he was a smith by trade. Perhaps that is why the Ephesian Jews chose him to be their spokesman; they thought that a fellow member of the guild would be heard.

Whoever he was, he hated Paul and the gospel. He did Paul "much evil." The Greek can also be rendered "many evil things." The word translated "evil" is *kakos,* which suggests depravity. We are not told how this evil man expressed his wicked nature in opposition to Paul.

Alexander likely opposed Paul in Rome at the time of Paul's first appearance in court. Perhaps he mobilized Jewish public opinion against Paul and Christianity and in support of Nero. The Jewish community in Rome, though powerful in its own right, might have been glad to have the spotlight removed from them and focused on the Christians. The Jews had tasted Roman anti-Semitism and were always nervous about it (Acts 18:2).

Nero was well acquainted with the Jewish community because he had married a Jewess; during their more compatible moments, he might well have listened to her Jewish views. Perhaps Nero welcomed and encouraged Jewish Alexander. His sneers and slanders might have been a balm to Nero's guilty soul during his crusade against the Christians. Nero might have been nervous about confronting Paul and might have wanted Alexander's help in the trial. Paul was no pushover, even for a Roman caesar.

Perhaps Alexander testified against Paul. He could have cited the Ephesian riot as a prime example of Paul's alleged incendiary, destabilizing sedition against Roman law and order. Alexander might have paraded a string of such incidents in Galatia, Macedonia, Corinth, and Jerusalem. In his account, he could have doctored the narrative, editing out references to Jewish instigation of the riots and portraying Paul as a lawless rabble-rouser and the chief proponent of an illegal religion.

Alexander might have found favor in Nero's eyes, but he was *a doomed man.* "The Lord reward him according to his works," wrote Paul (2 Tim. 4:14). If this Alexander was the one whom Paul had already handed over to Satan, the disciplinary action had not produced any positive change in him. He had gone from bad to worse. Yet, we note no element of malice or spite in Paul's words. He was simply thankful that God was still on the throne and that men like Nero and Alexander do not live forever.

Nevertheless, Alexander was *a dangerous man,* and Timothy needed to be warned. "Of whom be thou ware also; for he hath greatly withstood our words" (4:15). If Alexander was an Ephesian, he doubtless knew and hated Timothy too. Whether in Ephesus or in Rome, Timothy needed to be on his guard against this wily adversary. He had "withstood," the Greek word meaning "to set oneself against." It was used to describe the way the Egyptian magicians opposed Moses and contributed to the hardening of the pharaoh's heart (3:8). Alexander was guilty of doing the same. In deliberately setting out to oppose Paul and the gospel, the coppersmith strengthened Nero's wicked resolve.

3. Paul's heroism (4:16–18)
   a. Paul's loneliness (4:16)

Paul told Timothy, "At my first answer no man stood with me, but all men forsook me: I pray God that it may not be laid to their charge." Thus, Paul tasted the bitterness that his beloved Lord had tasted when, abandoned by all, He had stood alone before Caiaphas, Pilate, and Herod.

We can picture the scene when Paul first appeared before Nero. There sat the emperor in his robes of state. Bronze coins of his reign depict him as a bull-necked, beetle-browed, flat-nosed, and tough-mouthed man. His eyes were grayish blue. He was potbellied and spindly legged, and he suffered from bad skin and body odor. Standing around him were his counselors and cronies. Members of the imperial guard kept a close watch on one and all.

There Nero sat, the master of many legions. His political arm was long, stretching even to far-off Britain. There he sat, despicable and dangerous, with many crimes on his conscience. Even as he interrogated Paul, Nero's agents were combing the hills of Rome for men, women, boys, and girls who named the name of Christ. In their hideouts, God's blood-bought people, dreading discovery, were watching and praying. Was Nero the Antichrist? Some Christians thought so.

And there stood Paul. He had been hauled up from the pit. Cleaned, clothed, and under guard, he was brought before Nero. Paul was a Roman by citizenship, a Jew by birth, and a Christian by regeneration. He was a saint, but he was anything but attractive in appearance. His enemies said that his "bodily presence [was] weak, and his speech contemptible" (2 Cor. 10:10). Some Bible scholars think that he had a disfiguring eye disease; others think that he was an epileptic. In any case, he had been badly battered during his missionary years.

But Paul had a mind for the universe. Nero did not know it, but he was confronting a man who was possibly the most brilliant man in the world, a man whose keen mind was quickened by the omniscient Spirit of God. Not a man in Rome could have beaten Paul in debate. Nero, in spite of his decadence, was not without talent, but he was no match for Paul.

Moreover, Paul was fearless. He would be courteous, but he would never cringe (Acts 23:1–5). He had demonstrated his courage time and again. The sycophants and weaklings surrounding Nero were scared to death of the emperor, but Paul had no fear of anything that Nero could do to him. As the apostle stood there, he simply saw an unhappy, unholy man desperately in need of Christ. Paul was determined to make a bid for this sinner's soul (Acts 23:11; Eph. 6:18–20).

So we see them face-to-face at last: Satan's man and God's man; the most wicked man of earth and the most godly. What did Paul say to Nero—if he was allowed to say anything at all? Possibly, he told Nero what he had once told King Agrippa (Acts 26:1–29). If Paul was permitted to give his testimony and press home his point, he would have "reasoned of righteousness, temperance, and judgment to come" until Nero trembled as Felix had once trembled (24:25).

The one thing that Paul told us about that trial is that he stood there alone. "No man stood with me," he wrote in 2 Timothy 4:16. "All men forsook me." The word translated "stood with" here is *paraginomai,* which was used to denote the function of a person who came into court to defend the accused. Paul had no legal counsel, no advocate, no one to counter the lies and distortions of men like Alexander, who doubtless had been summoned to aid in the prosecution. The word translated "forsook" here is the same one that Paul had used in reference to Demas. In effect, the apostle was saying, "They all deserted me." He had to drain the dregs of that cup too. As a result, Nero strengthened his hand in wickedness and condemned Paul to death, but he left the time and manner of execution undecided.

One wonders if Nero ever slept soundly again. Just as the face of Stephen haunted Saul, surely the fact of Paul haunted Nero. He had never met such a man. Paul was a man who was unafraid, undaunted, and devastatingly honest. He was a man who looked him in the eye, wore good manners like a robe, spoke the truth in love, and—could it be?—spoke as though he actually loved his judge and accusers. In Paul's presence, Nero was the closest he would ever come to Christlikeness, the closest he would ever come to heaven. All of his life he had been surrounded by wickedness and depravity. He had met a few wise men, any number of clever men, and a sprinkling of brave men. Now he had met a good man, a man as much like Jesus as any man on earth could be. "Away with such a fellow from the earth," the Jerusalem mob had shouted (Acts 22:22). Nero reacted the same way.

b. Paul's Lord (4:17–18)

(1) The Lord's conscious presence (4:17a)

Was Paul really abandoned and left to face the Roman wild beast alone? No! The apostle's soul was comforted by the presence of the Lord. "The Lord stood with me," he said.

Suddenly, he became aware that Someone had come, all unseen, into that judgment hall. Paul did not have to face Nero the cruel and Alexander the coppersmith alone after all. Years earlier, Paul had looked into the Lord's face on the Damascus road. Now he knew that the Lord had come down from heaven to stand side by side with His embattled witness. Love, joy, and the peace that passes all understanding entered Paul's soul. His heart no longer raced. His thoughts cleared. His resolve stiffened. Jesus had promised His disciples, "Lo, I am with you always, even unto the end of the world" (Matt. 28:20); and Paul proved, as never before, this promise to be true. What need had he of legal counsel? The One who for years had been his Advocate with the Father (1 John 2:1) stood by his side to put the right thoughts into his mind.

(2) The Lord's conquering presence (4:17b)

Speaking of the Lord's presence at the trial, Paul added, "The Lord . . . strengthened me." The word translated "strengthened" here is akin to *dunamis* ("power"). The Lord clothed Paul with power; He poured strength into him.

Paul, after all, was only a man "subject to like passions as we are" (James 5:17). He was not impervious to fear. Before the trial, he must have trembled inwardly at the thought of the ordeal ahead of him. But when the One who had stood with Shadrach, Meshach, and Abed-nego in the fiery furnace (Dan. 3:19–25) stood with Paul in that corrupt Roman court, he was invincible. All that Nero could do was kill him, and the emperor could not even do that until the Lord allowed it.

(3) The Lord's confirming presence (4:17c)

Paul told Timothy that the Lord empowered him "that by me the preaching might be fully known, and that all the Gentiles might hear." The Lord gave Paul strength to proclaim the message even in that court and before that emperor. Paul had preached the gospel in many arenas. He had preached it in the temple court in Jerusalem to an infuriated mob. He had preached in on Mars Hill in Athens to a sneering court. He had preached it to Felix, Festus, and Agrippa. Now, having reached the supreme court of the Roman world, Paul preached the gospel fully and clearly to the highest peers of the realm, including Nero. This "preaching" was Paul's last message, as far as we know.

It is fitting that Nero should have at least one opportunity to hear the uncluttered, ungarbled gospel proclaimed fully and clearly before he himself was called to the Great White Throne of God. Paul's attitude was now that of Esther, who had "come to the kingdom for such a time as this." He could echo her valiant words: "If I perish, I perish" (Esther 4:14:16).

(4) The Lord's controlling presence (4:17d)

"And I was delivered out of the mouth of the lion," wrote Paul. Surely, Paul was referring here to Nero, who was ruled by no law other than his own passions. Perhaps Nero was goaded to madness by the lies and oratory of Alexander. Perhaps the emperor gnashed his teeth with rage over Paul's testimony.

Nero was quite capable of having Paul scourged to the bone, Roman citizen or not. Nero could have sent him to the arena. Nero could have defied law and convention alike and, scoffing at Paul's status as a Roman, sent him to a cross. Nero could have had him executed then and there. But Paul's hour had not yet come. He was immortal until his work was done.

(5) The Lord's continuing presence (4:18)

Back in his cell, Paul expressed confidence that the Lord would protect him from the king and preserve him for the kingdom: "The Lord shall deliver me from every evil work, and will preserve me unto his heavenly kingdom." Paul had seen enough of earthly kingdoms. He longed for the heavenly kingdom that was ruled by the One whose presence was with him. Paul might receive another hearing, but Nero would never let him live. Nero feared him and loathed him as only a truly wicked man can loathe a truly good man. However, Nero's power was limited. One mightier than he would draw a line in the sand and say to even the greatest of emperors, "Thus far, and no farther."

Nero was still capable of "every evil work." The word translated "evil" suggests active opposition to that which is good. The term conjures a picture of a person, swollen and pregnant with mischief, laboring to be delivered of some foul wickedness. Nero was such a person, and he had his mind focused on Paul. But the Lord was still with Paul, and not even Nero could get past Him. No plot formed against Paul could prosper.

The apostle had long since come to terms with death. It would simply open wide the gates of glory. Apart from the Rapture, Paul could expect death anyway as a matter of course. Considering all of his hairbreadth escapes, we might conclude that he had been living on borrowed time for years.

Knowing that there might be a rough path ahead, Paul still wrote, "The Lord shall deliver *[rhuomai]* me . . . and will *preserve* me." This word, also used in 4:17, is a tender word conveying the idea of rescue—the thought of being drawn to the rescuer and being moved out of harm's way. The Lord had delivered Paul when he was brought before the tribunal, and He would continue to deliver him as long as the occasion required it. The thought was that the Lord would keep him safe.

Doubtless, Paul was in dire peril. The persecution that was raging around him was monstrous. The most harrowing atrocities were being committed as a matter of course. Paul, however, refused to let his heart and mind dwell on his present perils. To brood over them might unman him. Instead, he fixed his mind on the Lord and His "heavenly kingdom." For years, Paul had prayed, "Thy kingdom come," and now it was drawing close. He had been a member of that kingdom for years (Col. 1:13), and now he was looking forward to entering through its pearly gates and taking up his residence in a land of fadeless day.

Paul burst into a doxology as he thought of the Lord, his companion in that horrible pit: "To [Him] be glory for ever and ever." Years earlier, he had met Him on the Damascus road and had known Him ever since as "the Lord from heaven" (1 Cor. 15:47). Now Paul would soon go home and see Him in all of His glory amid scenes of splendor that no words can describe (2 Cor. 12:2–5). Paul had lost sight of his earthly surroundings. His heart and mind were bathed in "joy unspeakable and full of glory" (1 Peter 1:8). All he could add was "Amen." For him, time had already been overtaken by eternity!

PART 4

Conclusion

2 Timothy 4:19–22

A. A salutation (4:19–20)

1. Notes (4:19)

Paul could not end his last letter without a personal reference or two, so he greeted a few of his friends who were with Timothy in Ephesus. He mentioned *some remembered helpers* ("Salute Priscilla and Aquila") and *a remembered household* ("and the household of Onesiphorus").

Paul first met Priscilla and Aquila in Corinth during his second missionary journey. The couple were Jewish refugees who had come from Rome at the time of the outbreak of anti-Semitism under Emperor Claudius. Because Priscilla and Aquila were tent makers, as Paul was, he had lived with them and labored at their looms while evangelizing in the city (Acts 18:1–3). When Paul was finished in Corinth, he took them with him to Ephesus and left them there to prepare the way for the gospel crusade that he would later conduct in that important city (Acts 18:19–21). Because they were early converts and well taught in the Word, they were able to give helpful instruction to as gifted a preacher as Apollos (Acts 18:24–26). Priscilla and Aquila were in Rome when Paul wrote his letter to the Romans; in it he acknowledged himself to be greatly in their debt (Rom. 16:3–4). When Paul wrote his last letter to Timothy, the couple were in Ephesus again, and Paul greeted them personally by name. As he did, many fond memories must have flooded his soul.

Paul had already praised Onesiphorus in 2 Timothy 1:16. Fearless of the consequences, he had visited Paul in prison. The mention of Onesiphorus's household is taken by some people to mean that this brave brother had recently died. Paul thought tenderly of both the man and his family.

2. News (4:20)

a. The abode of Erastus (4:20a)

Updating Timothy on news, Paul wrote that "Erastus abode at Corinth." This bit of information suggests that Paul had visited Corinth shortly before his arrest.

Erastus, the city treasurer of Corinth (Rom. 16:23), had accompanied Paul during his second missionary journey. The apostle had sent him and Timothy from Ephesus to Macedonia (Acts 19:22), perhaps in connection with the love offering for the poor in Jerusalem. Thus, Erastus and Timothy had escaped the riot that had broken out in Ephesus shortly afterward.

b. The ailment of Trophimus (4:20b)

Paul mentioned another news item: "Trophimus have I left at Miletum sick." Trophimus was an Asiatic and a resident at Ephesus (Acts 20:4; 21:29). As a member of the team that took the Gentiles' cash contribution to Jerusalem, he had traveled from Macedonia to Troas and from there to Miletus and Jerusalem. What happened to him after that is not known. Evidently, he traveled with Paul on his last journey to Rome. When Trophimus became sick, Paul was obliged to leave him in Miletus, not far from Ephesus. Probably, Paul expected Timothy to act on this news and see what could be done for a colleague in his time of need.

At one time, Paul could have healed Timothy, Trophimus, or anyone else, but the sign gifts—tongues, miracles, and healings—now seem to have been withdrawn from the church. As soon as the apostle John had written his books and departed to be with Christ, the gifts of apostle and prophet would also be withdrawn. The sign gifts had been given to authenticate Christianity to the Jews (1 Cor. 1:22), but the signs had been ignored. The national life was about to be terminated; there was no further need for the sign gifts. So poor sick Trophimus was left behind but was not forgotten.

B. A supplication (4:21a)

Paul made one last plea, full of pathos and yearning: "Do thy diligence to come before winter." The apostle was chilled to the bone in his dungeon. Paul thought longingly of his cloak (4:13) and wondered what it would be like when winter came.

If Timothy did not come before winter, it would be too late. Travel by sea would be impossible once winter came. Travel by land through highland passes could be almost impossible. And Paul doubted that he had long to live. Did Timothy arrive in time? Let us hope that he did! Let us hope that as soon as he read this letter he dispatched someone to Miletus to take care of Trophimus, packed his bags, bought his tickets, and set out for Troas and Rome.

C. A supplement (4:21b–22)

1. A final greeting (4:21b)

Paul, though left to fend for himself when standing before Nero, was not without friends in Rome. The apostle mentioned a few people in the beleaguered

Christian community still surviving the onslaught of persecution in Rome: "Eubulus greeteth thee, and Pudens, and Linus, and Claudia, and all the brethren." The use of the polysyndeton—separating each name from the others with the word "and"—reveals the thoughtful care with which he mentioned each name. We know nothing about these named people, except for speculations that Linus became the first bishop of Rome and that Claudia was the daughter of a British king who was an ally of Rome.

In addition to the mutual friends, there were "all the brethren." The church in Rome was surviving in spite of Nero's rage. The gates of hell could not prevail against it (Matt. 16:18).

2. A fitting good-bye (4:22a)

Paul bid Timothy a fitting good-bye: "The Lord Jesus Christ be with thy spirit." The apostle knew that Timothy would need a sense of the Lord's presence as he journeyed from the relative safety of Ephesus to the center of the firestorm in Rome. He would need more than all of his courage and all of his resolve; he would need the Lord.

The same Lord who was with Paul in Rome could be with Timothy in Ephesus, on the road to Troas, or on the ship bound for Italy. His port of entry might be Ostia (the seaport of Rome) or Puteoli on the bay of Naples, where Paul had once landed. Timothy would need the divine presence more and more if he disembarked at Puteoli and trudged the miles to the Forum of Appius, the Three Taverns, and Rome.

Before he reached Rome, Timothy could perhaps avoid all suspicion. Who would suspect that a leader of the Christian sect would deliberately travel to Rome when the sensible thing for Christians to do was to get out of Rome? But once in Rome, Timothy would face real peril. Spies swarmed the streets. Informers bought safety for themselves by retailing tips to the authorities. News would soon reach the security forces that a foreigner in town was asking for directions to the Mamertine prison. When Timothy showed up at the prison and asked to see Paul, he would surely need to be aware that Another was standing by his side.

3. A farewell gift (4:22b)

Paul closed his letter, saying, "Grace be with you. Amen." What other legacy did Paul have to leave? He had no gold or gems. The soldiers would cast lots for his cloak (if it arrived in time) as they did for the Lord's robe.

Paul's last words followed the apostolic precedent set by Peter in Acts 3:6: "Silver and gold have I none; but such as I have give I thee." Paul had grace, and grace was all that Timothy could possibly need. It was all that Paul needed; it was all that he had.

It was grace that had met Paul when he was the chief persecutor of the church. It was grace that had washed away his sins and written his name in the Book of Life. It was grace that had put him in the ministry and ordained him to be an apostle to the Gentiles. It was grace that had used him so mightily in so many ways for so many years. It was grace that had opened his eyes to heaven and then given him his thorn. It was grace that had brought him through so many perils. It was grace that had blessed his ministry and used it for the conversion and comfort of countless souls. It was grace that had opened his heart to a sense of the Lord's presence in his prison. What better gift could he give than grace?

"Grace be with you," Paul wrote. "Amen." And then the curtain fell. Paul had no more to say. His ministry was done.

The traditional date of Paul's martyrdom is June 19, A.D. 68. That same month, Nero committed suicide. Nero went to "his own place," as Judas did (Acts 1:25), from which some believe he will return as the Antichrist. Paul went to be with Christ and entered into "joy unspeakable and full of glory" (1 Peter 1:8). The Lord's smile and welcome were his. An abundant entrance was his. A crown of life was his.

We can imagine what happened on that fateful day when Paul left his dungeon forever. He said his last farewell to his beloved physician and was led to the place of execution. And there was the ax. Doubtless, Paul had some kind words for his executioner and a word of testimony about where he would be "in the twinkling of an eye," to use his own phrase (1 Cor. 15:52). Then he bowed his head to the block, closed his eyes, and opened them again to look straight into the face of Jesus.

We are reminded of the execution of Sir Walter Raleigh. When the ungrateful King James sent him to his death, the intrepid explorer faced his doom with unruffled calm. The headsman tried to ease Sir Walter's last moments by showing him the best way to lay his head on the block. Raleigh thanked him but said, "So the heart be right, it is no matter which way the head lies."

Paul might well have used the same words. His heart has been with Jesus now for nearly two thousand years. He is at rest, and his works do follow him (Rev. 14:13).